Our Lives, Our Fortunes, Our Sacred Honor

Capsule Portraits of Figures From the American Revolution

by Pierre Comtois

"Our Lives, Our Fortunes, Our Sacred Honor: Capsule Portraits of Figures From the American Revolution," by Pierre Comtois. ISBN 978-1-60264-312-3.

Manufactured in the United States of America.

Preface

Our Lives, Our Fortunes, Our Sacred Honor:
Capsule Portraits of Figures From the American Revolution

This book was a project born out of necessity.

As a long time reader of American history in general and the Revolutionary period in particular, I have always been interested in the Founding Fathers many of whose long and diverse careers fascinated me not only for their personal accomplishments but also for the way they seemed to intersect with one another. One Founder was personally acquainted with a number of others who in turn knew other Founders who in turn had met members of the first group. This tight circle of friends and colleagues was made possible because of the relatively small population of the infant United States and the even smaller circle of national and state leaders among whom the Founders moved. Thus Paul Revere knew Samuel Adams who knew John Hancock who knew George Washington who knew Alexander Hamilton, etc.

The problem was that in pursuing my interest in these Revolutionary figures, I found that aside from the biographies of such major figures as George Washington, John Adams, and Thomas Jefferson, and brief character sketches of others, personal histories of the more obscure Founders, including many of those who signed the Declaration of Independence, was completely lacking. Until the arrival of the internet, detailed information on many of those lesser known individuals was just not to be had for the casual history buff. And so, after many years of scouring bookstores looking for that handy but elusive single volume compendium of biographies, I finally came to the realization that if I wanted a book like that, I would have to write it myself.

But in embarking on the project, it had never been my intention to write a book based on original research involving digging into archival sources and unpublished letters. As a result, the following work is the end product of readings and delvings into a number of published sources from available books to the internet. What makes the "capsule biographies" I have written different however, is that the information on each subject was pulled from numerous places, collated, organized, and otherwise pieced together in a hopefully coherent whole for the interest of the general reader.

From the beginning, there was no question that the subjects to be covered in the book would consist of all the well known names from the American Revolution: James Madison, Benedict Arnold, Benjamin Franklin. The difficult decision was in choosing who among the lesser known Founders to include and as I researched each subject, more names would come to my attention. I ended up writing over 120 separate entries and that by no means exhausted the potential for more but I had to draw the line somewhere.

Adding to the difficulty of choosing whom to include, was my own rather broad interpretation of the term Founding Father. Some might restrict the term to a select few Revolutionary leaders such as those who signed the Declaration of Independence, or who served as officers in the Continental Army, or who framed the Constitution, but my definition of just who is deserving to be counted among that group is more inclusive: namely, anyone who participated even in the smallest way in the struggle to make America free, from the lowliest private in the Continental Army to the Indian fighter on the farthest edge of the frontier to the diplomat serving in Europe to the selectman working to meet his town's quota of supplies for the army.

While aware that such a broad definition would necessarily include those groups of people that often have not been covered in past histories including women, minorities, and the common soldier, I have decided not to include them here because to spotlight any example would necessarily give a false impression of the level of their participation vis a vis the greater majority of others. For instance, for every black soldier that may have fought in the war, there were 30 or 40 times as many whites. For every Joseph Plumb Martin, there were hundreds of other common foot soldiers and militiamen. Suffice it to say, that these individuals were Founders as much as their more famous peers but whose careers will have to be related by inference within the bodies of individual entries. Washington did not fight his battles single handed; farmers' crops did not grow by themselves; children were not raised without guidance. Thus, in choosing the subjects of the biographies included in this collection, I was guided primarily by my own interests and not such latter day movements as "political correctness" or historical "revisionism."

And so, taken from a personal evaluation of the Founders as figures from the country's lost heroic age, my approach is admittedly an eclectic one including those men commonly accepted as Founders and others who have hardly even been heard from. Although this approach did not necessarily forbid the inclusion of less respectable aspects of the Founders' lives, it also did not permit any judgment of their personal actions from a modern perspective. When it comes right down to it, the Founding Fathers were human after all, despite the seeming Herculean and outsize nature of their achievements. That said, this volume is not intended to glamorize the Founders; their often mighty deeds speak for themselves.

Pierre V. Comtois
June 2009

John Adams

It is probably true that of the entire population of the thirteen colonies at the time the first shots were fired at Lexington and Concord, less than half could be counted as being in favor of defiance of the king, let alone outright revolution. And while it was also true that anger and resentment toward England had been growing for years as a result of the passage by Parliament of a series of unpopular measures designed to coerce the colonists into paying higher taxes and quartering soldiers in their homes, political radicalization of America's nascent revolutionary leadership many times did not happen overnight. Discarding the attachments and loyalties of a lifetime was not easy and sometimes, as in the case of Pennsylvania's John Dickinson, it never happened.

Like Dickinson, John Adams was at first slow to embrace the radicalism already being pushed by his cousin Samuel Adams and other Massachusetts' Sons of Liberty. More interested in succeeding in the legal profession and perhaps securing himself an official position within the colony's government, Adams was slow to heed the entreaties of his cousin to join in the movement protesting Britain's oppressive measures against the people. Gradually, however, Adams was drawn in to the growing conflict, at first writing pseudonymous letters of protest in local newspapers and later coming out publicly on the issues. This, nevertheless, did not mean he intended to compromise on what he felt was right and in a dramatic move, Adams cemented a reputation for honesty and integrity by defending British soldiers accused of killing unarmed civilians in an incident called "the Boston Massacre" by local patriots. The streak of individualism that drew Adams to defend the soldiers was one that would define his entire subsequent career from his diplomatic successes in Europe to his disappointments as the second president of the United States.

Born in Braintree, Massachusetts in 1735, Adams' intelligence impressed his parents enough to send him to Harvard for an education. There, Adams developed an intense form of concentration that would serve him well in later years when his keen brain, saturated with an in-depth understanding of law, classical history, government, and political philosophy, would apply itself to the writing of *Thoughts on Government*, his collaboration on the Declaration of Independence and his various diplomatic triumphs. Graduating from Harvard, Adams began the practice of law but all the while his star ascended he was importuned by his cousin Samuel Adams to join local patriots in speaking out against what they saw as the growing oppression of Britain. At first reluctant to enter the fray, Adams' thoughts on the issues gradually evolved to the point where he was chosen to accompany his cousin to Philadelphia to attend the First Continental Congress in 1774. There, he met some of the leading lights of the growing revolutionary movement, including George Washington. Adams was chosen again in 1775 as the colony's represen-

John Adams

tative at the Second Continental Congress which took place soon after the historic events at Lexington and Concord. It was at the Second Congress that Adams emerged as an important figure in the revolutionary movement, taking the lead in nominating Washington as commander in chief of the new Continental Army and in 1776 finding himself joined with Thomas Jefferson, Benjamin Franklin, Robert Livingston and Roger Sherman to prepare a Declaration of Independence.

In 1777, Adams was appointed by Congress as a commissioner to France to join Benjamin Franklin in place of Silas Deane. It was the beginning of one of the most stressful times in the New Englander's life as he arrived in France with little knowledge of the language and dislike of the behavior both public and private of his diplomatic partner. Working on two fronts, Adams' first triumph was in securing from the Netherlands vital loans and treaties of commerce for the fledgling United States and later, defying both the will of French foreign minister the Comte de Vergennes and Congress by entering peace negotiations with Britain without the involvement of France. Together with Franklin and John Jay, Adams met with their British counterparts and by 1783 had come to agreement on the Treaty of Paris which among other things, fixed the westward boundary of the United States at the Mississippi River and granted fishing rights off the Grand Banks of Newfoundland.

In 1785, Adams followed Franklin to Britain where he replaced him as United States minister to the Court of St. James. His service coming to an end in 1788, he returned home to Braintree in time to be chosen the country's first vice-president with the election of 1789. Largely out of the loop during the eight years of Washington's presidency, he assumed the office himself in 1797 at a time of increasing domestic acrimony. Fellow patriots who had once been allies on the field of combat and in the halls of Congress had begun to divide themselves into rival political factions led by Thomas Jefferson, Adams' vice-president, and Alexander Hamilton, former Secretary of the Treasury who had left office with Washington. As leader of the Republicans, Jefferson was deeply suspicious of a strong central government and saw Adams, who had once been a close friend and colleague, as a tool of the Hamiltonian Federalists. Hamilton, an exponent of a strong federal government, thought Adams somewhat of a bumpkin and through the president's cabinet, attempted to control national policy himself. Buffeted from both sides of the political fence and pounded mercilessly in the press, Adams also had to contend with an increasingly belligerent France which had undergone its own bloody revolution and a stubborn Britain which continued to refuse to abandon western lands that had been ceded to the United States with the Treaty of Paris.

By the end of his term in 1801, even being the first president to govern from the new federal city of Washington was not enough to lift Adams' lagging spirits. It was true that he had brought France to the peace table after a dangerous period of quasi-war and strengthened the nation's defenses, but his term of office ended with the dismissal of two of three disloyal members of his cabinet, an eleventh hour appointment of a slate of federalist judges, and the bitter taste left behind in the wake of the Alien and Sedition Act.

With the Federalists in disarray and behind the scenes machinations by Hamilton, Adams failed to win enough votes for a second term as president. It was just as well. Tired and with the end of his public career well in sight, Adams retired to his home in Braintree, this time for good. Although his final years were of growing appreciation for his achievements as a statesman, Adams himself gave the country one last gift: an extraordinary body of correspondence with Thomas Jefferson, with whom he had finally come to a friendly understanding. And so the years passed, until the afternoon of July 4, 1826, the fiftieth anniversary of the Declaration of Independence. On that day, Adams breathed his last, but not before declaring that "Jefferson survives!" It was the greatest of ironies that on that special day, his old friend and political rival had himself expired under the impression that Adams still lived.

Samuel Adams

In every radical movement or political revolution throughout history there have been fiery leaders and rabble rousers who could whip people into a frenzy of agitation and inspire them into taking action against their oppressors. But seldom in revolutionary history, whether the French Revolution, the Spanish Civil War, the English Civil War or the various peasant uprisings or Communist Revolutions of Russia and China has a leader been immune to the temptations of power. Throughout history, such mass movements have all too often proven the dictum that power corrupts and absolute power corrupts absolutely. The American Revolution however, remains as that rare mass movement of a people that did not descend into tyranny; where its leaders did not succumb to the allure of personal power and that the original aspirations of the people, their yearning to throw off the shackles of an oppressive government and be free to shape their own destiny were preserved. Of course there were those conventional minded revolutionaries who could only think in terms of royalty, replacing one king for another, and the more numerous faction that did not completely trust the will of the common people to govern themselves; but for the most part, the leaders of the American Revolution remained faithful not only to the high flown language of freedom they had used to define the movement, but resisted being seduced by power itself. And while George Washington remains the most famous example of a leader who turned his back on personal power, Samuel Adams faced temptations from both sides of the Revolution that he could very easily have exploited in his position as a charismatic and well respected leader. Unlike other revolutionary movements before and after, it was the decisions of both men to resist the siren call of power that exemplified the integrity of the Founding

Fathers and guaranteed the eventual success of the American Revolution.

America's most forceful and easily most colorful political personality must have been born a revolutionary because years before even James Otis began to actively challenge royal authority in Massachusetts, Samuel Adams had submitted a graduation thesis at Harvard College entitled "Whether it be Lawful to resist the Supreme Magistrate, if the Commonwealth cannot otherwise be preserved." That was in 1740 when the future firebrand was only 18 years old. Born in Quincy, Massachusetts on September 27, 1722, Adams probably took an early interest in social affairs from his father who was active in local politics. Graduating from Harvard, the intelligent but indecisive Adams bounced from one job to another, failing as manager of a brewery as well as tax collector and a misfortune in business later lost him his inheritance, relegating him permanently to the status of a man of lesser means. The problem with Adams' not being able to hold a job was his growing interest in politics, which over the years demanded more and more of his time and attention. Ironically, as his reputation grew, he found that the plain dress and the status he occupied as a member of the lower middle class helped in making him popular as a man of the people. As a result, by 1748, Adams had become well known in Boston as a public debater and after forming his own political club, used its weekly broadside, the *Independent Advertiser*, to voice his opinions in print. But Adams' political skills and acumen really came into their own following the French and Indian War when discontent by many colonial veterans over the high handed manner in which they'd been treated by their British superior officers began to be transferred to such local representatives of the crown as the royal governor. This attitude crystallized in 1764 with the widely opposed Stamp Act passed by Parliament in order

Samuel Adams

to raise money from the colonies to pay for the war and current defense needs. Adams led the charge against the Stamp Act claiming Parliament had no right to tax the colonists. With his popularity at a peak, Adams was elected a member of the colony's legislature in 1765 and took the lead, over older revolutionaries such as James Otis, in urging a rejection of colonial representation in Parliament, no doubt realizing that any vote by the colonies could be overridden by the vast majority of British members. Increasingly radicalized, Adams became perhaps the first man in America to advocate independence from Britain and began in earnest to organize such incubators of revolution as the committees of correspondence and safety and to recruit like minded young men such as Joseph Warren, John Hancock and his cousin, John Adams.

A flurry of letters and official documents flowed from Adams' pen both as a member of the legislature and anonymously in local newspapers and it was he who first suggested the convening of a Continental Congress. By 1770, his reputation as a rabble rouser and organizer of sometimes violent street protests was such that he was widely suspected to have been the instigator behind the infamous Boston Massacre, the name he gave the incident in which British soldiers fired upon and killed a number of civilians. While Adams' personal involvement in the Massacre has been contested ever since, what has never been in doubt is the dramatic face to face meeting between Adams and royal Governor Thomas Hutchinson in which Adams demanded the removal of all troops from Boston. A cowed Hutchinson complied. Following that political success, Adams became involved in the planning and execution of the Boston Tea Party and later, was chosen as a delegate to the first Continental Congress. By that point, Adams' reputation was such that he topped the list of men wanted by royal officials for treason against the crown. When a number of attempts at bribing him with money and rank failed, orders were issued by British General Thomas Gage for Adams' arrest and he, along with Hancock, became one of the targets for the British incursion into the Massachusetts countryside in 1775 which resulted in hostilities that finally lit the fuse of revolution.

At the time, Adams and Hancock were staying at a home in Lexington when they were warned by Paul Revere that they had only minutes to spare before the arrival of British soldiers sent into the area to search for rumored military stores. Escaping just in time, they failed to witness the first confrontation between British troops and American minutemen on Lexington's town green. In a desperate attempt to salvage something from the disastrous events that followed, Gage granted amnesty to all known revolutionaries with the exception of Adams and Hancock. But by then, the two men were out of the colony and taking their places as members of the Continental Congress then meeting in Philadelphia.

At the Congress, Hancock was named president while Adams joined his cousin John as a member of the Massachusetts delegation. From the beginning, there could be no doubt in anyone's mind about Adams' position on independence from Britain ("Our unalterable resolution should be to be free."), but that momentous decision would have to wait another year before the rest of the colonies could catch up to him. Catch up to him they finally did however, and Adams joined his fellow congressmen in signing the Declaration of Independence on August 2, 1776.

Although Adams continued to serve with the Congress until 1781, the period of his greatest contributions to the Revolution was over. In 1779, he returned to Massachusetts to attend the convention that framed the state's own constitution which he, as a member of the sub-committee that wrote the first draft, was instrumental in fashioning. By contrast, Adams was suspicious of the federal Constitution much as he had been of the Articles of Confederation which, as a member of a special committee, he had helped create. Eventually, however, after he was assured of the addition of a Bill of Rights, he came around to accepting the new Constitution. In 1789 he was chosen to serve as lieutenant governor of Massachusetts and succeeded Hancock as governor in 1794. Adams retired from most public activity in 1797 and after a near lifetime of devotion to the cause of American liberty, died on October 2, 1803.

Ethan Allen

Unlike patriots such as John and Samuel Adams and Patrick Henry, many leaders of the American Revolution had other motives for resisting royal authority in addition to the purely philosophical. Some were financial, some included resentment at legal constrictions preventing settlement of western lands, others saw the chance to escape from beneath oppressive laws and regulations governing everything from taxation to religious freedom, and some yearned for military glory. But sometimes individual revolutionaries had more complicated, even inexplicable motives for joining the struggle against Britain, motives less idealistic than opportunistic. Such may have been the case with Vermont's Ethan Allen who, despite showing great courage and initiative in the war effort, was not above dealing with the enemy when it came to interests closer to home.

The man who would later become a legendary Vermont hero was not born in that state, but in Litchfield, Connecticut, on January 10, 1738. When Allen was two years old, his father removed the family to what was known at the time as the Hampshire Grants. Growing into a large, garrulous man, Allen learned the woodland skills needed for frontier life and although he had a start at formal education, it was curtailed upon the death of his father. In the late 1750s, he served in the French and Indian War before returning to the vicinity of Bennington where the rest of his family lived. But it was in the Grants that Allen was plunged into a political struggle between the colonies of New York and New Hampshire, each of which claimed the Grants. Ignoring New

Ethan Allen

(Demanding surrender of Ft Ticonderoga)

York's claims, New Hampshire had been busy selling land grants to settlers in the disputed region, including the Allen family who invested heavily in the area's real estate as the Onion River Land Company. Unfortunately for the Allens and other settlers who had bought their land from New Hampshire, the king of England had decided in favor of New York's claims for the region and soon, they were subjected to a heavy burden of taxes and fees as well as harassment by New York militia and revenue agents come to force payment of the money or confiscate their land. With a big investment in northern Vermont, the Allens had much to lose should New York declare their deeds invalid and so, to protect themselves and their land, they took the lead in forming a local militia called the Green Mountain Boys led by the hulking Ethan who was elected as colonel. Thus, upon the outbreak of the Revolution in 1775, Vermont had a ready made military force close by one of the most strategic locations in North America: Fort Ticonderoga, just over the border in New York. Fired by a resentment toward an overbearing England and authorized by the colony of Connecticut to take the fort, Allen was about to lead 230 of his Green Mountain Boys on the mission when he was intercepted by Gen. Benedict Arnold who insisted that he lead the assault due to having authority from the Massachusetts Committee of Safety. "Colonel Allen is a proper man to head his own wild people, but entirely unacquainted with military service," remarked Arnold in a report to the committee. Allen did not quite see things that way and questioned the fact that unlike himself, Arnold had arrived without any men to help him take the fort. In the end, Allen agreed to allow Arnold to accompany the raid but without command authority and early on the morning of May 10, 1775, about a third of the force crossed Lake Champlain and took the fort's undermanned garrison by surprise. Rushing through the open gate, Allen met the fort's commander and shouted at his bellicose best "Surrender in the name of the great Jehovah and the Continental Congress!" The fort, a key position commanding the entire Hudson River valley, had been captured without a shot being fired.

Following the seizure of Ticonderoga, Allen had a falling out with the Green Mountain Boys and was voted out as their leader. At loose ends, he attached himself to American General Philip Schuyler's army as it moved up from New York in preparation for an invasion of Canada and an attack on Montreal. Allen, always strong headed and independent, proved difficult for his superior officers to keep under control with Schuyler himself writing that he "dreaded his impatience of subordination." His impetuosity finally caught up with him when, on a mission well in advance of the army to rouse native Canadians to join the American cause, he decided to try and take Montreal himself. Recalling the ease with which Ticonderoga had fallen and hoping that the city's predominantly French inhabitants would rally to the American side, Allen crossed the St. Lawrence River with a force of 30 Americans and 110 French Canadians and, drawing up before the city on September 25, 1775, demanded its surrender. This time, however, Allen was facing a city of 5,000 people and not a garrison of only 32 soldiers as at Ticonderoga. His demand received only a tremendous volley of fire in response and as he and his men retreated, they found themselves trapped against the river with no alternative but to throw down their arms. Placed in irons, Allen was taken to England for trial and later transferred back to America where he became part of a prisoner exchange on May 6, 1778. At Valley Forge, he was finally commissioned a colonel in the Continental Army but never officially served with it.

In the meantime, with the United States having declared independence from England, all immediate authority over disputes between the former colonies was ended. Amid the legal chaos, the residents of the Hampshire Grants led by Allen's brother Ira, met and on January 17, 1777, declared their own independence from both New York and New Hampshire. Later, at the Windsor Constitutional Convention held on July 8, 1777, the new entity was named Vermont and, with the refusal by the Continental Congress to recognize its action, became an independent republic. That was where matters stood when Allen returned home and was appointed commander of the military forces of the Commonwealth of Vermont whose primary mission was to patrol the border between Vermont and Canada for signs of renewed enemy activity. Aware that Vermont might be too weak to survive on its own and frustrated by New York's continued interference in Congress, Allen and his neighbors became involved in secret negotiations with Sir Frederick Haldimand, governor of Canada on the possibility of the new republic being annexed by Canada. With Allen's spoken position that he had no intention of "betraying the trust reposed in him" by the people of Vermont, it is not at all certain that these overtures amounted to anything serious however with the possibility that they were made with the idea of pressuring the Congress to accept Vermont as a state. In any case, the whole affair became moot when America won the war and New York, concerned about the growing power of the South if Kentucky was admitted as a state, lost interest in its claims on Vermont. As a result, in 1791, Vermont ended fourteen years of independence and entered the Union as the fourteenth state. Unfortunately for the Allens, who had invested heavily in improving their lands, independence and later statehood did little to improve their financial fortunes while Allen himself did not live to see statehood. Growing philosophical in retirement, Allen, who had never been formally educated, wrote a book entitled *Reason, the Only Oracle of Man* which angered religious leaders because of its criticism that they failed to recognize the natural rights of their congregants. In 1787, amid the furor caused by his book, Allen settled on a farm outside Burlington located along the Onion River. It was there that he died two years later on February 12, 1789.

Benedict Arnold

After 230 years of excoriation, any American would be hard pressed to accept Benedict Arnold as a hero, a man whose name has become a synonym for treason and black betrayal. But trite as it sounds, there were extenuating circumstances. Flawed by overweening pride and an extremely thin skin, it seems almost inevitable in hindsight that Arnold would be driven to treason after being denied reward for repeated acts of bravery on the battlefield and being passed over for promotion in favor of officers less skilled in strategy and tactics but with more seniority and better political connections. Which is not to say that Arnold himself held no blame for his traitorous acts. Always ambitious and equating material gain with personal success, Arnold longed to gain entry into the upper classes of colonial society. So important was that desire that in order to attain it, he was prepared not only to do whatever it took to earn the cash to buy his way in, but to sacrifice his honor and even his country to do it. Not satisfied with the slow pace involved with a successful apothecary business, he became involved in local smuggling operations and later, as an officer in the Continental Army, he took advantage of his position to make money at the government's expense. Still later, hobnobbing with Loyalist sympathizers, he vaulted into the top rung of Philadelphia society with his marriage to a

Benedict Arnold

woman 20 years his junior. His subsequent actions, involving a traitorous deal with the enemy for money and position in return for betraying his country, was only the last act in a foredoomed drama. But his sordid final months in the Continental Army and his heinous acts upon becoming an officer in the British Army only serve to accentuate earlier deeds that are among the most storied of the revolutionary era. The contrast only serves to make the career of Benedict Arnold all the more tragic in that if it had not been for his misplaced pride and ambition, he would surely be recognized today as one of the towering figures of the Revolution.

Indications of the negative streak in Arnold's character were present even at the youngest age when he was considered a problem child in need of discipline. Born on January 14, 1741 in Norwich, Connecticut, Arnold's restless nature was perhaps exacerbated by a downturn in his family's fortunes, an alcoholic father, and a number of siblings who died of sickness. Concerned about her son's behavior, Arnold's mother persuaded relatives to take on the boy as an apprentice in their apothecary business. Although Arnold learned the trade and performed his work well, his heart was not in it and he tried more than once to escape by joining the colonial militia during the French and Indian War. Foiled in his early attempts at gaining military glory, Arnold still yearned to strike out on his own. With the death of his parents, he inherited some money and used it first to shop for inventory in Europe in order to stock his own apothecary and then to invest in shipping where he soon traded his clerk's apron for a sea captain's cap. Independent at last and with his sister employed as a clerk, Arnold was married in 1767 and became one of the colony's richest men after becoming involved in small time smuggling operations. A confrontation with royal authorities over contraband goods found aboard one of his ships placed him squarely in defiance of British policies and inspired the radical streak that led him to join the ranks of the rising revolutionary movement. By the time of Lexington and Concord, he was a captain in the local militia and wasted no time in marching to Massachusetts to participate in the siege of Boston.

It was while in Massachusetts that he remembered Fort Ticonderoga from the time he had fled the militia while posted there during the French and Indian War. Conceiving the idea of seizing the fort before its British garrison learned of the outbreak of hostilities, he petitioned the Massachusetts Committee of Safety for permission to make the effort himself. The committee agreed and Arnold set off at once for New York. There, he discovered another man on the same errand. New

Hampshireman Ethan Allen who, along with his Green Mountain Boys, had received his authorization from an agent of John Adams, a member of the Continental Congress which he considered superior to the Massachusetts Committee of Safety. Finding himself in an inferior position (not only did Allen seem to have stronger credentials, his Green Mountain Boys outnumbered Arnold 250-1), Arnold had no choice but to settle for sharing command of the expedition. And that was how matters stood on May 10, 1775 when the small force of Americans captured the great fort without a fight making available its desperately needed cannon for use in the siege of Boston.

But his participation in the capture of Fort Ticonderoga also resulted in personal animosity between Arnold and fellow officers as well as in strained relations with Massachusetts and Connecticut patriots that ended in a lingering resentment at what Arnold considered a lack of appreciation for his efforts. It was while fuming over these sleights that he was promoted to Colonel and appointed by commander in chief George Washington to lead an invading army into Canada. Happy to have an independent command and an opportunity to display his martial skills, Arnold threw himself into planning for the campaign and in the late fall of 1775, led his army of 1,100 men into the Maine wilderness. It was the beginning of one of the epic struggles of the Revolution during which the soldiers endured freezing temperatures, near starvation and deadly sickness. At last however, severely weakened but urged on by an indomitable Arnold, the army finally reached Quebec. There, they were joined by a second army led by Gen. Richard Montgomery which had advanced up the St. Lawrence River and captured Montreal. After laying siege to the city, the Americans' long planned attack took place during a snow storm on the night of December 31, 1775. Although begun with vigor, the effort failed when Montgomery was killed and then Arnold severely wounded. Although Virginian Daniel Morgan tried to keep the assault moving, the initiative had been lost and the Americans were forced to retreat, first from Quebec, and then from Canada itself.

Over the following months into the summer of 1776, Arnold was once again embroiled in controversy having been accused of plundering Canadian civilian stores and wound up in a court martial. He was finally cleared of all charges after Gen. Horatio Gates came to his rescue. At loose ends again, he was dispatched by the army to Lake Champlain to help counter a growing British naval threat in the area. With hundreds of experienced Marblehead men, he managed to build a small but serviceable navy of 15 ships that met a fleet of larger British war vessels off Valcour Island. There, on October 13, 1776, Arnold's force was defeated as expected, but the action, as well as the building of his fleet, delayed British intentions and forced them to abandon their plans for the remainder of the year, a decision that would later contribute to the enemy's first major defeat of the war. However, despite his resourcefulness at Valcour Island, Arnold was once again overlooked for promotion early the next year when Congress elevated five other officers with less seniority. Incensed, Arnold talked of quitting the army and decided to go to Philadelphia personally to seek answers from Congress. On the way however, he was distracted by a British attack on Danbury, Connecticut that left the town burned to the ground. Arnold led much of the local resistance and after incredible displays of reckless bravery and inflicting heavy casualties, chased the enemy back to the sea. For that action, and with support from Washington, he was promoted to major general. Mollified, Arnold accepted an appointment to the staff of Gen. Philip Schuyler and immediately left for upstate New York.

Schuyler's headquarters was not a happy one. Fort Ticonderoga had recently fallen to a British army of almost 6,000 men led by Gen. John Burgoyne and news had just arrived of the siege of Fort Stanwix, 110 miles to the west, by an army of 1,800 British, Tories and Indians. The enemy, commanded by Col. Barry St. Leger, had arrived at the gates of the fort after defeating a relief force of 800 militia under the command of Gen. Nicholas Herkimer in an ambush at Oriskany. If the fort and its 750 defenders fell, it would open the way for the completion of a plan that would find the Americans squeezed between Burgoyne in the north, St. Leger in the west, and a third British army advancing up the Hudson River valley from the south. The siege of Fort Stanwix had to be lifted and the British under St. Leger stopped. Thus, in late August, Arnold was ordered west with 1,000 men to relieve the western outpost. But time was of the essence and, fearful that he might not arrive in time to save the fort, Arnold took advantage of the Indians' fear of a local madman to send him ahead and allow himself to be captured. The ploy worked and when questioned about Arnold's advancing force, the man said the army had as many men as there were leaves on the trees. Frightened, the superstitious Indians abandoned the fight and fled leaving St. Leger too weakened to face both Arnold's army and the men still inside the fort. And so, without firing a shot, Arnold lifted the siege of the fort and for the second time in two years, succeeded in contributing a major factor in foiling Burgoyne's invasion of New York.

Arnold returned to Schuyler's headquarters fired up with his victory in the west and eager for more action when he discovered that due to the loss of Ticonderoga and the continued American retreat south, the New Yorker had been replaced by Horatio Gates. With a confrontation between Burgoyne's army and that of the United States' looming at a place called Saratoga, Arnold was placed in command of the army's left wing but when he asked permission to attack the approaching enemy at Freeman's Farm, was refused. All day on September 19, 1777, after contact had been made, Arnold kept feeding more units into what had become a holding action by the Americans. As the battle progressed however, he sensed an opportunity for victory and urged Gates to let him attack the enemy head on, but Gates still refused. In the end, although Burgoyne had held the ground at Freeman's Farm, his loss of almost a third of his army made it less than a completely satisfying victory. Believing the success of the day's action had been due to his own aggressive moves during the battle, Arnold became incensed when he learned later that the timid Gates had given him none of the credit when he made his report to Congress. Seething with anger, he confronted the general on the issue and was relieved of his command. Reluctant to leave with a major engagement pending, Arnold tried unsuccessfully to persuade Gates to take a more active approach toward the enemy. Finally, on October 7, it was Burgoyne who acted first, emerging from his camp at Freeman's Farm to approach the Americans atop Bemis Heights. As fighting began, Arnold's impetuous nature and burning desire always to prove himself got the better of him and, observing the distant battle from horseback, dashed off to the sound of the guns.

When Arnold arrived at the scene of the action where Morgan was directing the American fire, he rode out ahead of the troops encouraging them to regroup and attack. Men of the Connecticut units taking part in the fight, recognizing him, gave a cheer and with Arnold in the lead, charged a Hessian redoubt and easily captured it, turning the tide of the battle. Arnold however, found himself pinned beneath his fallen horse with the leg he had injured in Canada broken. Arnold's rallying of his men and charge had signaled the end of Burgoyne's army as the British began their retreat back north the next day. On October 17, with food having run out, Burgoyne offered his surrender to the Americans.

Having avoided the amputation of his injured leg, a crippled Arnold at last left Gates' command and returned to Washington at Valley Forge where he signed an Oath of Allegiance to the new United States.

Unable to fight because of his injury, Washington made Arnold military commander of Philadelphia, which had been lately abandoned by its British occupiers. But something had happened to Arnold since the battle of Saratoga. Upon reaching Philadelphia, he rented one of the most splendid homes in the city and began associating himself with members of the town's upper classes who only recently had participated in many of the glittering balls, fetes, and masques put on by their British occupiers. Although warned that even the appearance of impropriety would endanger his reputation, Arnold continued his visits with the suspected Tories. Indeed, it soon became clear that the general was even more interested in Peggy Shippen, daughter of one the city's most prominent men and a woman who had spent an inordinate amount of time flirting with British officers and one, Captain John Andre, in particular. His first wife dead, Arnold pursued Shippen and married her even while he involved himself in shady business deals for which he was eventually brought up on charges. Acquitted on some, but found guilty of using government wagons and personnel for personal business, Arnold grew increasingly resentful at his treatment and began a secret correspondence with the very Andre, now in charge of British spying activities, whom his wife had once known.

In 1780, Washington appointed Arnold as commandant at West Point, an important choke point along the strategic Hudson River, after he had begged off a more prestigious field command. It was while there that he began preparations to hand over the post to the enemy in exchange for money and a high ranking position in the British Army. On the fateful night of September 23, Andre was captured by highwaymen loyal to the American side and turned over to the army. On him, hidden in a boot, were found papers from Arnold giving away defense plans for West Point as well as a record of a recent meeting with Washington. "My God! Arnold has gone over to the British! Whom can we trust now?" demanded a distraught commander in chief upon hearing the news. Meanwhile, Arnold had escaped to a waiting British warship and on October 2, Andre was hanged as a spy. From that time on, Arnold would become the most hated man in America, his reputation, so fairly won on numerous campaigns and battlefields, squandered for gold and misplaced pride.

Compounding his infamy, Arnold became a brigadier general in the British Army and participated in a number of minor spoiling actions in Virginia and his home state of Connecticut where he struck New London only ten miles from his former home. There, Arnold's men forced the surrender of Fort Griswold and once inside, slaughtered the defenders even as their general added to his villainy by setting the town afire. When the war ended, Arnold found that he had only a traitor's reward: infamy in his homeland, suspicion and distrust among the British, and descent into poverty. In failing health, he died destitute in London on June 12, 1801, forgotten and uncared for except by his immediate family.

Josiah Bartlett

More often than not, heroes of the Revolution were drawn from the common folk rather than from the intelligentsia, the military, government, or the wealthy. And frequently in such cases, they became known to history through deeds of martial prowess rather than the quill. And as for personal risk, it often took more courage for such people to stand and be counted than it was for those with better access to resources and influence.

Josiah Bartlett

Such a hero was Josiah Bartlett, a physician who practiced medicine in Kingston, New Hampshire before the Revolution broke out. Bartlett, the son of a simple cobbler, was born on November 21, 1729 in Amesbury, Massachusetts. Displaying some intelligence and a good memory in his school work, he was apprenticed to study medicine with a relative when he was sixteen. By 1750, he had completed his medical training and, moving to Kingston, New Hampshire where more family members lived, he began his own practice and married his cousin, Mary. Bartlett always had a streak of independence in him and when his neighborhood was struck with a wave of fever, he cured himself with a natural treatment based on the idea that the body signaled what it needed to recover from an illness and all a physician needed to do was to heed those warnings. After recovering from his own sickness, he used the treatment on others and succeeded where those of his competitors failed. It was an idea that he would later apply to politics, believing that like the body, ordinary folk knew what they needed in the way of good government without the naysayers of the establishment from thousands of miles away telling them what they ought to think. The performance during the epidemic increased his local popularity which was only reinforced when a throat ailment swept through the community and again, ignoring the treatment prescribed by other doctors, Bartlett recommended the use of Peruvian bark which worked.

With a thriving medical practice, Bartlett built a large house in Kingston which in time would prove more than useful for his twelve children and the meetings of local physicians that he hosted. By 1765, Bartlett was well known and was appointed to the provincial legislature, an office he held until the outbreak of war between the United States and England. As the years passed, Bartlett's independent streak made itself apparent in politics. He began to speak out against royal authority and, notwithstanding the fact that the colony's Governor John Wentworth appointed him a judge and commander of the local militia, sided increasingly with local patriots and served on the colony's Committees of Correspondence and Safety while continuing as a member of the Provincial Congress. In response, Bartlett was dismissed from the bench and his home destroyed in a mysterious fire. In 1774 he was chosen to represent New Hampshire at the First Continental Congress, an appointment he was forced to forego while he sought new living arrangements for his homeless family. With the construction of a new house, his domestic situation improved and by the time of the Second Continental Congress, he was able to attend and ended up voting for independence and becoming the first delegate to sign the Declaration of Independence on August 2, 1776 following President of Congress John Hancock.

Soon after the Declaration was signed and the Articles of Confederation approved, Bartlett resigned from Congress and in 1777 accompanied Gen. John Stark's New Hampshire militia in the capacity of medical officer when it marched to Vermont and the battle of Bennington. In the spring of the following year, he was once again elected to

Congress but before the year was up, found himself back in New Hampshire where he once again became involved in local politics serving for the next ten years as a judge in the lower courts and then the state's Supreme Court. The move would mark the end of Bartlett's role on the national stage except perhaps for his participation as a member and sometime chairman of New Hampshire's convention that ratified the United States Constitution in 1788. The death of his wife in 1789 depleted much of his desire for public service and after refusing to run for the new United States Senate, in 1790 Bartlett accepted the position of governor (or president as the position was then called) of New Hampshire. In 1791 Bartlett founded the New Hampshire Medical Society and retired as governor in 1794. He died the following year on May 19, 1795.

Daniel Boone

America's most famous frontiersman, Daniel Boone, was perhaps the type of man who should never have married. The lure of the wilderness was too strong and his insatiable curiosity to always see what was on the other side of the mountain led him to embark on "long hunts" that lasted months, sometimes years before he returned to civilization. More at home with other men with the same rough hewn qualities or even the savage Indians that populated the lands that he roamed, Boone did his wife and many children no favors by being absent from home so long, especially in a day and age where life on America's frontier was hand to mouth and dependent on settlers raising their own crops or hunting for their food. Without a man in the home, survival became that much more precarious. In his defense, however, Boone's wilderness skills and Indian fighting capabilities were valuable qualities needed by everyone on the frontier not just his own family. Thus, he was often called upon to take part in reprisal raids on nearby Indians or hunting down war parties that had kidnapped local residents. In a country where law and civilization were weak if not nonexistent, Boone became a community builder, not only establishing settlements, but taking part in local government as well. And when the Revolution broke out, he and his neighbors hardly noticed as they were already in the middle of an Indian war that had begun years before. The major

change caused by the war in the east was that already scanty ammunition and militia units be-
came even scarcer on the
frontier and settlers were
thrown for the most part
onto their own resources.
Meanwhile, the British, in
an effort to open a second
front in the war, worked to
incite the Indians to greater action and although
they themselves were
seldom seen in uniform on
the frontier, their surro-
gates in the form of Indian
chief Joseph Brant and the
traitorous Girty brothers
seemed to be everywhere.

Born in a log cabin
along the Schuylkill River
in Exeter Township, Penn-
sylvania on October 22,
1734, Daniel Boone grew

Daniel Boone

up only with what education he learned from his own parents which,
like most frontier families, included simple figures and reading and
writing from the Bible. For the most part, his early life was taken up
with hunting and woodcraft, skills crucial to his family's survival and
that would prove important in his later career. When he was sixteen, his
father moved the family to Rowan County in North Carolina where
Boone worked as a wagoner and blacksmith. The year before, he had
gone on his first long hunt and found that adventure more to his liking.
Meanwhile, at his new home, Boone gained a reputation for marksman-
ship and made hunting his livelihood. The French and Indian War,
however, interrupted his new career, and he was with British Major
Gen. Edward Braddock's army when it met defeat while marching on
Fort Duquesne. When he was aged 22, Boone married Rebecca Bryan,
a partner whose patience and strength would prove invaluable to a man
like himself who would later be absent from home for great lengths of
time and who would insist on moving his family far beyond the areas
of established settlements.

In 1769, after settling his family back in Wilkesboro, North Carolina, Boone was visited by a friend named John Findley who asked him if he would be interested in joining him to look for a way across the Appalachian Mountains into Kentucky, the fabled hunting grounds of the local Indians whose law forbade permanent settlement within its borders. Having already visited the region once two years before and aware of its rich population of game, Boone joined the party and soon helped to blaze a trail through the Cumberland Gap and into the Kentucky country. What began as a months long hunting trip ended two years later after Boone's party was scattered and he himself captured by Indians not once, but twice. Before it was over, Boone had spent the last weeks of the hunt on his own, exploring the wilderness with hardly more than his rifle and a bedroll. The experience merely served to whet his appetite for Kentucky, which he found to be a sportsman's paradise of wild game.

In 1773, Boone made his first attempt to bring his family and other settlers to Kentucky but was stopped by an Indian attack in the Cumberland Gap that took the life of his eldest son. Settling temporarily on the Clinch River on the Virginia border, Boone was asked to go back to Kentucky and warn hunters and surveyors there that the Shawnee were on the warpath. His warnings came none to soon as, with the start of Lord Dunmore's War, he was forced to help defend the Clinch River settlements against Indian attack. Named a captain in the local militia, Boone was still determined not to waste any more time moving his family to Kentucky despite continued hostilities. Joining a real estate developer called the Transylvania Company, he helped to clear the Wilderness Road through the Gap and, building a stockade fort on the Kentucky River, founded Boonesborough.

Having brought his family to Kentucky at last, life at Boonesborough was precarious at best. In addition to building their homes and clearing the land for crops, the settlers had to always keep a wary eye out for Indians, angry at the violation of their hunting grounds by uncaring white men. Soon, Indians began to raid outlying cabins, murdering the men and often carrying women and children into captivity. In 1776, the year that the thirteen colonies declared independence from British rule, Boone's daughter Jemima and two of her friends were kidnapped by Shawnee warriors. Keeping their wits about them, the girls managed to slow down the Indian's pace while at the same time leaving clues for the pursuers they knew would be on their trail. A couple of days after the raid, Boone, leading a party of settlers, caught up to the war party and rescued the girls. Two years later, Boone himself was captured while hunting for a party of 30 men he had led to Blue Licks to collect salt. The Shawnee war party was led by Chief Black Fish and accompanied by two of the infamous Girty brothers, George and James. Impressed by his woodcraft, bold talk, and especially with his help in getting his men to surrender, Boone was adopted into the tribe as the son of the chief. Boone remained with the tribe for almost four months, waiting for the opportunity to escape. Time finally ran out after he discovered that the Shawnee, with the encouragement of the British, planned to attack Boonesborough. Slipping from the Indian camp, his absence was discovered and he was soon being trailed by a relentless party of warriors. What followed was an epic five day chase beginning in the vicinity of Detroit where Boone was forced to draw upon every bit of experience he had in order to elude and finally out distance his pursuers and arrive at Boonesborough in time to warn its inhabitants of attack. Taking charge of the defenses, Boone helped its inhabitants to withstand a 10 day siege by an army of over 400 Indians led by his adopted father who had come under the instructions of British Lt. Governor of Detroit Henry Hamilton, who, unbeknownst to his savage allies, would be captured at Vincennes a few months later on February 25, 1779 by another frontiersman, George Rogers Clarke.

When Boone arrived back at the settlement, he discovered that his wife and children, assuming he had been killed after Blue Licks, had retired to the safety of North Carolina. In 1779, after clearing his name at a court martial proceeding where he had been charged with aiding in the surrender of the men at Blue Licks and later attempting to arrange a peace treaty with the enemy without authorization, he returned his family to Kentucky along with a large group of additional settlers. But instead of heading to Boonesborough, Boone guided the party to the north side of the Kentucky River and founded Boone's Station. The next year, Boone and his brother Edward brought the war to the natives when they joined raiding parties that attacked the Indians in the Ohio country. After Edward was killed in battle with the Shawnee, Boone was elected to the Virginia legislature and this time found himself captured not by Indians but by the British when they invaded the state and forced the legislature, as well as Governor Thomas Jefferson, to flee for their lives. Having remained behind to secure public records, Boone was captured but released on parole by the British.

Returning to the frontier, Boone arrived in time to become one of the commanding officers at the Battle of Blue Licks in 1782. There, a force of less than 200 hundred reckless frontiersman eager for battle, ignored Boone's advice and threw themselves directly into a raiding party of 600 Indians and British who had prepared an elaborate trap for them. Before the battle was over, 72 Americans were killed, among them Boone's own son Israel, who died in his father's arms. Although he was forced to join in the panicky retreat from the battlefield, Boone immediately accompanied a second army of 500 men who returned to Blue Licks to bury the fallen and then proceeded to attack and burn out a number of Shawnee villages and their accompanying crops. The Battle of the Blue Licks, fought on September 10, 1782, turned out to be the last pitched fight of the Revolutionary War but far from the end of hostilities between white man and red on the frontier. After the war ended in 1783, Boone moved his family again, this time to Limestone on the Ohio River where he employed himself at different times with surveying, hunting, real estate speculation, and even keeping bar. It was the next year, in 1784, that Boone's name became a household word and his life as a woodsman, hunter, and Indian fighter came to the attention of every American upon the publication of John Filson's incredibly popular *The Adventures of Daniel Boone*.

Although the Revolutionary War may have ended with the Treaty of Paris and the British retreat back to their forts north of the Ohio River, it was not so easy to halt the primitive forces the enemy had unleashed when they encouraged the Indians to begin attacking the frontier settlements. And so, in 1786, a middle aged Boone, now a lieutenant colonel, once again led attacks on Shawnee villages in the autumn and the next year helped to arrange a prisoner exchange between the two sides. Once more elected to the Virginia legislature, Boone alternated his official duties with a cycle of moves that took his family ever farther west. He was pushed clean out of Kentucky when it became the fifteenth state and land claims began to be investigated. It was soon discovered that Boone's claims could not be proved and he lost everything. At the same time, an arrest warrant was issued against him for outstanding debts. To escape, he moved his family yet again, this time to the banks of the Ohio River. In 1797, his son Daniel Morgan Boone had gone to look over land in Spanish controlled Missouri and sent back a favorable report. A short time later, the entire Boone clan was invited to relocate to Missouri by the region's governor. Seemingly unwelcome in the state he had given so much to establish, Kentucky's most famous son left it in 1799 and traveled down the Ohio River and reunited his family in St. Louis. There, under Spanish authority, Boone became a magistrate for the Femme Osage District and was rewarded with land for his services. But again, as happened in Kentucky, when

Missouri became part of the United States after ratification of the Louisiana Purchase, he lost or was forced to sell all.

Over the next few years, Boone would continue to fight to retain the rights to his land in federal court but in 1813 he was struck with an even greater misfortune when he lost his courageous wife Rebecca. The following year, by special act of Congress, Boone was allowed to keep some of the land he claimed and went to live with his son Nathan. Healthy almost to the last, the aging Boone continued enjoying the outdoors as much as he could, participating in his last hunt in 1818, only two years before his death in 1820. The great frontiersman and Indian fighter was buried beside his beloved Rebecca in a small burial ground near the farm of his daughter Jemima, the girl he had once rescued from capture by marauding Indians.

Carter Braxton

Born to privilege on September 10, 1736, Carter Braxton, a signer of the Declaration of Independence, was the son of politically connected parents who spent the first part of his life living in the lap of luxury before his support of the Revolution brought him low.

Braxton grew up on his father's estate at Newington Plantation, in King's County, Virginia before being bundled off to the College of William and Mary for the completion of his education. Before he graduated in 1755, his father died and he inherited the family's holdings and vast wealth. That same year, he made an advantageous marriage to Judith Robinson, a wealthy heiress and settled down at Newington to raise a family and manage his plantations. But tragedy struck only two years later when his wife died in childbirth and Braxton took to the sea, traveling to England for two years. When he returned to Virginia in 1760, it was to Elsing Green in King William County, a new home built in his absence and a second marriage, this time to Elizabeth Corbin, the daughter of the colony's receiver of customs, a connection that would prove useful in the future.

By 1761, Braxton was a settled member of the powerful planter class and followed his peers into the colony's legislature as representative from King William's County. As controversy grew around the British Parliament's attempts to tax the American colonies, Braxton, aware of how such taxes would affect the sale and profit of the agricultural produce of his farms, found himself drifting into opposition. By 1765, he was prepared to stand with fellow legislator Patrick Henry when the young firebrand introduced his Stamp Act resolutions for approval by the colonial government. From that point on, Braxton became a committed patriot supporting anti-importation resolutions and stands against British claims of authority over the colonies. In 1774, after the House of Burgesses was dissolved, Braxton continued to meet with fellow legislators in defiance of the royal governor's action and his participation in revolutionary committees increased. Matters seemed to come to a head the following year when the exiled legislature decided to join other colonies in defiance of England and to continue to have its delegates participate in a Continental Congress. Meanwhile, Virginia patriots voted to prepare the colony for armed resistance and passed legislation encouraging the production and stockpiling of war materiel. The colony's governor, Lord Dunmore, learning of the action, ordered the colony's supplies of gunpowder removed from the mainland and stored in a warship offshore. The move enraged local patriots who, led by Patrick Henry, threatened to go on a rampage if the powder were not returned or at least paid for. Full scale violence was only avoided when Braxton arranged with his father-in-law, the colony's receiver of customs, to have the government pay for the powder.

Carter Braxton

But the narrow escape came too late for America as a whole, as almost simultaneously, open warfare broke out far to the north in Massachusetts when farmers fired on British troops at Concord Bridge.

Hostilities only added urgency to the business of the Continental Congress while Braxton, after seeing how easily men could be turned into a mob during the gunpowder crisis, still had his doubts about democracy and separation from England. Nevertheless, when he was chosen to replace the deceased Peyton Randolph as a member of Virginia's delegation to Congress, he accepted. Arriving in Philadelphia early in 1776, Braxton joined Congress just in time to become suspicious of New England's democratic ways and to participate in debate on independence, adding his voice to those urging caution. But after an unsuccessful invasion of Canada by Continental troops, the landing of thousands of British soldiers in New York, and an attempted enemy naval assault on Charleston, South Carolina, those voices were definitely in the minority. And so, when a Declaration of Independence was submitted to Congress for approval, Braxton was among the signers, placing his name to the historic document on August 2, 1776. But despite his support for independence, Braxton's career in Congress was cut short soon after the signing when he was removed from Virginia's delegation. Still wary of open democracy, he had expressed his fears publicly in advance of a planned convention where the formation of a new state government was to be discussed and as a result, lost his popular support. Among his peers, however, he retained favor and with their help, was elected as a member of the new state legislature later in 1776.

Although Braxton served in state government in one capacity or another for the rest of his life, a mixture of patriotism and bad financial decisions had destroyed his once considerable wealth. During the war, he had lent money in support of the revolutionary struggle and invested in privateers almost all of which were sunk or captured by the enemy. When the war ended, Braxton was repaid by the government in near worthless Continental currency and was unable to repay his creditors. In 1786, he sold most of his property retaining only Chericoke, a home he had built in 1767 not far from Elsing Green. But busy as he was in office, he chose to retain more modest housing in Richmond where he died of a heart attack on October 10, 1797.

David Brearly

Although many of the Founding Fathers could be said to have taken up arms against the British for reasons of law and the rights of Englishmen, David Brearly was one of those who chose to fight on almost purely philosophical grounds regarding the purpose of law as the guarantor of individual rights. In the end, he placed himself at personal risk by defying the popular will of his fellow Americans and upholding his fundamental belief in the rule of law.

Born on June 11, 1745 at Spring Grove, New Jersey, Brearly was familiar with the Trenton area by the time he entered the College of New Jersey (later Princeton). There, he became familiar with the precepts of western jurisprudence, the history of philosophy, and the great writers that gave rise to the Enlightenment. His mind fired by the role of law in government and its relationship to the natural rights of man, Brearly left college before graduation in order to pursue a legal career. Eventually, he passed the bar and went into practice for himself in Allentown, New Jersey.

David Brearly

It was his interest in philosophy and the origins of the rights of Englishmen as embodied in the Common Law that led directly to Brearly's decision to join the ranks of local patriots. Doing so, he stood in defiance of those measures passed by the British Parliament that he believed were a betrayal Americans' rights as Englishmen. At one point, he became so outspoken in the patriot cause that William Franklin, New Jersey's royal governor, threatened to have him arrested. By 1776, with warfare against England having begun in Massachusetts the year before, Brearly openly supported a call for independence from Britain and was appointed colonel in a local militia unit. At first concentrating on training and equipping his company, it was not long before Brearly was ordered by the colony's Committee of Safety to interdict Loyalist activity in New Jersey and to disarm the Tories where he could. Although he recognized these activities as clear violations of his long held belief in the rule of law, Brearly nevertheless justified them as being necessary in a time of national emergency. Thus, it was probably with mixed emotions that he was recalled from these duties after a British fleet was sighted off the coast of New York. At that point, Brearly's militia unit was drafted to serve as the colony's regiment in the new Continental Army under Gen. George Washington and assigned to guard New Jersey's coastline. But after the enemy had driven the army from Long Island and was threatening to sweep north out of Manhattan, the regiment found itself transferred to man the defenses on Harlem Heights. The effort failed however, and Brearly's regiment was one of those that joined Washington's retreat to White Plains.

With the army's defeat in New York, the Continental Army needed to be reinforced and Congress authorized the creation of more regiments. When New Jersey was asked to supply a new regiment, Brearly was promoted to lieutenant colonel and briefly placed in command of the 4th New Jersey. But with the need for experienced officers in the 1st New Jersey then just returned from service in Canada, Brearly was soon transferred. As second in command of the 1st Brearly worked to rebuild the unit's fighting ability while at the same time patrolling the no man's land of upper New Jersey against British patrols, roving bands of Loyalists, and criminal bushwackers. At this time, following Washington's victories at Trenton and Princeton, New Jersey became a battleground for the contending forces pending the next large scale movement by the enemy. That movement came on August 25, 1777 when the British sailed 15,000 men up Chesapeake Bay and brought them ashore at Head of Elk, Maryland.

Perceiving that Philadelphia was the object of the enemy's advance, Washington rushed the army to the Brandywine River to block the invasion with Brearly's regiment taking up positions at a place called Chad's Ford. On September 11 the British moved against the ford in a seeming attempt to force its passage, but the move was only a feint with the real attack coming farther upstream where the enemy had found an undefended crossing and threatened the entire American flank. Placed in an impossible position, Washington was forced to call a retreat and leave Philadelphia to the British. As the enemy settled down in the city for a comfortable winter, the Continentals froze at Valley Forge. Come spring however, morale among the Americans had again risen and Brearly's regiment was there when Washington chose to attack the British at Monmouth as the enemy marched out from Philadelphia in June of 1778. Following Monmouth, the British settled once more in New York and turned their attention to the southern theater. With the north suddenly quiet, there was less need to maintain as many men in the field and when the opportunity came to retire from the army, Brearly decided to leave.

Returning to his law practice, Brearly nevertheless kept a hand in with the local militia so that by the war's end, his had become a household name in New Jersey. So much so that in 1779, he was chosen as the new state's chief justice. No sooner had he taken his seat on the bench however, than he became embroiled in a case whose precedent would have profound repercussions on the national scene. At issue was an appeal by John Holmes of a lower court ruling that found him guilty of smuggling. Holmes' appeal was not on the smuggling charge but on being tried by a jury of six men instead of twelve as stipulated in the state's constitution. Despite the expected outcry from an enraged populace, Brearly's respect for the rule of law compelled him to find in the defendant's favor. The constitution was the ruling document and as such, he declared the law passed by the state's legislature allowing for only six jurors in cases of smuggling unconstitutional. It was the first ruling in the country that established judicial review of laws passed by a legislature and one that would have its effect on the Supreme Court of the United States when that body was established nine years later with the ratification of the federal Constitution.

With Brearly's historic decision, his respect for the rule of law, and his expressed wariness that the Articles of Confederation binding the thirteen American states were too weak to protect individual rights, it came as no surprise that after he was appointed to represent New Jersey at the Constitutional Convention of 1787 he would support some kind of stronger federal scheme of government. While participating little in the great debates that took place during the convention, Brearly's influence was nevertheless felt in committee and in his defense of the interests of small states such as New Jersey versus the larger. At one point, he even suggested that the boundaries between the states be redrawn so as to make them all of equal size. In the end, he judged the compromises that created the Constitution properly balanced to protect the rights of all the nation's citizens and signed the finished document.

Later, he would defend the proposed Constitution at New Jersey's ratification convention and had the satisfaction of seeing the state become the third to vote in its favor on December 7, 1787. With the Constitution's passage, Brearly first served as a member of New Jersey's Electoral College voting for his old commander George Washington as the country's first president. Soon after, he accepted an appointment as a federal district judge for New Jersey but was only able to serve in that position for a year before his death in Trenton on August 16, 1790.

Aaron Burr

In the dark underside of the Revolutionary era, the reputation of Aaron Burr rivaled that of Benedict Arnold; but it was not always that way. Early in the war, Burr served with distinction as a soldier under the command of Gen. Richard Montgomery and was present when the general was killed during the forlorn assault on Quebec. It was only after the war when he entered the cauldron of New York politics that Burr's ambition exceeded his judgment. Angry and frustrated, he ended by killing political rival Alexander Hamilton in one of the most infamous duels in American history.

Burr was born in Newark, New Jersey on February 6, 1756 the son of a minister and descendent of religious icon Jonathan Edwards. Two years later, he was orphaned and taken in by an uncle. A precocious child, it was a

Aaron Burr

foregone conclusion that Burr would attend the College of New Jersey (later to be renamed Princeton) where both his grandfather and father had served as president; but a first application made when Burr was only 11 years old was rejected. Trying again at 13, he was accepted and began his studies as a sophomore. At first intending to follow a clerical path like his father, Burr later changed his mind and began to prepare for a legal career.

Graduating in 1772, Burr was still reading law when the Revolutionary War broke out and like other young men, rushed to Massachusetts to join the army then surrounding Boston. Possessing an aristocratic streak perhaps instilled in him by his pedigree, the young Burr went straight to the top, applying for an officer's commission from George Washington, the newly appointed commander in chief of the Continental Army. When nothing came of his application, Burr attached himself to the command of Benedict Arnold in 1775 and accompanied him through the Maine wilderness for an invasion of Canada. By the time that epic wintertime trek ended before the gates of Quebec, Burr was a captain and still with the army, which was by then a shadow of its former self; but when a second army under Gen. Richard Montgomery joined Arnold from the south, Burr switched allegiances. He was at Montgomery's side when the general was killed leading a charge on a blockhouse outside the city on December 31, 1775. The defenders had fired a cannon loaded with grapeshot that downed every man but Burr and a French guide. After Montgomery died in his arms, Burr tried to drag the fallen officer's body to safety but did not have the strength. The next year, having been promoted to major, Burr joined Washington as a member of his personal staff. The assignment however, did not last long as he left the staff after only ten days to serve with Gen. Israel Putnam and took part in patrolling a no man's land between British and American lines north of New York City. During the subsequent battle for Manhattan, Burr fought at Harlem Heights and later helped to quell a mutinous regiment at Valley Forge. At the Battle of Monmouth, he had a horse shot out from under him.

Promoted to major, but suspecting that he was being held back, Burr decided in 1779 to end his military career and return to his law studies. He passed the bar in 1782 and the same year married Theodosia Prevost, a woman ten years his elder and the widow of a British army officer. Although Burr began the practice of law in Albany, he quickly moved his business to New York where it really took off allowing him to afford a lifestyle that appealed to his sense of self-importance. His success in business soon translated into political ambition and he was twice elected to the state legislature in 1784 and 1798 and in 1789, served as New York's attorney general. By then, no one involved in New York's political scene could fail to notice Burr's rapid rise in the public spotlight and if Alexander Hamilton had not been aware of him until then, Burr must certainly have caught his attention when in 1791, he defeated Hamilton's wealthy father-in-law for a seat in the United States Senate. The victory was more than a simple defeat for the Federalist Party that by then had coalesced around Hamilton, it was a challenge to Hamilton's preeminent position in the Byzantine world of New York politics. As Secretary of the Treasury in President Washington's cabinet, Hamilton was certainly one of the most powerful and influential men in the country and not to be easily challenged. In addition, like Burr, Hamilton was also an immensely successful attorney as well as a political foe of the Clinton family clan that had traditionally controlled state politics in New York. Perhaps already suspicious of Burr from the time when he had spent only 10 days on Washington's wartime staff, Hamilton (who had been on staff for years and served as one of the general's closest confidants) probably needed little excuse to form a negative opinion of the former New Jerseyite.

With his rise to public office, Burr had managed to almost single handedly invent the kind of machine that would dominate American urban politics for the next two centuries bringing together a hodge podge of supporters among New York's working classes who identified themselves with Jefferson's small government Republicans. They, in turn, were naturally opposed to Hamilton's Federalist supporters largely made up of the wealthier upper classes who preferred a central government that took a more active role in regulating trade, the economy, and the flow of money. At the time, New York had already become a magnet for investors with its nascent stock market and newly established Bank of New York and so it seemed inevitable that the two sides would clash in the streets of the city with their leaders, Hamilton and Burr, trading invectives in denunciatory speeches.

The contest between the two parties came to a head in the presidential election of 1800 when Hamilton tried to convince Governor John Jay (his partner in the Bank of New York) to have the legislature overturn the results of New York's elections which, as a victory for the Republicans, ensured that the state's 12 electoral votes would go to Thomas Jefferson and Burr who, it was generally understood, were running for president and vice-president respectively. But despite Jay's refusal to do as Hamilton asked, the national election did not go as expected. When the states' electoral ballots were counted, it was found that Jefferson and Burr had tied with 73 votes apiece, throwing the election into the House of Representatives. It was at that point that Burr's ambitions got the best of him. With enemies already on his right in the form of Hamilton and the Federalists, he could not afford to have more on his left with the Republicans. But that is exactly what happened when it appeared that he reneged on an agreement with Jefferson to run as his vice-president and did nothing to encourage the electors dedicated to his candidacy to swing their votes to the Virginian. The struggle in Congress went on for 36 ballots until Hamilton, fearing a Burr presidency more than a Jeffersonian one, joined a movement behind the scenes to influence key votes that had been dedicated to President John Adams. The result was a Jefferson victory that left Burr politically isolated as vice-president.

The effects of his decision to remain silent during the election of 1800 not only cost Burr any influence in Jefferson's administration, but also possible election as governor of New York. Running as an independent candidate in the elections of 1804, Burr was openly opposed by the Clintons and secretly by Jefferson who conspired to destroy his candidacy with a barrage of personal attacks in the press. In the meantime, Burr's frustration grew and in casting about for some release, fastened upon his old enemy Hamilton, who was rumored to have worked against his presidential ambitions as well as having calling his reputation into question. Using a newspaper article that quoted his rival as saying that as "a man of irregular and insatiable ambition" he could not be trusted, Burr sent a note to Hamilton demanding an apology. It was the opening move of the formal dueling process and recognized immediately as such by Hamilton. Despite that knowledge however, Hamilton refused to give the apology. In a series of back and forth communications conducted by seconds, the two men moved inevitably to their historic encounter beneath the heights at Weehauken, New Jersey. There, on July 11, 1804, Burr met Hamilton, shot him, and left the scene immediately by boat, learning only later that his opponent had died. Although legal in New Jersey, political enemies and supporters of Hamilton in New York had no trouble charging Burr with murder. The affair forced the vice-president to flee to South Carolina for a time but when things cooled down, he returned to Washington where dueling was not against the law and resumed his official duties, at one point presiding over the impeachment trial of Samuel Chase, an associate justice of the Supreme Court.

Completing his term as vice-president and realizing his political capital in the east was exhausted, Burr secretly met with the British minister to the United States to sound out the possibility of monetary support for a scheme to carve out an empire from the newly purchased Louisiana Territory and setting himself up as its head of state. Burr next met with an old wartime companion, Gen. James Wilkinson, who had since risen to the position of commander in chief of the army and governor of the Louisiana Territory. Wilkinson, already a spy in the employ of the Spanish, seemed enthusiastic about cooperating in the plan. Thus encouraged, Burr left for the frontier but his progress down the Mississippi River did not go unnoticed and was followed with interest by his political foes who soon began to hear rumors that he planned to raise a private army for a filibuster into Spanish territory. No stranger to such plots, having toyed with a scheme promoted by northern politicians to split New England and northern New York from the union following Jefferson's election as president, Burr should have exercised more caution in his activities. As it was, bringing in Wilkinson proved to be a big mistake. Already working both sides of the fence, the fearful general had no trouble turning state's evidence against his friend, leading to Burr's arrest in 1807. Taken from Mississippi and brought east to Richmond, Virginia, Burr was to stand trial for treason in one of the most famous cases in American jurisprudence. Now at last, Jefferson had his old enemy where he wanted him; unfortunately for the president however, the trial would be presided over by chief justice John Marshall who was no friend of the administration. In the end, the government failed to prove its case against Burr for lack of witnesses and though a charge of misdemeanor still remained, the New Yorker was essentially a free man.

The exposure of his plan of conquest cost Burr his few remaining sympathizers and left him without a future in the United States. Finally in 1808, he left the country for England but found little interest there for plots involving the seizure of land at the expense of the United States. Four years later, he returned to New York where he succeeded in having charges for the murder of Hamilton removed from his record and resumed the practice of law. He had just begun to get back on his feet when he learned that a ship upon which his daughter was traveling was lost at sea. Burr carried on for another twenty years until, weakened by a pair of strokes, he died at Port Richmond, Staten Island, New York, on September 14, 1836.

Charles Carroll

Made up of human beings, the societies of the original thirteen colonies were anything but uniform: in politics, in work, and most especially in matters of religion. When British colonists first crossed the Atlantic to North America, for many of them, the primary purpose was to escape the internecine struggles of religious faction in Britain and to establish their own communities whose affairs would be conducted according to the precepts of their own beliefs. Puritans did so in Massachusetts Bay, Quakers in Pennsylvania, the Church of England in Virginia, and Catholics in Maryland. But even with an ocean between them, colonists soon discovered that it was not enough to insulate them against the prejudices of the Old World. In England, the seventeenth century was dominated by the struggle for power between fundamentalist Protestant sects and the episcopacy represented by the Church of England and to a lesser degree, Roman Catholicism. In that struggle, Catholics lost out and became doomed to a second class citizenship that lasted until the nineteenth century. In America, the same struggle took place with the result that Protestants escaping from Anglican Virginia settled in Maryland and, soon outnumbering the original colonists, followed the example of their British brethren and disenfranchised the Catholics. That was where matters stood at the time of Charles Carroll's birth, when a lingering suspicion and prejudice persisted against the 10,000 or so Catholics then living within the thirteen colonies. Suspicions that were not helped by the presence of a Catholic Spain in New Orleans and the large population of French Catholics in Canada for whom Britain had guaranteed freedom of worship with the Quebec Act of 1774. In addition, rowdy, insulting festivals such as Pope's Day were still celebrated in many colonial towns in which Catholics and their beliefs were regularly mocked and ridiculed, adding fuel to the public's prejudices. Thus, the career of Charles Carroll became a celebration of two kinds of liberty, that of Americans' freedom from British oppression and the beginning of the acceptance of Catholics as full members of the new United States.

Not that it would be easy. Catholics would find the road to complete acceptance a long one, stretching well into the twentieth century. But all journeys have a beginning, and the one for Catholics in the United States began on September 19, 1737, the day Charles Carroll was born.

As the heir to perhaps the largest fortune in the thirteen colonies, it was ironic that in the years preceding the Revolution, Carroll could not vote or hold office in his native Maryland. Although it would no doubt have happened anyway, part of the reason was due to the outspoken nature of his grandfather who had been outraged by the injustice; a rebellious streak that the younger Carroll seemed to have inherited but that only manifested itself upon his return from Europe where he had spent twelve years being taught by Jesuits at St-Omer in French Flanders and the College Louis le Grand in Paris before studying law in London.

Charles Carroll

With growing resentment at the repeated attempts by the British Parliament to impose taxes upon the colonies, Carroll was finally moved to overcome his enforced political neutrality after Maryland's Governor Robert Eden overruled the colonial assembly in 1770 to retain a higher fee schedule that public servants used to charge residents for their services. "War is now declared between the government and the people," declared Carroll, who challenged the ruling in a series of newspaper articles he signed as "1st Citizen." His performance won the admiration of local patriots and thrust Carroll into the front rank of the colony's revolutionary movement.

But it was with his election to the Maryland Convention that Carroll at last shattered the prohibition against Catholics participating in state government. From there, he was appointed as an unofficial member of the colony's delegation to the Continental Congress whose instruction to resist any call for colonial independence Carroll opposed. It was while serving with the Congress that Carroll was chosen, along with Benjamin Franklin and Samuel Chase, to go to Canada and try to enlist its support in the struggle against Britain. But French-Catholic suspicions of the predominantly Protestant colonies to the south and the failure of an American attempt to invade Canada doomed the mission to failure.

Upon returning from Canada, Carroll worked in Maryland to convince fellow patriots there to support independence from Britain and was rewarded for his efforts both with support for his position and by being elected as a full member of the colony's congressional delegation. Thus it was that Carroll was present that day on August 2, 1776, when the official copy of the Declaration of Independence was signed, risking not only his life, but a personal fortune that was far in excess of any of his fellow signers.

It was while serving on the congressional Board of War that Carroll was elected as a delegate to Maryland's constitutional convention and was instrumental in devising how the state's senate was to be formed. In 1778, he resigned his seat in Congress to enter state politics, becoming a member of Maryland's new senate. Ten years later, he found himself holding two offices at once: his seat in the Maryland legislature and that of congressman in the United States Senate which had been created under the country's new Constitution. Like many of his fellow patriots, Carroll had always been wary of popular democracy, fearing the sort of unthinking, prejudiced mob rule that had oppressed Catholics such as himself for years and so, trusting to a more enlightened elite, aligned himself with the new Federalist Party under the leadership of Alexander Hamilton who advocated a strong central government. But if forced to choose, Carroll's loyalties, like many of his contemporaries, were with his state first, and in 1792, after Congress voted to disallow holding state and federal positions at the same time, the Marylander chose to give up national office and retain his seat in his state's senate, a position he held until 1801.

As a Federalist, Carroll was pessimistic about the nation's future after Thomas Jefferson won the election of 1800. The leader of the anti-federalist Republican Party, Jefferson favored a weak central government and the granting of more direct power to the people. But as the years passed, and the Virginia dynasty that held the presidency from 1800-1825 did not spell doom for the United States, Carroll found himself growing more optimistic about the nation's future. Although still not completely accepted, with the freedom of religion enshrined in the nation's Constitution, the rights of Catholics were guaranteed while their numbers continued to grow with increased immigration, the purchase of the Louisiana Territory, and the future annexation of much of the Spanish Southwest. Meanwhile, on the Fourth of July, 1828, at the dawn of the machine age, Carroll had the honor of laying the cornerstone of the Baltimore and Ohio railroad, just two years to the day after the twin deaths of Thomas Jefferson and John Adams. But at the time, Adams' dying reference to "Jefferson still survives" was wrong on two counts: Jefferson was already dead and Carroll, who would become the sole surviving signer of the Declaration of Independence, still lived. In fact, Carroll endured until 1832, by which time he had become a near legend among a new generation of Americans who were not even born when the Revolutionary War ended in 1783.

Samuel Chase

At first glance, Samuel Chase might not seem to be a hero, at least not in the traditional sense of a man of action. Although he spent most of his career in courtrooms and committee meetings, the fact that he risked his life when he signed the Declaration of Independence says something about his personal courage. But there are other kinds of courage than the sort found on the battlefield, like the kind of courage it takes to stand up for what you believe even if it makes you unpopular with your friends. Which was what happened to Chase, always a headstrong, independent man, when he stood in opposition to ratification of the United States Constitution and later, while a member of the Supreme Court, being impeached for daring to express his fear of a democracy that placed too much power in the hands of ordinary people instead of reserving it to society's elite whom he believed more trustworthy.

Born on April 17, 1741, Chase was raised in the city of Baltimore, Maryland where he was educated at home by his father before going on to study law at Annapolis. Graduating from law school at the age of 20 and deciding to remain in Annapolis to practice his profession, he quickly gained a fiery reputation that upset many people in that quiet community. It was a trait he would cultivate after he became a member of the Maryland General Assembly and began to oppose royal authority in such matters as the Stamp Act and the power of Parliament to tax colonists without their consent. An active member of the local Sons of Liberty, Chase came rapidly to the attention of colonial authorities as a dangerous, swaggering, firebrand who was not averse to participating in the occasional riot such as an assault made on governmental offices that resulted in the destruction of the tax stamps. Making no secret of his extracurricular activities, Chase defended them as the action of "men of reputation and merit," a sentiment which would prove ironic when, over thirty years later, he would be publicly rebuked for expressing just the opposite opinion.

As the efforts of Britain to tax the people continued, the anger of local residents grew until, with the closing of Boston harbor in 1774, their indignation was such that calls were made to hold a special convention of all the colonies. Among those chosen to represent Maryland was the well known Chase who became a delegate to the first Continental Congress. Although strongly resenting what they considered the high handed methods of Parliament, members of Maryland's revolutionary movement were not prepared at that time for a formal break from the mother country. Chase, however, in agreement with fellow patriot Charles Carroll, was in no doubt of his own position, renouncing early in 1775 any loyalty to Britain. Consequently, after serving as a member of an unsuccessful delegation charged by Congress to persuade the inhabitants of Canada to join in the revolution and having served on more congressional committees than anyone except possibly Massachusetts' John Adams, Chase returned to Maryland and worked to convince his fellow citizens that their only recourse in the dispute with Britain was to seek independence. Succeeding in his task, Chase

Samuel Chase

returned to Congress and in 1776 joined Carroll in signing the Declaration of Independence.

After independence, Chase served in Congress until 1778 applying himself in a successful effort to prevent a reconciliation with Britain that would have compromised the nation's newly won independence. He also joined in a defense of George Washington against enemies who sought to replace him as the army's Commander in Chief. Casting a pall over his Congressional career and the sterling reputation he had won as a staunch advocate of the principals of the Revolution was his participation in a scheme to corner the market in flour and being branded as a war profiteer. The use of privileged information for personal aggrandizement, which Alexander Hamilton said, gave Chase "the peculiar privilege of being universally despised," was shockingly out of character for the Marylander who, as a result, was removed from the state's delegation to Congress. The affair marked the beginning of a change in his personality, a hardening of his more conservative attitudes, perhaps caused by the bitterness of being censured, that seemed to build on his always headstrong, opinionated character. Still commanding a measure of respect, Chase spent the years after 1778 in a number of official capacities including justice of both the Maryland criminal and general courts until being nominated by President Washington, to the Supreme Court in 1796. Accepting the office placed Chase, now a staunch Federalist in support of a strong central government, in the odd position of sitting on a court created by a United States Constitution whose ratification he had vigorously opposed.

It was his position as a Federalist and a judge on the powerful Supreme Court that placed Chase directly in the sights of Thomas Jefferson when the Virginian succeeded John Adams as the nation's third president. Jefferson, leader of those opposed to a strong central government, had been appalled at Chase' behavior in a pair of trials conducted against newspaper publishers charged with violation of the Alien and Sedition Acts. Determined to rid the high court of a political enemy, Jefferson arranged to have Chase impeached. The immediate trigger for the move were some intemperate remarks Chase, in his capacity as judge, had charged to a Maryland grand jury that proved to be too much for the Republicans and embarrassing to the Federalists. Chase, who had already narrowly escaped removal from his state positions on two separate occasions, advocated a change in the structure of both state and federal government and condemned the repeal of the Judiciary Act of 1789 which removed 16 federal judges from office, an ill disguised attack not only against his colleagues on the Supreme

Court who upheld it, but on the president himself. "The change of the State constitution, by allowing universal suffrage," said Chase, "will...rapidly destroy all protection of property, and all security to personal liberty; and our republican constitution will sink into a mobocracy, the worst of all possible government." What he said was also the worst thing Chase could have uttered in a nation whose politics had firmly shifted away from federalism to populism. It was the opening the Republicans needed to attack Chase, remove him from the bench, and leave the field clear for the person some said was their real target: John Marshall, the rising star of the federalist leaning high court and political enemy of the president.

If such was indeed the plan, Republicans must have been disappointed with the outcome of the impeachment trial which ended in 1805 with Chase acquitted of all the charges made against him, including those involving his conduct of the Alien and Sedition Acts trials. A final charge dealing with his outburst before the Maryland court failed for lack of a majority vote in the Senate. Though acquitted, his unyielding nature and strong opinions that were increasingly in opposition to the growing movement for popular democracy prevented Chase from completely restoring the reputation he had before the Revolutionary War ended in 1783. Even his last years on the Supreme Court were eclipsed by a growing illness that prevented him from fully participating in the court's deliberations and the rise of John Marshall as Chief Justice. Chase, however, continued to serve his nation to the bitter end, dying in 1811, still a member of the Supreme Court.

Benjamin Church

The life of Benjamin Church began in almost as much mystery as it ended with much of what was left in between equally uncertain until after his strange disappearance and presumed death in 1776.

Although it is known that Church was born in Newport, Rhode Island in 1734, little else is certain about his early life save that he was the offspring of a respected family and that later he was educated at the Boston Latin School and graduated from Harvard College in 1754. Gravitating toward medicine, he studied under Charles Pynchon before traveling to Europe to complete his education in the most up to date methods of treatment. Later, he met his wife in England and finally returned to Massachusetts where he began his own medical practice.

In 1760, Church probably had not begun to think about local politics when he wrote a pair of popular poems in honor of the coronation of King George III, but by 1765 and the subsequent furor roused by Parliament's passage of the Stamp Act, he had turned his skill with a pen to the patriot cause. Writing for *The Times*, a paper Massachusetts royal Governor Francis Bernard singled out as especially subversive, Church came to the attention of patriot firebrand Samuel Adams who brought him into the Sons of Liberty and the company of other patriots such as John Hancock, Paul Revere, and Joseph Warren. Unbeknownst to them however, Church had fallen heavily into debt after building himself a huge house in Raynham, a situation that forced him to seek funds beyond what he earned even as a successful physician. As it turned out, his needs (and perhaps the promptings of his English born wife) led him perhaps as early as 1771 into secret intercourse with British authorities in Massachusetts. It was information that he supplied which resulted in the British march to Lexington and Concord in the spring of 1775 and ultimately, the "shot heard 'round the world." But in the late 1760s, when Church may have made his earliest contact with royal authorities, none of that was known.

In 1770, he was on the scene in the aftermath of the Boston Massacre to treat the injured and in 1772 became a member of the Committee of Safety where he worked to prepare the colony for war and even signed the order appointing Benedict Arnold a colonel in the Massachusetts militia and instructing him to raise a force for the seizure of Fort Ticonderoga. His posi-

Benjamin Church

tion on the committee gave him access to particularly sensitive information, information that he passed on to the British occupying force by way of a mistress he kept in the city. In the meantime, Church continued to cement his position in the patriot cause with his writings and a memorable speech given on the third anniversary of the Boston Massacre. But despite his high standing among the rank and file, there were those among the inner circle of the Sons of Liberty who began to suspect his loyalties. The British seemed unusually well informed about what was discussed at secret meetings held by local patriots at the Green Dragon Tavern, their favorite watering hole, and word may have been received by Revere, who ran spies in Boston, that the doctor's personal accounts included occasional infusions of cash that could not be accounted for through his normal medical practice. While Revere kept his suspicions to himself, Church continued to command the esteem of his fellow patriots as he was rumored to have participated in the Boston Tea Party and in 1774, was chosen as a delegate to the Provincial Congress which met in defiance of the governor's suspension of the legislature.

After the debacle suffered by the British at Lexington and Concord and a Boston that had turned into an armed camp besieged by thousands of local militiamen, Church suddenly determined to enter the city for what he claimed was a search for medical supplies. When he returned to American lines, he was faced with questions about having been seen leaving the headquarters of British General Thomas Gage. At the time, Church said that he had been captured and brought in for questioning, but a friend reported to Revere that when he left the headquarters, it was in the manner of a guest rather than a prisoner. The incident was dismissed, at least publicly, and Church continued his activities among the patriots even being appointed Surgeon General and director of hospitals upon formation of the Continental Army and the arrival of Gen. George Washington as commander in chief.

It all came crashing down however when Church entrusted a ciphered note to his mistress for delivery to an officer on the staff of General Gage. Unable to deliver it herself, the woman entrusted it to a friend named Godfrey Wenwood to complete delivery. Suspicious, Wenwood confided with still a third person who opened the note and advised that it be handed over to patriot officials in Rhode Island. Startled by the code in which the letter was written, Wenwood was directed by Rhode Island patriots to Gen. Nathanael Green, then with the Continental Army positioned around Boston. Finally, at the end of September, 1775, the incriminating note finally reached Washington's headquarters. Decoded, the message gave details about American defenses outside the city, plans for the invasion of Canada and the mood of Congress. Immediately, an order was given for the arrest of the mistress and although Washington wrote to John Hancock that she "was proof against every threat and persuasion," the woman finally broke early the next morning and confessed that the note had come from Church. Now it was the doctor's turn to be taken into custody but an attempt to search his papers was thwarted when it was discovered that his home had already been visited by an accomplice who managed to take away any incriminating evidence. In a subsequent court martial before Washington, Church was found guilty of "criminal correspondence" with the enemy and in a separate hearing before the Provincial Congress, where Church insisted that "the warmest bosom here does not flame with a brighter zeal for the security, happiness and liberties of America, than mine," the finding was confirmed.

Sentenced to life imprisonment, Church was first taken to Norwich, Connecticut for confinement but later moved back to Massachusetts when the British abandoned Boston. In Waltham, he barely escaped a maddened crowd by climbing out a rear window of his prison and in 1777, a claim of illness earned him a reprieve and banishment to the West Indies. He boarded a ship and set sail but the vessel never arrived at its intended destination. It, the crew, and Church himself, vanished and were never heard from again.

Abraham Clark

Although there is no evidence that Abraham Clark ever expressed any deep philosophical positions on the great issues raised by the Revolution, "the poor man's counselor" was genuinely a man of the people, sympathies that he shared with many other Founding Fathers and that, perhaps more than anything else, motivated this quiet, retiring farmer to be one of the earliest to embrace independence.

Born on February 15, 1726 the sole offspring of an Elizabethtown, New Jersey farmer, Clark was not a strong child and was soon judged by his father as unsuited for labor intensive farming life. Instead, recognizing in his son an aptitude for mathematics, the senior Clark thought the surveying profession might be a better fit and hired a tutor to teach him the basics. Eventually, Clark did become a surveyor but a natural interest in study also attracted him to the law and so, when his tutoring days ended, he continued to pore over legal books on his own. Later, combining his surveying activities with a nodding acquaintance with the law, he felt confident enough to begin advising his neighbors on issues involving boundary disputes. Although it was likely that Clark never passed the bar, his opinions were highly prized by residents around Elizabethtown and were often dispensed without charge or in exchange for produce. As a consequence, he became known as "the poor man's counselor" and earned a reputation for trustworthiness and magnanimity. Those qualities, borne out of a genuine concern for the welfare of others, were what probably drew Clark into the patriot orbit early in the Revolutionary struggle. His popularity and integrity were such that he soon found himself appointed as the clerk of the colonial legislature and later high sheriff of Essex County even as he served on New Jersey's Committee of Safety and became more deeply involved in revolutionary activity. In 1775 he was elected to the Provincial Congress which met in defiance of royal authority and from there, in 1776, was chosen as one of the delegates to the Continental Congress.

Abraham Clark

In company with Richard Stockton, Francis Hopkinson, and John Witherspoon, Clark's delegation had been picked specifically to replace New Jersey's first group of representatives who had proven to be not sufficiently zealous in the cause of independence as their constituents preferred. For his part, Clark had no intention of disappointing those who sent him to Congress and, likening the action as "embarking on a most tempestuous sea" fraught with danger, voted unhesitatingly to cut ties with England and signed the Declaration of Independence.

In the following years, Clark divided his time between the Continental Congress and New Jersey's new state government even as he fretted over his home which lay in the path of the British army as it contended with George Washington for control first of New York, and then of the New Jersey countryside. In addition, Clark was also concerned for the welfare of his wife and ten children, at least two of whom, serving as officers in the Continental Army, were captured by the enemy and imprisoned. Making their situation worse was the fact that the two men were held prisoner in the *Jersey*, one of a number of decommissioned sailing vessels in New York harbor used to confine prisoners of war. Locked away in the hold of these floating hulks, prisoners were barely fed, forced to live in their own filth, and subject to all kinds of diseases. As a result, few prisoners lived to be freed at the end the war. Learning that his sons were being held in one of these hell holes, Clark became wracked with worry, especially after learning that one of them had been locked in solitary confinement with the only food available being what fellow inmates could squeeze through a keyhole in his prison door. Although Clark had always avoided using his position to improve the lot of his sons in the army, he was finally moved by this latest extremity to ask his fellow congressmen if anything could be done. Congress notified British officials that should the condition of the young Capt. Clark not improve, similar treatment would be afforded their own officers in American hands. As a result, Clark's son was released from close confinement.

When the war ended in 1783, Clark returned to New Jersey where he served in the state legislature. In 1786, he was chosen to represent the state at the Annapolis Convention called by James Madison and Alexander Hamilton to consider inadequacies in the Articles of Confederation, the federal structure under which the thirteen states were then governed. That conference ended with the recommendation that a Constitutional Convention be held in Philadelphia where changes intended to strengthen the Articles of Confederation could be made. Although illness prevented Clark from representing New Jersey at the Constitutional Convention held in 1787, it did not prevent him from coming out in opposition of the new federal instrument that emerged from the Convention. A delegate to New Jersey's ratifying convention, Clark continued to oppose approval of the United States Constitution until a Bill of Rights was included, a position he held in common with many other Founding Fathers and which later became enshrined as the first ten amendments to the Constitution. With the new federal government in place, Clark was elected to rejoin Congress where he remained until retiring in the autumn of 1794. Unfortunately, Clark had not been home to Elizabethtown for long before he died of sunstroke on September 15, 1794.

George Rogers Clark

The Revolutionary War was a struggle fought not only on the battlefields of New York and New Jersey, the plantations of the Carolinas, the high seas, the halls of Congress, and the palaces of Europe, it also encompassed a frontier that stretched 1,500 miles from Canada to Florida. Included in that area was the Old Northwest from which would be carved the current states of Kentucky, Ohio, Wisconsin, Indiana, Illinois and Michigan. Farther to the east, the frontier also extended into the western portions of Pennsylvania, Virginia and New York and in the south, to territory within the current states of Tennessee, Mississippi and Alabama. All throughout those vast regions of untrammeled forest and mountains, advancing white men and native Amerindian tribes had been in an almost continuous state of war that began when the first Europeans arrived on the Atlantic coast of North America in the early 1600s. It was warfare frequently fought without mercy or pity displayed on either side and a struggle that was destined to continue for at least another 100 years after the conclusion of the Revolution.

Sometimes referred to as "the dark and bloody ground," by the time of the Revolution, Kentucky had become the epi-center of this seemingly endless contest for mastery of the wilderness and, over the decades, white men who had chosen to settle on the frontier and challenge the Indians for supremacy had long since learned to fight in the native style. Learning their enemies' skills at hunting and woodcraft, Americans were quick to add them to their own organizational and technological strengths. Less admirable were the Indians' more cold blooded traits involving hideous torture of captives and a pitiless form of warfare that did not distinguish between soldiers and noncombatants, habits that over the years were acquired by many white men as well. And so, while Americans and British in the east met each other in combat arrayed much as military units did on European battlefields, warfare in the west, which, despite British involvement as part of their overall effort to defeat the new United States, continued as it ever had, brutal, desperate and bloody, with few rules to constrain excesses on both sides.

Such was the environment in which one of the greatest heroes not only of the American Revolution, but of all American history came to prominence. Born November 19, 1752 on a 400 acre family farm not two miles from where Thomas Jefferson was born almost ten years earlier, George Rogers Clark was one of ten children whose education was probably received at home (although some evidence exists that he may have had a limited amount of formal schooling). In addition to book learning however, Clark was also taught the surveying trade by his father and, living in the Virginia back-country, shooting, riding and hunting no doubt came as a matter of course. But as manhood approached, the lure of adventure and striking out on his own became too strong and soon Clark was surveying land and guiding settlers into the forbidden Kentucky country, both illegal activities under the British government's enforcement of the Proclamation Line that barred settlement across the Appalachian Mountains. In 1774 his participation in Lord Dunmore's War that ended in the defeat of the Shawnee at Point Pleasant cemented Clark's reputation as both a warrior and a leader. With Kentucky relatively safe from Indian attack, he was chosen by the people there to make their case with the Virginia legislature for recognition as a county or a new colony. Clark's efforts proved successful and Kentucky was not only declared a new county of Virginia, but given 500 pounds of gunpowder for its defense.

The ammunition was put to good use over the following year when hostilities opened in Massachusetts between colonists and Britain

George Rogers Clark

and as part of their overall response to the widening conflict, the English began to encourage the western tribes to fight with them against the encroaching Americans. And so, as Indian attacks all along the frontier intensified and burned out cabins and slaughtered corpses littered the back country, residents turned naturally to men like Clark for leadership.

It was amid the escalating horror and fighting on the frontier that Clark learned from informants that the British were definitely involved in arming and encouraging the raiding Indians. Furthermore, he also heard that one of the enemy's most notorious soldiers, the Lt. Governor of Detroit, Col. Henry Hamilton, known all along the frontier as "the hair buyer" for the bounty he paid Indians for American scalps, was present west of the Ohio River in the Indiana country. Knowing how much it would mean for boosting morale on the frontier, Clark proposed to Virginia Governor Patrick Henry an attack on the tiny Illinois settlement of Kaskaskia and eventual capture of Fort Sackville located up the Wabash River at Vincennes. If successful, not only would victory and capture of Hamilton dampen Indian enthusiasm for the war, but a British retreat leaving American forces in control of the northwest would almost guarantee that the Ohio country would become part of the United States if a peace treaty were ever to be signed. Possession, after all, was nine tenths of the law.

Enthralled by Clark's vision and assurances of victory, the state legislature approved the plan and authorized the frontiersman to raise a force of 350 men for his expedition. But with war raging all over the thirteen colonies and on the high seas, even Clark's reputation was not enough to attract more than 150 men for the mission and when the full scope of the plan was revealed to them, Clark had to use every bit of his persuasive powers to keep many from turning back. It was the first, and not the last time, that Clark would need to resort to cajolery, bluster, and appeals to their vanity and courage, even at one point daubing himself like an Indian and performing a war dance, to keep his weary men moving forward.

Thus began one of the epic endeavors of the Revolutionary War which, unlike a similar attempt to seize Canada, ultimately succeeded and ended up doubling the size the infant United States. It succeeded because of one man, whose indomitable will drove his men on, hurling them hundreds of miles into an enemy occupied wilderness and eventual victory against a fortified position taken in the dead of winter. Leaving the settled frontier in the spring of 1778 and reaching Kaskaskia in July, Clark informed the French residents of the recent alliance between France and the United States and promised them that he would have "nothing to do with churches more than to defend them from insult; that by the laws of the state [their] religion had as great privilege as any other." That declaration and assurances of their rights as full citizens of the infant United States, said Clark, "seemed to complete their happiness" and secured for him the residents' allegiance against the British. With the help of a local Catholic priest, Clark's tiny force was able to move quickly, winning the friendship of the French inhabitants of Cahokia as well as other nearby towns and seizing Fort Sackville without a struggle. Over the ensuing months, Clarke consolidated his position in Illinois by convincing the local Indians not to interfere in his contest with the British, but word of his success reached Hamilton who moved south from Detroit to reoccupy the fort at Vincennes. There, the British general made a crucial error. He decided to remain at the fort through the winter pending the arrival of reinforcements. Realizing that his puny force of just 172 men, of which half were French volunteers, would be no match for a larger force of professional soldiers, Clark determined to attack Hamilton at Vincennes before spring.

It took every bit of Clark's persuasive powers to keep his men moving forward through a countryside drowned in icy water, but at last, after marching and slogging for 17 days across 240 miles of frozen wasteland, the American force reached Vincennes and, after a rendezvous with a previously dispatched boat of supplies, lay siege to the surprised garrison in Fort Sackville. As a demonstration of the futility of resistance, Clark had a number of Hamilton's captured Indian allies brought before the fort and, before the horrified eyes of the garrison, proceeded to have them killed one by one with the blow of a tomahawk to the head. After such a grisly display of frontier ferocity and the resulting desertion of his Indian allies fearful of the Virginian's reputation, Hamilton realized that his reduced force stood no chance of holding out. After three days of siege, he met with Clark who "had just come from his Indian triumph all bloody and sweating" and was washing the gore from his hands in a pool of rainwater and tendered his surrender. With the hair buyer taken prisoner and sent to Williamsburg, the United States' claim to possession of the whole northwest was sealed.

Representing the high point in his public service and action during the Revolution, Clark followed the capture of Vincennes with other, lesser campaigns in the west including the defense of St. Louis in 1780 and a series of actions in attacks against Kentucky that lasted until the end of the war. In 1784, he was named principal surveyor of public land and appointed to the Board of Commissioners of Indiana where he helped in apportioning land in compensation for veterans. Clark himself was constantly pursued by creditors for expenses he personally incurred during the war; expenses for which he was never compensated either by Virginia or the federal government. In the end, the man who won millions of acres for the United States, ended up with only the land he settled on in Clarksville, Indiana overlooking the Falls of the Ohio where twenty-five years before, he had begun his march to Vincennes. It was there, in 1809 that he suffered a stroke and, after having fallen into a fire, necessitated the amputation of his right leg. Later, while living with his sister's family in Louisville, Kentucky, he suffered a third and this time fatal stroke in 1818. "The mighty oak of the forest has fallen," concluded Judge John Rowan at Clark's funeral. "And now the scrub oaks may sprout all around."

Seldom has fate allowed a single man to make such important contributions as to effect not only the course of history, but the lives of millions yet unborn, but the American Revolutionary War was a singular event in that it produced so many individuals who did just that. And George Rogers Clark, "father of the western country," was one of the few who towered even above that pantheon of titans.

George Clymer

A framer of both the Declaration of Independence and the United States Constitution, George Clymer was most effective acting in the background; on committees and organizing public opposition to various attempts by the British to impose unpopular laws. Although his patriotism and enthusiasm for independence were initially inspired more by self-interest then altruism, a genuine concern for the well being of his fellow citizens soon became the overriding factor in his zeal for revolution.

Clymer was orphaned barely a year after his birth in Philadelphia, Pennsylvania on March 16, 1739. Delivered into the hands of an uncle who was also a successful merchant, Clymer received his education while clerking in the company's counting house. Later, he became a full partner in the firm and when his uncle died, inherited his fortune.

As a rising young professional, Clymer naturally drew the attention of Philadelphia's business community as well as the eye of the occasional young lady. Eventually, he married one, Elizabeth Meredith, at whose home he was also introduced to a wealthy southern planter named George Washington. After his marriage, he joined his in-laws to form a new company, Merediths & Clymer and by the eve of the Revolution, was one of Philadelphia's biggest taxpayers.

Long before that however, Clymer's political instincts had been aroused when the British Parliament began passing measures designed to raise more revenue from the American colonies in order to help pay for the recently concluded French and Indian War. Americans, including Clymer, did not see things that way. To them, the new laws were examples of unfair taxation made on a people who had no say in their imposition. In addition, taxes such as those on stamps and tea, interfered with private business, costing merchants like Merediths & Clymer money. As a result, Clymer found his resentment for Britain growing and became increasingly involved with patriot activities such as leading the effort to force the resignation of those designated by the crown to collect the tax on tea. Successful in that endeavor, Clymer soon found himself holding seats on a number of patriot committees including the Philadelphia Committee of Safety and became an officer with the Associators, the city's militia company.

By 1775, Clymer's patriotism as well as his business background proved ideal for the position of continental treasurer, an office created by Congress to attend to the economic affairs involved in conducting a revolution. Among the first things Clymer did on the job was to back up a new Continental currency using his own considerable fortune. His performance as treasurer brought him even more notice and in 1776 he

George Clymer

was chosen as a member of the colony's delegation to the Second Continental Congress. There, he became an early advocate for independence and had no reservations about signing the Declaration of Independence after a final draft was prepared in committee. Fellow signer Benjamin Rush described him as "a cool, firm, consistent Republican who loved liberty and government with equal affection" and "under the appearance of manners that were cold and indolent, he concealed a mind that was always warm and active towards the interests of his country."

With formal independence declared, Clymer fell to work with a will, becoming a member of a number of important committees making an especial mark in those covering military affairs. Although the well being of the common soldier drew a good deal of his attention, his business background was also of vital help to his friend Washington, now commanding general of the Continental Army. Clymer worked with Washington to improve the commissary system to insure the flow of supplies to the army would continue uninterrupted. So dedicated was Clymer to these tasks, that he risked capture by the invading British when he chose to remain behind in Philadelphia along with Robert Morris to attend to issues of supply. On a separate front, concerned about the enemy's support of bloody Indian raids on the frontier, Clymer prevailed upon Congress to sponsor a military expedition into the Northwest with the aim of capturing Detroit and neutralizing British influence among the tribes. Although that effort failed, it may have led directly to personal catastrophe when British forces approaching Philadelphia, veered from their intended line of march to ransack his country home. In that incident, Clymer's wife and children barely escaped in time to take cover in a nearby forest.

Leaving Congress in 1780, Clymer was elected to Pennsylvania's legislature the following year where his humanitarian spirit prompted him to support a number of reforms including the new state's penal code. In 1787, he was picked as a member of Pennsylvania's delegation to the Constitutional Convention, one of only six signers of the Declaration to attend. Although speaking little, Clymer did express reservations about allowing the entry into the union of new states formed out of the untamed west on an equal footing with the original thirteen. In political alignment however, he sided with James Madison and Alexander Hamilton in support of a strong central government.

In 1789, with the passage of the Constitution, Clymer was elected as his state's first member of the House of Representatives and although maintaining his loyalty to Washington, soon drifted from his previous Federalist leanings into the camp of Thomas Jefferson's Republicans. He saw revolution brewing in France as being borne out of the same desires that had inspired America's struggle with England and his sympathy for the French only reinforced his concerns for ordinary Americans. Also, as Treasury Secretary Hamilton's plans for the economy of the United States grew ever more grandiose, Clymer became increasingly convinced that his fellow citizens needed protection from the seeming avariciousness of his fellow businessmen.

Refusing to serve for a second term in Congress, Clymer accepted an appointment from President Washington as the country's chief tax collector, a job Clymer soon found not to his liking when his son was killed in the military effort to suppress the tax revolt known as the Whiskey Rebellion in 1794. Resigning, Clymer next agreed to help in negotiations with the Cherokee and Creek Indians in Georgia before finally retiring from public office in 1796. Retirement however, did not mean Clymer remained idle. Always having been interested in the arts and sciences, he agreed to act as the first president of the Philadelphia Bank, the Philadelphia Academy of Fine Arts, and as vice-president of the Philadelphia Agricultural Society, positions he continued to hold until his death at Sommerseat, his estate in Morrisville, New Jersey, on January 23, 1813.

William Dawes

As personalities emerge from the "fog of war," conflicting recollections and the perspective of time, many of the participants of the American Revolution have, over the years, achieved the status of hero and celebrity. Such was the case with Paul Revere whose "midnight ride" was made famous by the poem of Henry Wadsworth Longfellow that generations of Americans were taught to recite. But in her own poem published in 1896, Helen F. Moore asked "'Tis all very well for the children to hear; Of the midnight ride of Paul Revere," but what of his companion and partner, William Dawes?

Born in 1745, William Dawes was employed as a tanner and shoemaker when he became involved with the Sons of Liberty. At the time of his ride, Dawes was not actually a resident of Boston having moved his family west to Worcester after an incident involving an insult to his wife by a British soldier. The owner of a horse, he soon found himself, like Revere, doing duty as an express rider delivering messages between prominent patriots such as spymaster Joseph Warren and Samuel Adams. Unlike Revere, however, Dawes never became intimately involved in the patriot movement, he belonged to few if any committees and was not known to have written any fiery letters to local newspapers or published any pamphlets pseudonymously or otherwise. What he did do was to capitalize on his naturally open and friendly nature to ingratiate himself with any British soldier he happened to meet, an effort that succeeded sufficiently to allow him easy passage in and out of Boston when someone he knew happened to be on guard duty at Boston Neck south of the city. So successful was he in these efforts that once, he was even able to sneak away two small cannon and later contraband gold pieces he used as buttons on his clothing. Apparently he enjoyed his role as a patriot spy, acting the drunk or pesky peddler in order to slip past the guards against the day when an emergency might arise and one of his acquaintances was not on duty. That time arrived on the night of April 18, 1775 when Dawes was summoned by Warren and asked to take his horse and ride westward

William Dawes

to the town of Lexington to warn patriot leaders Samuel Adams and John Hancock of an impending foray by the British out of Boston, possibly aimed at capturing them.

Warren instructed Dawes to take the land route south of the city that he had been accustomed to take, and swing south warning the residents of Cambridge, Roxbury, Dedham, Watertown and Framingham that the enemy was on the march. In the meantime, to increase the chance of success, he would send Paul Revere on a shorter route across the Charles River to Charlestown north to Medford on the same mission. Dawes left immediately and luckily, one of the soldiers he had befriended was on duty at the Neck that night. When Dawes joined a group of soldiers as they crossed the checkpoint and headed out of town, his acquaintance raised no objection. Managing to draw as little attention to himself as possible, Dawes eventually lost the soldiers and managed to alert the minuteman companies in the towns along the way to Lexington which he reached about 12:30 a.m. on April 19, just half an hour behind Revere. After warning Adams and Hancock and taking time for food and drink, he and Revere conferred and agreed that a known cache of arms and ammunition at Concord, about ten miles from Lexington, was just as likely to be a target of the British as capturing notorious patriots. Deciding that it would be prudent to ride ahead and warn the town of the possible danger, Dawes and Revere headed for Concord. On the way, they met up with a local physician and Son of Liberty named Samuel Prescott who was returning to Concord after an evening spent with his girlfriend. Outside Lexington however, while Dawes and Prescott roused the occupants of a nearby home, Revere ran into a British patrol and before he could warn the others, he and Prescott were surrounded and captured. Dawes, lagging a bit behind his companions, managed to slip away down a side road and into the shadows of a nearby farmhouse. Realizing he was pursued and that his horse was all but spent after the night's long ride, Dawes took a chance and shouted as if his pursuers had been surrounded by militiamen. In the darkness, the ruse worked and the soldiers returned to the main road but in calling out, Dawes' mount suddenly reared, throwing him from the saddle. At that point, having lost a valuable watch in the long grass and possibly his horse as well, Dawes decided to call it a night and headed back to Lexington.

In the meantime, more suspicious than ever that the enemy did not intend to stop at Lexington, Revere and Prescott determined to attempt an escape of their own. At a signal from the doctor, they dashed off but as Prescott leaped a stone wall to safety, Revere was caught in the sites of a half dozen pistols. Forced to remain in the custody of the British patrol, Revere never made it to Concord and was released later in the morning after his captors decided they had more pressing concerns than to hold a local civilian. Making good his escape, Prescott, more familiar with the local terrain, went cross country and arrived in Concord in time to arouse the militia just hours before the British column out of Boston and late of Lexington Green arrived on the outskirts of town.

When the immediate danger was over, Dawes returned to the scene of his near escape, recovered his watch and, presumably, his horse. Later, he became one of the thousands of militiamen who surrounded Boston and saw some action during the battle of Breed's Hill. After the war moved south, he went into business as a supplier to the Continental Army and died, still relatively obscure, on February 25, 1799.

Silas Deane

One of the most controversial of the Founding Fathers, Silas Deane was sent to Europe early in the Revolutionary War as a quasi-secret agent and ambassador without portfolio to negotiate with France for the delivery of military supplies and to sign up freelance professional soldiers for service in the Continental Army. When joined later by other patriots, he was suspected of financial malfeasance and recalled. Deane's career was a good example of the pitfalls that in other revolutionary movements cost victims their heads.

Born to a blacksmith in Groton, Connecticut on December 24, 1737 Deane had a solid early education before entering Yale College. There, he studied the law and after graduation in 1758, passed the bar two years later. Deane may or may not have practiced the law following college, but if he did, it was only briefly as he soon married a wealthy widow and became a merchant in Wethersfield, Connecticut. His business brought him to the notice of his neighbors and he was elected to the colony's legislature in 1772 where he was caught up in rising resentment toward Britain as Parliament attempted to impose a number of tax raising measures followed in 1774 by a series of "intolerable acts." With his opposition to the measures well known, Deane joined the Connecticut Committee of Safety and was on board when Vermonter Ethan Allen was commissioned to seize the British fort at Ticonderoga. Chosen to represent the colony, Deane then became a delegate to the First Continental Congress in 1774.

With the outbreak of hostilities in Massachusetts in early 1775 and the formation of the Continental Army under Gen. George Washington, the need for military supplies became acute and Deane was chosen by Congress to sail to France ostensibly as an innocent businessman but actually as an unofficial representative and financial agent for the thirteen colonies. Not having been appointed an official ambassador, Deane's authority was murky at best as he ended up working with the French through an agent named Pierre Augustin Caron de Beaumarchais who had set up a dummy company called Roderique, Hortalez et Compagnie to cover a program aimed at exchanging military supplies for tobacco or simple payment. Working through French foreign minister the Comte de Vergennes, Beaumarchais nevertheless had the ear of the French king and advocated active support for the Americans. "You will only preserve the peace you desire, Sire, by preventing it at all price from being made between England and America, and preventing one from completely triumphing over the other," wrote Beaumarchais in a letter to Louis XVI.

In September of 1776, after the signing the Declaration of Independence, Congress ordered both Benjamin Franklin and Arthur Lee to France

Silas Deane

as official ambassadors of the new nation. At the same time, Deane's status was clarified as he was also given ambassadorial rank; but his earlier activities in arranging for military supplies from France and freely signing up foreign mercenaries such as the Marquis de Lafayette, the Baron von Steuben, and Thomas Conway raised questions and suspicions. Eventually, after working with Lee and Franklin in negotiating formal treaties of alliance and commerce with France that were signed on February 6, 1778, Deane was accused by Lee of outright profiteering in his previous dealings.

Recalled as a result, Deane returned to the United States aboard a French battleship to attend an investigation by Congress for financial misconduct. According to Beaumarchais, who had first made contact with the Americans through Lee, the Virginian's accusations were based on personal jealousy rather than hard evidence against Deane. "Mr. Arthur Lee…ended up by becoming (Deane's) enemy, as always happens in little minds more concerned to supplant their rivals than to surpass them in merit," wrote Beaumarchais. Tied up in the accusations was the matter of missing funds and disagreement between Lee and Deane over payment for the supplies provided by France to the United States. While Deane claimed they were meant to be purchased, Lee insisted they were a gift and suggested that if payment were made by Congress, the money would find its way into Deane's personal accounts. Not helping Deane was the fact that while conducting the affairs of the United States, he had been involved in personal business on the side, and may even have invested in the London stock exchange, which may or may not have become entangled with his public duties. But after taking his case to the public and with fellow commissioner Benjamin Franklin and revolutionary stalwarts John Adams and John Jay in his corner, Deane was awarded $10,000 in back pay and given permission by Congress to return to Europe to put his affairs in order. Instead, perhaps feeling betrayed after having his honor questioned, he retreated to the Netherlands where he remained until the end of the war.

With his faithfulness to the Revolution still under a cloud, Deane's reputation was given a body blow after British foreign minister Lord North leaked damaging letters written by Deane at the minister's behest. The letters clearly showed that Deane had tried to persuade various patriot leaders back home to abandon the Revolution and support reconciliation with England. By the time the war had ended, Deane, finding himself impoverished and in desperation, decided to leave the Netherlands. Making his way to Deal, England, he boarded a ship for Canada; but on September 23, 1789, even before his vessel had cleared the harbor, he died suddenly.

John Dickinson

The unacknowledged leader of the go slow, "what's the rush?" school among the Founding Fathers, John Dickinson's *Letters from a Farmer in Pennsylvania* were among the most forceful of early Revolutionary documents speaking out against British oppression and earning their author a worldwide reputation. Later, as a member of the Continental Congress, the fire that smoldered in Dickinson's *Letters* cooled somewhat as he fought to resist the drift to independence and argued instead for reconciliation with the king. Bowing to the majority when independence was finally chosen, he continued to be an active force in Congress and state politics.

Born to wealth on November 8, 1732 on his family's estate near Trappe, Talbot County, Maryland, Dickinson moved to Dover, Delaware in 1740 at a time when the area was still part of Pennsylvania and known as the lower counties. There, his education began until he was moved to Philadelphia to be tutored in the law. He finished his legal studies in 1753 when he traveled to London to attend the prestigious Middle Temple. By the time he returned to Philadelphia in 1757, his reputation preceded him and he quickly

John Dickinson

became one of the city's most prominent attorneys. By 1760, he had entered politics as a representative of the lower counties in the Pennsylvania assembly. At that time, relations between the Penn family, the colony's proprietors, and much of the ordinary population had degraded and a fierce struggle for the future of Pennsylvania had begun.

Politicians had to choose sides and Dickinson's respect for the law (and perhaps the fact that he had married into the family) placed him squarely with the Penns and the Proprietary Party against that belonging to a rising Benjamin Franklin. In the end, the conservatives lost and so did Dickinson, who was voted out of office in 1764.

But although he was out of local politics, Dickinson was unable to remove himself completely from national issues such as the Stamp Act, a tax collection measure passed by the British Parliament unpopular with Americans. Dickinson emerged from his public retirement with a pamphlet entitled *The Late Regulations Respecting the British Colonies* that advocated extreme measures to force Parliament to repeal the Stamp Act. On the strength of his convictions in the matter, he was chosen to represent Pennsylvania in a Stamp Act Congress that was to meet in New York in 1765 and for which he penned a *Declaration of Rights*. Over the next several years, as relations with Parliament failed to improve, Dickinson once more took pen to paper and wrote a series of newspaper articles that became known as *Letters From a Farmer in Pennsylvania to the Inhabitants of the British Colonies*. In them, he argued against Parliament's continued efforts to find ways to tax Americans and advocated resistance and cooperation among the thirteen colonies. Little noticed at the time was his call for settlement of the issues short of violence. The articles proved immensely popular and were reprinted in newspapers throughout the thirteen colonies and even brought to France and England by Franklin. Dickinson became a national hero and was given an honorary degree from the College of New Jersey and his portrait engraved by Paul Revere.

Dickinson's literary efforts culminated in 1768 when he advocated a boycott of goods imported from England as well as a ban on exports there following passage of the Townshend Acts. By that time, Dickinson's past transgressions had been forgiven and in 1771 he was returned to the Pennsylvania legislature on whose behalf he wrote a petition to the king pleading for a redress of wrongs. But, just as he sided with the proprietors during his first stint in the legislature, Dickinson remained respectful of the sources of authority and refused any use of force by Americans in defiance of the king. That position once more cost him popular support and did not endear him to local patriots. By 1774, Dickinson's stature had been greatly reduced but he still found himself a member of Pennsylvania's Committee of Correspondence and for a short time, as a member of the First Continental Congress where he wrote an *Address to the Inhabitants of Quebec* and joined Thomas Jefferson in writing the moderate leaning *Declaration of the Cause and Necessity of Taking up Arms.*

War finally broke out in Massachusetts when minutemen opened fire on British troops at Lexington and Concord. In response, Congress created the Continental Army and appointed Gen. George Washington to take command of the forces surrounding Boston. Meanwhile, before Washington could arrive on the scene, the battle of Breed's Hill was fought just outside the city. Those events however, were still not enough to change Dickinson's conviction that peace and reconciliation must continue to be pursued even as more radical patriots from Massachusetts and Virginia called first for armed resistance and then for independence. As a member of the Second Continental Congress, he frustrated the growing sentiment for independence by leading the effort for reconciliation with Britain and called for an eleventh hour "olive branch petition" to be sent to the king pleading for some sort of compromise that could defuse the crisis. Advocates for independence reluctantly agreed to the measure with the understanding that it would be the last stand of those opposing a final break with England. Ultimately, the petition was ignored by the king and when a motion for independence was finally brought before the Congress in 1776, Dickinson again sought delay with a long speech that reiterated all the arguments that had already been made against the move. The action only confirmed in fellow delegate John Adams' opinion that Dickinson was but a "piddling genius" ruled by the pacifistic feelings of his Quaker in-laws. Finally, when a preliminary vote for independence was presented to Congress, Dickinson voted against it. The next day, in a vote taken by Congress as a whole, the motion passed unanimously after Dickinson and fellow delegate Robert Morris absented themselves in order to avoid casting ballots against it. Later, when the time came to sign the Declaration of Independence, Dickinson again refused to participate. The move once more cost him his office and he was not reappointed to Congress. As a result, Dickinson also resigned his seat in the Pennsylvania legislature that he had held concurrently and retired to his home in Delaware.

Three years later, Dickinson reappeared as a member of Congress and, respecting the earlier vote for independence, worked to help draw up the Articles of Confederation and later became one of its signatories. In 1781, Dickinson became president of Delaware, which had become a state in its own right when its boundary disputes with Pennsylvania and Maryland were finally settled with national independence. But with citizenship still being a fluid thing, Dickinson soon found himself back in Pennsylvania and serving as that state's governor from 1782 to 1785. Once more representing Delaware, he attended the Annapolis Convention in 1786 where, after concluding that the Articles of Confederation had proven inadequate for the purposes of a federal government, members agreed to hold a follow up Constitutional Convention in Philadelphia to be held the next year.

Although Dickinson was appointed by Delaware to the Constitutional Convention, he was forced to leave early but not before helping to formulate the compromise that would guarantee a balance of power between large and small states and making known his support of a revised framework for a new federal government. After the convention, Dickinson became a strong advocate for the proposed Constitution and he once more appeared in newspapers under the pseudonym of Fabius in support of its ratification by the states. His support of a strong central government however, waned as the years passed until he drifted into the Republican camp on the strength of its position favoring revolutionary France over England. Later, when it became apparent that the revolution had descended into bloody chaos, he changed his mind and even advocated an alliance between the United States and England against France. Soon after ratification of the Constitution, Dickinson retired from politics, settled at his Delaware estate and devoted himself to writing and serving as president of the board of trustees of Dickinson College that was named in his honor and to which he donated much time and effort as well as his personal library. He died at his home in Wilmington, Delaware on February 14, 1808.

William Henry Drayton

On the eve of the Revolution, William Henry Drayton had it all: wealth, connections, a beautiful young wife, royal favor, and important positions in the government of South Carolina. And although he stood against opposition to England early on, he soon turned against Britain in favor of American independence thus placing his family's fortune at risk and losing any influence he might have had with royal authority.

Drayton was born on September 17, 1742 to wealthy and politically connected parents at Drayton Hall located on the banks of the Ashley River in South Carolina. When he was eleven years old, he was shipped off to England to begin his education first at the Westminster School and then at Balliol College in Oxford. Only returning to America ten years later in 1764, Drayton married wealthy heiress Dorothy Golightly and took up study of the law. After the Stamp Act crisis of 1764, Drayton entered the public discourse with a series of letters written under the pseudonym of Freeman opposing calls for a Stamp Act Congress as well as American intransigence against what he perceived to be British rights. It was an unpopular stand to take and Drayton was forced to travel to England in 1770 until things at home cooled down. While overseas, he was presented to the king and when he returned to South Carolina two years later, was appointed to the colony's privy council by his uncle, Governor John Bull. That triumph was followed in 1774 by appointment as an associate judge in the colony's court system. It was ironic then that soon after his last appointment, Drayton, perhaps fed up with a system of patronage that made whatever government position he occupied dependent on not being re-

William Henry Drayton

placed by some political appointee from England, again used the Freeman pen name and wrote a pamphlet entitled *The American Claim of Rights* which essentially repudiated his earlier position and called for the assemblage of a Continental Congress. The brazen declaration was interpreted as disloyalty to the crown and Drayton soon found himself removed from his royal offices.

The action only served to further radicalize Drayton who became a member of South Carolina's Committee of Safety in 1775 as well as a legislator in the provisional congress that replaced the discredited crown approved legislature. It was in his capacity as a member of the Committee of Safety that Drayton left Charleston on August 2, 1775 for a delicate mission to the colony's back country to win local support for the struggle against Britain. In a cause led primarily by rich "rice kings," the Revolution was suspect on the frontier and Drayton had a difficult time on the stump arguing with Tory leaders. Failing to convince them of the rightness of the Revolutionary cause, Drayton returned with 1,000 militia and in a strategy of divide and conquer, managed to get the Tories to sign the Treaty of Ninety Six which guaranteed their neutrality in any conflict with England. The treaty however, did not solve the problem and almost as soon as Drayton returned to Charleston, there was a general uprising by the Tories that took months for patriots to suppress. It was a harbinger of things to come when the Carolinas would be torn by virtual civil war after the region was invaded by the British some four years later. In the meantime, Drayton was named president of the provincial congress and it fell to him to order Col. William Moultrie to defend the colony against an expected British attack by sea.

In February of 1776, Drayton became one of the earliest patriots to call for a formal split with England and put his money where his mouth was by helping to draft a state constitution that would be only the second in the nation's history following that of New Hampshire. He finished his work by signing the document into law on March 26, 1776 a full three months before the Continental Congress declared America independent from England. In the new order of things, Drayton was not only chosen as the first chief justice of South Carolina's court system, but also appointed to its privy council and new legislature, making him a member simultaneously of all three branches of the state government. Drayton inaugurated his historic achievement on April 23, 1776 with a ringing speech whose echoes reached across all thirteen states and into the halls of the Continental Congress where it had a galvanizing effect on those Founding Fathers then debating the merits of a Declaration of Independence.

After joining fellow patriots in cheering for the Declaration when it was read beneath Charleston's Liberty Tree, Drayton was appointed in 1778 to represent South Carolina in the Continental Congress. Arriving in York, Pennsylvania where the Congress had fled following a British threat to invest Philadelphia, Drayton was immediately plunged into the swirl of administrative activity with membership in a number of subcommittees including those for Indian Affairs, Commerce, and Foreign Affairs. One of his responsibilities involved straightening out the supply system for Gen. George Washington's starving troops at Valley Forge, a task he succeeded in doing by removing corrupt middlemen. The workload, unfortunately, perhaps contributed to Drayton's sudden and unexpected death on September 3, 1779 hardly more than a year since his arrival in Congress.

William Ellery

Not all of the Founding Fathers were born firebrands, taking immediately to the streets at the first sign of injustice or firing off heated broadsides against royal authority. Some took years, even decades before finding the station in life for which they felt properly suited. Take William Ellery for instance, who lived quietly working in his family's mercantile business before entering the legal profession at the age of 37 and finding himself in the thick of revolutionary activity.

Born in Newport, Rhode Island on December 22, 1727, William Ellery was a member of a prosperous mercantilist family whose early schooling was conducted by his Harvard educated father. When he was judged ready, the younger Ellery was also sent to Harvard where, excelling in Latin and Greek, he graduated in 1747 before returning to Newport to attend the family's mercantile interests. By 1764, Ellery had acquired quite a name for himself apart from his role in the family business first by being named a naval officer for the colony and then by becoming involved in a controversy surrounding the location of the future Brown University.

William Ellery

That year also marked a number of other more personal milestones including the death of his first wife (who left him six children) and his father (who left him a tidy fortune). With a comfortable inheritance,

Ellery suddenly found himself free from the dull life of an accountant and at the age of 37, switched careers and entered the legal profession, beginning his practice in 1770.

It was perhaps while he was still employed in the mercantile business that Ellery's sympathies for the revolutionary cause were first aroused as the various attempts by the English Parliament to tax the colonists would have been felt most directly by local businessmen. Sympathies that, as Rhode Island's naval officer, would have been misplaced when the king's revenue sloop, *Gaspee*, was attacked by the residents of his own home town on June 9, 1772. It seems that in his eagerness to stop local smuggling, the overzealous captain of the *Gaspee* had taken to harassing every ship in Narragansett Bay and angering local merchants with the resultant interference with local shipping. In response, when the *Gaspee* found itself grounded a few miles outside Providence, angry residents rowed out and set the helpless ship afire. By that time however, Ellery had already divorced himself from association with royal authority and had become active with the local Committee of Safety and although he had been passed up the first time for membership in the colony's congressional delegation, he was later chosen to replace Samuel Ward for the Second Continental Congress and joined fellow delegate Stephen Hopkins in Philadelphia just in time to participate in the debates surrounding the issue of independence and in signing the formal Declaration on August 2, 1776. A famous observation credited to Ellery at the time was his claim that he took care to stand in such a way so as to be able to observe the faces of his fellow congressmen as they signed their "death warrant" and claimed that he could read every kind of emotion in them save fear.

While serving in Congress, Ellery was also a member of various committees including those responsible for communications between the states, fiscal policy, the acquisition of military supplies, and naval affairs. He was an outspoken advocate of an alliance with France and hoped to eventually see Canada and the Floridas join the thirteen colonies in revolt. In the wake of the Silas Dean affair and the various squabbles and complaints among the country's various European ambassadors, he became a member of the committee charged with reviewing the country's foreign policy system and was on hand when its recommendations for reorganizing the diplomatic corps were later presented to Congress.

Ellery served in Congress until 1786 during which time, Rhode Island was invaded and occupied by the British and his home in Newport burned in retaliation for his position as an important rebel. Subsequently, he worked with the Congress to provide relief for Rhode Island after the enemy had left while also supporting a failed effort for passage of a measure that would have ended slavery in the United States. Returning to Rhode Island, Ellery was appointed chief justice of the state's Superior Court and later, after George Washington became the nation's first president, collector of customs for the town of Newport. He was still serving as collector when, at the age of 93, he died peacefully in his Newport home on February 15, 1820, a copy of Cicero's *De Ofliciis* still in his hands.

William Floyd

Although possessed of great native intelligence and resolute manner, William Floyd seemed to owe the success of his early public career at least as much to good connections as to his limited exposure to formal education. If so, the confidence placed in him by New York's power brokers as well as the more ordinary citizens who knew of his staunch opposition to Britain turned out to be well founded as Floyd dared much and suffered much in his dedication to the Revolution.

William Floyd was born on December 17, 1734 the son of a wealthy Brookhaven, Long Island landowner. Displaying a good deal of native intelligence that promised a successful career in any profession he chose to pursue, Floyd nevertheless ended up getting only a scanty education due to the early death of his father and not much later, his mother. The responsibility of managing the family's estate on Long Island fell immediately upon his shoulders and, forced to leave school, Floyd became a farmer and one of Long Island's most prosperous and influential local citizens. As time passed, his managerial skills proved more than adequate and he filled out the gaps in his education with frequent soirees at his home involving New York's leading men. As time went on and the British Parliament began to implement a series of measures intended to coerce the American colonies into paying more in taxes, local businessmen who had to raise their prices to cover them and a citizenry who had to pay the increased costs began to agitate for their repeal. Depending on the sale of livestock, grain, lumber and other products from his farmlands, Floyd counted himself among those businessmen unhappy with British policies and when protesters began to coalesce into groups such as the Sons of Liberty, Floyd became one of their most outspoken supporters.

With his reputation established among local patriots, Floyd was chosen by the people as one of the colony's delegates to the First Continental Congress. Arriving in Philadelphia in time for the session that began in 1774, he was immediately assigned to a number of committees. At the same time, he was appointed an officer in New York's Suffolk County militia and although he saw little action, he eventually rose to the rank of major general. Back in Philadelphia, as a member of Congress, he had no trouble siding with those who agitated for a complete break with Britain and when the time came, supported independence. Ironically, even as he placed his name to the Declaration of Independence, his family was being chased from their Long Island estate by victorious British troops who then used his home as a headquarters building for the remainder of the war. Floyd's travails were made complete when, forced to support his family on the meager salary provided him as a member of Congress, his wife Hannah died suddenly in 1781 while the family was still homeless in Connecticut.

William Floyd

In 1777, following his term in Congress, Floyd was elected to the senate of the new state of New York where he served through 1778 and again for a run that lasted from 1784-1788. In between, finding his property somewhat run down after being occupied by the enemy for so long, Floyd deeded it to his son and ventured to the western part of New York where he bought land along the Mohawk River and began spending portions of each year afterward improving it. After the United States Constitution was ratified, Floyd was returned to Congress in 1789 to represent New York. Unlike many in the northern states however, he sympathized with the sentiments of Thomas Jefferson who yearned for a country made up of simple farmers rather than businessmen and a government that ruled with a lighter hand than political rival Alexander Hamilton would prefer. Floyd remained in Congress until 1791 and after failing to win reelection, went back home to settle on his new farm in Westernville, Oneida County, New York. In 1795 Floyd mounted an unsuccessful bid for lieutenant governor and in 1808 was once again a member of the state senate. In between, he found the time to help write the state's new constitution before finally retiring to his Mohawk River estate. There he concentrated on cultivating the land until his death on August 4, 1821.

Benjamin Franklin

One could be forgiven for assuming that by the time of the Revolutionary era, the career of Benjamin Franklin was about to draw to a close. After all, he was almost 60 years old when Parliament began to issue a series of measures aimed at drawing increased revenue from the American colonies. When the unpopular Stamp Act first raised the ire of his fellow colonists, Franklin was already renowned in both Europe and America for his wit, his political acumen, his many inventions, and his scientific achievements. But by the time he was chosen by Pennsylvania to represent its interests in England, it seemed as if his career had passed its zenith and he was positioned to enjoy a comfortable sinecure to while away the remaining days of his retirement. As things turned out however, nothing could have been further from the truth. Soon, Franklin found himself drawn in to the events surrounding the Revolution and embarked on the second half of his long and amazing career.

Although forever associated with colonial America's first city, Franklin was not born in Philadelphia but in Boston in 1706 and only moved to Pennsylvania in 1723. Largely self-educated, he left school at the age of 10 to begin working first with his father and then with a brother who published a newspaper. Differences of opinion between the two siblings soon prompted Franklin to leave Massachusetts for similar work in Philadelphia which offered wider horizons for an ambitious young man. There, he was noticed by the royal governor of Pennsylvania who sponsored his first trip to England where he spent two years studying printing methods before returning to America in 1726. It was soon after his return that Franklin managed to acquire an interest in the *Pennsylvania Gazette* and turn the newspaper into a showcase for his remarkable literary talents. Later, his local fame went intercolonial with his wildly successful *Poor Richard's Almanack* which he published for an amazing 25 years. But his personal fame had not yet reached its fullest extent. Successful in business, Franklin decided to retire from active employment and devote himself to study and the pursuit of science. It was the age of the Enlightenment where many men of leisure spent their time poring over volumes of natural philosophy and political science and conducting solitary experiments in scientific research. Often, important discoveries were made by individuals working in personal laboratories or in testing ideas on their own. So it was for Franklin when, while flying a kite during a thunderstorm in 1752, he proved that lightning was an electrical discharge. The discovery made him a celebrity in the scientific circles of Europe and resulted in his being made a member of the British Royal Society and later the French Academy of Sciences. Franklin added to his scientific reputation with a string of useful inventions including the lightning rod, bifocal glasses, and a new kind of stove. But even as his interest in science grew, he took a more active role in the social life of Philadelphia: he was named the city's postmaster general, helped to found the Academy of Pennsylvania, started a circulating library, and began a debating club that evolved into the American Philosophical Society. Amid all that activity, he still found some time to get married and write his autobiography.

But Franklin did not work in a vacuum. As a former newspaperman and later with his assignment to and reorganization of the post office, he could not help but become involved with local politics. Ally-

Benjamin Franklin

ing himself with Joseph Galloway, he became the leader of the Assembly Party which opposed the colony's powerful Penn family, the original proprietors whose ancestors had been given authority over Pennsylvania by royal decree. Franklin's immediate reason for moving against the proprietors was their refusal to act against Indians raiding the colony's frontier during the French and Indian War of 1755 but general resentment in the colony to the Penns' tax exempt status and a desire to see the family ousted in favor of rule by direct royal authority was a contributing factor to his party's success.

With its growing strength, the Assembly Party sent Franklin to England in 1757 to plead its case against the Penns. Winning the support of the mother country, Franklin remained in England for nearly five years, returning to America only in 1762. But his arrival in the colonies would have been a good deal more uncomfortable if he had continued along a path of appeasement to Britain's attempts to tax his fellow Americans. When word of his support for the Stamp Act reached the colonies where furor among patriots had grown to fever pitch, Franklin's house had to be guarded against angry mobs. Learning of the temper of the people back home, Franklin quickly backtracked and, in testimony before Parliament, explained why Americans resented the taxation measures. He also warned that if attempts to restore such measures continued, the result could be a severing of relations between America and Britain. Somewhat self-servingly, Franklin issued his testimony before Parliament in pamphlet form which resulted not only in the restoration of his reputation, but established him as a leader in the coming Revolution.

Upon returning to America, Franklin remained only briefly before going back to England two years later as colonial agent for Pennsylvania, Massachusetts, New Jersey, and Georgia. When patriot leaders called for a Continental Congress to meet in Philadelphia, Franklin was recalled to participate as a member of his colony's delegation. Thus, he was present in 1775 to join John Adams, Thomas Jefferson, Robert Livingston, and Roger Sherman as a member of the committee that drafted the Declaration of Independence. On July 2, 1776 he added his signature to the document that made a fact of his prediction to Parliament almost ten years before.

In acknowledgment of his popularity in Europe as well as his long experience in negotiating with governmental authorities, Congress chose Franklin, along with Arthur Lee and Silas Deane, as a diplomatic representative to France. In 1778, following the American victory at the battle of Saratoga, Franklin signed a Treaty of Alliance with France on behalf of United States. Although wildly popular among the French and with an ability to move easily in diplomatic circles, Franklin was criticized as being too circumspect by John Adams, who arrived later to replace Deane. Adams thought Franklin had not been forceful enough with French Foreign Minister the Comte de Vergennes whom he rightly regarded as concerned more about the welfare of France than of the United States. There was also a personality clash between the two men. Although respectful of his accomplishments, Adams considered Franklin too involved with the French social scene and not enough with his diplomatic duties, while Franklin thought Adams too severe. As the war progressed and Britain's position became more untenable, it was Adams' position that negotiations with Britain should be opened on a unilateral basis without the participation of the French despite the fact that doing so would be a direct violation of the will of Congress. Franklin at first disagreed, but eventually came around and in 1783, joined Adams and John Jay in signing the Treaty of Paris, effectively ending the Revolutionary War.

Franklin returned home in 1785 and was promptly elected President of the Pennsylvania Executive Council followed by his appointment two years later as a delegate to the Constitutional Convention called by Congress to remedy deficiencies in the Articles of Confederation. Instead, meeting in secret session, the convention, led by James Madison, created a whole new document, an instrument that not only strengthened the bonds among the states, but created a strong central government made up of a balance of power between legislature, judiciary and executive. Although he did not approve of a strong central government, Franklin nevertheless looked upon the completed instrument with optimism and fought for its adoption in the subsequent struggle over ratification by the required majority of states.

After a lifetime of accomplishments spread over two separate careers...literary/scientific and political/diplomatic...Franklin died in 1790 at the age of 84.

Elbridge Gerry

The Revolution could not have been successful if it were not for the participation of many men of diverse talents from lawyers and merchants to shipbuilders and soldiers. One man who managed to find his own particular niche was Elbridge Gerry, a man of contradictory moods that often left many of his fellow patriots either unsure of his position on various issues or frustrated at not being able to count on his support; a situation that would leave Gerry, who signed the Declaration of Independence and eventually rose to the position of vice-president of the United States, with few political allies.

Born in Marblehead, Massachusetts on July 17, 1744 to a wealthy shipping family, Gerry was the third of twelve siblings and as a matter of course, was sent to Harvard to receive an education. Starting out with the intention of becoming a physician, Gerry later changed his mind (a mercurial characteristic that was destined to give him trouble during his political career) and decided instead to enter the family business upon his graduation in 1765. After working several years as a merchant, and making a tidy profit for himself, Gerry decided to enter politics and was chosen to represent Marblehead in the Massachusetts General Court or legislature in 1773. There, he was picked by Samuel Adams (who was always on the lookout for fresh, young talent with a streak of rebelliousness in them) as a member of the new Committee of Correspondence that had been formed in response to continuing attempts by the British Parliament to tax the American colonies.

Adams' choice of Gerry to join the patriot ranks was a prescient one as the very next year, after the British had closed Boston harbor in retaliation for the colony's continued defiance of its will (of which the Boston Tea Party was an egregious example), the young shipping magnate used his connections to arrange the transportation of goods through Marblehead. Although Gerry had had his disagreements with the patriots, including his protest of the Tea Party, he continued to be actively involved in such resistance organizations as the Committees of Correspondence and Safety and Supply, and membership in the Massachusetts' Provincial Congresses. In fact, he had attained such a level of notoriety among officials in Boston that he felt compelled to flee in his nightshirt just ahead of British troops passing through Menotomy on their way to Concord and Lexington in April of 1775. "…he knew and embraced truth when he saw it," fellow patriot Benjamin Rush once wrote of him. "He had no local or state prejudices," and was "a genuine friend to republican forms of government."

Recognized for his patriotic zeal, Gerry was honored by Massachusetts in being chosen to represent the colony in the Continental Congress. Although his absence from that body prevented him from signing the Declaration of Independence with his fellow congressmen on August 2, 1776 he did manage to place his name on the historic document about three months later on November 19, 1776. But not all was sweetness and light between Gerry and his fellow congressmen. Serving on a number of committees including treasury and one charged with the purchase and distribution of supplies for the army (despite a conflict of interest due to his being one of those doing the supplying), Gerry's positions often seemed contradictory to his peers. Finally, Gerry simply left Congress in 1779 to return to the Massachusetts legislature and his own private business (that included some very lucrative privateering on the side).

After the war, Gerry went back to Congress where his contradictory nature proved not only unchanged, but exacerbated with a streak of suspicion and distrust of political authority first aroused by the British and now transferred to the government created under the Articles of Confederation. Unable to deal with the limitations of the Confederation and yet distrustful of a strong central government, Gerry once more left Congress and returned to Massachusetts to be married. In 1787, he was elected as a delegate to the Constitutional Convention where he became deeply involved in what has become known as the Great Compromise that gained the support of the southern states and their agreement to end the importation of slaves by 1808 in return for allowing five slaves to be counted the same as three white residents in determining the size of a state's population for purposes of taxes and representation. Gerry did not like the Compromise but supported it in the interests of keeping all thirteen states together. As for the Constitution itself, Gerry was not

Elbridge Gerry

satisfied, fearful of a number of its provisions including those involving the judiciary and popular representation as well as the lack of a Bill of Rights. He also felt that parts of the document were too ambiguous. Thus, when he returned to Massachusetts, he became one of its most ardent foes. True to form however, he changed his mind about the Constitution and after throwing it his support during the ratification process, was elected to the new United States' Congress.

Soon, however, the country's political landscape began to change as those who felt varying degrees of support for the Constitution coalesced into parties; the Republicans, who were fearful of a strong central government and the Federalists who were not. Those who felt that Gerry's initial opposition to the Constitution indicated sympathy for the Republican cause were disappointed when it turned out that he strongly supported it. Gerry, always wary of his rights as a citizen and seemingly never content if there was an opportunity to make political enemies, soon grew suspicious of the Federalists and after leaving Congress in 1793, allied himself ideologically with the Republicans.

As armed conflict loomed between Britain and a revolutionary France with the United States caught in the middle, Gerry was asked by President John Adams, his friend and old traveling companion when the two were members of the Continental Congress, to join John Marshall and Charles Cotesworth Pinckney on a special diplomatic mission. Since Marshall and Pinckney were known to be Federalists, Adams had asked Gerry, whom he knew and felt he could trust, to be a member of the team in a spirit of bipartisanship. The three commissioners left for France in 1797 and in the course of negotiations, were approached by Jean Conrad Hottinguer, Pierre Bellamy, and Lucien Hauteval, representatives of French foreign minister Charles Maurice de Talleyrand whom the commissioners dubbed X, Y, and Z. In secret dispatches sent to Adams, the commissioners revealed that through his representatives, Talleyrand had demanded a bribe of $250,000 for himself and a $10 million loan to France to make up for alleged insults made to the country by President Adams. Outraged, the Americans had refused to cooperate with Pinckney allegedly declaring "Millions for defense, but not one cent for tribute!" When the commissioners' report was finally made public in the United States, the XYZ affair as it became known, aroused similar indignation and spoiled much of the country's good feelings toward France. Under those conditions, it was poor judgment on Gerry's part to remain in France after his two fellow diplomats had already left, even though he may have been given good reason by Talleyrand, who hinted that peace between France and the

United States depended on his continued presence. When he returned to the United States after an embarrassed Adams ordered him home, Gerry endured the slights and insults of an angry public to report to the president that France was ready to talk peace. As a result, after sending a second team of negotiators to Europe, Adams ended his presidency in 1800 with the Treaty of Mortefontaine or the Convention of 1800, which ended the undeclared naval war between the United States and France that had been going on since 1798.

In disfavor with strongly Federalist Massachusetts as a result of his behavior in France, Gerry's initial run for governor of the state in 1800 met with failure. A number of subsequent attempts ended with the same results until, with the rising popularity of the Republicans and growing animosity toward Britain, he was finally elected in 1810. Later in his two terms as governor, Gerry's name became forever after synonymous with political underhandedness when he signed into law a redistricting measure that ensured a Republican majority in the state's legislature. Because the resulting district seemed to be in the shape of a salamander, such geographical convolutions created solely for political gain became known ever after as "gerrymandering." His personal fortune dwindling and suffering from increasing ill health, Gerry was nevertheless nominated to serve as vice-president under James Madison in the election of 1812. But the resulting victory was short lived for the aging merchant who suffered a fatal heart attack on November 23, 1814 while on his way to preside over the United States Senate.

Nathanael Greene

An interesting way to consider the career of Nathanael Greene is by looking at it as being the reverse of George Washington's. Where Washington had had military experience prior to being named Commander in Chief of the Continental Army, Greene was an amateur who, like Henry Knox, learned whatever he knew about warfare from books. Where Washington had already achieved a degree of national fame for his role in the French and Indian War, his social standing in Virginia, and his role in its legislature, and the Continental Congress, Greene was unknown outside of Rhode Island. Where Washington was a southerner called to command in the North, Greene was a northerner when he was sent to take over command in the South. But Greene was a fast learner, a man who understood his soldiers and someone who could inspire the loyalty and devotion of those he commanded, all qualities that would serve him in good stead when he took over the most difficult theater of the war and succeeded in winning it back for the nascent United States. By the end of the war, Greene had risen from an obscure Rhode Islander with a game leg and no reputation to speak of to a soldier second only to Washington himself in the love and esteem of his countrymen.

Greene was born in the town of Potowomut, Rhode Island on May 27, 1742. The son of a Quaker minister who was also the head of a well to do manu-facturing and mercantilist family, Greene had a no-frills education that con-sisted of reading, writing,

Nathanael Greene

and the kind of mathematics suited to a man of business. Greene's in-terests, however, diverged radically from those of his father and he developed a voracious literary appetite that compelled him to earn money however he could to buy books. Although interested in different subjects, it was not until he attended a local parade that he became fas-cinated by military history and tactics, an interest that would lead to his greatest success and his greatest defeat in the years ahead. This interest in things military would continue when Greene took a seat in the Rhode Island General Assembly and grew with each attempt by Britain to impose unpopular tax measures on its colonies. In 1774, with tensions increasing between the colonies and the mother country, Greene helped to form a local militia unit called the Kentish Guards upon which his fitness to serve was immediately challenged due to a limp he had suf-fered from ever since childhood. Outraged that his abilities should be questioned, friends rushed to his support and the objections were quashed just in time for the legislature to promote him from its commit-tee in charge of preparing the colony's defenses to brigadier general in command of its three regiments of Continental troops. No sooner had the action been taken than fighting between British troops and minutemen broke out in Massachusetts.

Immediately, Rhode Island heeded the call to arms and Greene led the colony's militia to Boston arriving too late for the battle of Breed's Hill but in time to help keep the British penned up in the town. By the time that Washington was appointed to command the Continental Army and arrived on the scene, Greene had already established a reputation for efficiency and an ability to work with men from different colonies. It took little time for Washington to recognize the value of those qualities and to form a friendship and a confidence in Greene that would grow stronger as the years passed.

When the British evacuated Boston, Greene was placed in charge of the city until the army moved south to New York. Later, Greene was ordered to prepare the defense of Long Island but missed the actual battle due to illness so that his first taste of action came on September 16, 1776 at the battle of Harlem Heights. Failing to hold New York, however, Washington retreated to New Jersey where Greene was tasked to secure the Jersey shore. Left behind at Greene's urging, was a 3,000 man force to garrison Fort Washington on the Manhattan side of the Hudson River. It was Greene's contention that the position was unassailable and that when the British were forced to attack it, they would suffer casualties on the order of those they received at Breed's Hill. Unfortunately, things did not turn out that way. Instead, the fort was surrounded and captured. It was a stunning defeat made all the harder to endure in the wake of the Americans being driven from Long Island, a mistake in judgment by Greene that had grown out of inexperience and an over reliance on book learning.

Greene's practical education then began in earnest as he helped command the retreat across New Jersey and then took a prominent role in the hugely psychological victories at Trenton on December 26, 1776 and at Princeton a few days later. At the battle of Brandywine on September 11, 1777, Greene saved fellow General John Sullivan's command at Sandy Hollow by holding the line against the enemy long enough for Sullivan's men to retreat past him to safety. It was a masterful display of military skill and courage that did little to prepare Greene for his next assignment as Quartermaster of the Army.

Though not as exciting as combat, the quartermaster's job was just as important to Washington who was in dire need of someone he could count on to fight another kind of battle with bureaucrats in the Congress and state politicians for desperately needed supplies to feed and equip an army that was freezing and starving in winter quarters. Green's energy and dedication went far to straighten out Washington's supply problems and eliminate the waste and corruption that had plagued the distribution system when he found himself once more on the field of combat at the battle of Monmouth on June 28, 1778 and two years later at Connecticut Farms on June 7, 1780. It was not until three days after the battle of Springfield on June 23, 1780 that Greene finally got around to resigning as Quartermaster.

Later in 1780, in the wake of the stunning revelation of fellow General Benedict Arnold's treason, Greene was placed in charge of trying Arnold's British contact, Major John Andre, as a spy. After he had seen Andre hang, Greene was given command of West Point, the stronghold that Arnold had plotted to surrender to the enemy. Meanwhile, as these events had taken place, the United States had suffered a crushing defeat on August 16 at Camden, South Carolina when Major General Horatio Gates, still basking in the glow of his perceived victory at Saratoga, New York, force marched an army of 3,000 men through nearly impassible country and blundered into a waiting British army. "For God's sake…send Greene," was Alexander Hamilton's plea to Congress following the disaster. It was a recommendation that came as no surprise to Washington who had advised the same thing before the politicians had given the southern command to Gates.

It was fortunate that Greene had served so long with Washington and seen first hand the difficulties faced by the commander in chief just in keeping an army in the field, let alone succeeding against a larger, better equipped and trained professional army. That experience would serve him well when he faced the challenges that plagued the southern theater of operations. In the wake of Gates' defeat at Camden, whatever organized resistance that remained in the south was scattered and weak with most offensive action being conducted by small units of militia commanded by such officers as Gen. Francis Marion, the Swamp Fox, who mostly operated independently of one another. Striking where the enemy was weak, these bands would emerge from swamps and forests to fight a guerilla war against isolated British or loyalist forces across a harsh landscape criss-crossed by scores of rivers and streams. Added to the difficulties imposed by a hot, wet, tangled geography that contrasted sharply with the orderly towns and farmland of the north, was the fact that loyalist sentiments in the Carolinas and Georgia were much stronger than they were along the shores of the Hudson River. Thus, the war in the south had assumed more the look of a civil war than a revolution with most of the fighting being done between Americans, often among members of the same family.

Forewarned of the chaotic and desperate situation, Greene, unlike Gates, prepared the groundwork for his southern campaign by sending representatives to each state to raise men and supplies while he went ahead to meet with the partisan captains of the local militia bands and the remnants of the Continental Army which he characterized as "wretched beyond description." Most importantly, after he had begun to assemble a new army, Greene was able to bring Brigadier General Daniel Morgan out of retirement and back into the fight. Realizing however, that an acute lack of supplies and an army composed mostly of undisciplined militia would be no match for a stand up fight with the British, Greene decided upon a risky plan of dividing his forces into two columns and using them to lure the enemy ever deeper into the wilds of the Carolinas. Crossing numberless streams and covering hundreds of miles over trackless forest and swamp while at the same time keeping up a series of harassing attacks at the enemy's flanks, Greene hoped to wear out the pursuing British and compel them to extend their supply lines to the breaking point.

Finally, one pursuing British force under Lt. Col. Banastre Tarleton caught up to Morgan's wing of the army and on January 17, 1781, at the battle of the Cowpens, the Virginia veteran showed how a combination of undisciplined militia and experienced Continental troops could be used together to defeat a more professional army. The victory set the stage for Greene's own encounter with Lt. Gen. Charles Cornwallis on March 15, 1781 when, after reuniting with Morgan's army and following the retreating British from the Dan River in North Carolina, he met the enemy at a place called Guilford Courthouse in South Carolina. There, with an army of 4,200 men, he followed the same order of battle used by Morgan at the Cowpens and would have won the fight but for his dwindling supply of ammunition and a desperate move by Cornwallis who ordered his cannon to fire into the ranks of his own men in order to prevent an imminent American breakthrough. As a result, Cornwallis was left in possession of the field but with the loss of a quarter of his 2,000 man army, it came at a cost too high to claim complete victory. Licking his wounds, the British commander would abandon the Carolinas for Virginia leaving Greene to roll up a string of outposts left to fend for themselves.

In a series of engagements, Hobkirk's Hill on April 25, 1781, the Siege of Ninety Six over three days in May, 1781 and the battle of Eutaw Springs on September 8, 1781, Greene was unable to win a clear cut victory but the increasing confidence of his army and the concomitant loss of men and morale among the British and their loyalist allies combined to eventually bring the whole of the southern countryside under the authority of the United States. By that time, Cornwallis had surrendered his army to Washington at Yorktown and soon, even the cities of Charleston and Wilmington were free of occupation.

By the summer of 1783, the Treaty of Paris had been signed ending the war and a victorious Greene appeared before Congress to resign from the army. A grateful south, mindful of the enormity of Greene's success in the Carolinas, expressed its thanks by granting him a cash award and 24,000 acres of prime land in Georgia. For his part, Greene had fallen in love with the south and determined to make his home on the land that was given him and become a planter. And so, on the banks of the Savannah River, the Greene family made its home calling it Mulberry Grove while the former general applied the same diligence he displayed on the battlefield to raising vegetables and fruit trees. It was an idyllic life that Greene seemed to have every intention of making permanent. Unfortunately, it was not to be. On June 19, 1786 he suffered a stroke after spending too much time in the hot Georgia sun inspecting a friend's rice paddies. Holding on for a few hours, he managed to reach Mulberry Grove before he died.

Button Gwinnett

The only signer of the Declaration of Independence to have been killed in a duel, Button Gwinnett's gravesite is undetermined and even his signature is one of the rarest among the Founding Fathers. Neck deep in political controversy, Gwinnett added to the mystery of his life by ending it early, only a year following the signing of the Declaration.

Born on April 10, 1735 in Gloucester, England, little else is known of Gwinnett's life before he stepped off a ship in Charleston, South Carolina. By then, he was already 30 years old and it is a safe bet that he did not leave England because of success in business. Wasting little time in South Carolina, Gwinnett soon moved on to Savannah, Georgia where he tried his hand at shopkeeping. Unsuccessful, Gwinnett next managed to borrow a sum of money and bought himself a 36 square mile island called St. Catherine's and proceeded to raise crops and cattle with an eye to joining the state's successful planter class. To that end, he also entered politics first as a justice of the peace and then as a member of the colony's legislature. Unfortunately, Gwinnett had as little luck as a planter as he had as a store owner and was forced to sell St. Catherine's in 1773. Almost destitute, he gave up politics in favor of earning a living but was drawn back by local physician Lyman Hall who succeeded in radicalizing Gwinnett's politics with a litany of injustices streaming from the British Parliament between 1765 and 1774.

Never having thought much about the growing struggle with England, Gwinnett threw himself back into politics with a will, beginning with an important meeting held at Savannah's Peter Tondee Tavern in July of 1774 where Parliament's "intolerable acts" were hotly debated by local patriots. Identifying himself with the people of Georgia's politically radical countryside, Gwinnett inadvertently set himself against Savan-

Button Gwinnett

nah's more conservative business sector that included the powerful McIntosh family. The division between the two factions only widened over the next two years as word was received that war had broken out in Massachusetts and the Continental Congress that had been meeting in Philadelphia assumed greater importance in its direction. Meanwhile, with Hall away as a member of Georgia's delegation to Congress, Gwinnett assumed leadership of the colony's radical contingent. Impatient with the cautious attitude of Savannah's "city party" and concerned that a man of the wrong political persuasion might be chosen to lead Georgia's military forces, Gwinnett rallied the colony's more ardent patriots and succeeded in getting himself appointed as commander. But Gwinnett had misjudged the power of his opponents and after furious protest, he was forced to give up command and instead, accept election as a delegate to the second Continental Congress. Arriving in Philadelphia in June of 1776, he was just in time to vote in favor of the Declaration of Independence. On August 2, he added his signature to the famous document and soon after returned to Georgia.

Back home, Gwinnett still harbored hopes of military glory, but was frustrated once again, this time by two members of the McIntosh clan, brothers George and Lachlan McIntosh, political rivals with the city party. Determined to gain the upper hand in the state once and for all, Gwinnett concentrated his efforts in gaining political control of Georgia and succeeded in packing the legislature with supporters. As a result, he was chosen as speaker of the House and in 1777 became involved in the creation of the state's new constitution. His meteoric rise to political power did not stop in the house however. After the death of Archibald Bulloch, who had been president of the state's Council of Safety, Gwinnett was chosen to fill out his unexpired term. With the legislature out of session and his dreams of martial glory still unfulfilled, Gwinnett was determined on leading an army into British East Florida and received authority from the Council to organize one. But then followed a series of political missteps as Gwinnett ordered the arrest of George McIntosh for treason and then failed to raise enough militia for the expedition. As a result, he was forced to ask Gen. Lachlan McIntosh for help in conducting the invasion. McIntosh, in command of the state's Continental troops, assumed control of the expedition but on April 15, 1777 Gwinnett arrived in Sunbury with what militia he could muster and immediately called a council of war. Unable to take a politician with no military experience acting as if he was in command of the offensive, McIntosh and his officers refused to attend the meeting. The next day, McIntosh began to move his men south and after learning that Gwinnett was refusing to follow, requested that the supplies for the expedition be released to him. Once again, Gwinnett stepped in to foil his rival by ordering the quartermaster not to give McIntosh the supplies. With the invasion halted, accusations were soon being flung in both directions with McIntosh calling Gwinnett a "scoundrel and lying rascal." Although Gwinnett was charged with malfeasance and later cleared, his honor had been insulted and it was perhaps inevitable that in such a highly charged political atmosphere, a collision was unavoidable. Challenging McIntosh to a duel, Gwinnett met his rival on ground just outside Savannah on May 16, 1777 and after the powder smoke had cleared, both men were found to have been wounded: McIntosh in the leg and Gwinnett in the hip. Gwinnett's wound however ultimately proved fatal and he died three days later on May 19, 1777.

Nathan Hale

When the Revolutionary War broke out in 1775, Americans found themselves at war without a means to collect information on the activities and plans of their enemies. Throughout history, nations and armies have always found the need for accurate information at least on the whereabouts of an enemy force if not timely warning of its intentions. Long established nations such as Britain and France, by the eighteenth century, already possessed sophisticated methods of gathering intelligence with spies, informants, and soldiers on the frontiers of empire. The thirteen American colonies had nothing like that except maybe a handful of frontiersman familiar with wilderness warfare. But being able to track Indians across miles of forest was of little use in the settled east. Thus, when Washington assumed command of the Continental Army surrounding Boston, he found that he knew next to nothing about the enemy located just on the other side of Dorchester Heights. To solve the problem, he created his own intelligence network with himself as spymaster. Having begun from scratch however, his assets were strictly amateurs; local residents eavesdropping on British soldiers. Looking elsewhere for potential agents, Washington decided to seek them from within the ranks of the army where, presumably, men who were no less amateurish in the spy game might at least provide some degree of resourcefulness; men such as Nathan Hale, who was destined to become the war's first out and out hero.

Before the war however, Nathan Hale would not have seemed to fit anyone's definition of a hero. Born June 6, 1755 in Coventry, Connecticut, Hale was sent to Yale College at the age of 14 with the expectation that he would become a minister like his father. Instead, after graduating in 1773 at the top rank of his class, he decided to become a teacher. Hale was teaching grammar school in New London, Connecticut and serving in the local militia when rising tensions between the colonies and Britain reached a boiling point and a shooting war began in neighboring Massachusetts. Soon after, a town meeting was held in New London and when a 20 year old Hale had stood up and declared that any support given to fellow Americans must not end until independence from the mother country was achieved, he was promptly commissioned a first lieutenant in the 7th Connecticut Regiment.

After a brief period of waiting and drilling, Hale's unit was finally called up by George Washington, the Continental Army's new commander in chief, and reached the vicinity of Boston in September 1775. Over the next six months, into the spring of 1776, Hale worked to whip his unit into shape according to the standards of military discipline demanded by Washington and returned briefly to New London in order to drum up new recruits. In March, even as Washington was fortifying Dorchester Heights with the cannon brought from Fort Ticonderoga by Henry Knox, Hale's unit participated in a raid on the outskirts of Boston to burn homes being used by the British as housing for its officers. The two events only hastened the enemy's decision to evacuate the city by March 17.

Nathan Hale

After a promotion to captain and a brief furlough home that would sadly prove to be his last, Hale joined the rest of the Continental Army in marching south to New York which was expected to be the next place the British would strike following their evacuation of Boston. Over the spring and into the summer, Washington began to prepare for the defense of New York; an unwise decision what with an untrained army and an enemy who controlled the sea, but he had orders from the Continental Congress not to allow the colonies' second greatest city to fall into enemy hands without a fight. Late in August 1776, the British invaded Long Island and proceeded to push the inexperienced Continental Army across the East River into Manhattan. The next month, the enemy humiliated the Americans by literally frightening them from their positions and capturing New York City without a fight. Hunkered down behind his defense lines along Harlem Heights, a frustrated Washington could only look on as British Gen. William Howe's troops began making themselves comfortable for the winter.

Hale, meanwhile, after distinguishing himself in the retreat from Long Island and in a raid on a British war vessel that netted some much needed supplies, came to the attention of Lt. Col. Thomas Knowlton, a fellow resident of Connecticut and leader of a newly organized body of rangers. Knowlton, impressed by Hale's dash, asked him to join his unit and the former schoolteacher accepted. At about that same time, in a meeting with his officers, a worried Washington complained that he needed more information about enemy intentions and proposed to run spies into the city to find out whatever they could. Someone suggested that perhaps volunteers for the dangerous duty might be found from among Knowlton's rangers but when the request was made to them, no one was willing to go. Finally, however, filled with patriotic zeal, Hale spoke up and declared that he would take the chance. Warned by Capt. William Hull, a friend from his old regiment, that acting the role of a spy was extremely dangerous, Hale explained that the information needed by Washington was urgent and that getting it was worth the risk.

On September 12, only three days before the British landed in the American rear at Kip's Bay, cutting off New York City from the rest of Manhattan, Hale caught a ride on a local schooner and entered enemy lines bearing his Yale diploma and disguised as an unassuming school-teacher looking for work. Completely unprepared for the task ahead of him, the amateur spy moved about the town making his observations and writing them down in Latin. Without any contacts, he was forced to hide the papers in the heels of his shoes so when he was inevitably discovered, he had no hope of plausibly denying the evidence of hidden, uncoded messages on his person. There are many stories of how Hale was caught: he signaled to the wrong ship on the night appointed for his return trip to friendly lines, he was recognized by a cousin who turned him in, he revealed his mission to an acquaintance he met in the city and thought could be trusted. However it happened, it could not have come at a worse time than on September 21. The night before, a fire broke out that threatened to burn the whole city to the ground, a fire that was said to have been started by local patriots as they escaped from town. Such an action was not calculated to make Howe a happy man, so when Hale was brought before him with the incriminating evidence of his written notes and admitting that he was an officer in the Continental Army, the general ordered him hung as a spy the next day, September 22.

The decision came with little deliberation let alone the formality of a hearing; Hale was even denied a visit by a clergyman or the comfort of the Bible before the execution. Respecting the courage with which Hale had received his sentence and taking pity on his dishonorable treatment, Captain John Montresor allowed the American use of his tent to write a final message to his mother (which was later destroyed). "...he was calm," said Montresor, "and bore himself with gentle dignity, in the consciousness of rectitude and high intentions." When the time arrived for the execution, Hale was escorted to an artillery park located near an apple orchard and hanged from a tree with little fanfare. It was Montresor, meeting later with Hull under a flag of truce, who described the details of Hale's death and his last, immortal words: "I only regret that I have but one life to lose for my country."

Lyman Hall

Far ahead of the curve, Lyman Hall found little support in his native Georgia either for resistance against British oppression or independence. As a result, he ended up leading a sometimes lonely crusade that not only prompted him to join the Continental Congress as a nonvoting member representing only his home county, but also to advocate for the secession of St. John's Parish from the rest of Georgia and uniting it with a more radical South Carolina.

But one of Georgia's most famous Founding Fathers came to that state only later in life. Born in Wallingford, Connecticut on April 12, 1724, Hall headed to Yale College to prepare for a career as a clergyman. Graduating in 1747, he became a Congregationalist minister and began preaching in Bridgeport. There, something went wrong and he soon found himself dismissed from practice. Fences were soon mended however, and by 1751, Hall was back in the pulpit. He was not there long when, after getting married, he decided to find a more lucrative career. He settled for medicine and after studying for a couple of years with a local physician, returned to his hometown and went into practice for himself. Being an ambitious young man, Hall decided to move his practice somewhere with less competition and took his family to South Carolina where he established himself among a group of transplanted Yankees.

In 1752, Hall made yet another move, following some members of the community to Georgia, the last of the thirteen original American colonies to be established. Intended to act as a buffer between England's mid-Atlantic colonies and Spanish Florida, Georgia at that time was still relatively unpopulated and the least developed of the seaboard colonies. Settling in newly founded Sunbury in St. John's Parish, Hall bought himself a nearby plantation and called it Hall's Knoll where he began to grow rice. Continuing to practice as a physician, he was radicalized in the 1760s when the troubles with England began. As the years passed and conflict over Parliament's attempts to tax the colonies continued, St. John's Parish, along with the district around Savannah, became hotbeds of resistance with Hall assuming a leadership role. Disgusted with the tepid response by his fellow colonists at various conventions held to discuss the increasing friction with Britain, Hall supported an effort to have St. John's secede from Georgia and unite with the more radical South Carolina. When its request was refused, the parish held its own convention and in 1775 Hall was dispatched to Philadelphia to represent St. John's as a non-voting member of the Continental Congress. Later that year, the rest of Georgia finally came around and voted to make Hall's position official and sent two more delegates to join him, Button Gwinnett and George Walton. Gwinnett was especially welcome as he was somewhat of a protégé of Hall's. Together, the three men would later vote for and sign the Declaration of Independence.

Although he was appointed to serve in Congress until 1780, Hall decided to return to Georgia in 1777 as the threat of enemy invasion of the new state became imminent. Back home, he joined Gwinnett's battle with the McIntosh clan, political rivals based out of Savannah, a situation that ended badly for his friend when Gwinnett was killed in a duel with Continental Gen. Lachlan McIntosh. When the British finally

Lyman Hall

arrived in Georgia in 1778 they seized Savannah, forcing Hall, who had been branded a traitor for signing the Declaration, to flee the state. With their hold on Georgia secure, the British began to move north, threatening Charleston and before that city was eventually forced to surrender, Hall had once again moved on, this time to Philadelphia and ultimately to safety with his family in Connecticut.

Hall was finally able to return home in 1782 where he discovered that not only had Hall's Knoll been burned to the ground, but so had a second home in Sunbury. Taking up residence in Savannah, Hall resumed the practice of medicine and worked to restore his property. In 1783 he was elected to the state's legislature and the next year served as governor. The ensuing years were taken up with duties as a judge and trustee for what would later be known as the University of Georgia. Much of Hall's time was also spent litigating the will of his friend Gwinnett who was killed in a duel with political rival Lachlan McIntosh in 1777. In 1785, Hall sold Hall's Knoll and bought Shell Bluff Plantation outside Augusta where he died on October 19, 1790.

Alexander Hamilton

Alexander Hamilton has the distinction, along with Benjamin Franklin, of being one of the most famous and capable heroes of the Revolutionary era who was never elected president but should have. A man of courage, conviction, principal, vision, and above all, genius, Hamilton's path to national leadership was thwarted by his great friend and mentor George Washington when the latter chose him as the country's first Secretary of the Treasury. The appointment thrust Hamilton into a maelstrom of political infighting that found his policies increasingly at odds with those of his great rival, Thomas Jefferson. The result was that Hamilton tended to polarize public opinion rather than unite it, a situation that eventually ended in the creation of the nation's first political parties: the Federalists and the Republicans. In the end, Hamilton was considered by the public as too much a partisan of the Federalist cause, a cause whose support, though strong at the start, eroded early and then lost permanently with the election of 1800 when Jefferson was made president. By that point, Hamilton's reputation had become so politically charged, he could never hope to win a national election. In hindsight however, Hamilton's political defeat during his lifetime was only a temporary one as his visionary plans for setting the United States on a sound fiscal foundation and initiating long range plans that boldly encouraged business and manufacturing, would become a personal triumph that would propel the new nation, made up mostly of raw frontier and farmland, into the front rank of industrial super-states only 150 years later.

But for a man whose figure today looks out like a patron saint over Wall Street, the nerve center of world finance and home of the New York Stock Exchange, Hamilton's beginnings were inauspicious ones. Born on January 11, 1755 on the island of Nevis in the West Indies, Hamilton was the illegitimate issue of James Hamilton and Rachel Levien. Compounding the unfortunate circumstances of his birth, Hamilton lost his mother early and his father became a bankrupt and disappeared. But the young Hamilton had a few things still in his favor: genius, ambition, and opportunity. At the age of twelve, he was taken

Alexander Hamilton

on as an apprentice accountant by a local importer and soon having proved his worth, the impressed owners decided to contribute to a fund collected to underwrite Hamilton's formal education.

Sent to the North American colonies, Hamilton entered New York's King's College in 1773 and although a good student, he soon became distracted from his studies by the rising tide of revolt in the colonies. He joined other students in an amateur military unit and when hostilities broke out between the colonies and Great Britain, he became a captain of artillery. Seeing action during the dismal New York campaign in which the British pushed the Continental Army clear into neighboring Pennsylvania, Hamilton came to the attention of George Washington and was offered a promotion to lieutenant colonel and a staff position with the commander in chief. He served four years as one of Washington's aides de camp during which time he and the commander in chief developed a close, father/son relationship, a situation that made it all the more difficult when they at last parted. Hamilton, who early on had expressed a keen desire for military glory, chafed at the restrictions placed on him as a simple aide. He wanted action, and he wanted it before the war ended. To that end, he used a minor disagreement with Washington to request a transfer to a line unit. The application was granted just in time for Hamilton to lead a dangerous and successful charge against an enemy redoubt before British defensive positions at Yorktown. The event proved to be the climax of his military career and with the war clearly winding down, Hamilton chose to leave the army to take up the practice of law in New York.

The choice of the law was a logical one for an ambitious young man who had recently married Elizabeth Schuyler, daughter of Gen. Philip Schuyler, one of the most influential men in the new state of New York. It was a simple matter for someone of Hamilton's proven abilities to master the admittedly limited requirements of an eighteenth century legal education and in a matter of a few months he had established himself in practice and with the help of his connections, soon became involved in the political life of New York that included a term of service in Congress. It was his experience in Congress that dissatisfied him with the limitations and confusion resulting from the Articles of Confederation under which the newly independent colonies operated. The experience prompted Hamilton to become a strong and vocal advocate for change. In particular, he supported the creation of a new federal governmental structure with strength enough to bend the relationship between the states to its will. Finding sympathetic allies, Hamilton called for a convention to discuss the possibility and the Annapolis Convention, held in 1786, was the result. There, Hamilton met James Madison and the two like-minded men united in support of a Constitutional Convention that would be gathered for the purpose of fashioning a new federal government. That demand became a reality when the states approved the idea and the new convention was held in Philadelphia the following year. Once again, Hamilton was appointed as a member of New York's delegation but despite his keen interest in the subject, failed to attend many of the sessions. Although in favor of a central government much stronger than most of his peers preferred, Hamilton enthusiastically embraced the proposed federal structure that emerged from the convention, becoming the first to publicly defend the new Constitution in a newspaper article. That piece became the basis of a remarkable literary collaboration between himself, Madison, and John Jay, with Hamilton contributing the bulk of the entries. In a series of articles that have since become known as *The Federalist Papers*, the three men addressed every aspect of the argument for a constitutional government with a well reasoned and richly detailed knowledge of history, philosophy, and political systems. But equally important was the fact that in their calculations the question of human frailties was not ignored and was taken into account in discussions involving the checks and balances built into the constitutional plan. Their efforts were successful, and after a suspenseful period of debate among the states, and the addition of a Bill of Rights, the Constitution of the United States was finally adopted.

With Washington the universal choice as the country's first president, it came as little surprise to anyone that the former commander in chief chose Hamilton to be a member of a small group of his closest advisors. It was in the capacity of Secretary of the Treasury that Hamilton's career would reach its zenith and become the instrument of his political marginalization. Hamilton prepared himself for his new duties by reading all he could find in matters relating to finance which of course, had much to do with Great Britain, the most successful economic model of the time. His admiration of Britain's economic success aroused suspicion in many, including Secretary of State Thomas Jefferson, that Hamilton had grown uncomfortably sympathetic with the nation's former enemy and so, when his first recommendations as Secretary of the Treasury were made, they touched off a firestorm of protest. One of those recommendations, summarized in his Report on the Public Credit, included the concept of assumption, which allowed the federal government to assume the outstanding debt incurred by the states during the war by offering interest payments to bond holders. Many states, such as Virginia, were against assumption because they had already repaid their debts but Hamilton believed that the acquisition of a modest public debt by the federal government was a good thing and would help in attracting lucrative loans and investment from Europe which in turn could be used by the new nation to build an infrastructure friendly to business. It was a visionary plan that initially failed passage in Congress due in large measure to those such as Jefferson who could only see it as the beginning of a contest between the rich, money holding interests, and everyone else. In the end, however, Hamilton's plan prevailed as behind the scenes negotiations resulted in a compromise allowing passage of the Assumption Bill in return for passage of a Residence Bill that would set the location of a proposed federal capital city in the South.

Later, when Hamilton's Reports on Manufactures and National Bank ended with the recommendation that the country establish a national bank (based on his experience in helping to found the Bank of New York), protective tariffs, and encourage diversification in manufacturing, Jefferson felt his earlier fears justified. Adding to the Virginian's disquiet, Hamilton had drawn support for the measure through persuasive arguments that his fiscal recommendations were allowed under the Constitution because of its "implied powers" and the responsibility it gave to federal officials to "promote the general welfare." As a result, the two men's opposing opinions soon polarized into two political camps with Jefferson at the head of the Republicans who supported a weak central government and Hamilton as the leader of the Federalists who advocated a strong federal government. From then on, the two sides went at each other tooth and nail with the Federalists maintaining the upper hand through Washington's term as president (for whom Hamilton wrote his famous Farewell Address) but slowly losing influence through the subsequent administration of John Adams.

Recovering from sickness and tired of the constant political battles, Hamilton decided to resign as Secretary of the Treasury in 1795 and return to New York. From there, he continued to advise Washington and later, to meddle in federal affairs through his influence with President John Adams' cabinet ministers. With Jefferson's election to the presidency in 1800, the influence of the Federalists, and by extension Hamilton, was almost completely ended. Hamilton's last triumphs came with his refutation of notions by resentful federalists to sunder the union and his successful behind the scenes machinations that foiled the ambitions of political rival Aaron Burr to renege on a promise to Jefferson not to stand in his way of becoming president. Hamilton's scheme to thwart Burr was only the latest and most dramatic in a rivalry between the two New Yorkers begun when Hamilton early on judged correctly Burr's unscrupulous nature. Their struggle to dominate the politics of New York ended on a field in Weehauken, New Jersey on July 11, 1804 when Burr shot Hamilton in a duel. Never intending to shoot Burr himself, Hamilton died the next day.

Hamilton's death was universally deplored, even among his enemies, who realized the important role he had played in the nation's birth. Madison, who took Hamilton by surprise when he turned away from federalism to follow Jefferson, acknowledged his personal integrity and genius. But although Hamilton experienced disappointment in many of his objectives and the National Bank he founded was eventually abolished by Andrew Jackson, the ultimate purpose of his efforts to set the nation on a strong economic foundation have since proved correct with many of his capitalist principals now enshrined in a free market system that spans the globe.

Wade Hampton

Born in Halifax County, Virginia in 1754, Wade Hampton was a member of the kind of pioneering family that characterized the restless energy of the American people in the eighteenth century. Confident in themselves and their destiny, they constantly pushed at the western boundaries of the thirteen colonies letting neither the king's proclamation barring settlement west of the Appalachian Mountains nor the threat of wild Indian tribes deter them. To be sure, many of the early pioneers had no choice; they were the victims of a society where land ownership was the only way for the unskilled to avoid destitution. There were others however, who already owned land but whose ambitions were greater than simply subsistence farming. And with land on the frontier as cheap as it was or just there for the taking by anyone willing to hazard the risks of failure or death at the hands of the Indians they displaced, it presented the possibility for increased wealth that made the gamble more than worth it. Such a person was Hampton's father, who took his family to Spartanburg, South Carolina where he established a large farm in the Piedmont forest country. But building the farm and then holding it against local Indians angered at the encroachment upon their traditional hunting grounds came at a high price.

In July of 1776, with the Revolution barely a year old and a Declaration of Independence only recently signed in Philadelphia, Anthony Hampton, his wife and some of his children were killed by marauding Cherokee Indians. The family's struggle against the Indians, with little help from the ruling government in England as well as the restrictions placed on Americans by the Proclamation Line both probably had a great influence on Hampton's decision to support the Revolution as they did for most others living on the frontier. In the internecine warfare that would come to characterize the war in the south, a clear demarcation would develop between those residents living on the frontier and those farther east: most of the loyalists were to be found on the seaboard where day to day dealings with the British were more intimate while the strongest support for the patriot cause was located inland among small landholders like the Hamptons.

Battle of Eutaw Springs

When hostilities broke out between Americans and British, Hampton, who, like most other frontiersmen, was an excellent rider and hunter, well versed in the ways of the forest, volunteered his services on the side of revolution. Rising to the rank of colonel, he led his own cavalry unit and saw action under Generals Francis Marion and Thomas Sumter. The climax of Hampton's service in the war came on September 8, 1781 at the battle of Eutaw Springs. After a year of military setbacks, from outright defeats such as those at King's Mountain and the Cowpens, and technical victories such as Guilford Courthouse where he was left in command of the field but at heavy cost, British General Lord Charles Cornwallis was ready to give up on the lower south and take his army to Virginia. As he moved north, Cornwallis left a few units behind to protect his flanks which in turn became targets of opportunity for a Continental Army that had been growing in strength even as it suffered grievous shortages in supplies.

Under the command of Gen. Nathanael Green, the Continentals had adopted the hit and run tactics developed by Francis Marion to keep the British on the defensive, but as Cornwallis began his retreat from the Carolinas, set piece battles became more frequent. Finally, Green learned that a 2,400 man force under British Lt. Col. Alexander Stewart was encamped on the south bank of Eutaw Creek. With his own army of just 2,000 men, Green formed a line of battle east of the creek and, following Morgan's order of battle at Cowpens, set his militia units in front with the regulars in reserve. The North Carolina militia were placed in the center of the line with those of South Carolina to the right and left. Anchoring the left were the men of Hampton's cavalry unit. The battle opened after the North Carolinians stood up and fired taking the enemy completely by surprise. The unexpected shooting sent the British reeling back in disorder with the Americans pressing their advantage. On the left, where Hampton's unit moved forward under the command of Lt. Col. John Henderson, it was met with heavy fire from the British right wing under Major John Majoribanks. "Never was the constancy of a party of men more severely tried," stated American Colonel Otho Williams in his after action report. During the fighting on the left, Henderson was critically wounded, affecting the confidence of his men. Assuming command, Hampton rallied the troops and was able to keep the attack going until a cavalry charge by Lt. Col. William Washington on Majoribanks' position could be affected. Unfortunately, Washington's horsemen were caught in a crossfire that broke up their attack and it was all Hampton's men could do to cover their retreat. Remnants of both units then regrouped to resume the attack but by then, things began to fall apart along the rest of the American line.

Seeing the British in full retreat and sensing victory, the near starving Americans came upon the enemy encampment and, unable to resist, quit the battle to plunder for food and clothing. The distraction weakened the American drive and gave the British the opportunity to counterattack. After that, it was all the more disciplined units could do, including Hampton's, to cover the retreat. In the end, despite hand to hand combat by Hampton's men, the British counterattack succeeded in hurling the Americans from the field and back into the nearby forest. It was another technical victory for the British who suffered 866 casualties to that of 522 Americans, but it was enough to force Stewart to abandon the countryside for the safety of Charleston.

With the war winding down, Hampton himself retreated to the family farm and divided his concentration between service in South Carolina's state Assembly and managing his properties. Satisfied with the Articles of Confederation and suspicious of replacing one distant government with another, he grew to oppose ratification of the United States Constitution but when his state chose to support the document, he did not allow his earlier opposition to prevent him from accepting a seat in the country's new Congress. Serving in the House of Representatives from 1795-1805, Hampton again was obliged to divide his time between his public duties and his own business enterprises and by the turn of the new century had transformed his family holdings in the Piedmont to an agricultural empire that would eventually stretch all the way to Louisiana.

In the meantime, however, Hampton was called upon once more to exercise his military skills in the War of 1812 when he was appointed colonel in 1808 and promoted to brigadier general the next year. Stationed at first in New Orleans, his irascible temperament alienated his officers and he was eventually replaced by the conniving Gen. James Wilkinson, a former governor of the territory who had only recently been cleared of conspiracy charges related to a plot by Aaron Burr to conquer the southwest. The snub to his honor forever tainted Hampton's attitude toward Wilkinson (who later became an informant for the Spanish) and became a major factor in a failed campaign to invade Canada in 1813. In that instance, Hampton, who had been promoted to major general, commanded one of two armies that were meant to cooperate in an attack on Montreal. On October 26, 1813 an advance party comprising of about half of Hampton's 4,000 man army met a force of British soldiers a third their strength at Chateaugay, New York and were repulsed. The unexpected setback unnerved Hampton who immediately ordered a retreat back to Plattsburgh. Without Hampton's support, Wilkinson ordered his 8,000 man army to fall back as well and the whole plan to attack Montreal fell apart. Throughout, Hampton further tarnished his reputation by refusing to cooperate with the hated Wilkinson, who had been placed in command of the operation, going so far as to accept orders only from the Secretary of War himself. In the wake of these events, and an official review of his behavior, Hampton resigned his commission in 1814 and returned to South Carolina where he resumed his agricultural pursuits. By the time of his death on February 4, 1835 he had become one of the richest men in the United States owning estates and plantations all over the south. The owner of over 3,000 slaves, he was one of the first to experiment in growing cotton and cultivated sugar in Mississippi and Louisiana.

John Hancock

Besides being familiar with the public as the name of one of the country's premier insurance companies, the name of John Hancock has also become synonymous with a person's signature, and with good reason. After years of defying king and Parliament as well as British law with smuggling operations that made him one of the richest men in the thirteen American colonies, Hancock had developed a brash ego, perhaps a necessary characteristic for a successful law breaker, one that inspired him to sign his name twice the size of his fellow signers of the Declaration of Independence so that "John Bull can read my name without his spectacles." But the same qualities and interests possessed by Hancock also represent the mixed motives of many of the Revolutionary generation in which self-interest walked hand in hand with a belief in the principle of liberty and a burning desire to be free of arbitrary state power. And so, although Washington had investments in western land made inaccessible by British law and Hancock

John Hancock

earned his living by smuggling proscribed merchandise into the country, the danger to their lives as well as their fortunes was very real. In fact, in signing the Declaration of Independence and joining other patriot leaders in pledging "our lives, our fortunes, our sacred honor," Hancock was charged with treason by the Crown.

One of three children, Hancock was born in Braintree, Massachusetts on January 23, 1737, the son of a clergyman. Upon the death of his father seven years later, Hancock's life was radically changed when he was adopted by a wealthy uncle who owned a number of sailing vessels that plied the South America/Caribbean/New England shipping lanes. After graduating from Harvard in 1757, his uncle sent him to England to round out his education with some taste of the larger world. There, Hancock attended the coronation of his future nemesis, George III, who at the time was almost his own age. It was probably only after he returned to the colonies and assumed duties in his uncle's business that Hancock learned the true source of his patron's wealth: smuggling. In 1764, Hancock's uncle died, leaving his riches and business empire in the hands of the 27 year old youth.

The next year, Hancock entered politics in a run for the Massachusetts House of Representatives but was defeated by Samuel Adams. Despite his loss, Hancock nevertheless sided with Adams in the Stamp Act crisis and in 1766, with the support of the patriot firebrand, stood for election a second time and won. Soon after, the British Parliament passed the Townshend Acts that placed added duties on selected imports such as tea and precipitated a personal crisis for Hancock that succeeded in catapulting him into the front rank of revolutionaries. It happened in 1768 when a Hancock owned ship, the *Liberty*, entered port in Boston and declared a cargo of Madeira wine. The problem, according to royal customs inspectors, was that the declared cargo was well below the ship's storage capacity. Under the protection of a British war ship, royal officials seized the *Liberty*. The action ignited public protests, some violent, which forced customs officials and their families to retreat to an island fort in Boston harbor. Patriots exploited the affair in its opposition to the Townshend Acts and eventually Governor Thomas Hutchinson ordered all charges against Hancock dropped and the *Liberty* released. But by then, much of the damage had been done and royal officials had succeeded in radicalizing one of the most powerful men in the colony.

Now a popular and undisputed leading figure in the patriot cause, Hancock was named president of the Massachusetts Provincial Congress in 1774, the governing body that had replaced the Massachusetts House upon its dissolution by General Thomas Gage, commanding officer of British forces in occupation of Boston. In 1775, Hancock was named as a delegate to the Second Continental Congress, but before he was due to attend, war broke out in April and he and Samuel Adams (both wanted for treason) narrowly escaped capture in Lexington with the timely warning of Paul Revere. The next year, in Philadelphia, Hancock assumed the presidency of the Continental Congress and guided it to its momentous climax when the Declaration of Independence was ratified. Now one of the most wanted revolutionaries in America, Hancock placed his famous signature at the foot of the document in letters large enough, he said, for John Bull to read it without his glasses.

Although Hancock had gone from one important post in the nascent Revolution to another, one plum evaded him, that of commander of the Continental Army, a position he coveted but one which was denied him by his closest political allies. It was John Adams' belief, seconded by his cousin Samuel, that in order to demonstrate that the war effort was truly one involving all of the thirteen colonies, a southerner needed to be named to the post and nominated Virginia's George Washington to command the new national army that was then comprised mostly of New Englanders. Disappointed and estranged from the Adamses, Hancock resigned from Congress in 1777 and, returning to Massachusetts, participated in the creation of the new state's constitution. In 1778, he fulfilled his dream of martial glory by leading a 5,000 man army into Rhode Island in an unsuccessful attempt to free the state from British occupation. In 1780, he capped his public career by being elected for the first of nine consecutive terms as governor of Massachusetts. He died in office in 1789.

Josiah Harmar

After enjoying a distinguished career as an officer in the Continental Army, Josiah Harmar's reputation was tarnished, as had so many others both before and after him, when a force under his command met defeat at the hands of Indians in the post-war northwest territory.

Born in Philadelphia, Pennsylvania on November 10, 1753, Harmar was brought up as a Quaker but spurned the sect's teachings about non-violence when, in the spring of 1775, farmers in Massachusetts fired on British troops and ignited the Revolutionary War. That autumn, Harmar was appointed a captain of the 1st Pennsylvania Battalion. The next year, he entered the Continental Army as captain of the 3rd Pennsylvania Regiment and by 1783, had worked his way through a succession of commands to the rank of colonel. Harmar began his career in the army with Gen. George Washington and Continental forces operating in New York, New Jersey, and Pennsylvania. Then, following Gen. Horatio Gates' failure to contest British occupation of the southern states, he was attached to the command of Gen. Nathanael Greene who was appointed in place of the disgraced Gates. Harmar served with Greene until 1782 and following the surrender of British Gen. Charles Cornwallis at Yorktown, was dispatched to England by president of Congress Thomas Mifflin to deliver the ratification of the Treaty of Paris. Although Harmar was the first of three messengers traveling by separate ships to reach London, he still arrived a full month later than the agreed upon deadline for submission of the ratification decision. But the tardiness of his arrival mattered little as the British were in little mood to continue the war.

That same year, 1784, he married and became a senior officer in the new United

Josiah Harmar

States Army. Ordered to the northwest frontier as military commander of the newly created 700 man 1st American Regiment, Harmar served under Gen. Arthur St. Clair who had been appointed governor and set about contending with the ongoing struggle between settlers and Indians in the disputed Ohio country. With little first hand knowledge of the Indians, Harmer built a number of forts in the region and was present at the signing of a treaty at Fort McIntosh in 1785 which promised the Indians peace in exchange for land forfeited by their alliance with the British during the Revolution. To enforce the treaty, Harmar built Fort Harmar and sent troops to the north side of the Ohio River to remove settlers from Indian territory. But as was often the case on the frontier, treaties had little effect on the situation with Indian tribes such as the Miami, Wyandot, and Shawnee unwilling to join their former British allies in defeat following the Revolution. Led by Miami chieftan Little Turtle, the various tribes united in a broad effort to resist further settlement of the Ohio country. By 1790, treaties had failed and Harmar was ordered to launch a punitive expedition against the Indians north of the Ohio River. Marching out of Fort Washington with an army of 1,400 men, mostly local militia, Harmar's force succeeded in destroying a number of Indian villages. The easy march inspired overconfidence in the army and when its commander ordered a smaller detachment out to look for the main body of Indians, it was ambushed and lost almost 200 men. While retreating back to Fort Washington, Harmar allowed a second unit of 360 men to proceed with another search and destroy mission but that one too ended in disappointment when 60 regulars were cut off from the main body and slaughtered. Back at Fort Washington, Harmar injudiciously celebrated with a victory dinner and tried to put the best light on the disastrous campaign to Secretary of War Henry Knox. Rebuked, Harmar asked for a court of inquiry to review his conduct during the campaign and was cleared of fault with the blame for failure placed on the quality of the militia under his command.

Harmar retired from the army in 1792 and after a stint as adjutant general of Pennsylvania, tried his hand at business before he died in Philadelphia on August 20, 1813.

Benjamin Harrison

Benjamin Harrison must certainly be counted among the "Virginia Dynasty" of early American political leaders, he was also the progenitor of a dynasty of his own, becoming the father, grandfather, and ancestor of a number of descendents who would play important roles in the history of the United States including his own son, William Henry Harrison, who became the ninth President.

Harrison was born at Berkeley, his family's plantation in Charles City County, Virginia on April 5, 1726. When he was a young man, he followed a liberal arts curriculum at the College of William and Mary. However, he was obliged to leave school in 1745 without graduating due to the sudden death of his father and the need for him to tend to the affairs of the family plantation. Some years later, he emerged from his work to be married and accept election to Virginia's legislature, the House of Burgesses. There he remained from 1749 to 1775, seeing the colony move from loyalty to the English crown to open rebellion. But for Harrison himself, the journey from loyal subject to revolutionary was a slow one and one he was reluctant to make.

As the owner of one of the colony's largest estates, he had a vested interest in the status quo, even though he could see the validity in the positions taken by more ardent patriots. In 1764, Harrison served on a committee that drafted an official protest to the king about a Stamp Act being proposed by the English Parliament. If passed, the act would force a tax on the American colonies that they had no say about. Later, Harrison partially supported a list of resolutions submitted by fellow legislator Patrick Henry balking only at language that called for active measures to resist the tax. Although Harrison may have been seen at the time by such younger men as Henry and Thomas Jefferson as an old stick in the mud, he proved his patriotic bona fides when he refused a bribe from the colony's governor and joined the growing revolutionary movement. From there, Harrison became a member of Virginia's Committee of Correspondence, and participated in local and provincial con-

Benjamin Harrison

gresses. By 1774, Harrison's reputation as a patriot was such that he was chosen as a member of the colony's delegation to the first Continental Congress joining such illustrious company as George Washington, Patrick Henry, and Richard Henry Lee. Later, he was on hand outside Boston when he accompanied a committee of fellow congressmen to Gen. Washington's camp to help lay plans for the creation of a Continental Army.

In 1776, Harrison was present in Congress during the deliberations regarding separation from Britain and sealed his patriotic credentials by joining his fellow members in voting for and signing the Declaration of Independence. He even joked that his weight would guarantee him a swift death at the end of a hangman's rope! The next year, Harrison exchanged his seat in Congress for one in Virginia's new state legislature. In 1782, his stature had grown such that he was elected governor, occupying the position until 1784 when he gave up the office to Patrick Henry. Returning to the legislature, Harrison remained there until 1791, punctuating his stay in 1788 by also serving as a representative to the state's ratifying convention for the United States Constitution. By that time, Harrison's old conservatism had begun to reassert itself, joining others such as Henry and Richard Henry Lee in opposition to the Constitution. Against his advice, Virginia ratified the instrument and, before his death on April 24, 1791, Harrison, gracious in defeat, gave the document his full support.

John Hart

Even though all of the signers of the Declaration of Independence risked their lives, their property, and their sacred honor in the cause of American freedom, few ever had to face the stark choice of either living up to that stirring vow or turning their backs on it. For those few who did, reactions varied. For Richard Stockton, captured, imprisoned, and maltreated, signing a loyalty oath to the king seemed the right thing to do at the time while for others such as John Hart, the risk of death by exposure to the elements rather than capture by the enemy was the preferred choice.

Born in 1713 (the exact date is unknown), Hart began life not the scion of some great family but the son of a simple farmer in Hopewell Township, New Jersey. Educated only in the basics of reading, writing, and arithmetic, Hart was expected to follow in his father's footsteps and help manage the family farm. There he worked until 1739 when he married Deborah Scudder (with whom he would have 13 children) and used his savings to buy 193 acres of land on the north side of Hopewell Township. It would be the beginning of a long, but steady climb to prosperity for Hart. In 1746, he pitched in to help his father repurchase the family farm when questions about its ownership were raised. In 1747, Hart, himself a Presbyterian, earned a reputation for magnanimity when he donated a portion of land to his Baptist neighbors for construction of a church. Grateful for his patronage, members of the church were perhaps instrumental in helping him win election to his first government job as freeholder for Hunterdon County. In 1751, he added to his standing in the community by partnering with his brother for the purchase of a grist mill. Four years later, with a growing reputation as a successful businessman as well as farmer, Hart gave up his position as freeholder and in 1757 became a justice of the peace. In 1761 he was elected to New Jersey's colonial legislature where he served for the next ten years. There, dealing first hand with royal authority and unpopular edicts handed down by Parliament, Hart found himself becoming increasingly radicalized. Thus, by the time Parliament issued the Stamp Act, Hart was one of the first to call for the thirteen colonies to gather at a Stamp Act Congress to discuss the issue. On the domestic front, Hart sold his mill in 1766 and in 1772,

John Hart

after leaving the legislature, bought another 230 acres of land and became Hopewell Township's major landowner. Adding to his growing real estate empire, Hart joined with his son-in-law in purchasing an entire mill and farm complex and solidified his position in the community as a successful businessman.

Meanwhile, however, events outside Hopewell continued to move forward. Already a member of New Jersey's Committees of Correspondence and Safety, Hart was chosen as a member of the committee whose purpose was to choose delegates to represent the colony in the Continental Congress. Next, he was elected to the colony's Provincial Congress which began meeting in place of the colonial legislature.

Finally, there came the climax of Hart's public career and the event which would throw his personal life into chaos.

In 1776, Hart was chosen as a delegate to the Second Continental Congress and arrived in Philadelphia just in time to add his signature to the Declaration of Independence. About that same time, the British, after having swept the Continental Army from New York, invaded New Jersey and with the help of local Tories, began to target patriot owned property for spoliation. As a known signer of the Declaration, Hart's property became the object of particular attention but luckily it never suffered complete destruction. But the worry over the threat of attack and looting proved too much for Hart's wife, whose health was ruined. Luckily, Hart soon had reason to return to New Jersey after he was elected to the new state's legislature and became its Speaker. Dividing his time between the legislature and Hopewell, Hart was at home when his wife died on October 8, 1776. It was hardly a month later when German mercenaries in the employ of the British returned to the neighborhood and, fearing for his life, Hart took to the nearby woods. Now in his early 60s, with his family scattered among friends and relatives and outside temperatures dropping quickly, Hart hid out in the forest, sleeping in caves for a week or so until things cooled down enough to return home. In the meantime, Gen. George Washington had restored patriot confidence in the Revolution with a Christmastime victory at Trenton followed by the battle of Princeton early in the new year. The twin actions persuaded the enemy to pull out of New Jersey, allowing Hart to emerge from hiding and recall the state's legislature into session. As winter gave way to spring, the enemy retreated from New Jersey and Hart invited Washington to use his farm to bivouac his 12,000 man Continental Army. It was while camped there that Washington began planning the next part of his campaign and on June 24, 1778 decamped and left for the battle of Monmouth which took place only a few days later. Meanwhile, Hart continued to serve in the state's legislature and when he returned to Hopewell that autumn, kidney stones prevented him from resuming his duties in the following session. On May 11, 1779 complications derived from the stones finally killed him.

William Heath

Not all military leaders of the Revolution were battlefield Napoleons. Although most were fired by a belief in the patriot cause, that zealotry did not necessarily translate into military genius. Some officers such as John Stark and William Prescott were natural born fighters and others such as Benedict Arnold and Nathanael Green, were brave as well as resourceful. Others however, were merely competent and as the conflict widened, they would be shaken out with the experience of combat, each to find the place where their particular talents were best suited. Some would rise in the ranks of combat generals, while others became quartermasters and administrators. Still others, such as William Heath, inexperienced except for what he had taught himself from

British evacuation of Boston

books, overweight and with a tendency toward laziness, eventually found his niche commanding troops in the necessary but dull duty of guarding supply lines and lines of communications far from the front.

Born on March 7, 1737 in Roxbury, Massachusetts, William Heath was raised on a farm that had been in the family for a hundred years. Heath loved the agrarian life and the basic education he received in reading and sums would, with a single exception, prove enough for him. Fascinated by war and combat, he began to read anything he could get ahold of on the subject and later, applied his enthusiasm in helping to organize a local militia unit. It was after being elected to the colonial legislature in 1761 that Heath became increasingly aware of the rise in popular dissatisfaction with the British Parliament and its string of tax raising measures that residents considered oppressive. Sensing perhaps that relations between Massachusetts and England could go from bad to worse, Heath decided to step up his efforts to train and organize more militia companies in preparation for whatever might ensue. As a result of his involvement, by 1770, he had risen from captain of the Suffolk County militia to Colonel and then commander of a Boston artillery company. That same year, as he became increasingly active in the revolutionary movement, Heath began to write articles dealing with military preparedness for local newspapers under the name of A Military Countryman and by 1774 was serving on the colony's Committee of Correspondence as well as its Committee of Safety (the patriot body that dealt with intelligence and military affairs) and was chosen as a delegate to the Provincial Congress. It was while serving with the congress in 1774 that he was commissioned as one of several generals of militia.

When war finally broke out at Lexington and Concord, Heath was the first officer of rank to arrive on the scene and immediately tried to take control of the situation. His efforts, however, proved unnecessary as the militiamen's instinctive strategy of sniping from cover and leapfrogging ahead of the retreating enemy column as it snaked its way back to Boston worked well enough. Anticipating the enemy's movements, Heath had men race ahead to tear up the planking of the only bridge that led across the Charles River. Unfortunately, when they were removed, the men failed to take the planks away and when the British arrived, a few men simply crossed the remains of the bridge, retrieved the planking, and replaced them. On the other side, local militia planned to hold the road to Charlestown but, unused to the sound of shots fired in anger, quickly dispersed when the soldiers came too close. At that point, fearful that the enemy now occupied a more favorable defensive position within the city's limits, Heath ordered the militia to halt its pursuit. It was his plan to keep just enough men to make sure that the British remained bottled up in Boston, but his orders for the rest of the militia to disperse fell on deaf ears and soon, the city was completely surrounded by thousands of militiamen who had no intention of leaving.

In the days following the running battle, Heath was superceded by Maj. Gen. Artemas Ward as commander of the state's militia and later, when George Washington arrived on the scene as commander in chief, was transferred from his position with the Massachusetts militia to the Continental Army and given responsibility for the center of the American line at Cambridge. After the British had evacuated Boston, Heath accompanied the army to New York and shared in the frustration of the retreat from Long Island to Manhattan. When talk was afoot to abandon New York City and retreat still further up Manhattan into New Jersey, Heath opposed giving up the important seaport but with the enemy in control of the coast and able to come ashore at any point, there was too much danger of the army being surrounded and cut off from the mainland if it remained in New York. Finally, the two sides confronted each other at White Plains but even with armies of about equal size, victory once again went to the British. Chased into New Jersey, the army was at last able to halt its retreat as the year wound down and the campaigning season ground to a halt. As 1777 began, Washington determined to keep the enemy off balance with a number of movements including an assault on Fort Independence located just above King's Bridge, New York and held by 2,000 Hessian soldiers. Chosen to lead the attack against the fort was Heath, but through inaction and confused commands regarding the disposition of his 6,000 man army, the overly cautious Heath failed to press home an attack. Instead, he issued a demand for the fort's surrender, a threat he apparently had no intention of going through with, then wasted ten days outside the fort until an enemy foray chased off some of his militia. Finally, with the arrival of wet and stormy weather, he ordered a retreat. As a result of the aborted attack, Heath became the subject of a severe reprimand from Washington himself who called the expedition "fraught with too much caution."

Following the Fort Independence fiasco, Heath was removed from command of troops in the field and ordered to take over the eastern department from Artemas Ward, an area that included New England, which by then had receded as an active theater of the war. It became even more so in the autumn of 1776 with the defeat of British Gen. John Burgoyne at the battle of Saratoga which Heath learned about as he led a division along the Hudson River, shadowing a British fleet moving north in support of Burgoyne's ill fated army. With the defeat, Burgoyne and his army ended up in Heath's charge as they were escorted to Boston for confinement. In 1779, Heath was ordered to take over command of West Point and the upper reaches of the Hudson Valley following the discovery of plans by a treasonous Gen. Benedict Arnold to hand over the strong point to the enemy. In 1781, while Washington marched the main body of the Continental Army south to Yorktown, Heath was named commander in chief of all forces that remained in the vicinity of New York, charged with doing what he could to maintain the charade that the army had not left for the South.

With the subsequent victory at Yorktown and the end of the war, Heath, for a time, retired to his farm in Roxbury until he was chosen in 1788 to serve as a delegate to the state's ratifying convention for the new United States Constitution. He then became a state senator in 1791 and a judge in the newly formed Norfolk County in 1793. He turned down a nomination for lieutenant governor in 1800 and although he identified himself politically with Thomas Jefferson's Republican Party, he broke ranks after President James Madison chose to lead the nation into the War of 1812. Throughout the years however, Heath worked on his memoirs of the Revolutionary War which finally saw print in 1798 as *Memoirs of Major-General William Heath, Containing Anecdotes, Details of Skirmishes, Battles, etc., During the American War*. Heath died at his farm in Roxbury on January 24th, 1814.

Patrick Henry

If Samuel Adams can be considered the northern firebrand of the Revolution, then for sure Patrick Henry was his counterpart in the South. Henry also resembled Adams in that when independence had finally been won, his early support for revolution turned to caution. The man who once declared "Give me liberty, or give me death!" would become wary and even suspicious over ratification of the Constitution. Creating a new form of government was a step that later generations would come to see as quite natural in the country's evolution but to those living in an era when the ideas of Jean Jacques Rousseau permeated the culture, a strong central government seemed to threaten a return to bondage. "We are in a state of nature," declared Henry at the first Continental Congress, referring to the limbo that existed between rejection of royal authority and declaring independence. Thus, Henry joined many of the Revolution's most ardent supporters who, once free of the constrictions of royal authority, became reluctant to bind themselves to another form of government, even one of their own making.

Henry was born as one of eleven children on May 29, 1736 in rural Studley, Hanover County, Virginia, receiving his earliest education from his father who taught him Latin and Greek. Although the young Henry was apprenticed as a store clerk when he was 15, his fortunes quickly turned when he married Sarah Shelton who brought to the union a 600 acre tobacco plantation called Pine Slash. Quitting his job as store clerk, Henry immediately took to the duties of farmer. Unfortunately, the change in career came just as the colony was experiencing an unusual drought. Failing to make a living off the land, Henry turned to the law. Self-taught, it was a measure of the plain dressed young man's determination that within a few

Patrick Henry

years he was ready to be examined. In 1760, he passed the bar and wasted little time in hanging out a shingle. His subsequent success came much to the consternation of Thomas Jefferson whom he had met at a house party some years before. Although Jefferson would come to admire Henry's zeal for independence, he grew increasingly suspicious of him as his political power in the state increased. But in the meantime, it was as an attorney that Henry's talent for oratory and logic became evident. In case after case, his arguments before the court were made with such eloquence and fervor that he soon earned a reputation as a very successful attorney. His early career climaxed in 1763 with his defense of the "Parson's Cause" in which he argued that the king had no right to abrogate a law passed by the colony's duly elected officials regulating the price of tobacco with which the local clergy was paid. In the course of his argument, Henry labeled the king a "tyrant" and established himself as an opponent of royal authority.

In 1765, on the strength of his reputation and growing notoriety, Henry was chosen to serve in the Virginia House of Burgesses and almost immediately solidified his reputation as being an outspoken opponent of the crown. Most famously, his name became attached to the Virginia Resolves, which he had drawn up and defended as an argument against implementation of the Stamp Act. "Caesar had his Brutus, Charles the First had his Cromwell, and George the Third..." he began, coming as close to outright treason as anyone dared before finishing with "...may profit by their example!" His ringing words came in a speech in the Burgesses urging acceptance of the Resolves by legislators. "If this be treason," he concluded, "make the most of it!" When he had finished, the resolutions were accepted and Henry found himself one of the colony's most influential politicians as well as a leader in the Patriot cause.

Involving himself more deeply in the growing opposition to British authority, he was outraged when Virginia's royal governor, Lord John Dunmore, dissolved an increasingly hostile legislature in 1774. In response, Henry led the effort to reconvene the body at nearby Raleigh Tavern in Williamsburg and one of the measures issued from that session was a proposal that representatives from all the colonies meet in Philadelphia to form a Continental Congress. Henry joined fellow Virginians, Richard Henry Lee, Peyton Randolph, and George Washington among others as a delegate and the four arrived in Philadelphia ready to support any decision to resist efforts by king and Parliament to unjustly force their will upon the American people. The argument in favor of resistance advocated by the Virginians and their allies from Massachusetts won the sympathy of many of their fellow delegates but there was still a general reluctance against consideration of such a radical step as breaking away from Britain. And so, upon adjournment, the Congress had decided on last minute appeals to the crown to see if the situation could be salvaged. Henry, however, was not satisfied and back in Virginia, recommended that the colony prepare for active resistance. At a Revolutionary Convention held in Richmond on March 23, 1775, barely weeks before shots were fired at Lexington and Concord, he warned those in attendance that Britain would never surrender to the colonies' wishes and as a result, Americans must prepare to defend their rights. As for himself, declared Henry, "Give me Liberty or give me death!"

No sooner had those ringing words been uttered, than Henry led the local militia in an effort to reclaim public munitions stores that had been impounded by Lord Dunmore in anticipation of its being seized by radicals. It was only the intervention of Peyton Randolph, who had accompanied Henry to Philadelphia and had been one of the attorney's who had examined him for the bar that averted possible violence by assuring the crowd that the governor could be persuaded to return the munitions. Despite the fact that he had been declared an outlaw by Dunmore, Henry was named colonel of the First Virginia Regiment and then, despite having no military experience, commander-in-chief of the Virginia militia. But wary of his inexperience as well as his hot temper, local officials decided to keep Henry from actually taking the field. In the end, Henry resigned his commission, and concentrated instead on helping to fashion the state's constitution and becoming Virginia's governor in 1776. While serving his first three one year terms, Henry did all he could to support the war effort including securing the western frontier by providing military support to George Rogers Clarke in his battles against the Indians and eventually, his expedition to the Illinois country.

In 1779, Henry stepped down from the governor's office in favor of political rival Thomas Jefferson who continued many of his predecessor's policies. An unfortunate event later in Jefferson's term involving an invasion of Virginia by a renegade Benedict Arnold at the head of a British army resulted in accusations that the governor had ill prepared the state for self-defense and that he himself had run in the face of the enemy. They were accusations Jefferson's political enemies, including Henry, would use against him for the rest of his public career. In the meantime, Henry had married his second wife, Dorothea Dandridge, upon the untimely death of Sarah in 1775 and returned to the state's legislature. In 1784 he was restored as governor for two more years but, wary of giving up the freedoms he had championed for so long and suspicious of the motives of James Madison, refused to take part in the Constitutional Convention of 1787 which was called with the intention to fine tune the already existing Articles of Confederation and not create a whole new federal government. But when the results of the Convention did indeed yield a new Constitution, Henry led the fight against its ratification. Unrepentant, he soon retired, dividing his time between his estate at Red Hill and other residences while fending off requests from President George Washington and later John Adams to take a position in the new federal government including those of Secretary of State and Chief Justice of the Supreme Court. Eventually, however, the excesses of the mob during the French Revolution drove him into the ranks of the supporters of a strong central government and at the suggestion of Washington, he decided to run again for Virginia's legislature this time as a Federalist. Although he won the race, he was never able to take office, dying suddenly on June 6, 1799.

Nicholas Herkimer

Born in Little Falls on an indeterminate date sometime in 1715, Nicholas Herkimer was the eldest of thirteen children, the son of a well to do landowner and trader in New York's Mohawk Valley. Following his father into the family business, Herkimer (the family's name was an anglicized version of the German Herchheimer), was given a plot of land where he built a good sized home commensurate with his station in the local German community. Never formally educated, when he spoke English, it was with a thick accent that was likely barely understood at times by his non-German speaking neighbors. During the years that young Herkimer was growing up, the Mohawk Valley was a raw frontier with the danger of Indian attack, and its accompanying savagery and mercilessness, always a possibility. As a result, the Herkimer home at Little Falls was fortified and doubled as a fort in times of emergency and every able man was obliged to serve in the local militia.

By 1758 the rivalry between Britain and France boiled over and became the French and Indian War. Being the eldest in one of the area's most prominent families, Herkimer was named a lieutenant in the militia and helped in the defense of Fort Herkimer when the enemy attacked German Flats. The end of the war however, was far from a guarantee against attack from the large and sullen Indian population that still remained. Meanwhile, Herkimer returned to his farm and no doubt concentrated on business and family matters for several years until news began to filter into the Mohawk and Schoharrie Valleys of trouble brewing in the east as the English Parliament began to impose a series of tax raising measures designed in part to have the thirteen American colonies help pay for the recent war with the French. But the manner in which the laws were passed and enforced without any kind of input by the colonies, enflamed American passions which soon hardened into resistance.

In response, by the mid-1770s, committees of correspondence began to spring up in every colony keeping patriots everywhere informed on the latest doings of the English and what was being done to counter them. As the chairman of the Canajoharie district Committee of Safety, Herkimer was well aware of the rising opposition to British policies and in 1775 retained a position in the Tryon County militia as a colonel of the first battalion. It was in that same year that the colonies' resistance to England became a shooting war when minutemen in Massachusetts opened fire on British troops seeking military stores in the towns of Lexington and Concord. With tensions rising, the first concern of frontier leaders was to secure the border areas from potential Indian attack. To preempt that possibility, in his capacity as a patriot leader and officer in the militia, Herkimer arrested Sir John Johnson, the son of Sir William Johnson, the long time British Indian agent in the area.

Johnson, however, was freed on the promise that he stay out of the rising conflict but he soon broke his word and was forced to flee to Canada. After that, everyone on the frontier began to choose sides with many of those still loyal to the king (including one of Herkimer's younger brothers) joining Johnson's Royal Greens or John Butler's Tory Rangers to take part in raids against their former neighbors.

As part of his effort to defuse the Indian threat to the frontier, in the spring of 1777 Herkimer, who had been promoted to brigadier general of militia the previous autumn, decided to meet along the Un-

Nicholas Herkimer

adilla River with Indian leader Joseph Brant, whom he had known for years. After keeping Herkimer waiting for a week, Brant arrived in company with a band of warriors and while Herkimer held back his 380 militiamen, the two unarmed men approached each other across an open field and began to parley. The meeting, however, proved a disappointment to Herkimer as Brant declared that he would remain loyal to the king and each parted wondering if the next time they met would be on the battlefield. The answer was not long in coming as later that year, Herkimer learned that a force of 1,800 British regulars, Loyalists, and Indians under the command of Col. Barry St. Leger had left Fort Oswego with the intention of attacking Fort Stanwix (renamed Fort Schuyler) on the Mohawk River.

Leger's movement was part of a larger scheme by the British that was intended to split the thirteen colonies in half with a drive by Gen. John Burgoyne from Canada south along the Hudson River to Fort Ticonderoga while a similar thrust by Gen. William Howe was made up the Hudson River from the south. If successful, the three prongs from north, south and west would converge on Albany and complete the dismemberment of the infant United States. Whether Herkimer at the time knew of the part Leger was to play in the larger plan of attack is of little import as he immediately called up every available militia-man in Tryon County with the intention of marching to the relief of Fort Stanwix. As he waited for his men to assemble, Herkimer, sent a message ahead to the fort's 750 defenders with a plan that would re-quire them to make a sortie from the fort to draw the attention of the enemy as the relief force attacked their rear. With luck, the enemy, taken by surprise, would scatter. The plan failed however due to the slow progress of the militia some of whose officers grew impatient and began to doubt Herkimer's patriotism. Angered that his honor could even be questioned, Herkimer ordered the army of about 800 men to move more quickly. Meanwhile, having received word of Herkimer's approach, Leger had detached a mixed force of Johnson's Royal Greens, Butler's Tory Rangers, and Brant's Indians to set up an ambush at a place called Oriskany Creek.

There, on August 6, 1777 the Americans soon appeared follow-ing the creek into the steep sided ravine. Suddenly, shots rang out, men fell, and they were surrounded by the blood curdling yells and shouts of the Tories and their Mohawk and Seneca allies who fired down on them from three sides. But the trap had been sprung too early by Brant's impetuous warriors and while 200 men not caught in the am-bush panicked and fled for their lives, the remaining Americans hun-kered down and began to return fire. Among the first casualties of the battle was Herkimer himself who took a ball in the leg. Dragged by his men to the protection of a tree, it was said that while he calmly filled his pipe with tobacco, he gave orders for the American defense which quickly centered on seizing the high ground. Experienced in wilderness warfare, the men soon broke into small groups of twos and threes and, moving from the cover of trees and rocks, began to return fire. Eventually, both sides were close enough to engage in hand to hand combat with tomahawks, knives, and rifle butts the weapons of choice. Then, as the fight neared its climax, it began to rain. Having suffered about 400 casualties and learning of a sortie from the fort led by Lt. Col. Marinus Willett, the enemy began to retreat and soon melted away into the surrounding forest. It would be left to Gen. Benedict Arnold traveling north with 1,000 men under separate orders from Maj. Gen. Philip Schuyler to trick St. Leger into believing that a second, much larger relief force was on the way and compel him to abandon the siege and withdraw back to Canada.

The Battle of Oriskany was judged a victory for the Americans on the strength of their being left in possession of the field, but they suffered heavy casualties and did not have the strength to continue on to Fort Stanwix. After the battle, Herkimer was carried the 35 miles back to his home at Little Falls where his leg wound refused to heal. An attempt to have it amputated was unsuccessful and as the wound continued to bleed, Herkimer read aloud from his Bible. He died on August 16, 1777 only ten days after the conclusion of the battle.

Thomas Heyward

Born to great wealth and privilege on July 28, 1746, Thomas Heyward, Jr., was raised on his father's Old House plantation in St. Helena's Parish, South Carolina. An ambitious father and his own native intelligence allowed Heyward to excel at a private academy where he mastered Latin and Greek that in turn gave him entry to schooling in England at the Middle Temple. There, Heyward applied himself, was accepted at the bar, and became a lawyer. His education was completed on a grand tour of Europe where he observed first hand the excesses of the continent's ruling aristocracy, exposure that perhaps shaped his later attitude toward royal authority after he returned home in 1771. There, Heyward had barely begun to practice law for himself when he won his first office in 1772 as a member of South Carolina's provincial assembly. In 1773 he enhanced his personal fortunes by marrying Elizabeth Matthews, the daughter of another wealthy planting family. In the meantime, efforts by Parliament to enforce a slate of new measures intended to raise taxes paid by colonists only confirmed Heyward's opinion of the contempt the English ruling class held for the common man in general and Americans in particular. By 1775, his resentment growing as the royal governor attempted to enforce the new taxes, Heyward moved into the camp of the growing patriot movement and was serving on South Carolina's Committee of Safety when he was appointed by a provincial convention to take over for John Rutledge as a member of the colony's congressional delegation. He arrived in Philadelphia just as Congress was in the midst of debating whether the thirteen colonies should separate themselves from England. When it came time to decide, Heyward approved and signed the Declaration of Independence and later, the Articles of Confederation.

Heyward served in Congress until 1778 when he left to help draft a state constitution and to take up duties as a judge for the new government of South Carolina, not an easy job. Although the southern states at the time were not much different from those in the north in having their populations divided between patriots and loyalists, the internecine warfare that became part of the war for independence would turn out to be far more pronounced in the south especially after it was invaded by large British armies as the war went on. The enemy decided to move its offensive operations south partially because of reports that support for the crown was much stronger there than in the north, a belief that was not completely unfounded. It was amid such divided loyalties and strongly held beliefs that Heyward presided as judge and after the investiture of South Carolina by the British, held court in the trial of several men accused of trafficking with the enemy. Found guilty, they were exe-

Thomas Heyward

cuted within sight of the British lines, an event that did not endear Heyward to the enemy.

Later, Heyward traded his judge's robes for a musket serving as a captain in the local militia and joining Col. William Moultrie at Port Royal Island in 1779. In command of an artillery unit, Heyward was slightly wounded in battle just outside Beaufort but was back in action for the defense of Charleston when, in the spring of 1780, the British came ashore and surrounded the city. When the city surrendered, Heyward was captured along with 5,000 other militia and Continental soldiers among them, fellow signer of the Declaration Edward Rutledge. Conveyed to St. Augustine, Florida as a prisoner, Heyward languished there for almost a year, entertaining himself by composing alternative lyrics to such songs as "God Save the King" for the entertainment of his fellow prisoners. It was only after he was released in Philadelphia as part of a prisoner exchange that Heyward discovered that his home at White Hall had been overrun by the enemy and his slaves confiscated and resold in the Indies. Heyward himself had almost drowned on his way from St. Augustine and only managed to survive by grabbing hold of the rudder of the ship he had been sailing on after having fallen overboard. Completing his misfortunes, his wife died around this time as well.

By 1781, Heyward was back on the bench in South Carolina where he remained until he retired in 1798. In 1790, he was called to participate in the state's ratifying convention for the Constitution where he voted in its support and later participated in the founding of the Agricultural Society of South Carolina for which he also served as president. He remarried, and after several years in retirement on his estate, Heyward died on March 6, 1809, the last of the state's signers of the Declaration.

Joseph Hewes

Born on January 23, 1730 of parents who had barely survived being ambushed by Indians as they moved from Connecticut to New Jersey, Joseph Hewes would rise from stolid Quaker beginnings, to successful merchant, southern gentlemen, and patriotic revolutionary by the time of his early death at the age of 50.

Educated in New Jersey's public schools, Hewes entered Princeton College to prepare for a career as a merchant. Following his graduation, he moved to Philadelphia and took a position in a counting house where he received practical experience to go along with his book learning. Soon after, he took what he had learned, invested his savings, and eventually built up a prosperous business of his own. Perhaps unsatisfied with the crowded and highly competitive atmosphere prevalent in the largest city in the thirteen colonies, Hewes decided to take his business as far

Joseph Hewes

away from Philadelphia as possible, or nearly so. Moving to Edenton, North Carolina in 1760, Hewes established himself there as a merchant with his own shipping line and prospered. Along the way, he made many new friends so that by 1766 he was popular enough with the locals to have himself elected to the Provincial Assembly remaining there until 1775 when it was dissolved by the royal governor. It was in Edenton that Hewes first met and befriended John Paul Jones, a youthful Scottish immigrant with seafaring experience who harbored deep resentment for Britain. Moving in circles occupied by North Carolina's wealthy planter classes, Hewes also learned to enjoy dancing and other social activities, pleasures frowned upon by his Quaker faith and that would contribute to his eventual break with the Society of Friends. Finally, it was while in Edenton too that Hewes suffered the greatest tragedy of his life when his fiancé suddenly died just before she was to marry him. Hewes never recovered from the loss, remaining unmarried for the remainder of his life and throwing himself into his work and the rising revolutionary cause.

As a merchant, Hewes was acutely aware of the various taxes the British Parliament tried to impose on the colonies including the infamous Stamp Tax. That, and the increasingly arrogant attitude taken by royal authority in North Carolina contributed to his radicalization prompting him in 1773 to become a member of the colony's Committee of Correspondence.

That association led the next year to his being chosen as a member of North Carolina's delegation to the Continental Congress. There, Hewes supported efforts to prevent the import of British goods and in 1776 submitted North Carolina's Halifax Resolves which proclaimed the colony's support for independence. At the time, Hewes was still cautious about pursuing separation from England but after debate had gone on for some time on the issue, he was convinced otherwise. As a man who had offered few words on the floor of Congress, he had begun to despair over tensions between those members who supported independence and those who opposed it. Finally, however, he threw up his hands in a dramatic gesture and declared that the arguments in favor of independence had won him over. "It is done!" he said. "And I will abide by it." And so, when the time came to place his name on the Declaration of Independence, he did so. Afterwards, he supported measures to block the import of British goods to America despite their harmful effects to his own business and even broke with his Quaker faith after the Society of Friends held a convention that denounced independence and war with England.

Upon independence, Hewes, his mercantile experience valued by Congress, was appointed to the Marine Committee where he became indispensable in the creation of a Navy and other maritime issues. Although admired by fellow committee member John Adams, the two clashed over the appointment of captains for the nation's new warships. Recalling his friendship with John Paul Jones, Hewes championed naming the young seaman as one of the captains but Adams, after supporting George Washington, a Virginian, for command of the Continental Army, felt that Naval appointments should belong to New England men. In this instance, Hewes lost the debate and Jones had to settle for a mere lieutenancy. Hewes' advocacy of Jones however, would be vindicated on September 23, 1779 when the young captain won the most famous sea battle of the Revolution off the coast of England at Flamborough Head.

Despite his contributions in Congress, Hewes was recalled by North Carolina and returned to the new state's legislature in 1778. The next year, he was again chosen to represent the state in Congress and though ailing, accepted the appointment. No sooner had he arrived in Philadelphia however, than his health failed. Bedridden on October 29,

Hewes died days later on November 10, 1779. At a funeral attended by Congress, the Pennsylvania legislature, foreign dignitaries, and numerous residents, Hewes was laid to rest in a local cemetery.

William Hooper

William Hooper, who is said to have been the first of the Founding Fathers to predict independence from Britain and later signed the Declaration of Independence, paid for his daring with the complete destruction of his property after it was captured by invading British soldiers. Separated from his family and forced into hiding while prostrate with malaria, Hooper was a Founder who ended his life in a far worse position than when he started on the road to rebellion.

Although he was later sent to Philadelphia as a member of North Carolina's delegation, Hooper was not a native of that colony having only arrived there in 1764. He was born in Boston, Massachusetts on June 28, 1742, the son of a clergyman who had hoped that his son would follow his example as a man of the cloth. But after spending three years at Harvard and graduating in 1760, Hooper decided to take up the law instead. Adding to his father's distress, the young man moved into the office of James Otis, an early leader of the patriotic movement against royal authority in the colony. Perhaps imbued with some of Otis' rebellious attitudes and looking afield for a place where he could build his own practice with the least competition, Hooper decided to move to North Carolina, which might as well have been on the moon so far as his family was concerned.

Accordingly, Hooper arrived in Wilmington, North Carolina in 1764, the year the infamous Stamp Act was passed by Parliament along with other measures such as the sugar and currency acts. Hooper, apparently, had little trouble in acclimating himself to southern life or ingratiating himself with his new neighbors as his legal practice proved successful and he won the attention and later the hand of Ann Clark, the daughter of one of the colony's oldest families. With his wife's modest fortune, Hooper established himself at Finian, a country estate a few miles outside of Wilmington and built up a clientele consisting of the area's wealthy planters. The planters showed their gratitude in 1770 when they lobbied for his appointment as the colony's deputy attorney general. Eager to prove his loyalty to North Carolina, Hooper sided with royal Governor William Tryon against an uprising in the western part of the colony by backwoodsman organized as "Regulators" who were protesting high legal fees and what they felt was an oppressive local government. Advocating the use of force to suppress the movement, Hooper marched west with the militia that eventually put an end to the rebels at the battle of Alamance.

After his role in having the Regulators suppressed, Hooper was rewarded in 1773 with an appointment to the colonial assembly. But if local leaders thought the Boston native was firmly in their pockets, they were mistaken. As time passed, Hooper became disenchanted with royal authority and its supporters, a disenchantment that climaxed in the struggle over a new law needed to keep the colony's court system up and running. With the previous law due to expire, a replacement needed to be voted on but this time, the legislature sought to add property owned by non-residents to the list of those that could be confiscated for payment of debts, including that owned by residents of England. The measure was opposed by the governor and while lawmakers wrangled, the colony was thrown into legal turmoil for years. For his part, Hooper's finances took a hit but he refused to give up any idea of surrendering the principal that the legislature alone had the right to regulate such matters and not an authority representing a faraway king.

That legal battle brought Hooper much attention among local patriots and was only enhanced when he led the effort to keep the legislature in session after the governor had ordered that it be dissolved.

William Hooper

Evidence of Hooper's increased radicalization was presented in a letter he wrote a friend in 1774 in which he predicted eventual separation of the colonies from Britain, a prophecy that later earned him the sobriquet of "Prophet of Independence."

In 1774 the legislature voted to hold a provincial assembly that in turn appointed Hooper as a member of the colony's delegation to the Continental Congress. Arriving in Philadelphia, Hooper took part in debates and worked in committee even as he continued to travel back and forth to North Carolina to maintain his participation in the colony's legislature. But the years in which the North Carolina court system had been inactive had cost Hooper's legal practice dearly and by 1776 he was obliged to spend more time at home at the expense of his congressional duties. Later that year however, he had the opportunity of seeing his prediction of 1774 come true when he joined his fellow congressmen in signing the Declaration of Independence. At the end of that year, Hooper was reelected to Congress but decided to turn down the honor in favor of continuing as a member of the state legislature and attending to his personal affairs. Before he left Philadelphia however, he and fellow North Carolina delegate John Penn prevailed upon John Adams, who had impressed them with his ideas on government, to write them down so that they might use them as guidance when they returned home to help write a new state constitution. Adams did so and wrote what he later entitled his *Thoughts on Government*, which would be used as the basis not only for the new constitution of Massachusetts, but those of a number of other states as well.

Hooper's plans for his return home were interrupted in 1780 when the war came to North Carolina in the form of an invading army under British Gen. Charles Cornwallis moving north after handing the American Gen. Horatio Gates a devastating defeat at Camden, South Carolina. In the face of the threat, Hooper decided that his family would be safer in the city than in the isolation of Finian and accordingly moved them to Wilmington. But then, while he was out of town on business, the enemy struck and seized the capital. What resulted was personal calamity for Hooper who ended up separated from his family for almost a year and being laid up for part of that time with malaria. Sick and cut off from his home and family, Hooper became completely dependent on the good graces of friends for sustenance and when enemy forces finally abandoned Wilmington, he returned only to discover that his home and property had been completely destroyed. Rejoining his family in Hillsborough where they had fled, he never returned to Finian.

Although Hooper continued in the state's legislature, his political fortunes began to wane after the war. Recalling how he had once been dragged through the streets and beaten by Regulators, Hooper was wary of the excesses of democracy and advocated restraint of the popular will, a position that earned him the distrust of the common people. But despite his reputation as a conservative, he fought for ratification of the United States Constitution and following its passage, was named in 1789 as a judge on the federal court, a position he held for less than a year before ill health forced him to retire. Hooper died at his home in Hillsborough the next year, on October 14, 1790.

Stephen Hopkins

Some of the Founding Fathers had lengthy careers long before their roles in the Revolution and in fact, by modern standards, were well past the age of retirement when independence was declared. And yet, not only were they willing to risk their lives in defiance of the mother country, but their attitudes were still elastic enough to entertain as fantastic a notion as separation from England and the novel prospect of a government that allowed the people to rule themselves.

Stephen Hopkins, a well read, self-made man was one of those people. He was born in the Scituate section of Providence, Rhode Island on March 7, 1707 and although a descendent of the colony's first governor, belonged to a family of only modest means. Although he attended only local schools excelling in mathematics, he was for the most part, self taught, managing to learn the surveying trade which he practiced when his responsibilities as a farmer did not interfere. Thus life for Hopkins may have continued indefinitely but for the separation of Scituate from Providence. With the creation of the new township, Hopkins was chosen as town clerk, then justice of the peace, and in 1731 was sent to the colonial legislature as its representative. In 1733, he became chief justice of the court of common pleas. With more and more of his business taking place in Providence, Hopkins eventually decided to move there permanently and in 1742, built himself a new home in the city and with his brothers, entered the booming sea trade by investing in the construction and equipping of trading vessels. In 1751, he began a three year stint as chief justice of the colony's Superior Court and by 1754, on the eve of the French and Indian War, was appointed as a commissioner to attend the Albany Congress in New

York. There, he took part in negotiations with local Indian tribes and met fellow delegate Benjamin Franklin of Pennsylvania. It was from Franklin that Hopkins first heard the idea of having the thirteen colonies join in a single union, a notion perhaps inspired by the example of the Iroquois Confederacy or Six Nations of Indian tribes the two men were sent to deal with. In any case, Hopkins joined his name with that of Franklin in suggesting a plan of union for the colonies which was accepted by the Congress at Albany but ultimately turned down by the various colonies. Bolstered by his own political reputation as well as the esteem gained by his trip to Albany, Hopkins returned to Rhode Island in time to be elected to his first single year term as the colony's governor in 1755, an office he would hold for roughly the next twelve years. Being a governor under the umbrella of royal authority however, did little to restrict Hopkins' ideas about the relationship between America and England. In 1764, amidst the Stamp Act crisis, he published an essay entitled "The Rights of the Colonies Examined" that addressed attempts by Parliament to impose its will upon the colonies and made an early call for some kind of self-government. In 1774, following a call from the citizens of Rhode Island for an intercolonial congress and its swift endorsement by other cities, Hopkins was chosen as one of Rhode Island's delegates to the First Continental Congress held in Philadelphia.

Stephen Hopkins

Already an advocate of independence, Hopkins would have to wait with other congressional firebrands until England rejected a last minute plea for reconciliation before a vote on the subject could be taken. By that time he had become reacquainted with his old friend Franklin whom he joined in signing the Declaration of Independence in 1776. When the time came, the seventy year old Hopkins had to steady his own hand as he affixed his signature to the historic document, risking hanging if the cause of American freedom was ever lost. "My hand trembles," Hopkins was heard to have said as he held his palsied hand, "but my heart does not." With independence finally declared, Hopkins served on a number of committees while in Congress including that which framed the Articles of Confederation. By nature of his seafaring experience, he was also heavily involved in the committee charged with the establishment of a Continental Navy where he was joined by Massachusetts delegate John Adams who would only have good words to say about the convivial Hopkins. Returning to Rhode Island upon completion of his final service in Congress, Hopkins rejoined the new state's legislature where he held on until 1779. Retired at last, he died after a lengthy illness at his home in Providence on July 13, 1785.

Francis Hopkinson

Like Benjamin Franklin, an acquaintance of his father's, Francis Hopkinson might be considered an American renaissance man. An attorney, he was also an accomplished writer, poet, painter, and musician as well as an inventor, mathematician, and part time astronomer, and in his short life also came up with the basic design for the flag of the United States thereby becoming entangled in one of the earliest examples of bureaucratic red tape in American history.

When Francis Hopkinson was born in Philadelphia on October 2, 1737 his father was already a well established attorney in the city having emigrated there from England only six years before. But by the time Hopkinson had entered his teens, his father had died and it was up to his mother to see to his education, a task she accomplished nicely with the help of Benjamin Franklin, who had befriended her husband when the two had worked together to found the College of Philadelphia. Impressed by the young Hopkinson, Franklin saw to it that the boy was accepted at the college where he performed well and from which he graduated in 1757. Following college, Hopkinson decided to take up the law as his father had and after studying for a time under an eminent attorney, passed the bar in 1761. The law, however, may have been only of secondary interest to Hopkinson who discovered early on a flare for the written word. Poetry and satire would be his chosen form of literary expression but songwriting too would draw his attention with the first being written in 1759. In 1764, the restless Hopkinson left the law behind and found employment at the Library Company of Philadelphia (also founded by his father) and stayed a year before giving it up to see more of the world.

In 1766, Hopkinson sailed for Europe where he spent some time in Ireland before settling in England for the better part of a year. There, he indulged his tastes in the latest trends in music and art while also making contacts among influential members of society including his mother's uncle, the bishop of Worcester, trying to wrangle himself a comfortable, and profitable, position as collector of customs back home. His efforts, apparently, were initially unsuccessful because when he did return to Philadelphia, he took up the law again while keeping a small store on the side. Finally however, his lobbying efforts in England paid off when he was appointed collector of customs first in Salem, New Jersey (where he met and married Ann Borden, the daughter of a wealthy local family), and

Francis Hopkinson

then in New Castle, Delaware. Eventually, Hopkinson decided to settle near his wife's family in New Jersey and once again took up the practice of law. In 1774, his connection to Franklin continued to pay off when he was chosen by the man's son, Governor William Franklin, to serve on the colony's provincial council. But over the years, despite his connections and hobnobbing with those in royal authority, Hopkinson found it increasingly difficult to resist firing off satirical barbs in such a target rich environment. One of his earliest and most famous satires, *A Pretty Story*, considered the relationship between Great Britain and its American colonies. Although mostly written under pseudonyms, his efforts did not go unappreciated first by his royal employers who fired him as collector of customs in Delaware and then by local residents who were growing impatient with what they considered oppressive parliamentary edicts such as the Stamp Tax and other "intolerable" measures.

Such was Hopkinson's reputation as a patriot, despite his use of pseudonyms, that he was even chosen as a member of New Jersey's delegation to the Continental Congress arriving in his old home town of Philadelphia in 1776, just in time to hear John Adams sum up the case for a permanent separation from Britain and to join in signing the Declaration of Independence. Hopkinson, along with fellow delegates Richard Stockton and John Witherspoon, was apparently chosen for his support of independence, in contrast to the colony's previous delegation whose members were unsympathetic to the idea. Returning home to Bordentown, New Jersey, Hopkinson arrived just in time to whisk his family away before a squad of Hessian soldiers in the employ of the British swooped down and ransacked his house. Although his well stocked library became a casualty of war, Hopkinson was later surprised when at least one volume found its way back into his possession along with a name on the flyleaf of the soldier who had stolen it and a note of admiration for the owner's good taste in books! Later, Hopkinson may have had his revenge on those who ravaged his home with the appearance in 1777 of *I Issue This My Manifesto*, a satirical poem poking fun at a proclamation by British Gen. John Burgoyne commending the king's justice and mercy. In 1778, Hopkinson was still in fine form when he wrote the popular *Battle of the Kegs* (a poem commemorating an early effort by Americans to sink British warships off Philadelphia using contact explosives floated downstream in wine kegs) and perhaps the most famous ditty of the Revolution that explained why British Gen. William Howe seemed to lack enthusiasm for the war: "Sir William he, snug as a flea/Lay all the time a snoring,/Nor dreamed of harm as he lay warm/In bed with Mrs. L---ng."

Serving in Congress for only a few months, Hopkinson was there long enough to be assigned to the Continental Navy Board where, among his other duties, he found it necessary to create a national ensign, or flag that would fly on the new nation's naval vessels (somebody had to do it!) What Hopkinson came up with was a flag very similar to the modern Stars and Stripes: a banner sporting red and white stripes with a blue field in the upper left hand corner spangled in stars representing the original thirteen colonies. At the time, Hopkinson never gave the matter much thought; designing the flag was just one in a number of projects he had worked on around the same time including designs for currency and the Great Seal of the United States. It was only in 1780, after he had moved back to Philadelphia and had taken a job in the Continental Loan Office that it occurred to him that some compensation might be due him for his design ideas. Consequently, he filed a claim with the government and there followed months of delay as the request was bounced from one committee and board to another until it was finally decided that Hopkinson had done the work only as part of his duties as a member of the Navy Board and so was not entitled to any special compensation.

In the meantime, Hopkinson had quit the Loan Office and taken a position as judge on Pennsylvania's Admiralty Court. In 1787, fearful that the Articles of Confederation would not be enough to keep the country from flying apart, he participated in New Jersey's ratifying convention, supported ratification of the United States Constitution and upon its passage, organized and led a huge, "federal procession" in Philadelphia to celebrate the event. His vigorous support of ratification aside, Hopkinson for the most part avoided politics which probably made an attractive candidate to President George Washington who appointed him a federal judge for the district of Pennsylvania. He had barely begun to serve on the bench however, when he died suddenly of a stroke on May 8, 1791.

John Eager Howard

Unlike many of his contemporaries, John Eager Howard never graduated from college or attended a university, but an inborn intelligence and an unerring conviction in what was right endowed him with the qualities to succeed as a soldier of the Revolution and a public servant after independence had been won.

Howard was born to wealth at Belvidere, his family's home outside Baltimore, Maryland, on June 4, 1752. Educated by private tutors, he never attended a formal school and would no doubt have spent his life helping to maintain his family's holdings and perhaps moving into colonial politics as was to be expected of a member of the upper class, but in 1775 the Revolutionary War interrupted and changed all that.

Commissioned a captain of infantry, Howard was placed in charge of a company of the 2nd Maryland Brigade, part of the "flying camp" reserves under Gen. Hugh Mercer. In 1776, Howard and his men found themselves in battle at White Plains after the British army had overrun Manhattan and in the wake of defeat and retreat from New York, the flying camp was reorganized with the Marylander promoted to major and reassigned to the 4th Maryland regiment. It was while in command of the 4th that Howard saw action in the battles of Germantown in Pennsylvania and Monmouth in New Jersey. By 1778, already displaying a fondness for the bayonet charge that would stand him in good stead in the South, Howard had been moved up in grade to lieutenant colonel and placed in charge of the 5th Maryland Regiment. It was with the 5th that he was ordered to the southern theater with an army under the command of Gen. Horatio Gates that was intended to help bolster American resistance to repeated attempts by the British to exploit a perceived weakness in patriotic will in Georgia and the Carolinas. Unfortunately, Gates' overconfidence and his decision to divide his army in the face of an enemy force of unknown size, resulted in a resounding defeat at Camden, South Carolina on August 16, 1780. During the battle, the enemy shattered the American lines and sent its remnants reeling.

With the South open to British depredation, the war there devolved into guerilla tactics and swift raids by small but mobile partisan bands. That was where matters stood when Gen. Nathanael Greene took over from Gates with the assignment of rebuilding the army and leading a counterattack into the south. As Greene followed a hit and run strategy while slowly increasing the size of his forces, he allowed many of his officers, especially those familiar with the territory and the ways of the south, to operate more or less independently

John Eager Howard

when opportunity permitted. Such was the case when, on January 17, 1781, Gen. Daniel Morgan, a hero of Saratoga, decided to turn and face British Lt. Col. Banastre Tarleton who had been dogging his trail for days. Choosing his ground carefully, Morgan decided to make his stand at a place called the Cowpens and, arranging his 1,000 men in two lines, took the unusual step of placing his least dependable militia units at the front. Knowing that these men were the most likely to break and run upon a good volley from the enemy, all he asked of them were "two good fires" before they retired from the field. In the meantime, Howard and his regiment of Marylanders and Virginia militiamen were stationed on the right wing of the American second line and as the British emerged from a distant tree line, they made ready to fight. Composed of about 1,100 men including regulars and the members of Tarleton's Tory Legion, the enemy's infantry began to advance and for the Americans, all went according to plan as the militia duly gave their two fires and retreated in order, but did not flee, the battlefield. By then, the two sides had collided as British regulars and American Continentals in the second line engaged in hand to hand combat. At that point, in an attempt to turn his line to prevent being flanked by enemy reserves, Howard ordered the men on the extreme right to bend back so as to keep their foe in sight. But somehow, the order was misunderstood and his men began to retreat instead. Fortunately, there was no panic and Howard managed to retain good control of his men the whole time and after Morgan had noticed the movement and ordered them to halt atop a small rise overlooking the battle, the Marylander was able to comply. After halting his men, Howard turned them about, and had them direct a volley of fire into the enemy flank. As dozens of men fell under a hail of lead, Howard saw a chance to take advantage of the surprise his men had created and ordered an immediate bayonet charge. The tactic worked; the enemy flank was turned and the battle won. Following Cowpens, it seemed that Howard was everywhere: with Greene at Guilford Court House on March 15, 1781; and the South Carolina battles of Hobkirk's Hill on April 15; at Ninety Six in the summer of 1781; and at Eutaw Springs on September 8, 1781 where his regiment was reduced to 30 men and he himself was badly wounded in a final, desperate charge.

His injuries forcing him from the army, Howard returned to Maryland just before the end of the war. In 1788, he entered national politics by being elected to Congress and the next year was recalled to become governor of Maryland serving until 1791. In 1796 he turned down an offer by President George Washington to serve as Secretary of

War for a seat in the United States Senate where he remained until 1803. Before that, he once more turned down a request by Washington to appoint him a general when war with France seemed imminent in 1798. When war finally came in 1812, it was not with France but with Britain whose soldiers captured and burned Washington D.C. In the ensuing panic that gripped nearby communities, Howard was ready to defend Baltimore against attack and urged local leaders not to surrender to the enemy. In 1816, Howard made his final bid for national office when he failed to win the position of vice-president on the Federalist ticket. Retiring to Belvedere, he died there on October 12, 1827.

William Hull

After the Revolution, many of those who served in the army found it difficult to live up to the heroism they displayed on the battlefield. Such a person was William Hull who received the accolades of Congress for his service but when given command responsibility of the entire Northwest Territory during the War of 1812, he failed miserably and his name, somewhat unjustifiably, became a byword for ineptitude and cowardice.

Hull was born on June 24, 1753 in Derby, Connecticut and attended Yale College with the intention of preparing for the ministry. Before graduating in 1772, he changed the focus of his studies by switching to the law and passed the bar in 1775. That year, hostilities between Britain and its thirteen American colonies broke out at Lexington and Concord and Hull joined thousands of other young men who joined local militia units and marched off to war. For his part, Hull began his military career as a captain of the Seventh Connecticut Regiment but was quickly promoted through a number of battles including those of White Plains, Trenton, Princeton, and Monmouth. When Generals George Washington and Anthony Wayne planned a surprise assault on the British positions at Stoney Point, they decided that only the army's most experienced units would take part and Hull's became one of them. Hull was still a captain when he was told by Yale classmate, Nathan Hale, of his intention to enter enemy occupied New York as a secret agent. Wary of the enterprise, Hull warned his friend of the danger but to no avail; Hale went to the city, was discovered, and hanged as a spy. It is to Hull however, that the nation is indebted for preserving Hale's last words: "I regret that I have but one life to give to my country."

By the time he left the army in 1779, Hull had reached the rank of lieutenant colonel and had been recognized by Washington and Congress for his feats on the battlefield. Marrying a woman from a well to do Massachusetts family, he moved to Newton and settled down to practice law. In 1787 his military experience was called upon to take command of an army raised to help put down a rebellion in western Massachusetts led by Daniel Shays; later, he was appointed as a member of a diplomatic team sent to Canada. Returning to Massachusetts again, he became a judge and was elected to the state's legislature. Finally, in 1805, he was appointed by President Thomas Jefferson as governor of the newly organized Michigan Territory.

As governor, it was one of Hull's responsibilities to deal with the Indians but in arranging treaties securing land for settlement, there were always elements that refused to recognize what other Indian leaders had agreed to. Consequently, when hostilities against Britain were resumed in the War of 1812, general discontent on the frontier guaranteed that

William Hull

the United States would have to fight not only England, but the Indians as well. When the war broke out, Hull had hoped for appointment as Secretary of War but had to settle instead for a general's stars and command of the Northwest. Securing a deal in which he could keep his position as governor while serving in the field as military commander, Hull prepared for an invasion of Canada. Asking for reinforcements and a navy to protect the great lakes, he received very little and ended up having to rely on volunteers from among the settlements, the traditional source of military manpower on the frontier. What is more, he entered the war at a disadvantage: while the British commander of Canada learned quickly that a state of war existed, Hull found out about it much later, having received notice from Congress through the slow moving postal system. And so, facing an enemy that had had much more time to prepare, Hull assembled an army and began a march to Fort Detroit. From there, he crossed into Ontario, Canada in July of 1812 and, besieging Fort Malden, demanded its surrender. He had not yet received a reply when news began to filter in of British victories on the American side of the border and, fearful of a general Indian uprising in his rear, ordered a retreat back to the United States and the protection of Fort Detroit. There, he became the victim of British cunning and was soon convinced that he faced a far superior force under the command of British commander Sir Isaac Brock. Actually, both sides were of about equal size, but it was Hull who lost his nerve and the campaign. His surrender of Fort Detroit on August 15, 1812, made without firing a shot, was an ignominious development in the history of American arms and amid the outrage that followed, Hull was court martialed on charges of cowardice and neglect of duty. Found guilty and sentenced to death, he was given a reprieve by President James Madison on the strength of his services during he Revolution. Although history would later find him not completely at fault for the conditions that existed on the United States/Canadian border during the War of 1812, Hull retired to Massachusetts as one of the most despised men in the country. In retirement, he would write books attempting to clear his name and explain his actions but by the time he died on November 29, 1825 his reputation still retained much of the tarnish it had gained as a result of the surrender of Fort Detroit.

Samuel Huntington

Samuel Huntington shared with many of his fellow Founding Fathers a similar career track that began behind a plough and, through mostly his own effort, ended in the most exalted public offices of the new United States. Chosen as a delegate to the Continental Congress, Huntington became its president and continued to serve in that capacity after the adoption of the Articles of Confederation and through the darkest hours of the Revolution.

Born in Windham, Connecticut on July 3, 1732, Huntington was one member of a large family that earned its living from the land and while elder brothers were sent to school to prepare them for the ministry, Huntington remained behind to help his father on the farm. But the desire for learning was strong in Huntington and whenever he could, he visited the local pastor to borrow books from his library (and, apparently, to woo the minister's daughter whom he later married). In time, he discovered in himself an interest in the law and after learning all he could on his own, passed the bar by the time he was 23 years old. Although he began his own practice in Windham, he soon decided to test the waters elsewhere and moved his business to the more upscale Norwich. There, at last, he made a name for himself and entered politics as the local tax collector, moderator of Town Meeting, justice of the peace, and in 1764 was chosen to represent the town in the colonial legislature. Later, he became an attorney for the royal government and in 1773 an associate judge on the superior court. But despite his rise in the hierarchy of the government, Huntington never lost the point of view of the common laborer and so his close association with royal authority, far from earning his respect, enabled him to see the harm such laws as the Stamp Act posed to ordinary people just trying to earn a living. As a result, he began to speak out against the attempts of Parliament to coerce the colonies into carrying a greater share of the tax burden, joined the Sons of Liberty, and earned for himself a good reputation among local patriots. So much so, that in 1775 the legislature named

Samuel Huntington

him as one of the colony's delegates to the Continental Congress where, the following year, he joined his colleagues in signing the Declaration of the Independence.

In 1779, Huntington was honored by his fellow congressmen when he was named their president and through two terms saw some of the most difficult years of the war. Years that included the invasion of the southern states where the enemy managed to destroy virtually all resistance; the Continental Army under George Washington still exiled from New York and reduced to hardly more than a handful of starving, freezing men; and devastating raids on the seaport towns of his own home state. In addition, Huntington was forced to contend with dissension in Congress, the reorganization of the diplomatic corps, a disastrous economy, and adjustment to the new Articles of Confederation.

Finally, in 1781, exhausted and his health failing, Huntington gave up the presidency and his position in Congress to return to a more tranquil Connecticut where he retook his place on the superior court bench. There was little rest for the weary however as only a year later, he was once more chosen to represent Connecticut in Congress but either for health reasons or disinclination, he failed to attend. Elected again the next year, he finally returned to Congress in the summer of 1783 but did not stay long, quitting in November and never going back. At home again, he was elected lieutenant governor in 1785, an office that also came with the position of chief justice of the state's superior court, and in 1786 he became governor. With his concern for the state's economy, strong support for freedom of religion and ratification of the Constitution, as well as his agreement with Alexander Hamilton's view of promoting domestic manufactures, Huntington proved to be a popular chief magistrate and easily won reelection as governor every year until his death on January 5, 1796.

John Jay

John Jay was one of those handful of Founding Fathers who seemed to have been everywhere and done everything during the Revolutionary era. Like Washington, Jefferson, Hamilton, and John Adams, Jay was an active participant in his own colony's early revolutionary movement; he was involved with the Continental Congress, the formulation of the Constitution, and helped to negotiate the Treaty of Paris. After the war, Jay helped shape New York's state government, served as the nation's first Chief Justice of the Supreme Court, returned to Europe as a diplomat, and ended his long career as governor of New York. In fact, the only place that Jay never saw action was on the battlefield! If the list of Founding Fathers could be narrowed down to a certain number of key men, then for sure, Jay would have to be counted among the top half dozen.

Born in New York City on December 12, 1745, Jay was a middle child in a brood of seven children and although he spent his youth on his father's extensive farm outside New York City, his early life was tragically marred when a number of siblings were struck by blindness or developed psychological problems in the wake of a small pox epidemic. At first taught at home by tutors, by the time he was 15, Jay was judged ready for admission to King's College where he prepared for a career in the law and graduated in 1764 giving a speech on the blessings of peace. After passing his bar exam, Jay entered a partnership with Robert Livingston, Jr., a member of one of New York's most prominent families and later, married Sarah Livingston, the daughter of the colony's governor, William Livingston. Thus socially connected, Jay branched out and began his own legal practice in 1771 and later served as a clerk for the boundary commission surveying the borders between New York and New Jersey.

Known as an advocate for peace, preferring negotiation over confrontation, Jay found himself involved in the growing revolutionary movement with the call for the establishment of a Continental Congress. Conservatives in the New York political establishment, wary of the intentions of more radical

John Jay

elements from Massachusetts and Virginia, chose him to be a member of a Committee of 50 who would choose the colony's representatives to the Congress. Jay himself was later chosen as a delegate to the Second Continental Congress where he continued to press for peace between the colonies and England but, whether by design or happenstance, missed the historic vote and signing of the Declaration of Independence when he absented himself to return to New York to attend a constitutional convention and to become the new state's first chief justice. Once independence was declared however, Jay devoted himself wholeheartedly to his nation's cause, even going so far as to urge Washington to burn New York City in order to deny it to the British for use as winter quarters.

Jay had returned to Congress in 1778 to serve as its president when he was later chosen to represent the new nation in Spain. His first diplomatic mission was typical of those early years of the war in that European nations were reluctant to be seen as supporting the United States for fear of angering a powerful Britain. Jay spent three years in Spain ("The people here are in almost total darkness about us...") before moving on to France to join Benjamin Franklin and John Adams in negotiations that eventually resulted in the Treaty of Paris and the end of the Revolutionary War. During that process however, Jay had brought with him suspicions about France which he felt had not pressed Spain enough about joining the war against Britain. He was right.

While France supported the United States' struggle against Britain, it was wary of creating a new power in North America. To that end, it had secretly negotiated with Spain to share domination of the Mississippi Valley, a situation that was vehemently opposed by Jay and Adams who fought with Franklin to enter negotiations with England without the knowledge of France. "...as an American I feel an interest in the dignity of my country, which renders it difficult for me to reconcile myself to the idea of the sovereign independent United States of America submitting, in the persons of their ministers, to be absolutely governed by the advice and opinions of the servants of another sovereign..." wrote Jay to Congress about its instruction that the American peace commissioners not make a move without the permission of France. Franklin eventually agreed with Jay and Adams to disregard the instructions of Congress and the three were successful in securing the country's claim for all the land from the Atlantic seaboard to the Mississippi River. Jay, however, might be considered responsible for missing an opportunity of doubling the size of the nation by refusing to join

Adams in a demand that Britain also cede Canada to the United States, dismissing it as a mere "few acres."

The end of the war did not mean an end to Jay's public career. When he returned to the United States in 1784, he found that he had been appointed by the Congress as its Secretary of Foreign Affairs. Immediately, he found himself involved with the unsavory business of negotiating with the Barbary pirates and dealing with the same officials he had confronted for years in Britain, France, and Spain, trying to get them to abide by conditions set in previous treaties. Together with the difficulties he encountered working with a Congress operating under the Articles of Confederation, his experience as Secretary of Foreign Affairs convinced him that a new, stronger form of central government was needed. Alexander Hamilton and James Madison, leaders in the movement for the creation of a strong federal government, found in him an ally. In 1787, after delegates to a convention in Philadelphia produced a Constitution that would establish a new framework for national government, Jay joined Hamilton and Madison in vigorous defense of the document that resulted in a long series of newspaper essays. Known collectively as the *Federalist Papers*, they became the most authoritative and exhaustive argument for a federal government ever written many of whose points, even today, are ignored at the country's peril. Unfortunately, illness prevented Jay from participating as fully as his partners, but in the end, his association with the project as well as his subsequent leadership in persuading New York to ratify the Constitution, resulted in his being appointed by President George Washington as the new nation's first Chief Justice of the Supreme Court.

Jay thus began the third phase of his public career riding circuit for the Supreme Court, establishing and defining much of its power and responsibilities as he did so. With popular discontent on the rise in France, Washington asked Jay to travel once more to Britain to discuss continuing violations of the Treaty of Paris as well as the hated practice of impressment where British naval vessels would stop American ships on the high seas and seize sailors claiming that they were deserters from the Royal Navy. What resulted caused a storm of controversy in the United States when it was learned that Jay's Treaty of Amity, Commerce and Navigation fell short in two areas crucial to both the northern and southern states: it left open the issue of impressments and did not address compensation for slaves freed during the war. The failure to solve the two issues as well as controversy surrounding Jay's appointment incited a growing dissatisfaction with federalist policies in two politically powerful regions of the country and spurred the creation of party machinery involving Republicans and Federalists.

When Jay came back from England in 1795, he found that not only had he become the object of intense controversy and vilification as a result of his treaty negotiations, but that he had also been nominated for governor of New York. With Hamilton's support and his control of the state's political apparatus, Jay was elected. After serving as governor for two terms and with the wane of federalist power with the election of Thomas Jefferson as President of the United States and George Clinton's reelection as the Republican governor of New York, Jay retired from politics in 1801 and devoted much of his remaining years to farming, supporting the growing anti-slavery movement, and acting as president of the American Bible Society. One of the oldest surviving members of the Revolutionary era Jay died at the age of 83 on May 17, 1829.

Thomas Jefferson

History has blown hot and cold over Thomas Jefferson. A controversial figure when he was alive, it took many years for his stature as a champion of democracy and the rights of man to develop to the point of immense respect that he has since been held around the world. But his reputation reached a peak in the immediate wake of the fall of communism in eastern Europe, after that, the revisionist trend in American and European history that had begun earlier in the twentieth century had gained such momentum that even such mighty figures as Jefferson were no longer immune from reappraisal. Not that he had lived a life free of error; there is plenty in Jefferson's career to warrant further speculation including his comparative inactivity during the Revolutionary War, his behind the scenes manipulations to attack political rival Alexander Hamilton, and his later contempt even for George Washington whose Federalist sympathies he could not tolerate. There was also Jefferson's dogged loyalty to the French Revolution even after its excesses became known, his political struggle with Supreme Court Justice John Marshall and his former Vice-President Aaron Burr, and even the contradictions in his own positions regarding presidential power. That said, his accomplishments in the name of liberty yet outweigh any questions that might be raised regarding his personal shortcomings including his writing of the Declaration of Independence, the *Notes on the State of Virginia,* and *A Summary View of the Rights of British America.* And his service to his country in Congress, as governor of Virginia, as ambassador to France, as Secretary of State, and President of the United States all speak to his public commitment. In addition, there was his creation of the University of Virginia and passage of the Virginia Statute for Religious Freedom which he wrote. All this and more has earned Jefferson his place in the top ranks of Revolutionary heroes.

Born at Shadwell, his parents' Albemarle County, Virginia plantation on April 13, 1743, Jefferson was raised a child of privilege in what was at the time, widely seen as the most prosperous and most powerful of the thirteen American colonies. As was the custom of the times, his early education was conducted by tutors and later continued at exclusive private schools. In 1760, Jefferson, already familiar with the classics of Greek and Roman literature, developed a life long interest in the sciences while attending the College of William and Mary from which he graduated in 1762. Attracted to the law, Jefferson spent the following five years studying under George Wythe, the colony's most prominent attorney. Passing the bar in 1767, he spent the next few years practicing law, inheriting Shadwell upon the death of his father, beginning construction of his mountaintop home of Monticello, and getting married to wealthy widow Martha Sayles Skelton.

Thomas Jefferson

In the meantime, Jefferson had assumed many of the public roles in Albemarle County that his father had held before him including a local magistracy and county lieutenant. Later, he took a seat in the colony's House of Burgesses that he held until 1774. Never much of a public speaker, Jefferson nevertheless could appreciate it in others and one of the young orators whom he admired in the Burgesses was Patrick Henry with whom he soon united in the spirit of rebellion against royal authority. Deeply familiar with the works of many Enlightenment philosophers such as Jean Jacques Rousseau, Jefferson was already sympathetic to appeals to freedom, individual rights, and national self-determination. In 1774, after the courts had been forced to close in response to revolutionary activity, Jefferson wrote his *Summary View of the Rights of British America* in which he denied any political connection to England save its king.

Impressed with his strong views, in 1775 local patriots chose Jefferson as one of Virginia's representatives to the Continental Congress and the next year, as a member of a committee that included Benjamin Franklin, John Adams, Robert Livingston, and Roger Sherman, he was deputed to write the first draft of the Declaration of Independence. Although some changes were eventually made to the document by Congress, what remained was essentially Jefferson's including its ringing opening phrases declaring that all men were created equal. In writing the Declaration, Jefferson said that his object was "not to find out new principles, or new arguments, never before thought of, not merely to say things which had never been said before; but to place before mankind the common sense of the subject, in terms so plain and firm as to command their assent...it was intended to be an expression of the American mind..."

Soon after the acceptance of the Declaration by Congress, a homesick Jefferson left Philadelphia to return to Virginia. Resuming his place in the new state's House of Delegates, he was subsequently elected governor and drafted a Bill for Establishing Religious Freedom. Finally enacted into law in 1786, the measure permitting freedom of conscience was considered by Jefferson one of the supreme achievements of his life. Although he was also successful in passing a law ending the system of primogeniture in Virginia, a second bill that would have created a public education system based on merit failed for lack of support. As governor during wartime, Jefferson tried to stretch Virginia's meager resources as much as he could, supporting the state's western counties against Indian attack while sending as many supplies as possible to the army fighting in the Carolinas. Consequently, when

Virginia itself was invaded first by a traitorous Benedict Arnold and then by a British army under Gen. Charles Cornwallis, there was little he could do to oppose them. When the crisis had passed, he came under fire by political enemies including Patrick Henry for running before advancing British soldiers and not doing enough to prepare the militia to defend the state. He left office just in time to preside over the death of his wife and make a start on his *Notes on the State of Virginia*.

Work on the book was interrupted when he was once again chosen as a representative to Congress in 1783 where among other things, he worked to create what would become the Northwest Ordinance, the historic document that would provide for the creation and acceptance of new states to the union equal to the original thirteen. The next year, he replaced Benjamin Franklin as commissioner to France and while there, developed a strong admiration for the French and their own revolutionary movement. After observing the ratification process for the Constitution from afar and corresponding on the subject with James Madison, its prime defender along with Alexander Hamilton, Jefferson returned to the United States in 1789 to find himself offered the post of Secretary of State by the nation's first president, George Washington. He accepted the position little knowing the rancor that would grow between himself and Hamilton who had been appointed Secretary of the Treasury. As time passed, he discovered that he and Hamilton shared opposing views not only on the Constitution but on the Revolution itself which Jefferson felt was fought to make the country safe for farmers and land owners such as himself and not for the interests of rich merchants and money lenders. Over the next few years, his behind the scenes battles with Hamilton grew more heated and made all the more galling to Jefferson with the New Yorker's string of victories involving the assumption of state debts by the federal government, the establishment of a national bank, and the establishment of a vast financial system that was immune from tinkering due to its intricate interlocking and mutually dependent parts. Alarmed at what he suspected were Hamilton's goals, namely to hand the country over to moneyed interests and developing a closer relationship to the country's former enemy England in opposition to his own sympathies for former ally France, Jefferson began a clandestine campaign not only to oppose Hamilton, but to thwart his policies. In the end, realizing that without Washington's support, he stood no chance against Hamilton, Jefferson resigned as Secretary of State and retreated to his mountaintop home where he quickly became the focus of a growing anti-Federalist network that would soon coalesce into a bona fide political party.

In the three years until he was elected vice president of the United States in the administration of John Adams, Jefferson waged a secret battle against Hamilton using as proxies newspapers and congressmen who shared his views. What resulted was a hardening of the political fault lines in the country and the creation of two distinct parties, the Federalists who supported Hamilton and a strong central government and the Republicans who favored Jefferson's ideal of a weak government and a more agrarian based economy. Although Hamilton had given up his position as Secretary of the Treasury by the time Jefferson arrived in Philadelphia to preside over the senate as John Adams' vice president, he continued to hold great influence through fellow Federalists in Congress and the president's own cabinet, all of whose members were more loyal to the New Yorker than to Adams.

Over the next few years, even as the clandestine war between himself and Hamilton continued in the public newspapers, Jefferson busied himself by writing a *Manual of Parliamentary Practice* and a number of papers detailing his various scientific interests and inventions. In 1797, a year after becoming vice president, he was chosen president of the American Philosophical Society (which he remained until 1815) and in 1798 secretly authored the Kentucky Resolutions in defiance of the Alien and Sedition Acts where he claimed the states had the right to reject any federal law they disapproved of. The Resolves failed in their purpose but Jefferson's ideas would inadvertently provide the basis for the notion of nullification used by the southern states to secede from the Union sixty years later.

Ironically, it was with the help of Hamilton that Jefferson won his first term as President of the United States in the election of 1800. Wary of Jefferson, but even more so of fellow New York politician Aaron Burr, whom he believed possessed no moral convictions, Hamilton used his influence to help win the vote for the Virginian. Calling his election a "revolution," Jefferson arrived in Washington signaling the beginning of the end of Federalist power. Hamilton himself was removed from the political scene in 1804 when he was killed in a duel with Burr. After that, Federalists retreated behind the walls of the judiciary for a last stand. In the meantime, Jefferson proceeded to set a new tone for the presidency marked by simplicity and a lack of ostentation. His first term opened with the first salvo in what would turn out to be an ongoing struggle with the judiciary, first in addressing the flood of last minute appointments to the bench by Adams of mostly Federalist judges and then a long term struggle with Chief Justice John Marshall involving attempts to remove him and restrict the court's authority over interpreting the Constitution. Jefferson also suppressed his scruples regarding a liberal interpretation of the Constitution and in 1803, concluded the Louisiana Purchase with France, paying $15 million for a land area of 828,000 square miles, more than doubling the size of the territorial United States. Before that, refusing to pay the tribute demanded by outlaw regimes along the North African coast, Jefferson ordered offensive operations against Tripoli that forced the pirates to negotiate and a treaty was signed in 1805.

Jefferson's second term as president was marked chiefly by the spectacular trial of Aaron Burr who was accused of conspiring to detach the western parts of the United States and/or conquer Mexico in an attempt to create for himself a separate nation. The subsequent trial for treason became another major confrontation between the president and Marshall, who presided over the trial and whose rulings eventually led to acquittal. The final months of Jefferson's presidency were clouded by growing hostility between Britain and France with the United States caught in the middle. Not wishing to go to war over increasing incidents of impressments; the searching of American vessels by Britain for "contraband" and the seizure of sailors under the claim that they were British or French deserters, Jefferson imposed an embargo on all American shipping to both France and Britain. But because the resulting effects did far more harm to the domestic economy than it did to the offending nations, he was forced to end the embargo before leaving office in 1808.

After his friend James Madison was elected to succeed him as president in 1809, Jefferson retired to his home at Monticello. But retirement proved little less exciting than his public life had been with a continual stream of house guests; his work in designing, planning the curriculum, and overseeing the construction of the University of Virginia; and wide ranging correspondence that finally included John Adams, his estranged friend with whom he had been a member on the committee that produced the Declaration of Independence and beside whom he had worked in Europe. As the years passed, Jefferson's reputation grew and his stature as a champion of liberty made his home a required destination for many overseas travelers. He spent more time reading his favorite books until finally donating his collection to the public making its 6,700 volumes the cornerstone of the Library of Congress. On July 4, 1826, the fiftieth anniversary of the signing of the Declaration of Independence, the infirmities of old age finally caught up to Jefferson who died at Monticello only hours before the death of fellow patriot John Adams in Massachusetts.

John Paul Jones

The Revolutionary War gave rise to many deathless phrases of defiance to royal authority that have ever since thrilled and inspired succeeding generations of Americans, phrases such as that boomed by Ethan Allen when asked upon whose authority he demanded the surrender of Fort Ticonderoga: "In the name of the Great Jehovah and the Continental Congress!" or Nathan Hale's "I regret that I have but one life to lose for my country!" just before he was hanged as a spy. But perhaps the most famous of all was spoken, not by a native born American, but a Scotsman named John Paul Jones, while on the burning deck of the warship *Bonhomme Richard*: "I have not yet begun to fight!"

Perhaps part of the reason for Britain's disdain for its American colonies was rooted in the fact that many of its citizens were low born in an age where class meant everything. Which class a man was born into determined not only his path in life but his place in the larger society. In eight-

John Paul Jones

eenth century Britain, classes were divided roughly among the aristocracy, the merchants, the various trade guilds, or the unskilled masses that either worked the land or acted as servants to the wealthy. Rarely would members of different classes move from one to another and the gulf between the aristocratic and the lower classes was especially vast. As a result, it was difficult for the rulers of Britain to take seriously the democratic aspirations of Americans whom they characterized as mere descendents of bonded servants, toilers of the land, small tradesmen, and the failed refuse of Scotland and Ireland who had escaped to the new world with only the rags on their backs. And as with all generalities, there was some truth to the belief. Many did immigrate to America in a desperate search for a new start and one of those searchers was John Paul who would soon change his name to the more familiar John Paul Jones.

Born in Scotland on July 6, 1747 young John Paul, the son of a landscape gardener, developed an early interest in the sea, spending any free time he had haunting the local dockyards at the nearby seaport of Caresthorne. His dream to go to sea became a reality in 1759 when he signed on as a seamen's apprentice with a trading vessel that took him for his first visit to the American colonies. Upon returning to Scotland however, he learned that the term of service on his apprenticeship was to be cut short due to some belt tightening on the part of the ship's owner. In a stroke of luck, Paul was able to sign on as third mate on a slaver and, later, as first mate on a second ship where he served as only one member of a six man crew taking over 70 slaves from Africa to Jamaica. But after two years in the trade, he quit in disgust and took passage from the West Indies on a merchant ship headed back to England. On the way, luck of a sort struck again as the ship's captain and second mate both died of illness and Paul was chosen to command the vessel until it reached port. There, impressed with his performance, the owners made Paul the ship's captain. Finally, in 1773 his luck ran out, or maybe it was simply his short temper and habit of treating crewmen with harsh disregard, when he was accused of murder upon the death of a sailor he had ordered flogged. Charged with the man's death, he was acquitted but his reputation was sullied; a second incident involving his killing of another sailor in a mutinous dispute over payment led him to flee to the American colonies to avoid prosecution.

In Virginia, where an older brother worked as a tailor, Paul changed his name to John Jones and explored the idea of becoming a farmer and even found himself briefly engaged. But as the colonies' disagreement with England became a war, he decided to take advantage of his naval experience and applied through acquaintances such as Thomas Jefferson, for a commission in the newly formed Continental Navy. Right from the beginning, there was eagerness by some in Congress to challenge Britain on the high seas, but others thought the very idea was preposterous: the country could barely keep its soldiers supplied, assuming the exorbitant cost of building capital warships capable of meeting those of the Royal Navy on an equal footing was plainly a waste of resources. Better to concentrate instead on the country's merchant fleet and issuing letters of marque for privateering. In the end, Congress decided to take both approaches and soon American privateers became a real thorn in England's side. Then, in November of 1775, Congress ordered the establishment of a Continental Navy and created a Marine Committee to oversee it. Five warships were soon commissioned, including the first, called the *Alfred,* which became Lt. Jones', now calling himself John Paul Jones, first assignment.

Acting in concert with other war vessels in a variety of missions that kept the American fleet close to home waters, Jones was soon promoted to captain and given command of the *Providence.* Learning quickly, he was able to adapt his experience of sailing ships to the requirements of naval warfare and, as a result, found himself advising the Marine Committee on broader naval matters. In 1777, he was sent to Portsmouth, New Hampshire to oversee the construction of his new command, the 18 gun *Ranger.* With preparations completed, Jones set sail for France and met with Benjamin Franklin who was serving there as American Ambassador. The next year, he left France for his first raid in British home waters where he attacked shipping and burned two forts at Whitehaven before moving up the coast to Scotland and then Ireland where he met and defeated HMS *Drake.* With 200 prisoners in tow, Jones returned to France victorious and immediately began making plans with Franklin for a second voyage.

With the *Ranger* in disrepair after its encounter with the *Drake,* the government of France gave Jones an old merchant vessel that he immediately began to refit as a warship including cutting out new gunports in its hull and bringing the number of cannon aboard to 42. Renaming the ship the *Bonhomme Richard* in honor of the French publication of Franklin's *Poor Richard's Almanac,* Jones left France in August, 1779 at the head of a small French financed fleet of four ships including the *Alliance, Pallas,* and *Vengeance.* Making its way up the English Channel, the American squadron took prizes and otherwise continued their depredations against the British homeland as Jones had been instructed to do before leaving the United States by Marine Committee representative Robert Morris.

It was after the squadron had entered northern waters on the evening of September 23, that it encountered a merchant fleet of 40 ships escorted by the 54 gun *Serapis* and 28 gun *Countess of Scarborough.*

As the defenseless merchant vessels moved inshore toward Flamborough Head, the two British battleships prepared to engage the Americans. "What ship is that?" demanded Captain Richard Pearson from out of the darkness as the *Serapis* drew abreast of the *Bonhomme Richard*. Then, receiving no reply, he gave the order to fire and unleashed a broadside that was met almost simultaneously by a cannonade from the American ship. With the wind in its favor, the American vessel was the first to recover and rammed its bow into the stern of the British vessel. That action notwithstanding, Pearson called out again, "Has your ship struck?" According to an account of the action by Lt. Richard Dale who took part in the battle, it was then that Jones uttered his deathless reply: "I have not yet begun to fight!" Further maneuvering brought the two ships closer together until, their rigging hopelessly entangled, they were made fast together, hulls flush. Over the next three hours, the battle raged with American sharpshooters positioned in the topsails sniping at anyone who showed themselves on the upper deck of the *Serapis*, cannon of both ships firing at point blank range below decks, and crews fighting desperately to keep fires from spreading into magazines. At last, near midnight, an American hand grenade fell into the powder room aboard the *Serapis* resulting in a huge explosion that finally took the fight out of the enemy. But the Americans hardly had time to celebrate their victory, nor that of *Pallas* over the *Countess of Scarborough* before they once again found themselves under attack, this time by one of their own ships as the *Alliance* began pounding the *Bonhomme Richard* with cannon fire. Coming as it did in the light of a full moon and with the all black hull of the *Bonhomme Richard* contrasting sharply with that of the yellow painted *Serapis*, the action by the French captain of the *Alliance* can only be explained in terms of either jealousy or madness. Jones himself, at least, had little doubt of the ship's treachery. "There was no possibility of his mistaking the enemy's ship for the *Bonhomme Richard*," he said in a report of the battle to Franklin. But victory came despite the friendly fire incident as well as numerous other American disadvantages including the bursting of two cannon early in the battle, an inexperienced and mostly foreign crew with no knowledge of English, the release of 200 prisoners in the middle of the fight, and a ship a good deal older than the newer *Serapis*. Due to Jones' determination and coolness under fire, the United States had won the bloodiest naval engagement of the war and proved that even though its navy was small, it was no less effective due to the skill and courage of its seamen. But victory at Flamborough Head came with a price: of Jones' 380 crewmen, fully half were killed or wounded.

With the battle ended, Jones watched as the battered *Bonhomme Richard* sank beneath the waves and, in command of the *Serapis,* sailed first to Holland then to France where he became a national hero. In 1780, Jones returned to the United States and received a commendation from Congress but none of the back pay owed him. Perhaps as compensation, he was given command of the country's newest battleship, the *America*, but more than a year later, his commission was rescinded and the *America* given to France. Disappointed, Jones requested permission to join an expected French attack on the West Indies, but when the plan fell through, he was sent instead to France to try and recover money earned for prizes captured in his raids on England.

After fruitless years of trying to recover prize money from France and Denmark and back pay from Congress as well as a promotion in an American navy where seniority was more important than merit, Jones gave up and accepted a commission in the Russian Navy where he once again displayed courage and skill fighting Turks on the Black Sea. Leaving Russia under a cloud, he made his way to France again where he died in 1792 of complications involving pneumonia. At the age of only 45, America's greatest naval hero was dead. Buried in an unmarked grave, it was not until 1905 that it was identified and his remains returned to the United States eight years later with full honors and reinterred on the grounds of the nation's naval academy in Annapolis, Maryland.

Jack Jouett

Although the most famous "ride" of the Revolutionary War, thanks to the poem by Henry Wadsworth Longfellow, was that of Paul Revere in 1775, there were no doubt many others across the thirteen states whose riders dashed on similar missions to warn friends and neighbors of the advance of enemy forces. One such was Jack Jouett, a towering militia captain who one day found himself in the path of the dreaded British Col. Banastre Tarleton as Bloody Ban conducted one of his lightning raids hoping to catch key Virginia legislators in their beds.

Born in 1754 in Louisa County, Virginia, by the time John Jouett, Jr. joined the local militia, he had grown to well over 6 feet in height and put on 220 pounds, mostly muscle. By the night of June 3, 1781,

Jouett had long since been appointed a captain of militia and had seen the enemy up close many times, but perhaps not as close as when Col. Banastre Tarleton, known widely as the butcher of the Waxhaws after refusing quarter to Americans who had tried to surrender to his Legion of Tory cavalry, rode past the Cuckoo Tavern in Louisa township. Jouett, in the area helping to round up supplies for the army, was startled at the Legion's sudden appearance but guessed immediately what its mission must be.

Earlier in the year, the state's legislature, the House of Burgesses, had moved from Williamsburg to Richmond in the face of threatening moves by the enemy. In April, the traitor Benedict Arnold invaded Virginia at the head of a British army and immediately drove toward Richmond prompting the legislature to move again, this time to Charlottesville. Then, in May, British Gen. Charles Cornwallis, in his drive up from the Carolinas, arrived in the vicinity of Petersburg in pursuit of the vastly outnumbered forces under the command of Gen. Lafayette. Driving the Frenchman away, Cornwallis suddenly pounced toward Charlottesville, probably hoping to bag such high profile targets as signers of the Declaration of Independence Governor Thomas Jefferson and legislators Patrick Henry, Thomas Nelson, and Benjamin Harrison. Expecting that they would take the Virginians' by surprise, Tarleton's Legionaires were dispatched to range far ahead of the army with the aim of catching the legislators before they could be warned. Traveling at night and covering almost seventy miles in a single day, they almost succeeded, reaching the Cuckoo Tavern by about 10 p.m. on June 3. Adding to Jouett's sense of urgency was the fact that the state was drained of fight-

Jack Jouett

ing men who were either in the north with Washington or on the run with Lafayette. The caliber of the few militia that remained was not high, due in some measure to the Jefferson administration's own failure to prepare the state for war. In short then, the legislators in Charlottesville were almost completely undefended.

No sooner had the Legion's 180 dragoons and 70 mounted infantry ridden out of sight, than Jouett mounted up and rode to warn the unsuspecting legislators. Using the main road to Charlottesville down which Tarleton had gone was out of the question so Jouett decided to make his 40 mile dash to Charlottesville cross country, not an easy task even by the light of the moon and a knowledge of the area. Heedless of his own safety, Jouett bulled his way through thickets and forested hillsides, leaping stone walls, plunging into hidden gorges and traversing little used pathways and trails until, early on the morning of June 4, he crossed the Rivana River at Milton Ford. It was past 4 a.m. by the time he arrived at Monticello, Jefferson's mountaintop retreat. His clothing was in tatters and his skin and face criss-crossed in bloody scrapes and scratches. In a way, he was lucky, because Tarleton had decided to stop at a number of places along the way including Castle Hill where he surprised and captured a number of lawmakers in their nightshirts. Although the delays gave Jouett the time he needed to complete his soon to be famous ride, the enemy still remained at his heels arriving at Monticello only a few hours later.

Despite the enemy's proximity and Jouett's warning however, there was no sense of urgency in Jefferson's household. After breakfasting with a group of fellow legislators who were staying with him at Monticello, Jefferson himself took the time to send his family off to a nearby plantation and collect his personal papers. He only stopped his work when a Capt. Christopher Hudson of the Continental Army appeared to warn him that the British were at the base of his "little mountain." Leaving his home at last, Jefferson looked back once but saw no indication that the enemy was near, but a second look moments later revealed the streets of nearby Charlottesville filled with Tarleton's men. The whole adventure would come back to haunt him as political enemies such as Patrick Henry, used the flight from Monticello to further damage a reputation already stained as a result of Jefferson's poor performance as governor in readying his state for war.

From Monticello, Jouett turned his exhausted horse about and rode on to the Swan Tavern in Charlottesville, owned by his father, where the balance of the legislators were staying and warned them to clear out. But his work for the night was not yet done. Donning a bright red coat, he led Tarleton's men on a wild goose chase giving more time for the legislators to escape and reconvene in Staunton. Because of his quick thinking and even quicker horse, Jouett managed almost single handedly to save the entire Virginia legislature from capture and possible execution as traitors by the vengeful British.

Although a thankful Virginia awarded him with a sword and brace of pistols, Jouett did not remain in the state following the war. He married a local girl and moved to Harrodsburg, Kentucky where he took up politics and thoroughbred horses. He was involved in the effort to make Kentucky a state, was a supporter of Andrew Jackson, and served four terms in the Kentucky legislature. He died at the home of his daughter in Bath County on March 1, 1822.

Simon Kenton

A friend and contemporary of Daniel Boone, Simon Kenton was well known on the frontier not by his real name but by the name of Simon Butler. Like Boone, Kenton was lured into the Kentucky wilderness at a young age and experienced many hair raising adventures as an Indian fighter and in battle against the British during the Revolution.

Kenton was born to a poor farming family in Fauqier County, Virginia on April 3, 1755. As one of nine children, he received no formal education and never learned to read or write. In 1771, when he was just sixteen, Kenton assaulted another boy in a jealous rage over a girl and believing he had killed him, fled west into the settlements. Changing his name to Simon Butler, he fell in with frontiersmen such as George Yeager and the soon to become notorious Simon Girty who told him tall tales of a place called Kentucky, a mysterious land beyond the mountains that teemed with game and wild Indians. It was with Yeager in 1775 that Kenton went down the Ohio River and up Limestone Creek to Kentucky where he staked his first claim and planted some corn. But the lure of what lay beyond the canebrakes became too strong. Soon, he gave up farming for the wandering life and learned the skills needed to survive in the wilderness from such pioneers as Daniel Boone and George Rogers Clark. Kenton's growing experience came in handy in the years that followed as relations between settlers moving into Kentucky and Ohio and Indians who regarded those lands as their personal hunting grounds erupted into bloody conflict. In 1774 Kenton hired himself out as a spy in the pay of a British army sent west under Virginia Governor Lord Dunmore to end the Indian threat. But Dunmore's campaign did little to quell the unrest and in 1777, the "year of the three sevens," one of the bloodiest in the history of the frontier, Kenton was on hand to save the life of Daniel Boone during a deadly hand to hand skirmish with Indians outside Boonesborough.

The next year, with the Revolutionary War raging across the thirteen colonies, Kenton joined George Rogers Clark on an expedition to the Illinois country for a surprise assault on the British outpost at Vincennes. In what would later be recognized as one of the truly epic military operations in history, the small band of frontier volunteers trekked across hundreds of miles of wilderness to the small French settlements of Kaskaskia and Caho-

Simon Kenton

kia and following their capture, crossed miles of frozen swampland for the assault on Vincennes itself. With the capture of the British outpost, Kenton was sent back to Kentucky to recruit more men but his efforts failed.

At loose ends, Kenton then joined others in an expedition against a large body of Shawnee known to be in the area and in the process was captured. When the Indians realized whom they had prisoner, there was great joy in the villages and Kenton was subjected to one of the most vicious series of tortures any man ever endured and survived. Very nearly at the end of his rope, he was saved by Simon Girty and adopted into the tribe before being once again condemned to die at the stake. But his luck had not yet run out. At the last minute he was saved again, this time by a Mingo chief named Logan who prevailed upon a French trader to buy the American and take him to Detroit. The deal arranged,

Kenton next found himself employed as a laborer for the British garrison at Detroit until managing to escape in 1779. Making his way back to Kentucky, he arrived just in time to help repel yet another Indian raid on the sparsely populated settlements before rejoining Clark as an officer of scouts.

After the war, Kenton established his own town in Kentucky called Kenton's Station and learned that the man he thought he had killed back in Virginia was still alive. Now able to live under his own name again, Kenton was made a major and in 1793 led a company of hand picked scouts ahead of an army commanded by Gen. Anthony Wayne who had been ordered to end the Indian menace in the Ohio country once and for all. Unfortunately, despite seeing plenty of action as the army moved north, Kenton was felled by sickness and discharged before Wayne's victory at Fallen Timbers.

By 1799, Kenton had married and made the first of several moves around the Ohio country. In 1807, he first met Shawnee war chief Tecumseh at a peace council and despite assurances of friendship, advised that the Indian leader be killed before he could stir up trouble on the frontier. When war did come, Kenton joined an expedition against Tecumseh led by Gen. Isaac Shelby and was on hand in October 1813 for the battle of the Thames where he later identified the body of the fallen chief.

Unfortunately, Kenton's later years often were not happy ones with the death of his first wife and the discovery that the thousands of acres of land he had claimed in his career had been improperly registered. The final blow came when the little property that remained to him was seized for back taxes. Impoverished, he was barely recognized as one of Kentucky's most famous sons when he tried to plead his case to the state's legislature. However, Kenton's story ended happily when some of his lands were returned to him and the Ohio legislature awarded him a pension. After making a profession out of escaping death, Kenton finally submitted peacefully in Logan County, Ohio on April 29, 1836.

Thomas Knowlton

Thomas Knowlton, along with William Prescott and John Stark, was the third militia officer to emerge from the battle of Breed's Hill not only as a genuine American hero but as a consummate professional. Like Prescott and Stark, Knowlton had served extensively in the French and Indian War where he garnered much valuable experience and just as his peers had retired to quiet lives of farming when the war ended, so did he. But when long simmering resentments finally broke out into open warfare at Lexington and Concord, his reputation as a military man made him the unanimous choice among the men of his local militia unit to lead them. Later, Knowlton became the commander of an elite corps of scouts for the Continental Army and the nation's first professional intelligence officer.

Knowlton was actually born in West Boxford, Massachusetts on November 30, 1740 before his parents moved the family to Ashford, Connecticut a few years later. In 1755, when he was just fifteen years old and yearning for adventure, Knowlton followed an older brother into the army and became a scout during the French and Indian War. By the time the war ended, Knowlton had infiltrated enemy territory a half

Thomas Knowlton at Breeds Hill

(in white shirt holding gun)

dozen times and been promoted to lieutenant. In 1759 he returned to Ashford, established his own farm and took Anna Keyes as his wife. Together, the couple raised nine children with Knowlton leaving home briefly 1762 to serve with the British against the Spanish in Cuba. Ravaged by disease, he was only one of a handful of men in his unit to survive the experience and ten years later he found himself elected as an Ashford selectman. But just as he was making the transition from soldier to politician, resentment over the English Parliament's attempts to tax the colonies boiled over in the spring of 1775 when a company of Massachusetts minutemen fired on a column of British soldiers at Concord Bridge.

With sentiments in Ashford strongly opposed to British high handedness, the town had already formed its own militia company and it was a foregone conclusion that Knowlton would be named its captain. As soon as word was received in Connecticut that hostilities had broken out in Massachusetts, the colony became the first to order militia units north in support of the uprising. As a result, it fell to Knowlton to lead 200 men of the 5th Connecticut Regiment from out of state into Massachusetts following the events at Lexington and Concord. Without uniforms or proper equipment, the militiamen arrived in the vicinity of Bunker Hill just as an army of farmers from miles around was coalescing to bottle up the British in Boston. With defensive lines being taken atop nearby Breed's Hill, Knowlton's men with two cannon were ordered by local commander Col. William Prescott to form a line along a fence that ran at the base of the hill. In command in the area of the fence was New Hampshire man John Stark who perhaps consulted with Knowlton on strengthening the defensive line running down to the edge of the Mystic River. Quickly, while some of his men erected a second fence running parallel to the first, Knowlton had others gather up freshly cut grass to pile up between them. While that was being done, rocks and stones were found to extend the defense line down to the water's edge. Thus, when the enemy attempted a flanking attack around the base of the hill, Knowlton's men were ready for them, safe behind their breastworks. So impregnable had their position turned out to be, that the Connecticut unit was able to hold its ground and cover the eventual American retreat from Breed's Hill. Although Knowlton's men accounted for scores of British casualties during the action, they lost only three of their own.

The unit's performance that day did not go unnoticed and when Gen. George Washington arrived to take command of the nascent Continental Army, Knowlton was promoted to major and ordered to join the 20th Continental Regiment. Soon after, he was given the risky assignment of penetrating the enemy's lines to infiltrate Charlestown and destroy any building that remained standing at the bottom of Bunker Hill while capturing any British soldiers he might come across. The mission went off without a hitch as Knowlton not only returned with captives, but accomplished the assignment in silence and without losing a man. Impressed with his performance, Washington asked Knowlton, now promoted to lieutenant colonel, to form a regiment of rangers, a special unit of picked men to act as scouts and spies for the Continental Army.

Under the direct command of Washington, Knowlton's Rangers, as the regiment was soon known, were given their first major assignment: to reconnoiter the area in New York around Long Island and Manhattan where the British were expected to strike next. As part of his efforts to gather intelligence on enemy intentions regarding New York, Knowlton called for a volunteer to enter New York City to see what could be learned. Stepping forward was Nathan Hale, a fellow resident of Connecticut who had been a teacher before the war. After warning the young man of the dangers involved, Knowlton gave him the assignment. Unfortunately, not long after, news arrived that Hale had been discovered by the British and hung as a spy.

Later that summer, on September 16, 1776, as the British invaded Manhattan and began to press its attack northward toward the American lines, a company of 150 of Knowlton's Rangers scouting ahead of the American defense works on Harlem Heights, stumbled upon an enemy outpost made up of British and Hessian soldiers. Immediately upon contact, an elite unit known as the Black Watch assembled and moved against the lightly armed Americans. Picked for their height and large build and outfitted in their distinctive uniforms, the men of the Black Watch were an imposing and fearful sight as they advanced with their rifles at the ready. Standing their ground, the rangers slowed the enemy advance but seeing that he would be surrounded if his men continued to hold the field, Knowlton joined a retreat back to the American lines. The British surged ahead, blowing their bugles as if they were chasing fox, an insult that filled the defending Americans with rage. In reply, Col. Joseph Reed implored Washington for the opportunity to strike back and as the enemy's advance had left some units overextended, Washington thought he saw an opportunity to cut them off. Under Reed's command, a party that included three companies of Virginians and Knowlton's Rangers left their positions to creep around the enemy's flank. In the meantime, a second unit meant to draw the attention of the enemy opened fire before Reed's men were ready. As the shooting became more general, Reed was unable to keep his men from being drawn to the sound of the guns and as a result, the enemy was struck in the flank rather than the rear. But despite the premature attack, between the two groups of Americans, the British were forced to fall back and after a mile or so, the Continentals were ordered to return to their lines lest the whole British army be drawn into a general engagement.

Unfortunately, when the powder smoke had cleared, it was found that Knowlton was among the American casualties. In company with his sixteen year old son Frederick, he fell mortally wounded with a bullet in his back. "...our greatest loss was a brave officer from Connecticut whose name and spirit ought to be immortalized," wrote Reed in a letter to his wife. "I assisted him off (the field) and when gasping in the agonies of death all his inquiry was if we had drove the enemy." Although Knowlton may have died with news of the enemy having been driven off, it was only a temporary victory as the Americans would eventually be forced completely off Manhattan and into New Jersey. But Knowlton's memory, like his country, would not die; and years later he would be recognized as the father of the United States Army Rangers.

Henry Knox

The American Revolution was not a planned affair. Men did not gather in local taverns or dimly lit back rooms to map out a strategy aimed at rebellion (although they *did* meet in those locations and some *did* hope for revolution and ultimate independence). When the war came, it came suddenly; after all, the British had conducted other forays into the countryside before Lexington and Concord and never met with serious opposition. Of course there was some organization to the resistance movement against the Parliament's efforts to impose, among other things, what was seen by the colonists as unfair tax burdens. The Sons of Liberty, led by Samuel Adams and Joseph Warren, orchestrated a campaign of perpetual agitation that was designed over many years to keep the public's outrage at the boiling point. Committees of Safety and Correspondence were set up, not just in Massachusetts, but in other colonies as well, a local spy system was put in place and eventually, a Continental Congress was called where all the colonies could gather, compare notes and plan for concerted action. And despite the fact that membership of local organizations included many professionals from physicians to attorneys to politicians, most had no experience either with revolution or nation building. And although talk of revolution had been in the air among radicals for years, the suddenness of Lexington and Concord thrust everyone into a situation where independence would be declared, a war would be fought, and a confederation forged over the course of only fifteen months. Through it all, there was little time to recruit experts, to find just the right men for all the things that had to be done. For the most part, those men would need to rise from among the people when the situation demanded, men such as Massachusetts' Henry Knox. Born in Boston on July 25, 1750, a middle child in a family of ten, there was nothing about the young Henry Knox to indicate that he would grow into a man capable of heroic deeds. Inclined to portliness, he never received a formal education. Instead, upon the death of his father and while still a youngster, he was forced to earn a living clerking in a bookstore to help support his family. But Knox was neither without personal energy nor a native curiosity and eventually had a bookshop of his own and was busily taking advantage of the fact to read everything he could get his hands on, especially books on military subjects. A witness to the Boston Massacre, sympathy for those in opposition to Britain inclined Knox to support the Sons of Liberty while his interest in things martial led him to join the Boston Grenadier Corps in 1772. He received his first taste of battle when he participated in action surrounding the battle of Breed's Hill and when Gen. George Washington arrived in Massachusetts to assume command of the troops surrounding Bos-

Henry Knox

ton, he made an impression on the Virginian and the two began a friendship that would last their entire lives. It was Knox, greatly interested in the uses of artillery in warfare, who suggested to Washington that if cannon were brought from Fort Ticonderoga, which had been captured by the Americans, and placed atop Dorchester Heights, the

British might be forced to abandon their occupation of Boston. Washington agreed, promoted Knox to Colonel, made him chief of artillery, and gave him the assignment to fetch the big guns.

The mission, completed despite the worst conditions imaginable, would place Knox alongside Benedict Arnold and George Rogers Clark, legendary heroes of the Revolution who also had overcome similar difficulties leading troops through the wilderness. To do it, Knox left Cambridge late in the year and, arriving in the vicinity of Ticonderoga, wasted little time in hiring carpenters to build 42 sleds and rounding up 160 oxen to pull them when they were done. By the end of December, with snow on the ground, the sleds were loaded with the fort's heavy cannon and the long train began the journey back to Boston. Over a frozen landscape, Knox and his men hauled 43 cannon and 14 heavy mortars almost 300 miles across icy streams, including the Connecticut River, and up and down the steep forested slopes of the Berkshire Mountains of western Massachusetts. "It appeared to me almost a miracle that people with heavy loads should be able to get up and down such hills as are here…," Knox wrote of his efforts. Finally, "after having climbed mountains from which we might almost have seen all the kingdoms of the earth," Knox delivered the hardware to Washington on January 25, 1775. With the artillery in place atop a hurriedly fortified Dorchester Heights, the British realized that their position in Boston was untenable and on March 17, evacuated the city without a fight.

The personal determination and organizational skills displayed by Knox in getting the cannon from Ticonderoga to Boston were characteristics that Washington would come to depend upon as the years of war dragged on but never more so than in those early months of the conflict. And so, while the army marched south to New York, Knox was ordered to remain behind to help shore up the defenses of Connecticut and Rhode Island. After rejoining Washington in New York, he helped perform the same duties there. Despite those efforts however, the heavily outnumbered Continental Army was forced to retreat before a British force of 30,000 soldiers. Adding to the army's problems was its mismatched collection of artillery whose pieces sometimes tended to self-destruct and which required a number of different kinds of ammunition, a supply problem that would plague Knox through most of the war. Following the battle of New York the British went into winter quarters, confident that the Americans were defeated. Sensing the enemy's complacency, Washington conceived a bold plan to cross the Delaware River and strike a Hessian garrison at Trenton, New Jersey. Knox was given the responsibility not only of getting 3,000 troops across the river and back again, but also of the artillery, which he had prepared with improved carriages for better mobility. On Christmas day, 1776, the army crossed the nearly frozen river and surprised the German mercenaries still recovering from their holiday celebrations. "The hurry, fright and confusion of the enemy was (not) unlike that which will be when the last trump shall sound," wrote Knox of the action. The victory at Trenton was followed quickly by a similar engagement at nearby Princeton before the Americans once more retreated across the river. But the twin victories provided only temporary relief as the British soon began to move again, this time toward Philadelphia, capturing the city on September 26, 1777.

The Americans' last major encounter with the enemy took place at Germantown in a battle that began well, but eventually miscarried. Among the tactical mistakes was the insistence by Knox, now a brigadier general, that the Chew House, a mansion inside which a body of British soldiers had holed up, could not be allowed to remain in the American rear. Valuable time, too much time as it turned out, was wasted in attempts to reduce the fortresslike home which withstood Knox' artillery even as fog and confusion halted the American advance and ended any chance for victory. With the campaigning season over, Washington pulled back and encamped for the winter at nearby Valley Forge. There, Knox helped in organizing the encampment and was sent back to Massachusetts to recruit for the army and establish the kind of arsenal in Springfield that he had recommended earlier to Congress in a report he titled "Hints for the Improvement of the Artillery of the United States."

Back at Valley Forge, Knox cooperated with the newly arrived Baron von Steuben in training the army and teaching the artillery how to coordinate with the troops, training that paid handsome dividends at the battle of Monmouth in the spring of 1778. But major action around Philadelphia was drawing to a close and Knox found himself increasingly involved in requisition and recruitment duties. In 1781, he accompanied the army to Yorktown where he was in charge of placing the artillery and following British Gen. Charles Cornwallis' surrender there, served for the remainder of the war as commander at West Point, New York. It was perhaps fitting that West Point would later serve as the location of the country's first military academy, the creation of which Knox had originally recommended in his "Hints" on artillery.

Following the war, Knox succeeded Washington as the army's commander in chief and in 1785 was appointed Secretary of War for the Continental Congress where he played an important role in the sup-

pression of Shay's Rebellion in Massachusetts and supported the creation of a stronger central government. In 1789, after the United States
Constitution was ratified Washington, who had been elected the nation's first president, asked his old friend to remain on duty and join his
cabinet as Secretary of War. Knox agreed, and over the next five years,
would oversee training of the militia, establishment of coastal defenses,
deal with frontier issues between settlers and Indians, and help federal-
ize the Springfield arsenal. He was also involved in the establishment
of the Society of the Cincinnati, a fraternity of former military officers
that would later be suspected as favoring the creation of a monarchy in
the United States. Finally, in 1795, tired of public service and eager to
spend more time with his large family, Knox asked Washington to accept his resignation. And so, at age 45, Knox returned home, but not to
Boston. Instead, he purchased a farm near Thomaston, Maine and
passed his remaining years concentrating on his crops, building boats,
and making bricks punctuated in 1798 with a brief reappointment as
general of the army. Sadly, his days of bliss were cut short on October
21, 1806 after he died of an intestinal infection.

Henry Laurens

It was rare, even during the Revolutionary era, that men who had
sworn their lives, their fortunes, and their honor to the cause of liberty
were called upon to sacrifice more than one of those possessions. To be
sure, having to give up only one should have been enough for anyone,
especially if it happened to be a person's life which, for a soldier, was what
was mostly on the line. But for a politician or a diplomat, the possibility of
having to give up one's life was a more remote possibility. Suffering the
inconveniences of long separation from family and friends, being on the run
from the approaching enemy and having a price on one's head were far
more likely possibilities. And although the career of Henry Laurens falls into
the second category, he was unique in not only having to put up with the
day to day privations of being a member of Congress, but also suffered
the loss of his home and having the dubious distinction of spending
over a year confined in the infamous Tower of London.   Born on
March 6, 1724 to well to do parents in Charleston, South Carolina,
Laurens was apprenticed early to a local mercantile firm and by the age

of twenty was judged sufficiently experienced to continue his business education in England. He remained in Europe for the next three years until 1747 when he returned to Charleston and began working to acquire his own fortune. Starting in the export and import trade that he knew well, Laurens worked hard and invested wisely and in 1750, married Eleanor Ball who yielded him twelve children of whom seven would die before reaching maturity. Of two surviving sons, John Laurens would gain renown in the coming Revolution along with his father. Before that time arrived however, the senior Laurens, whose Revolutionary career would primarily be a political one, paid his dues in the Cherokee War that began independent of the larger French and Indian War of 1754-1763 but soon became entangled in it. Serving in the local militia and rising to the rank of Lt. Colonel, Laurens fulfilled his martial duty against the Cherokee before being elected for the first of many consecutive terms in South Carolina's legislature. With the victory against the Indians, more land opened up for real estate investment and Laurens was one of many wealthy men who did so buying over

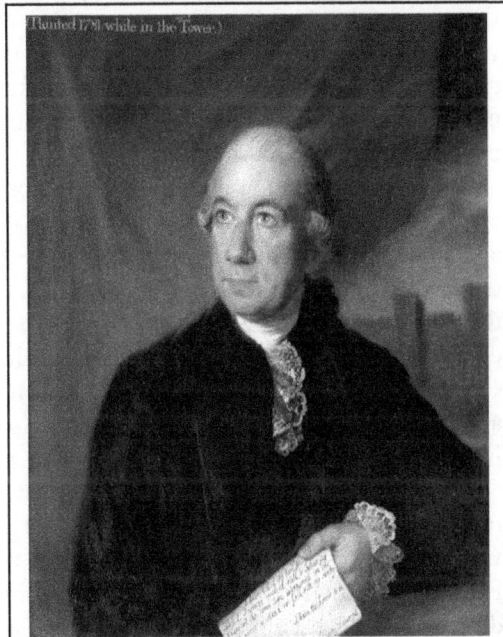

Henry Laurens

20,000 acres including a 3,000 acre farm he called Mepkin. Retiring from business around 1773, Laurens retreated with his family to the bucolic surroundings of Mepkin where he pursued the life of a local planter.

But life had a way of continuing on and soon Laurens' peaceful pursuits would be interrupted by the great events happening elsewhere in the thirteen colonies. To be sure, as a wealthy businessman with interests in shipping that plied the sea lanes between the colonies and England, he was keenly interested in whatever might interrupt that trade including ruinous laws passed by Parliament. Angered at repeated attempts by England to regulate colonial trade, Laurens challenged many in the court system and wrote arguments in pamphlet form against royal authoritarianism. These acts of defiance however, were not enough to free him completely from the suspicion of local patriots who saw his continued friendship with royal officials as disturbing. When the Stamp Act was passed by Parliament in 1765 there was rioting in many colonial capitals including Charleston. A rumor spread that Laurens had been commissioned as a stamp officer and an unruly mob, their faces disguised with soot and masks, assaulted his home demanding to be allowed in to search the premises for the hated stamps. At first, Laurens refused, but soon judged it wise to allow the search but when a demand was made that he swear there were no stamps on the premises, he adamantly refused. However, seeing that Laurens recognized most of them, the crowd declared its satisfaction as to his innocence and left without further violence.

With his position toward royal authority hardening, Laurens traveled to Europe in 1774 in order to supervise the education of his sons and while there, joined a group of fellow Americans in signing a petition addressed to Parliament protesting harsh measures taken against the port of Boston. As a measure of how far he had come in the confidence of his fellow citizens, he was chosen as a delegate to the South Carolina Provincial Congress the year after he returned from Europe and later, became a member of the colony's Committee of Safety. After independence was declared in 1776 and with the enemy threatening Charleston, Laurens was elected as the new state's vice president and then as a delegate to the Second Continental Congress. There, on November 1, 1777, he was elected president upon the resignation of John Hancock. Immediately, he was plunged into a maelstrom of activity directing various committees, signing official documents, and making important decisions affecting a wide range of issues from supplying the army to giving instructions to diplomats in France and Holland. Most importantly, Laurens presided over the debates that resulted in the adoption of the Articles of Confederation the first crude federal document under which the thirteen states would unite for the common defense and other national concerns.

On the other hand, Laurens also had to preside over hearings in the case of Silas Deane who, as a minister to France, had arranged for much needed supplies for the infant United States. However, charges surfaced that the deal, which Congress had believed was charity, was actually for cash and that Deane himself may have profited from it. The affair dragged on for months and bitterly divided Congress until Deane was forced to go public with his case, poisoning the waters even further. In the midst of the turmoil, a disheartened Laurens decided to step down from the presidency of Congress barely a year after assuming the office. He remained as a member of the South Carolina delegation until the fall of 1779 when his fellow congressmen appointed him as minister to Holland. Boarding ship, his journey had hardly begun before it ended under the guns of a British warship off Newfoundland.

Although Laurens managed to throw incriminating documents overboard, they were retrieved and he was arrested for treason. Taken back to England, he was denied diplomatic immunity, tried and thrown into the Tower of London where his health soon deteriorated. In the meantime, a rejection by Holland of a British demand that it refute its plans to help the United States with a loan as outlined in the papers taken from Laurens, resulted in a state of war between the two nations. Over most of the next fifteen months, Laurens himself was held incommunicado while officials offered him pardon if he would only serve the crown. Laurens refused and later withstood threats of worse treatment when he failed to cooperate in convincing his son, John, to abandon a diplomatic mission to France. Eventually, Laurens was allowed to draw upon his own account to provide himself with necessaries and later, was given writing materials which he used to send letters not only to his family, but to the newspapers. Those small favors, however, hardly mitigated the sad news he received of the death of his son John, who had returned to South Carolina only to be killed in a minor military action. Finally, on the last day of 1781 he was released from his confinement under bail put up by Richard Oswald, a wealthy merchant sympathetic to the American cause.

Eventually exchanged for British General Lord Cornwallis who had been captured by Gen. George Washington following his surrender at Yorktown, Laurens was then asked by a similarly sympathetic Lord Shelburne to approach John Adams in Holland about the possibility of opening up peace negotiations with the United States. With Cornwallis' defeat at Yorktown widely considered the last straw by many in Britain, talk of peace was in the air. It must have been with exquisite satisfaction that Laurens returned to Europe just in time to join old acquaintances such as Adams, John Jay, and Benjamin Franklin to wind up negotiations of preliminary articles to a possible treaty of peace. That November, after supporting Adams' demand for fishing rights off the Grand Banks and an article for the return of all American property taken by the British, including slaves, the instrument was signed. Further negotiations would eventually produce a document to be called the Treaty of Paris that officially ended the Revolution.

Upon his return to the United States and South Carolina, Laurens discovered that his beloved home at Mepkin had been destroyed during the war. While the main house was being rebuilt, he moved into a smaller building where he lived with the rest of his family. In the meantime, his health never having fully recovered from his ordeal in the Tower, he refused a number of offers to rejoin the Congress, to participate in the Constitutional Convention, or stand for election to the state's legislature. Laurens did serve briefly during the South Carolina ratifying convention of 1787 and cast his vote in favor of the Constitution that would replace the Articles of Confederation he had helped to create ten years before. Laurens died five years later, on December 8, 1792. His remains were cremated according to his wishes and buried at Mepkin.

John Laurens

In addition to early revolutionaries such as James Otis and older veterans of the French and Indian War such as George Washington, Daniel Boone, and John Stark, there was also a strain of youthful idealism and impetuosity that ran through the American Revolution represented by such younger men as Alexander Hamilton and Thomas Jefferson. But perhaps no person better personified that spirit than John Laurens. Taught in Europe, Laurens probably imbued much of his early republican spirit among the self-ruling cantons of Switzerland but an accompanying impetuosity was likely more of an inborn trait than a learned one. It was a part of his personality that would compel him to leave Europe and to return to America at the start of the Revolution, to display reckless bravery on the battlefield, to challenge long standing social taboos, and that would force him into an early marriage. In the end, it was all to catch up with him and cost Laurens his life in an unnecessary skirmish after the British surrender at Yorktown.

Born in Charleston, South Carolina on October 28, 1754, Laurens was the son of Henry Laurens, a self made man and at that time, one of the richest, if not the richest, men in the colony. At first taught by private tutors, young Laurens was taken to England by his father for the next phase of his education and from there to Geneva, Switzerland in 1774 where he was taught such varied subjects as classical and modern languages, physics and mathematics, philosophy, and law. In addition, he was also taught fencing and riding. Remaining in Geneva the next two years, he eventually traveled back to England where he completed his study of the law at the Middle Temple. It was while on this second stay in England that Laurens displayed some of the impetuosity that would lead to his untimely death years later. He met and secretly wed Martha Manning in a ritual he characterized at the time as a "clandestine celebration," revealing the union to the girl's parents only when her pregnancy forced the issue. The timing of the event was unfortunate in that it occurred just as the outbreak of hostilities between Britain and America was taking place in faraway Massachusetts, a clarion call that the hot blooded Laurens was unable to resist. Leaving his new bride in France, Laurens set sail for America, never to see his wife and child again.

Back in South Carolina, Laurens met with his father who had, in the meantime, been appointed as a delegate to the Continental Congress. Together, father and son then traveled to Philadelphia where Laurens' connections soon gained him a position as aide de camp to George Washington who had been named as commander in chief of the newly created Continental Army. Laurens' intelligence, openness, and energy made him a popular member of the general's "family" and best friend to an equally youthful Alexander Hamilton who, instead of resenting him as a rival, hero worshipped the older and more accomplished man and embraced him as a friend. And although both young men yearned for glory on the

John Laurens

battlefield, it was Laurens who managed to see the most action at places like Brandywine and Germantown where the southerner was slightly wounded while trying to set fire to a fortified mansion called the Chew House within which the enemy had holed up. Laurens also commanded infantry in the failed Rhode Island campaign in the summer of 1778.

Following the battle of Monmouth, where Gen. Charles Lee was found guilty of bad judgment rather than cowardice in his questionable decision to retreat at a crucial point in the fight, Laurens managed to become personally involved in the controversy. After his court martial, Lee published a tract that accused Washington himself of incompetence; a dueling offence if ever there was one. Washington however, felt that as commander in chief of the army, it was improper for him to reply and after refusing a challenge from Gen. Friedrich von Steuben, Lee accepted one from Laurens who had been on the field with him at Monmouth and had tried unsuccessfully to convince his superior not to retreat in the face of the enemy. The two men met again late in 1778 this time on the field of honor with the result that Lee was wounded in the exchange of shots and an agreement reached to carry the affair no further. Significantly, acting as Laurens' second, the action would be Hamilton's first experience with dueling but not his last.

As the war quieted down around New York and fearing that it would soon move south, Laurens conceived the idea of creating military units comprised entirely of black slaves who would serve in return for their freedom. It was Laurens' contention that blacks would fight out of the same republican ideals as whites. Congress approved of the notion and promoting the young man to lieutenant colonel, dispatched him to his native state to put the idea into action. Once again in South Carolina, Laurens was elected to the state's legislature in 1779 and it was there that he formally introduced his concept of an all black regiment not once, but several times. Unfortunately, the idea proved too extreme for his fellow politicians and each time it was rejected overwhelmingly. In the meantime, the war continued and was soon to be visited upon the southern states with full force.

The same year Laurens had arrived in Charleston and had been elected to the legislature, the city was threatened with attack by British Gen. Augustine Prevost who marched an army up from Savannah, Georgia, which was captured in December of 1778. With South Carolina's capital also threatened with capture and many of its leaders fearful of a general slave uprising, Governor John Rutledge proposed that the state remain neutral in the war in exchange for remaining unmolested by the enemy. Outraged, Laurens opposed any such deal and the timely approach of an American force under the command of Gen.

Benjamin Lincoln forced the enemy to retreat back to Georgia. Later, Laurens marched south at the head of an infantry column to join Lincoln in an attempt to recapture Savannah. But a plan to assault the city on October 9, 1779 with help from a French war fleet failed when the British were reinforced at the last minute. Laurens himself had taken part in the initial charge but his regiment reached no farther than a ditch along the enemy's defensive line whose opposite side could not be scaled without ladders. As a result, the attack disintegrated into confusion and it was all Laurens could do to lead his men out of the trap.

With the failure at Savannah, Laurens returned to South Carolina where he took part in the defense of Charleston after the British launched a second assault upon the city in the spring of 1780. Despite the efforts of its defenders, the fatal decision on the part of Lincoln to concentrate his army within the city led to its being completely surrounded by a numerically superior enemy of 10,000. In the end, the city and its 5,000 defenders, including Laurens, surrendered. When Laurens was eventually released in a prisoner exchange, Congress appointed him as a special minister to France on the strength of his many years experience while living on the Continent. Although his mission was a success, winning loans from the Netherlands and military supplies and assurance from France that its armed forces would soon return to join those of the United States, any satisfaction that he might have gained from it was mitigated by the knowledge that his father, captured by the British after the conclusion of a similar diplomatic mission to Europe, was languishing as a prisoner in the infamous Tower of London.

His revolutionary spirit undaunted, Laurens returned to the United States in 1781 just in time to rejoin Washington for the Battle of Yorktown. In command of one of several battalions charged with assaulting a pair of enemy redoubts outside the city, Laurens was present as his friend, Alexander Hamilton, finally saw action when he led a successful charge against one of the two outlying bastions. Later, Laurens had the honor of representing Washington in the negotiations that led to the surrender of the British army. But despite the momentous defeat of Lord Cornwallis at Yorktown and a tacit acknowledgment by British forces elsewhere in the country that the war was virtually over, the enemy continued to move about in places, probing and scouting. It was to counter these activities that Laurens, under the command of Gen. Nathanael Greene, ran a spy network outside Charleston to keep an eye on British troop movements around the city. On August 27, 1782, Laurens' men ran into one of these enemy patrols along the Combahee River foraging for supplies. Instead of keeping a discreet distance, Laurens joined his men in confronting the enemy. Known later as the battle of Chehaw Neck, the fight was actually nothing more than a skirmish that need not have happened. Nevertheless, one thing led to another, shots were fired, and when the smoke cleared, a ball had found its target in the 28 year old Laurens who fell from his saddle dead.

Arthur Lee

Due to his involvement with the Silas Deane affair, history has not treated Arthur Lee kindly in the course of his career as a revolutionary, relegating him to the status of a lesser light in the pantheon of Founding Fathers. The anonymity of Arthur and his brother William was compounded by the fact that much of what they did for their country took place out of the public spotlight. Unusual not only among their fellow patriots but Americans in general, the two brothers held promising positions in England itself, even entering politics there, and although Arthur was eloquent in his call for American liberty in many pseudonymous letters published in the English press, his efforts failed to bring him much notice with a wider public back home. His writings however, did draw the attention of those in Congress who appointed he and William as spies of sorts to relay any information on the mood and temper of the British people and their Parliament. In addition, living as virtual Englishmen in Britain, when the two brothers made secret contact with the French to acquire supplies for the war effort, they risked their lives as potential traitors.

Along with his older brothers, Richard Henry, Francis Lightfoot, and William, Arthur Lee was born at the family's Stratford estate in Westmoreland County, Virginia on December 20, 1740. Also like his brothers, after beginning his education at home, he was sent to England to complete it, attending Eton College and later the University of Edinburgh in Scotland where he graduated in 1765 as a physician. After a brief visit home, Lee returned to London at first to practice medicine but later switched gears and chose to study law at the Temple.

Graduating in 1770, Lee had already begun to practice the law when he accepted a commission from the colony of Massachusetts as its representative in London and it was perhaps this association that sharpened his awareness of Parliament's ill treatment of his fellow Americans. It was in these years leading up to America's break with England in 1776 that Lee embarked on a literary career concentrating on defending the colonies' position against the series of unpopular measures taken by Parliament that opponents claimed had been approved without the consent of those who would be directly effected. In scores of letters and tracts, including his most well known entitled *An Appeal to the English Nation* published in 1774, Lee established for himself a reputation as a patriot across the Continent and inspired sympathy for the American cause in many quarters. At the same time, in correspondence with Samuel Adams, he grew increasingly paranoid about the trustworthiness of those around him, an attitude that would later prove injurious to American efforts to gain recognition in Europe.

In 1775, amid rising tensions in the British capitol, Lee was appointed by Congress as its special agent in England and charged with gathering information on the thinking of local politicians and the mood of the public. More personally perilous was his contact with French secret agent and sometime playwright Pierre Augustin Caron de Beaumarchais who had become enthusiastic about supporting the Revolution. Aware of French desires to deprive Britain of its American colonies, Beaumarchais arranged for the secret

Arthur Lee

transfer of war materiel from France through a dummy corporation called Rodrique Hortalez et Compagnie. The scheme prompted the Congressional Committee of Secret Correspondence to send Silas Deane under cover to France as a typical businessman to arrange the purchase of more supplies and recruit European military talent for the Continental Army. Unfortunately, Deane's authority to do business with Beaumarchais inflamed Lee's jealousy. Soon after, a resentful Lee began to insist that the supplies he had initially been promised from the French were to be had for free and that charges subsequently billed by Hortalez et Compagnie were simply meant to line the pockets of Deane and Beaumarchais, claims the Virginian would later use to discredit Deane.

In the meantime however, the success of these ventures resulted in Lee's subsequent appointment by Congress as a commissioner to France along with Deane and Benjamin Franklin. Thus, soon after hostilities had begun between Britain and her American colonies at Lexington and Concord, Lee was at Versailles working to convince the French government to support the Revolution with money and supplies. Although Lee's later failure to gain public recognition for the infant United States from Spain and the Germanies can be partially blamed on their unwillingness to do so ahead of France, other reasons could have included the American's increasingly boorish behavior that Franklin described as "suspicious, malignant, and quarrelsome." After meeting him, John Adams had to admit that Lee could not "govern his temper" and "had notions of elegance, rank, and dignity that may be carried rather too far." In correspondence to French Foreign Minister Charles Vergennes, Beaumarchais characterized Lee's attitude as a combination of ambition and jealousy mixed with an unhealthy sympathy for Britain that he believed involved informing the enemy of the commission's activities.

With the British seemingly aware of the commission's every move, Lee's inability to get along with Deane and Franklin spilled over to his relations with the French court and complicated the team's efforts to gain aid and recognition for the United States. With his reputation called into question, Lee became embroiled in a struggle for professional and political credibility with his fellow commissioners, a struggle whose rancor eventually reached across the sea to Congress. A member of one of the most prominent families in Virginia and with influential friends in Congress that included his brother Richard Henry and Samuel Adams, Lee wasted no time in accusing both Franklin and Deane of profiteering. Franklin's reputation made the Pennsylvanian untouchable leaving Dean to face the brunt of the charges.

Recalled to America to respond to the accusations, Deane returned in style aboard a French battleship, token of the high esteem in which he was held by France. Characterized in a letter written to Congress by Franklin as "a faithful, active, and able minister," Deane nevertheless became embroiled in a long and nasty investigation that split the Congress and tied up its affairs for months. When the dust finally cleared, a shakeup of the country's diplomatic corps resulted in the loss of position for Arthur who decided to give up on diplomacy completely and return to Virginia in 1780.

At home again for the first time in over twenty years, it took little time for Lee, not only respected for his intellectual achievements and diplomatic career, but as a member of one of the most important families in the state, to find himself elected to the state's legislature where he served from 1782 to 1786. Concurrent with his time in the state house, Lee also served in Congress for two years where he was appointed Indian commissioner for New York and Pennsylvania before ending his public career as one of three members of the Board of Treasury that replaced Robert Morris in his capacity of Superintendent of Finance under the Articles of Confederation. Retiring to a life of study and correspondence, Lee died on December 12, 1792 at Landsdown, his home in Urbanna, Virginia.

Francis Lightfoot Lee

A middle son of one of Virginia's most famous, and seemingly most numerous, families, Lee was also the least flamboyant of the clan who hated anything to do with politics or even public life. And yet, the sense of honor and responsibility he felt as a leading member of his community prevented him from doing the thing he most wanted to do: remain at home seeking pleasure in reading, farming, and the company of his beloved wife. Yet, emerge from his idyllic country home he continued to do, as the rising tide of revolution made increasing demands on the services of men such as himself.

Francis Lightfoot Lee, known as Frank to friends and family, was born like his older brothers at Stratford Hall in Westmoreland County, Virginia on October 14, 1734. Unlike his brothers however, his father never sent him abroad for his education but instead, had him taught at home by a private tutor who nurtured in Lee a love of learning that would serve him in good stead over the years. Being rich, there was never any real need for Lee to be trained in any profession and so he never attended a college or university. Although he enjoyed the pleasures of life, Lee was more retiring than his brothers, preferring contemplation in a quiet library and talking over issues behind closed doors rather than in public debate. Those qualities however, did not prevent him from being chosen to head a local militia company after he had inherited Coton, an estate in Fairfax County which later became part of the newly created Loudoun County. In 1758, after he and his brother Philip Ludwell founded the town of Leesburg, he was elected to Virginia's House of Burgesses where he served for the next ten years. Finally, at the age of 39, Lee found love in 16 year old Rebecca Tayloe whom he married in 1769. The two were given 1,000 acres of land by Rebecca's father who also built them a home they called Menokin where Lee would spend the happiest years of his life.

Always a reluctant politician, Lee soon found himself drawn into the looming crisis with Britain after Parliament's attempts to tax the colonies were keenly felt by Virginia's tidewater community which relied on trade involving agricultural products sold in exchange for consumer goods brought from overseas. Compelled by economic forces and a keen awareness of his rights as an Englishman which he shared with friends Patrick Henry and Thomas Jefferson, Lee supported the Westmoreland Resolves that condemned the Stamp Act and threatened retaliation against any person who dared to be involved in its enforcement. Continuing his involvement with revolutionary activities, Lee joined others in calling for the Virginia Convention which, in 1774, chose him as a member of the colony's delegation to the First Continental Congress where his thoughtful manner and voting record that sometimes was at variance with that of his brother Richard Henry, left a favorable impression on peers such as John Adams.

Francis Lightfoot Lee

Returning to Congress in 1776, Lee helped write the Articles of Confederation and joined Richard Henry in voting for independence and then becoming a member of the elite group that signed the Declaration. Later, Lee was drawn into the dispute between his brothers William and Arthur and fellow diplomat Silas Deane that divided Congress for months and elicited from him an accusation that Deane's supporters represented a "very dangerous party who think it necessary to their designs, to remove all the old friends of Liberty and Independence."

Remaining in Congress until 1779, Lee finally decided to retire permanently from public life and return to Rebecca and Menokin. His time at home turned out to be shorter than he planned when he was chosen once again to represent Loudoun County in the new state's legislature. It was not until 1785 that Lee was able to leave office for good. Back at Menokin, he concentrated on managing his property, relaxing with his wife, and helping to raise the children of his younger brother William. Tragically, Lee, who was characterized by one of his nieces as being the "sweetest of all the Lee race," died of pleurisy on April 3, 1797 within a few days of the death of Rebecca, who died in the same manner.

Henry Lee III

A cousin of brothers Richard Henry and Francis Lightfoot, Henry Lee was a member of the numerous Lee clan and as the Revolutionary War proved, its most militarily accomplished. A natural horseman, Lee became a brilliant commander of cavalry but when the war concluded, found peacetime intolerable. He served in many important offices but complaints about his health seemed at least partially due to the sense of depression suffered by a man of action unable to adjust to a life of idleness. Never having completed the education that was to have taken him to England as it did his brothers, Lee lost a fortune and while in debtors' prison, wrote a history of the war's southern theater that for decades was considered definitive.

Henry Lee III was born at Leesylvania near Dumfries, Virginia on January 29, 1756. A lively, precocious child with distinctive blond hair and blue eyes, he was said to have learned to ride a horse by the age of 4 and, as an excellent judge of horseflesh, raising them by 12. Sent off to Princeton to complete the first part of his education, Lee graduated in 1773 but his naturally garrulous nature had already taken an interest in the growing political conflict that was brewing between Britain and its American colonies. As war clouds began to gather, Lee decided to forego the study of the law in England and to remain in Virginia. The storm broke in 1775 when fighting began in Massachusetts and an American army coalesced around British forces in Boston. Next, even as the Continental Congress appointed George Washington as commander in chief of the Continental Army, Lee was commissioned a captain in the Virginia cavalry.

In 1777, Lee's unit joined the 1st Continental Dragoons in Pennsylvania and in a number of sharp conflicts, Lee proved himself a competent and courageous soldier if an overly strict one. At one point, after recapturing a group of deserters and executing one out of every three, he decapitated another and paraded the severed head around his camp.

Henry Lee III

The incident brought him to the attention of Washington in a most uncomplimentary fashion but after receiving a written tonguelashing from the commander in chief, he was soon promoted to major and in 1778 commanded several units of combined cavalry and infantry on raids and spying missions behind enemy lines. In one of his more celebrated exploits, Lee proved his worth in a series of harassing movements that climaxed in the storming and capture of an enemy garrison at Paulus Hook, New Jersey on August 19, 1779. In that engagement, Lee commanded a unit of 400 men which he led through miles of mud and salt marshes in the dark of night with orders for complete silence. Arriving at the fort later than expected and fearing the rise of the tide, Lee divided his men into three columns and ordered an assault across an empty ditch and over a line of abatis. The operation was wildly successful with the Americans taking the enemy by surprise, killing 50 at bayonet point and capturing over 164 with the loss of only two men. The operation's success however, did not prevent Lee from being accused of incompetence during the operation. Cleared by a subsequent court martial, he was never completely able to wash away suspicions about the charges nor get over his later feelings of neglect and persecution in matters of promotion. Despite his resentments however, Lee was made lieutenant colonel following Paulus Hook and nicknamed "Light Horse" by his men. Later, he became a close friend of Washington's and, after being transferred to the southern department, also earned the affection of Gen. Nathanael Greene.

Working closely with Greene, Lee made himself indispensable as he continued the fast moving harassment tactics against British Gen. Charles Cornwallis in the Carolinas that he used with such success in the North. Over 1780 and 1781, his green coated Legion ranged across North and South Carolina where some of the most vicious and desperate fighting of the war took place not only with trained units of the British army, but also against smaller, loyalist militia who were often familiar with the swampy, forested countryside that provided plenty of opportunity for unobserved movements and ambush. At the Waxhaws, Guilford Courthouse, and Eutaw Springs, Lee's Legion was always in the thick of the action. Then, with Cornwallis' decision to take his army north to Virginia, Green made the tactical decision not to pursue and Lee advocated coordinated attacks on an isolated string of enemy outposts that stretched from the coast deep into the interior of South Carolina. With the plan approved, Lee's Legion joined forces with units commanded by Gen. Francis Marion and began to roll-up the garrisons from Ninety-Six to the outskirts of Charleston. But years of almost uninterrupted battle and seemingly endless skirmishing had placed such pressures on him, that even someone with Lee's temperament and constitution might reach a limit. And so, even though Lee said it was failing health that prompted him to resign his commission after Cornwallis surrendered at Yorktown, complaints of persecution, which he extended even to Greene, seemed to belie those claims.

Returning home, he married Matilda Lee, a cousin who had inherited her family's estate at Stratford Hall; but a life of idleness on a landed plantation soon palled for a man of Lee's temperament and after a while, he sought divertissement by plunging into the world of politics. In 1785 he was chosen to serve in the Continental Congress and after 1788 became a member of Virginia's legislature. In 1791 he was chosen as the state's governor and served in that position until 1794. But whatever joy the office might have given him was negated by the death of Matilda two years before leaving him to raise three small children. When his grief had eased, he met and married yet another heiress, Ann Hill Carter. He left the governor's office to command American forces that helped suppress the Whiskey Rebellion in western Pennsylvania, a task he completed without the loss of life on either side. In the fight to ratify the Constitution, he opposed his powerful cousin Richard Henry Lee in its support and was rewarded with a seat in the House of Representatives from 1799-1801. Finally, with George Washington's death in 1799, Lee was called upon to give a tribute to his old friend describing him famously as being "first in war, first in peace, and first in the hearts of his countrymen."

But seemingly at the height of his success, Lee was brought up short and soon after the conclusion of his congressional career, profligate spending and unwise real estate investments caught up with him, wiping out his fortune. Then, shortly before he was arrested and placed in debtors' prison, on January 19, 1807, Ann presented him with the last of their five children whom the couple named Robert Edward Lee. Whatever happiness Lee may have felt in the birth of his son, was mitigated by his time in prison that he nevertheless used constructively to write his *Memoirs of the War in the Southern Department of the United States* which was published in 1812. Released from prison, Lee discovered that an inheritance from Ann's father enabled the family to move to Alexandria where it could live in some comfort. Things seemed to be looking up for Lee when he was offered a commission to serve as a major general for the coming War of 1812. Unfortunately, failing health aggravated by a beating he received at the hands of an angry Baltimore mob after defending a friend in the name of freedom of the press forced him to turn the offer down in favor of seeking a more healing climate in the West Indies. But the change of scene failed to improve his condition and after a few years, Lee decided to return home. He never completed the journey, dying on March 25, 1818 at the Cumberland Island, Georgia home of the daughter of his friend Nathaneal Greene.

Richard Henry Lee

In contrast with the pace at which various patriots such as Gouverneur Morris or John Adams were radicalized or the hesitant John

Dickinson, who pushed the envelope of defiance before the war but who stopped short of the ultimate step of declaring independence from Britain after hostilities had begun, some revolutionaries seemed to breath fire from the very beginning. One such man was Richard Henry Lee who, either because of a liberal education or simple ambition or both, was prepared to take serious action against the mother country as early as the Stamp Act crisis when he threatened violence against royal officials. But even if there had not been an American Revolution, Lee would no doubt have still been unable to control his rebellious spirit or his need to be recognized as a man of importance. Tall and aristocratic with a gift for eloquence, the earliest impression he made as a public figure was as an office seeker but a speech he gave in the Virginia House of Burgesses urging the abolition of slavery showed that there was more to him than a seeker after opportunity.

Richard Henry Lee

Richard Henry Lee was born to wealth on January 20, 1732 at his family's Stratford Hall home located in Westmoreland County, Virginia. Lee's early life followed the typical pattern of the colony's landed class being taught by tutors at home before being sent off to Wakefield Academy in England to complete his education. Returning home in 1751, he was caught up in the fervor of the impending French and Indian War and took the lead in recruiting local youths to form a brigade of volunteers to join the army of Gen. Edward Braddock as it prepared to move against Fort Duquesne. Arriving at Braddock's encampment however, Lee and his volunteers were turned away. At loose ends, Lee drifted into the law and in 1757 was appointed as Justice of the Peace and then elected to the House of Burgesses, the colony's legislature. At first unsure and reluctant to speak yet at the same time yearning to make a mark for himself, Lee was finally moved to make his first big public speech on the issue of slavery. After introducing a bill that, if passed, would have placed such heavy fees on the importation of slaves as to discourage the trade, he rose in its defense declaring that Africans were "equally entitled to liberty and freedom by the great law of nature." This radical position was followed by demands for increased religious freedom and awarding more residents the vote. By the time Britain had begun its attempts to tax its American colonies for the cost of the French and Indian War as well the continuing expense of patrolling the frontier, Lee had begun to gain a reputation for radicalism that was confirmed during the Stamp Act crisis of 1765.

After a brief flirtation with becoming a stamp collector himself, Lee came to his senses and in association with Patrick Henry, helped to draw up the Westmoreland Resolves that vowed retaliation against anyone cooperating with the crown to collect or even pay the hated stamp tax. Lee proved his earnestness after he led an armed band to the home of a stamp agent and threatened him with bodily harm if he refused to give up his appointment. The man's cooperation having been acquired, the patriot posse then proceeded to destroy the agent's stamped papers in a bonfire. Later, Lee was censured by the royal governor and met with his fellow legislators at Williamsburg's Raleigh Tavern in defiance of an order dismissing the House of Burgesses.

Cementing his reputation with Virginia's royal authority as an agitator, Lee, aided by a number of family members, threw himself into the revolutionary cause with a will protesting the Townshend Acts to Parliament in 1767 and suggesting to local patriots, as Samuel Adams was doing in New England, that they establish Committees of Correspondence to share information among themselves. Soon, Lee had proposed the idea to correspondents in other colonies hoping to promote cooperation on matters of mutual interest especially in relation to Britain's continuing efforts to enact upon them what many saw as unjust laws. That inter-colonial effort bore fruit when in 1774 Lee, along with Patrick Henry, Peyton Randolph, and George Washington, was chosen as a member of Virginia's delegation to the First Continental Congress and discovered that he and the Adams' cousins John and Samuel, were on the same wavelength in regards to declaring independence from Britain. Seeing however, that the mood of many of their fellow delegates was still tentative, they agreed to dampen their calls for separation and back a final attempt at reconciliation with the mother country.

Lee was returned to Congress in 1776 with instructions to seek independence from Britain and found the attitude of most delegates had changed considerably since hostilities had broken out at Lexington and

Concord and the crown had firmly rejected the olive branch America had extended the year before. Throwing himself into a vigorous round of committee work, Lee not only drew up the orders under which Washington was to assume command of the Continental Army, but was given the task of writing a draft declaration of rights and independence which was used as the basis of the actual Declaration of Independence. On June 7, 1776, Lee submitted his draft declaration and, gesturing with a hand wrapped in a handkerchief to hide missing fingers lost as the result of a hunting accident, motioned that Congress pronounce independence from Britain declaring "that these united colonies are, and of right ought to be, free and independent states; and that all political connection between them and the state of Great Britain is, and ought to be, totally dissolved." The motion, which also included resolutions to enter foreign alliances and to form a confederation of the thirteen states, was seconded by his friend John Adams who then took on the bulk of its defense in debate after Lee was forced to return to Virginia to tend his ailing wife and help draft a state constitution. Eventually, the motion was tabled for three weeks and in the meantime, fellow Virginian Thomas Jefferson took Lee's place in committee and rewrote his initial draft document into what would become the Declaration of Independence. Accepted by Congress on July 2, it was ratified on July 4, 1776 with Lee as one of its signers.

Following independence, Lee worked even harder on scores of congressional committees and over the course of nearly four years succeeded in ruining his health. Retreating to Virginia to recoup, he resumed active participation in the state's legislature. With the state's finances in near collapse due to the ravages of raiding British armies and its responsibilities toward the war effort, Lee immersed himself in money matters involving the depreciation of paper currency, the public debt, and the repudiation of private debts owed to British merchants that he opposed. Largely successful in helping to restore fiscal stability to Virginia, Lee was chosen by Congress in 1784 to act as its president under the Articles of Confederation. Thus Lee returned to the national scene and eventually left office after a busy year that saw him establish many of the mechanisms and duties expected of a central government; mechanisms that would provide George Washington the foundation upon which to build a new federal system when he became the first chief executive to serve under the United States Constitution.

Back in Congress again, Lee was present in 1787 when the Constitutional Convention that had met in Philadelphia the same year, submitted the result of its deliberations for approval. Despite his earlier role in the creation of the Articles of Confederation, Lee was fearful of the tendency of any government to draw power to itself and expressed wariness at the federal scheme as embodied by the Constitution. As a result, he fought hard to keep Congress from ratifying the plan while at the same time calling for a Bill of Rights and other amendments designed to weaken its power over the people. Like many of his fellow patriots who had risked everything to defy what they believed to be an oppressive tyranny, Lee was wary of any system that might replace that tyranny with another. In the end, he decided not to stand in the way of a decision by Congress simply to defer approval of the Constitution to the individual states. In the debates that followed, he joined other prominent revolutionaries such as Samuel Adams and Patrick Henry in opposition to the proposed scheme of government and in his *Letters of the Federal Farmer*, echoed many of the suggestions made by John Adams in his 1776 tract *Thoughts on Government* (whose publication costs Lee had covered) and called again for the addition of a Bill of Rights to the document. After the Constitution had been ratified and a new federal system of government established, Lee was elected as one of Virginia's first senators and immediately sponsored another amendment to the Constitution guaranteeing that all "powers not delegated to the United States by the Constitution, nor prohibited by it to the States, are reserved to the States respectively, or to the people." By the time creeping infirmity forced Lee to retire permanently from the Virginia legislature in 1788 and from Congress in 1792, he had come to accept the Constitution and when he died on his estate at Chantilly on June 19, 1794, his sympathies rested with Washington's administration at a time of rising anti-federalist feeling.

William Lee

The next to youngest of the numerous Lee clan of Virginia, William was in many ways the most remarkable. At a time of rising tensions between Britain and America, Lee managed not only to ingratiate himself with England's merchant class, but was popular enough to become the second American to hold the office of Sheriff of London and the first to become a city alderman. But William, along with his brother Arthur, soon became involved in intrigues against the British and after they were appointed by Congress as diplomats to France, the enemy's spies followed them. More than at any other time or place during the Revolutionary War, the diplomatic front in Europe became a hotbed of espionage activity with secret agents from the much more sophisticated French and English moving like sharks among the less experienced Americans. The whole situation finally became so confusing, that the American mission collapsed in a tangle of mutual suspi-

Signing of the Treaty of Paris

cion and accusation that ended both William and Arthur's careers as diplomats and prompted a complete overhaul of America's diplomatic efforts overseas.

Like his brothers, Richard Henry, Francis Lightfoot, and Arthur, William was born at the family estate of Stratford in Westmoreland County, Virginia on August 13, 1739. Receiving his early education at home, Lee traveled to England in 1768 where he concentrated on business, entering the mercantile trade. It was perhaps a tribute to his open personality and winning ways that he soon ingratiated himself upon the people there and rose high in the estimation of many. In fact, such was his reputation that he was often considered more of an Englishman than an American and when his interests turned to politics, his outspoken opinions did his reputation little harm.

Being in business, Lee, like many of his fellow merchants, was aware of the regressive effect taxes had on trade and the uproar in

America over Parliament's various attempts to coerce the colonists into paying a range of new taxes pushed Lee into the Revolutionary camp. Speaking out against the tax measures, Lee's efforts urging the mercantile community to press their representatives in Parliament to repeal them paid off when all but the tax on tea were taken back. Parliament's repeal of the tax measures proved that the government's bellicosity toward the colonies was not monolithic and that a significant portion of the public was sympathetic toward the colonies. In 1773, Lee was chosen for the position of Sheriff of London and in 1775, the same year that hostilities opened between Britain and America at Lexington and Concord, he was elected a city alderman. The combination of his political positions as well as his favor among the business community and the public placed Lee in a very favorable position to help the revolutionary cause and together with his brother Arthur, who was a respected attorney and physician, became an important conduit to Congress for information regarding the mood of the English people and the plans of their government.

From that point, William and Arthur became de facto spies for the United States and began to hold clandestine meetings with those whom they thought could help their country. During these intrigues, which the brothers took on at the risk of their lives, Arthur met with French secret agent Pierre Augustin Caron de Beaumarchais to arrange for the acquisition of military supplies from France through a dummy corporation called Rorique, Hortalez et Compagnie.

In 1776, the year the thirteen colonies declared their independence from England, William accompanied his brother to France after Arthur had been named as one member of a three man diplomatic mission that also included Benjamin Franklin and Silas Deane. Their move to France however, was not made alone as a number of British secret agents followed them there and over the next few years, insinuated themselves in and out of the lives of the various commissioners. While Lee was aware of espionage attempts against the American mission and tried to warn Congress that the British were relying more on the money being spent on spies than soldiers to win the war, he himself was duped by American loyalist turned British secret agent Paul Wentworth who called upon the Virginian's residence in France and, finding him absent, took a calling card for later forging.

In 1777, William was appointed an official commercial agent to French ports for the Continental Congress and later was instructed to represent the United States in Germany and Austria. In that capacity, he journeyed to Holland, at the time, one of the world's great trading powers, and met with Jan de Neufville, on the surface merely an Amsterdam businessman, but actually an informal representative of the Hague. Through Neufville and Amsterdam pensionary Mynheer Van Berckel, William negotiated a tentative agreement calling for the Netherlands to lend the United States $10 million. The deal, however, came to nothing when Henry Laurens, who had been commissioned by Congress to finalize the agreement, was captured on the high seas and his papers seized. Laurens spent almost two years in the Tower of London and Holland found itself at war with England when it refused to reprimand Van Berckel.

The balance of William's diplomatic career was dominated by the feud between Arthur and Silas Deane over accusations of profiteering. The affair ended only after it had bitterly divided Congress and the diplomatic corps was reformed. When the dust cleared, William and Arthur found themselves without positions and the two men returned to Virginia. Although Arthur began a political career in the Virginia legislature and later in Congress, William married but died soon after on June 27, 1795.

Francis Lewis

One of those who suffered dearly for daring to sign the Declaration of Independence, was businessman Francis Lewis who lost not only a fortune during the Revolutionary War, but also his home and his wife.

Born in Landaff, Wales on March 21, 1713, Lewis experienced adversity early on in his life when his parents died and he was given into the care of relatives. Luckily, they were fairly well to do and saw to it that their nephew received a solid education first in Scotland and then at the Westminster School in London. When his school years ended, Lewis took work with a London based mercantile house for practical business experience. Thus, by the time he turned twenty-one and inherited a bit of money and land left to him by his father, he knew what to do. Converting the inheritance into cash, he invested the money in assorted merchandise and sailed for the American colonies where he had already made contact with his future business partner, Edward Annesly. Arriving in New York in 1735, Lewis did not stay long in that city, leaving some of his merchandise in the hands of Annesly and taking the rest with him to Philadelphia. A few years later, he returned to New York, invested his profits in shipping, and married Elizabeth Annesly, his partner's sister. As his business grew and he became more affluent, Lewis began accompanying his ships overseas, traveling to Europe and suffering shipwreck a couple of times. By the time the French and Indian War broke out in 1755, he had already managed to secure a contract to supply clothing for the British army and was acting as a mercantile agent under Col. Hugh Mercer when Fort Oswego fell to the French the following year. It was then that Lewis underwent perhaps the most harrowing experience of his life when, following the surrender, he escaped death after Indians burst into the building where the British were being held prisoner and slaughtered over 100 of the disarmed men before a furious French commander could stop them. When the carnage ended, Lewis was taken to Montreal with other surviving prisoners and eventually shipped off to France from where he was finally released in a prisoner exchange.

By the time Lewis returned home, his wartime contracts and the gift of 5,000 acres of land by the colonial legislature in recognition of his services had made him a rich man and he decided to retire from business. But retirement to his estate in Whitestone, New York did not mean a complete retreat from the affairs of the world. When Parliament began its efforts to impose new taxes on its American colonies following the war, it was felt most keenly by the business community and in growing resentment of British tactics, Lewis was increasingly radicalized and became an early member of the local Sons of Liberty. In 1765, the same year as his retirement, Lewis made his first foray into the public arena when he

Francis Lewis

was chosen as a representative to the Stamp Act Congress and later to the colony's provincial congress. Impressed by his performance there, residents chose him in 1776 to represent them again, this time as a member of New York's delegation to the Second Continental Congress. It was there that Lewis would take the action that would change the course of his life.

At first willing to work for reconciliation with Britain, with the failure of the olive branch petition in 1775, Lewis became convinced that there was more to gain by separating from the mother country than by remaining under its rule. Unfortunately, he had to wait for the rest of New York to catch up with his thinking and without instruction from home was unable to vote for independence or for approval of the Declaration of Independence when the time came. But his conviction on the issue was such that when the decision back home was finally made to embrace independence, he had no trouble signing the Declaration at a later date.

Fearful that becoming a known outlaw could mean serious repercussions, Lewis moved his family from their residence in New York City to Whitestone on Long Island. That move, however, proved futile as the British forced the Continental Army out of lower New York and occupied Manhattan as well as Long Island. Seizing Whitestone, they captured Elizabeth and imprisoned her under harsh conditions for months while leaving the estate a ruin. Sad though the fate of his home had been, sadder still was Elizabeth's death soon after her release from imprisonment as well as that of a son who had also been captured by the enemy. Although Lewis managed the twin losses and served briefly as a member of the board of admiralty in 1779, he never completely recovered from the blow to his finances that the war had cost him and even the date of his death has been in question with December 19 and 30, 1803 as well as December 31, 1802 given as the date.

Morgan Lewis

Born to a wealthy family and the son of a signer of the Declaration of Independence, Morgan Lewis nevertheless began his public career from the bottom, or pretty close to it, when he volunteered in a militia regiment helping lay siege to Boston in the months following the battle of Breeds Hill. And although his own intelligence and later service as an officer in the Continental Army would no doubt have gained him entrance to New York's political scene, having married a daughter of one of the state's most powerful and influential families did not hurt.

Lewis was born in New York City on the eve of the French and Indian War on October 16, 1754 just before his father, Francis Lewis, left for the frontier and later captured by the enemy. Receiving his early education at home, Lewis enrolled at Princeton University at first to prepare himself for the clergy but later, upon the advice of his father, for the law. Graduating from college in 1773, Lewis had just begun his legal studies when the long simmering resentments in the American colonies against Britain began to boil over. Then, before he could complete his education and appear before the bar, open war broke out in Massachusetts.

Giving up the pen for the musket, Lewis volunteered with a local militia unit and marched off to help in the siege of Boston. Elected captain of his regiment, he was later commissioned a major when the unit was absorbed into the newly created Continental Army. Perhaps because of some experience he might have earned through his father's mercantile business, Lewis was promoted and eventually transferred to the command of Gen. Horatio Gates as quartermaster for the northern army and was on hand in 1776 when the invading forces of British Gen. John Burgoyne were defeated at the battle of Saratoga. Following Burgoyne's capture, Lewis found himself in command at the ill fated battle of Stone Arabia in 1778 and its more successful followup at Klock's Field where he faced off against former British Indian agent Sir John Johnson and the notorious Joseph Brant. Later, Lewis saw action at the battle of Crown Point.

Morgan Lewis

Following the war, Lewis picked up where he left off in his legal studies and finally passed the bar in 1783. Related to the powerful Livingston family by marriage, he acquired his first taste of politics when he ran for and won a seat in New York's legislature and in 1791 became the state's attorney general. The next year, he was appointed chief justice of New York's supreme court presiding over a number of cases in which he came down against Alexander Hamilton, who, as leader of the Federalist party was one of the most influential men in the country. Finally, in 1804, Lewis was drafted to run against Aaron Burr for governor in a heated contest that Hamilton had been sure he would lose. But although Lewis lost the vote in New York City, he proved the favorite with the rest of the state and was swept handily into office where he made public education and beefing up the state's militia two of his most important concerns. Later that same year, after Burr had killed Hamilton in a duel at Weehauken, New Jersey, Lewis was pressed against his will by the vice president's political enemies to demand his arrest for murder and return to New York for trial.

Lewis happily divided his time between his duties as governor and farming at his Dutchess County estate until 1812 when President James Madison tried to lure him to Washington with an appointment as Secretary of War. Although Lewis turned down the offer, he came out of retirement to serve as a general in the army after hostilities broke out for the second time against Britain in the War of 1812. As quartermaster general, Lewis commanded in upstate New York, participating in a number of engagements including the capture of Fort George, Sacket's Harbor, and French Creek. Those engagements however, came in the face of operations by the United States along the Canadian border that proved mostly dismal in planning and execution.

After the war, Lewis added luster to his record by refusing to collect rent from tenants living on his land who had had family members serve in the army. As he aged, Lewis helped found New York University and spent more time on family affairs and membership in civic groups such as the Order of the Cincinnati for which he served as president and once gave a well remembered speech on the occasion of the one hundredth birthday of George Washington. Lewis died where he was born and raised, in New York City on April 7, 1844.

Benjamin Lincoln

At times during the Revolutionary years, it often seemed as if the right men were in just the right places at the right times. Furthermore, they seemed to appear with either exactly the proper experience or were able to rise to whatever the occasion demanded. Men such as George Washington, Henry Knox, Alexander Hamilton, John Stark, William Prescott, George Rogers Clark and even Benedict Arnold all filled that bill in one way or another, others however, who likewise found themselves in the right place at the right time, were never able to completely transcend their inauspicious beginnings and rise to greatness. Such was the case with Benjamin Lincoln, who, when war came, found himself an officer in the local militia just as a Continental Army began to coalesce around Boston. Drawn into the highest ranks of officers surrounding George Washington, he proved to be loyal and steadfast and a patriot with a good deal of common sense. Assigned to one of the most difficult commands of the war, his ultimate failure there did little to damage the high regard in which he, a New Englander, was held by the southerners he commanded.

Born on January 24, 1733 on a farm in Hingham, Massachusetts, Benjamin Lincoln began life as unprepossessingly as that of his later career as soldier and civic leader. Like most boys in colonial Massachusetts, he received only a basic education before going to work on the family farm. He had his first taste of public life when he followed his grandfather

Benjamin Lincoln

and father as the town's clerk and later as a militiaman. But ensconced as he was in his rural community, he could not remain isolated from the winds of discontent that swept through the colony in the 1760s and 1770s as Parliament attempted to impose its will on England's American possessions. He became a member of Hingham's Committee of Safety and adjutant of the 3rd Regiment of the Suffolk militia and by 1772, perhaps because of his proven fervor for the patriot cause, eventually its lieutenant colonel. After purging his militia unit's leadership of loyalist sympathizers, he became a member of the Massachusetts Provincial Congress and later, its president. It was in 1775 that he first met George Washington when the newly appointed commander in chief arrived in the vicinity of Boston to take charge of the thousands of militia units that ringed the city, trapping its garrison of British troops inside. Early the next year, with a strong recommendation from Washington, Lincoln was promoted to brigadier general and given command of the Massachusetts militia outside Boston.

After the British abandoned Boston, Lincoln accompanied his troops to New York, where the enemy was widely expected to strike next. In the subsequent battles for Long Island and Manhattan, Lincoln performed well and in October 1776, commanded the crucial right wing of the army at White Plains. In January of 1777, he joined in the siege of Fort Independence where he commanded one of three wings under fellow Massachusetts resident Major Gen. William Heath. It fell to Lincoln to approach the fort to demand its surrender, a demand that Heath apparently had no intention of enforcing. Lincoln's challenge was met with defiance and a subsequent sally from the fort saw the American besiegers scattered by a numerically inferior enemy force. Weeks later, as the weather turned nasty, Heath ordered the siege lifted, such as it was, and withdrew his army.

Although Heath's actions drew sharp criticism from Washington and the general was never again given a direct combat command, no dishonor was accrued to Lincoln. In fact, the next month he was himself promoted by Congress to major general and after spending the winter encamped in Pennsylvania with the rest of the army, was ordered to take command of an outpost at Bound Brook, New Jersey only a few miles up the Raritan River from the nearest British garrison. Provoked at the proximity of the American position, British General Charles Cornwallis advanced with 2,000 men almost as soon as the weather turned in April 1777. Heavily outnumbered, and taken by surprise when Cornwallis was able to cross the river unopposed, Lincoln managed to save his army from being surrounded until it could be reinforced by fellow general Nathanael Greene.

Popular among his men, Lincoln was sent back to Massachusetts to help recruit militia forces for fighting in New York where British General John Burgoyne was descending the Hudson with an army of 10,000. After capturing Fort Ticonderoga from the Americans on July 5, Burgoyne, in need of supplies, detached portions of his army to forage eastward into Vermont where Lincoln was headquartered. Swarmed by thousands of militiamen, the enemy detachments were stopped hard by Col. Seth Warner at Hubbardton and soundly defeated by Gen. John Stark at Bennington. Arriving on the scene too late to help, Lincoln ordered his army out to sever the northern supply route from Canada to Burgoyne's army. With the defeat of a separate army under Col. Barry St. Leger at Fort Stanwix and the failure of fellow Gen. William Howe to march up the Hudson River to his support, a weakened Burgoyne fell back to a place called Freeman's Farm near Saratoga Springs, New York. Joining an army under Gen. Horatio Gates at Saratoga, Lincoln once again led the right wing on the first day of battle when the two armies met and supported Gen. Benedict Arnold in his estimate of the developing battle. The next night, while leading a patrol to feel out the enemy lines, Lincoln was shot in the ankle when he came upon an enemy column in the dark. Taken back to Albany to recover from his wound, Lincoln missed Burgoyne's surrender on October 17, 1777 but was compensated by Washington, along with Arnold, with the gift of a set of epaulets and sword-knots for his heroics.

Returning to Washington later that summer, the time had come at last for Lincoln to be given his first truly independent command. It was his misfortune however, to be assigned the southern theater, a command that in time, would prove to be a graveyard of military reputations. Formally taking command of the theater on September 25, 1778, Lincoln reached Charleston, South Carolina on December 4, barely a month before the fall of Savannah, Georgia to the enemy. With a combined force of about 3,600 Continentals and militia units weakened by hunger and sickness from the sultry climate, harassed by local Tory units, and with little help from local governments, Lincoln nevertheless managed to throw up a ragged line of defense south of Charleston in expectation of a drive northward by the victorious British. His fears were confirmed when an enemy column did finally cross the state line from Georgia but it was rebuffed at Beaufort by a force under the command of Brig. Gen. William Moultrie on February 2, 1779. A second victory against a band of Tory militiamen at Kettle Creek helped local recruitment and, thus strengthened, Lincoln moved south in an attempt to retake Georgia. At first, the campaign met with success as the Americans captured Augusta from the enemy and won a few other battles but then, after suffering a defeat at Briar Creek on March 3 that cost a third of the army's manpower, the advance stalled. As the British pressed forward again, Lincoln, fearful of being outflanked, decided to fall back into South Carolina to protect Charleston. After the enemy failed to continue the pursuit, Lincoln moved south again, attempting to cut off enemy supply routes to the west. In the meantime, British Col. Mark Prevost bypassed him and headed for Charleston. It was a very near thing as the state's governor ordered a parley with the invaders offering them the state's neutrality in return for sparing the city. Luckily, Lincoln returned with his army just in time to prevent such talk from going any farther. Then, in September, Lincoln heard that a French fleet under Admiral Charles d'Estaing had arrived off the coast of Georgia and marched immediately to Savannah to join him. Though he protested a demand by the admiral for the surrender of the city in the name of the French king, he joined him in an attack on the city. Unfortunately, the assault was given away and in the ensuing battle, d'Estaing was wounded twice and the force of the allied attack dwindled away. Some ten days later, fearful of a change in the weather, d'Estaing reembarked his troops and sailed away.

Back in South Carolina again, Lincoln, fearful that they would try to surrender the state again, acceded to the request of local politicians not to abandon Charleston to an invading force of over 10,000 soldiers led by British Lt. Gen. Henry Clinton who appeared with a fleet in the city's harbor area in February, 1780. Unlike Moultrie's successful defense of the same harbor in 1776, this time the entrances were given up with little resistance and the enemy was able to bottle Lincoln and his army of 5,000 men in the city after cutting off the neck of land leading to the mainland. After barely a month of siege, Lincoln was forced to bow to the inevitable and on May 12, 1780, presided over the surrender of the single largest American force of the war.

Following his capture, Lincoln was paroled and on his way back to Hingham, stopped in Philadelphia to demand a court martial to clear his reputation after the surrender of Charleston. The hearing was never held and no blame was ever officially laid on Lincoln for the disaster. He was finally exchanged for Saratoga veterans British Maj. Gen. William Phillips and Baron Friedrich von Riedesel in the fall of 1780. Immediately, Lincoln set about recruiting again in Massachusetts and the next summer rejoined the main army in New York. In August, Lincoln led the Continental Army south to Yorktown and was on hand when Cornwallis surrendered. In fact, it was he who received the British commander's sword from his second-in-command Lt. Gen. Charles O'Hara after it was first offered to French Gen. Comte de Rochambeau in a calculated insult to Washington. When Rochambeau indicated that the sword should be presented to Washington, the commander in chief also refused to accept it and ordered it be given to his own second, Lincoln.

The next year, Lincoln was named Secretary of War under the Articles of Confederation, a position he held until the Treaty of Paris was signed on September 3, 1783 ending the war. Returning to Massachusetts, Lincoln was asked in 1786 to leave his farm in order to take command of the militia and put down a tax revolt known as Shays' Rebellion in the western part of the state. In a gutsy, winter campaign, Lincoln tried to get the rebels to surrender but was finally forced to hit them in a surprise nighttime attack at Petersham that dispersed the rag-tag army to the four winds. Early the following year, with a mixture of firmness and mercy, Lincoln succeeded in ending the revolt without bloodshed and when he returned home, became lieutenant governor of Massachusetts. In 1788, he took part in the state convention that ratified the United States Constitution and after being defeated for reelection as lieutenant governor, was given the lucrative post of collector of the port of Boston by President Washington. In 1793 Lincoln was asked to preside over treaty negotiations with Indians at Sandusky and in 1809, finally retired from public life. Lincoln died on his farm in Hingham on May 9, 1810.

Philip Livingston

Like Massachusetts' James Otis, Philip Livingston spent most of his public career in the pre-revolutionary era of colonial politics and before that, in private business where he became a successful merchant independent of his family's already considerable wealth. That background made men like him, although not unaware of the injustices being perpetrated on the colonies by Parliament, more cautious in approaching relations with Britain. Not immediately a supporter of independence, Livingston's innate sense of outrage over the crown's overt disregard for the concerns of Americans made it easy for him to fully embrace the concept when the time came to sign a Declaration of Independence.

Livingston was born in Albany, New York on January 15, 1716 and following suitable preparation, entered Yale College to complete his education. Graduating in 1737, Livingston returned to Albany where he added practical knowledge to his scholastic achievements by working with his father in the mercantile trade and by serving in a series of public offices. After making an advantageous marriage to Christina Ten Broeck, Livingston decided to strike out on his own. Moving to New York City, he found little difficulty in cracking the local mercantile scene by investing in the sugar trade that moved between the West Indies and the American colonies. Although Livingston's business showed steady improvement, it did not really take off until the outbreak of King George's War in 1744 when the young merchant made a fortune in providing supplies for the army and outfitting privateers to prey on enemy shipping.

Following the war, Livingston was sitting pretty, a position he only enhanced ten years later during the French and Indian War when he bought shares in a number of privateers and invested his profits in real estate. In the meantime, Livingston added to his luster by returning some of those profits back to the community in the form of donations to local churches, endowments to colleges, and helping to establish a hospital. Now one of New York's most prominent men, he found it a simple thing to enter the world of politics first as a city alderman in 1754 and then as colonial legislator in 1758. Six years later, he was involved in a written

Philip Livingston

statement protesting Parliament's attempts to tax its American colonies and in 1765 was a representative for New York at the Stamp Act Congress. But his resentment at the manner in which Britain was treating its colonies had not kept up with that of many of his fellow citizens and a division between local patriots and more traditional elements loyal to the crown found Livingston on the wrong side of the issue costing him his seat in the provincial assembly. But while Livingston may have been more cautious about maintaining relations with Britain than many of his peers, he was by no means an apologist. In the contention between local patriots and royal authority for the sentiments of the people that characterized the New York political scene, Livingston believed that Americans were owed the same rights as all Englishmen and did not hesitate to say so. As a result, he felt there was no contradiction between his loyalty to the crown and his membership in a number of unofficial committees created to offer organized resistance to British policies. In fact, it was one of these committees whose members voted to appoint Livingston as a member of New York's delegation to the First Continental Congress in 1774. Later, he returned to local government as a member of the Committee of One Hundred which served as New York's unofficial legislature in the months leading up to independence.

In the Continental Congress, Livingston's business experience came in handy on a number of committees including the Secret Committee charged with acquiring weapons and gunpowder for the new Continental Army, the Marine Committee that looked into the creation of a navy, and the Committee on Provisioning to supply the army. But it was in 1776 that Livingston provided his most signal service in Congress when he put aside any lingering loyalties he may have had for England as well as a profound wariness of democracy and signed the Declaration of Independence. Like many of the Founding Fathers, Livingston looked around and saw a lack of firm local leadership whose absence he feared could lead to anarchy and even civil war. Luckily, however, none of that proved true as the former colonies immediately began to create new state constitutions and in 1777, under New York's own, Livingston found himself sitting as a member of the state's newly composed legislature. The following year, he was also returned to Congress which had relocated to York, Pennsylvania after Philadelphia had been seized by the enemy. But by now, the effects of age had caught up to Livingston and he was warned by doctors that a journey to York would likely kill him. But once having signed the Declaration, Livingston's patriotic sentiments had been aroused and he insisted on taking his seat in Congress. Sadly, his doctors' predictions proved true and after a journey in which he visited with friends and family one last time, Livingston collapsed only a month after reaching York and died on June 12, 1778.

Robert Livingston

In addition to the more famous revolutionaries, there were many more who were less well known but equally dedicated. And although these lesser known participants lent their efforts in countless ways to the Revolution, often their greatest contributions came only after victory had been won and the ground prepared for a flowering of liberty that in turn would unleash a boundless energy in the American people for opportunism and ingenuity. One of those people was Robert Livingston who, after initial doubts, spent years in revolutionary politics and emerged in peacetime as a far seeing entrepreneur who recognized the potential in steam power and promoted its development. It was a venture that would eventually transform not only the day to day transportation needs of the new nation but would thrust the whole world into an industrial age only dreamed of by Livingston's fellow revolutionary and advocate of industry, Alexander Hamilton.

Robert Livingston

The son of one of New York's wealthiest families, Livingston was born in New York City on November 27, 1747 and educated at King's College where he graduated in 1764. Taking up the law, he practiced briefly with friend John Jay before striking out on his own and earning a reputation for legal excellence. His name coming to the attention of the colony's leaders, he was appointed recorder of the city of New York by Governor William Tryon in 1773 but due to increasing involvement with the revolutionary movement, was soon removed from office.

It was the commotion surrounding the implementation of the Stamp Act years before that first awakened Livingston's democratic instincts and, tempered by moderation, his patriotic sympathies won him an appointment to the Stamp Act Congress held in 1765 and attended by delegates from nine of the thirteen colonies. Later, he was elected to the colonial legislature, but his cautious attitude toward Britain became increasingly out of step with fellow New Yorkers who turned him out of office in 1768. Although still reluctant to embrace independence, Livingston moved further into the radical camp, enough so that he became a member of New York's Provincial Congress which in turn named him as a delegate to the Continental Congress in 1776. There, despite his having argued against resolutions proposed by Virginia's Richard Henry Lee advocating independence, he was chosen to join fellow members Benjamin Franklin, John Adams, Thomas Jefferson, and Roger Sherman in the committee that drafted the Declaration of Independence. He was able to avoid signing the historic document after it was approved by Congress due to having been suddenly recalled to New York. He arrived home in time to take part in voting that altered the colony's official status from that of province to state and to work with friends John Jay and Gouverneur Morris in the creation of a new state constitution which was accepted at the Kingston Convention the following year.

Livingston was returned to the Continental Congress in 1779 where he remained until 1781 when he became its secretary of foreign affairs under the Articles of Confederation. As secretary, he had the duty to inform the nation's ministers in Europe, John Jay, John Adams, and Benjamin Franklin, that they were required by Congress to keep the nation's French allies informed of their every move. In particular, the three ministers were dismayed to find that they were expected to receive the approval of French foreign minister Charles Comte de Vergennes' before making any decision regarding peace negotiations with Britain. Adams was so incensed that he was prompted to write a letter to Livingston informing him of the realities of international diplomacy. In any event, the three ministers decided to ignore their instructions and to negotiate and conclude a treaty with Britain on their own. When Congress learned of their actions, there was outrage among the supporters of France who feared that the insulted French would cancel much needed loans. Livingston however, advocated full disclosure and in the end, the incident had little effect on the country's relations with its ally.

Livingston relinquished the office of secretary when he was appointed chancellor of the New York court system in 1783, a post he held until 1801. He was an advocate of a strong central government and joined Alexander Hamilton in leading his state's debate on ratification of the United States Constitution in 1788. Later, as New York's chief justice, he had the honor of administering the oath of office to incoming President George Washington. Upon concluding his duty, he turned to the crowd and exclaimed: "Long live George Washington, president of the United States!" In 1794, Washington rewarded his enthusiasm by offering Livingston an appointment as minister to France, but preferring his duties in New York, Livingston turned him down. However, after initially refusing another offer by President Thomas Jefferson to serve as his Secretary of the Navy, Livingston, finding himself freed of his obligations in New York, agreed in 1801 to represent the United States as its minister to France.

Livingston arrived on station after the end of the bloody convulsions that had rocked France in the wake of its revolution and Napoleon Bonaparte had completed his meteoric rise to power. Somehow, he rose high in Bonaparte's esteem and so was in a good position when instructed by Jefferson to sound out the French government about its territory in Louisiana which France had recently acquired from Spain. In particular, Jefferson wanted free navigation of the Mississippi River or perhaps the purchase of a piece of land at the mouth of the river for use as a free port. Later, Livingston was joined by James Monroe who arrived in France with authorization to offer as much as $10 million for the purchase of New Orleans and West Florida. But by the time Monroe arrived in Paris, Napoleon had suffered reverses in his plans for North America and had made inquiries about how much the United States would be willing to pay for the whole Louisiana Territory. On May 2, 1803 Monroe and Livingston signed a treaty of cession that transferred an area of 828,000 square miles from France to the United States for a price of $15 million. The agreement would also cover $3.7 million in debt owed by France to American citizens. Before resigning from office in 1805, Livingston was also able to begin negotiations with France over its depredation of American shipping on the high seas.

Following his resignation, Livingston embarked on a tour of Europe and it was while visiting Paris that he met the young inventor Robert Fulton who was trying to drum up interest in his plan to adapt steam power to run ship engines. A dabbler in inventions himself, Livingston was impressed and, joining in a partnership with Fulton, prevailed upon the New York legislature to grant him exclusive rights to navigate the state's waterways for 20 years in return for certain performance standards involved with steam power. Over the following months, through trial and error, Fulton was able to refine his steam engine to the point where it finally exceeded the minimum four mile an hour speed that had been required by the agreement with the legislature. And so, in 1807, the inventor made history with the 150 foot paddle wheeler *Clermont* as it chugged up the Hudson River from New York City to Albany at five miles an hour.

Although Livingston decided to retire following Fulton's success, he never slowed down; he just shifted his interests. Concentrating on agriculture, he sponsored experiments with fertilizers and introduced new breeds of sheep to local farms. In 1788, he had become a trustee of the New York Society Library and in 1808, first president of the American Academy of Fine Arts. Livingston died at his estate in Clermont, New York on February 26, 1813.

Thomas Lynch

Only 27 years old when he signed the Declaration of Independence, young Thomas Lynch possessed every quality necessary to have risen high in the politics of his state and perhaps the nation when his life was cut short by a tragic accident at sea.

The only child of one of the wealthiest planters in South Carolina, Lynch was born August 5, 1749 on Hopsewee Plantation, his father's estate at Winyaw, Prince George's Parish. Early on, he attended a local private school before being sent to Eton and Cambridge University in England to complete his education. His performance in those schools was such that his father urged him to move on to the Middle Temple to earn himself a law degree. In time, he succeeded and returned home in 1772. After an absence of almost nine years, Lynch wasted little time in getting married and plunging into local politics.

At the time, the thirteen American colonies were already in the midst of a revolutionary fervor and Lynch's father, Thomas Lynch, Sr., was one of South Carolina's leading patriots. His father's reputation was such that the younger Lynch found it a simple matter to insinuate himself into the councils of local patriots. Beginning in 1774, he attended meetings of the provincial congress and was involved in the creation of South Carolina's constitution. On the national front, his father was appointed to serve on South Carolina's delegation to the Continental Congress. In 1775, impatient with his father's desire to pull strings to get him higher rank, Lynch joined the local militia as a captain and proceeded to travel around the colony raising troops for his regiment. It was while on one of those recruiting drives that he caught a fever which seriously weakened him and prevented him from fulfilling all of the duties required of a captain in the militia. In the meantime, his father suffered a stroke that prevented him from fully participating in the work of Congress.

Concerned for the welfare of their fellow planter, colonial officials appointed the younger Lynch to replace his father in Congress and to tend to his health while he stayed in Philadelphia. It was under those circumstances, that Lynch journeyed north and arrived in Congress just in time to attend the debates on the issue of separation from Britain coming down firmly against any move to include slaves as part of a state's general population for determining taxation. His opinion reflected those of his southern peers and when the suggestion was dropped, Lynch had no difficulty joining his fellow congressmen in signing the Declaration of Independence. But whatever satisfaction he may have felt in the signing, was tempered by the weakened condition in

Thomas Lynch

which Lynch found himself due to the fever he had suffered while serving in the militia. Unable to shake it, he prepared to accompany his father on the long trip home where it was hoped that they both would have a chance to recuperate. It was not to be however, as his father made it only as far as Annapolis, Maryland before succumbing. Saddened, Lynch continued homeward arriving at Peach Tree, his estate in St. James Parish not far from Hopsewee. There, his health failed to improve and doctors recommended that he seek a more favorable climate perhaps in the south of France. But as passage of the Atlantic would be risky for an American, especially one who had signed the Declaration, it was decided that Lynch would travel to the Caribbean instead. Accordingly, in late 1779, Lynch and his wife boarded ship and set sail…they and the ship were never heard from again.

James Madison

Being known as the "Father of the Constitution" may not have been as flashy as "Father of his Country" or "The Swamp Fox," but then James Madison was never what one might call a flashy guy. Small and slight of stature rather than robust, he once held a position in the local militia but never fired a shot in anger. A good student, he graduated from New Jersey's Princeton College but never pursued a career either in the law or the clergy. Instead, he entered local politics and became involved in the revolutionary ferment that swept Virginia before the outbreak of open rebellion. Madison's closest brush with colorful celebrity came in the battle to ratify the Constitution which he was instrumental in creating. Teaming up with contemporaries Alexander Hamilton and John Jay, he wrote at least 26 of 85 of the *Federalist Papers* that together, form the most important and articulate defense of republicanism and constitutional government ever written. But even with that grand accomplishment and the acceptance of the Constitution by the several states, Madison soon backed away from the federalism he had fought so hard to establish. Under the influence of Thomas Jefferson, whom he greatly admired and consid-

James Madison

ered a mentor, Madison's position on the role of a central government in the life of the new United States changed from support to suspicion and suddenly, former allies became political enemies and opposing positions solidified into the first political parties. Thus, closely associated with Jefferson's Republican Party, the unassuming Madison, near the end of his public career, found himself swept into the most powerful office in the land on the coattails of the author of the Declaration of Independence.

Madison was born in Port Conway, King's County, Virginia on March 16, 1751 and grew up on his family's 5,000 acre plantation in Orange County. Although his family home benefited from the labor of 100 slaves, slavery was an institution Madison grew to dislike. As with many of his southern contemporaries, he found that he could not live without it so long as he depended upon it for his livelihood.

After graduating in 1772 from the College of New Jersey (later known simply as Princeton), Madison returned home and, two years later, was named colonel in the local militia. In between, he served as a member of the Orange County Committee of Safety and in 1776, following the electrifying events at Lexington and Concord in Massachusetts, was elected to the convention that declared Virginia's independence from Britain and helped draft the new state's constitution. Always resentful of the snobbish airs of his fellow Virginia gentry, Madison became all the more impatient with the high handedness of British rule in the colonies. Inspired as much by Patrick Henry's stirring speech in Virginia's House of Burgesses as by a classical education that included many of the natural philosophers of the Age of the Enlightenment, Madison was fired with revolutionary zeal, working diligently as a member of the governor's council serving first under Henry and then more fatefully, Thomas Jefferson.

His work in local politics being recognized, Madison was chosen to represent Virginia in the Continental Congress beginning in 1780. It was while in Congress that direct experience of working under the Articles of Confederation convinced him that a new, stronger framework for cooperative government among the thirteen states was needed. Thus, after honing his political skills over four years in Congress, Madison returned to Virginia to begin laying the groundwork for support of a Constitutional Convention charged with finding ways to strengthen the union between the thirteen states. Unstated, was the intent of supporters to use the convention not simply to bolster the existing Articles of Confederation, but to create a whole new framework that would further centralize political power in a single national government. At the Annapolis Convention of 1786, Madison joined forces with Alexander Hamilton in calling for a Constitutional Convention to be held in Philadelphia, a suggestion that was approved by the various states and scheduled for the next year.

With Hamilton mostly a no show at the convention, Madison was able to apply his full energies toward his goal of creating a strong federal government. Together with his state's other delegates, Madison helped to draw up what became known as the "Virginia Plan" which outlined much of what he felt a new form of government should include. Of particular importance to Madison was a balance of power between the executive, the legislative, and the judiciary branches to ensure that no part of the new government could seize sole power and so tyrannize the people. The ultimate goal in fashioning the new scheme (which also included a bicameral legislature) was to give no group access to total control over the government. To get what they wanted, opposing groups would have to find ways to work together, to compromise and ameliorate their differences, thus ensuring that drastic change was unlikely to happen. Change, when it came, would be slow, even glacial, thus the nation would be protected against the intemperance of the mob. In this scheme, the judiciary would be a relatively passive branch of the government but what Madison failed to see was its later claim, under Chief Justice John Marshall, to being the sole arbiter of what was and was not allowed under the Constitution. It would take almost 200 years, but Marshall's interpretation of the judiciary's role in the federal government would result in near dictatorial power not only over the executive and the legislative branches of government, but over the entire population of the nation as a whole, completely thwarting and undermining Madison's and the Framers' original intent.

With a Constitution agreed upon by the Convention, the delegates returned to their respective states to begin the long political and ideological battle for its ratification that was by no means a sure thing. Teaming up with Hamilton and John Jay, Madison helped break down all the arguments for and against the new Constitution and each man took turns writing a series of exhaustive and often brilliant essays in defense of federalism. Full of the wide range of classical and contemporary philosophical thought that was familiar to most learned men at the time, the trio crafted 85 separate pieces that were then printed in newspapers across the country and eventually assembled as *The Federalist Papers*. Despite the letters, the fight to ratify the Constitution was not easy; many old Patriots spoke out against it including Patrick Henry in Virginia and Samuel Adams in Massachusetts, but one by one, each state voted acceptance until it was finally adopted with an additional Bill of Rights in the summer of 1788.

Selected by Virginia to be that state's first delegate to the new House of Representatives, Madison settled into his job nicely, writing President George Washington's inaugural address and advising him on his choices for cabinet appointments. Soon, however, trouble arose when Hamilton, the new Secretary of the Treasury, began to make his celebrated suggestions for putting the United States on a solid financial footing. Already having come under the influence of Thomas Jefferson through a series of letters the two exchanged over the course of the Constitutional Convention and ratification efforts, Madison had begun to have second thoughts about the need for a strong central government. He opposed Hamilton's position and when Jefferson returned from Europe, the two became far more intimate in their plans to oppose the New Yorker. Soon, this opposition hardened into the creation of the first political parties and fostered vituperative public denunciations between Jeffersonian Republicans and Hamiltonian Federalists. Through it all, Madison's hands were not left completely clean but by the end of John Adams' single term as president, the Republicans' stance had become the nation's and Jefferson was finally swept into the White House in the election of 1800.

With Jefferson in power, Madison was appointed Secretary of State and became involved in many key issues including negotiations for the Louisiana Purchase and war with the Barbary Pirates. Increasingly, however, the rising conflict between Britain and Napoleonic France came to dominate much of the administration's foreign policy culminating in the unpopular Embargo Act of 1807. Because he resisted the idea of armed conflict, Madison was convinced that enough pressure could be applied to the warring countries by economic means alone and thus supported a law that barred trade between the United States and the two European powers. Failure of the Embargo Act to accomplish its intended purpose and its repeal did not do the Republicans lasting harm however as Madison was elected to succeed Jefferson as president in the election of 1808.

Unfortunately, Madison's tenure in office was a less than happy one as Federalist political resistance hardened in the northeastern states and tensions within the Republican Party itself conspired to weaken his administration. In addition, the war in Europe continued to rage causing friction between the United States and Britain which was exacerbated by the impressment of American sailors on the high seas to serve in the

English navy. The refusal by the British to halt the practice and public outrage over the issue eventually forced Madison's hand and he declared war with England in 1812. Although most Americans were supportive of the war, the nation was ill prepared to fight a foe as powerful as the British Empire resulting in badly led and supplied armies made up mostly of volunteers being routinely defeated in repeated attempts to invade Canada. There were some triumphs at sea but they were more than wiped out in 1814 when the enemy came ashore in Maryland, marched inland and burned the nation's capital. The nadir was reached when Madison, after personally witnessing the defeat of American forces at the Battle of Bladensburg, found himself on the run from the advancing British. Although America began to see more victories on the battlefield later in the war, both sides decided that further conflict was not worth the effort and on December 24, 1814 a treaty of peace was signed. An important part of the agreement, besides ending the war, was final recognition by Britain of provisions in the Treaty of Paris that recognized the possession by the United States of the Old Northwest. And so, for the first time since the end of the Revolutionary War, British troops would no longer occupy forts on American territory.

With the experience of being a wartime president, Madison seemed to step back from the brink of orthodox Republicanism by using the power of the federal government to affect the economy. He advocated Hamilton's old idea of a National Bank, use of the tariff to protect American business, and improvement of the nation's infrastructure with federal aid. Overcoming his earlier unpopularity, Madison so strengthened his reputation that when he left office in 1816, his vice president and heir apparent, James Monroe was elected to take his place.

Retiring to his home at Montpelier, Madison occupied his time with agricultural pursuits and aided Jefferson in the establishment of the University of Virginia and then succeeded his friend as the school's rector. In 1829, he returned to public affairs as a delegate to Virginia's second constitutional convention where he attempted to effect political change in the state and to curtail slavery but failed. Though often laboring in the shadow of more famous contemporaries such as George Washington, Thomas Jefferson, or Alexander Hamilton, Madison's turn in the spotlight during the battles for ratification of the Constitution more than made up for his otherwise less than bombastic personality. In keeping with his retiring nature, Madison lived on quietly for another few years following Virginia's second constitutional convention until, in declining health, he died on June 28, 1836 among the very last of the Revolutionary generation.

Francis Marion

One of the most well known figures of the American Revolution and one of the few whose name has endured in popular folklore from the time immediately following the end of the war to the present day is that of Francis Marion, better known to history as the "Swamp Fox." Marion received his famous sobriquet from the British, whom he chased, harassed, and battled from his base of operations deep in the South Carolina swamps that he had known intimately since childhood. But Marion was not based in the swamplands for his health. Unlike the northern states the population of the southern states was more evenly divided between patriots and loyalists and in some counties, Tories even outnumbered patriots. As a result, when the British brought the war to the south, they found what appeared to be more fertile ground from which to conduct military operations. Recruiting among local loyalists British forces in the south were largely com-

Francis Marion

posed of native Americans, a situation that soon transformed the war in the south from a struggle against the British to virtually a civil war. As a result, battles between patriots fighting for their freedom from British oppression and loyalists fighting for their king became vicious affairs often tinged with personal retribution among the combatants. Thus, the scene was not set to the advantage of Marion and his fellow patriots: they were evenly matched or outnumbered by loyalists; the British held the major cities and frequently had the run of the countryside; and they were plagued by lack of men, supplies, and proper leadership that resulted in many losses on the battlefield. Which is not to say that all was bleak. Despite the loss of cities and sometimes whole armies, local patriots hung on, coming together when the need arose to confront the enemy and then melting away again, waiting for the day when real help would arrive from the north and the enemy could be confronted in the open. And in the back and forth fighting among the scattered villages of the Carolina and Georgia back country, the tactics that worked best were those of hit and run and no one was as good in that style of warfare as the "Swamp Fox."

Born around Georgetown, South Carolina in 1732, there was nothing about young Marion's appearance to suggest the reputation he would gain later when grievances between Britain and its American colonies burst into open warfare. But thin as he was and often sickly, he loved to explore the swamps near his home and later, to hunt and fish. His love of the outdoors was a manifestation of an adventurous spirit that first took him to sea at the age of 15 and later was tempered with early disappointment when the ship he had boarded for a cruise to the West Indies sank and he was obliged to spend weeks adrift on a raft with a few fellow sailors until finally coming to shore.

His brush with disaster however, did not dampen Marion's enthusiasm for taking risks and in 1760 he joined a company of militia commanded by an older brother for action against the Cherokee. Proving his mettle, Marion led a scouting party into an area likely to hold an enemy ambush and foiled a plan by the Indians to take a force of 1,200 British regulars by surprise. Of his company, he was one of only a handful who survived the resulting skirmish. Following the war, the next few years were quiet ones for Marion as he concentrated on farming and acquiring land in the Santee River area of South Carolina. In 1775, he was serving in the colony's Provincial Congress when news came from Massachusetts of the outbreak of hostilities between colonists and the British. With the start of the Revolution, Marion did not hesitate to side with the patriots and after being named a captain in the Continental Army, he reported to the regiment of Colonel William Moultrie, his former commanding officer during the Indian wars.

Immediately, Marion joined other militia units in the South Carolina backcountry in what was called the Snow Campaign aimed at rooting out enemies of the Revolution. After that, he seemed to be everywhere that counted: at the battle of Fort Sullivan in 1776 and Savannah, Georgia in 1779. But the fortune of war did not favor the south and by

1780 conditions in the southern theater seemed to have reached a nadir. American forces had been defeated and were on the defensive everywhere and on a more personal level, Marion himself broke an ankle after jumping from a second story window during the siege of Charleston and invalided out of the service. After he had recovered, Marion was promoted first to lieutenant colonel and then to general even as he began to gather a few friends around him to form the core of a new unit. Then, just as Gen. Horatio Gates arrived to take charge of the southern theater, Marion was given the assignment of scouting out and locating enemy positions. His arrival in the camp of the regular army prompted stares from his fellow soldiers: he and his men were "...distinguished by small black leather caps and the wretchedness of their attire," wrote Continental Army officer Col. Otho Williams, "...their number did not exceed twenty men and boys, some white, some black, and all mounted, but most of them miserably equipped; their appearance was in fact so burlesque that it was with much difficulty the diversion of the regular soldiery was restrained..."

Gates, meanwhile, had been assigned to shore up the southern resistance on the reputation of his victory at Saratoga, but in August of 1780 his army was decisively beaten by the British at Camden, South Carolina. Thus, with the south virtually defenseless and the enemy roaming the countryside at will, the only recourse for local patriot forces was to resort to hit and run tactics, striking only when the odds were in their favor. Operating out of the Santee River swamps he knew so well, Marion developed his own personal strategies which involved moving under cover of darkness, never camping in the same place twice, never attacking a superior force unless conditions were in his favor and keeping the final object of a mission to himself until the last minute. So successful were his efforts, that Marion became the most successful of the partisan leaders swiftly earning the nickname "Swamp Fox" from his most determined rival and arguably the most hated man in the south, Col. Banastre Tarleton who commanded his own band of ruthless Tory cavalry.

Wasting little time after the disaster at Camden, Marion and his men rode out from their base in the tangled cypress swamps and struck the enemy at Great Savannah, the home of Gen. Thomas Sumter, and released over 147 American prisoners being held there by the British. Later, a pursuit force made up of over 250 mounted Tories was repulsed at Blue Savannah by the vastly outnumbered Patriots. 1780 was a busy year for Marion as he continued to strike at the enemy with his small force whenever the opportunity arose. In October of that year, learning of the presence of a Tory patrol camped near Tearcoat Swamp, Marion took 150 men, surrounded and attacked the loyalists and scattered them to the four winds. His reputation among the enemy mounting daily, Marion's activity became intolerable to the British command which finally ordered its most feared operative to put an end to it. And so, Tarleton, followed by 400 Tories of his British Legion, rode into Marion's stomping grounds hoping to beard the guerilla leader in his den. But aside from being led on a merry chase, Tarleton was never able to catch "the damned old fox" and contented himself with terrorizing the local population with home burnings before giving up.

In 1781, after Major Gen. Nathaniel Greene had been ordered to take charge of the southern theater, Marion cooperated in the general's long range plan to avoid a major confrontation with the British until he had a chance to build up his own army. Hit and run tactics were the order of the day as Greene lured British Gen. Charles Cornwallis deeper and deeper into the countryside. One of many skirmishes took place at Quinby Bridge where Marion's brigade came under Sumter's command who, against the advice of the Swamp Fox and Lt. Col. Henry Lee, ordered a frontal attack on a superior enemy position. The ill fated action resulted in many unnecessary deaths, devastated Marion's brigade, and ended Sumter's questionable military career. After Quinby Bridge, Marion became the target of British Col. John Tadwell Watson and his 500 man Tory regiment. On March 6, the two sides met at Wiboo Swamp where Watson was lured across a narrow causeway and ambushed. Another clash took place a few days later at Mount Hope Swamp where Watson was prevented from crossing the Black River at Kingstree by Marion's sharpshooters. Watson had planned on continuing his pursuit but all he received were more casualties at the hands of Marion's riflemen and eventually, his force swiftly diminishing, he was chased from the swamps. At Georgetown, Marion once again trounced a superior enemy force in the harrying manner used against Watson prompting Captain Tarleton Brown to write: "Upon him depended almost solely the success of the provincial army of South Carolina, and the sequel has proven how well he performed the trust reposed in him." In May, 1781, the Swamp Fox assisted in the seizure of a number of British strong points including Fort Mott on the Congaree River where Marion defied fellow officers in ordering a halt to reprisals being made on captured loyalists. On September 8, 1781 Marion led his brigade on the right wing at Eutaw Springs where he joined the main Continental Army under Greene in a battle that could have been won if not for the desperation of the half starved and clothed men who could not resist looting captured British supply wagons. After Eutaw Springs, the war in the south wound down rapidly with Marion seeing his final action at Fair Lawn in August of 1782.

With the end of active hostilities, Marion joined the state's legislature for two terms before accepting command of Fort Johnson. Always opposed to any kind of retaliation against former enemies, he was appointed as South Carolina's representative at the Constitutional Convention of 1790 before retiring permanently to his home at Pond's Bluff. He died there on February 27, 1795, his reputation for personal bravery, patriotic fervor, and tactical brilliance in his many campaigns secure in the admiration of his fellow citizens.

John Marshall

One of the most far reaching events of the Revolutionary era did not take place on a battlefield or the halls of Congress or the palaces of Europe or even at the Constitutional Convention, but rather before the bench of the Supreme Court. Conceived by framers of the Constitution such as James Madison and Alexander Hamilton as little more than an arbiter of federal law and for settling disputes between states, it was not until Chief Justice John Marshall redefined the court's role that it was able to attain parity with the executive and legislative branches of the government. With the case of Marbury v Madison, it was Marshall's opinion that it was the unique function of the Supreme Court not only to settle disputes, but to pass judgment whether or not measures passed by Congress were allowed under the Constitution. As a result, for almost 200 years, the court served as a check against Congress and the president as the politics of the nation grew ever more polarized. Confidence in the integrity and neutrality of the court in its new role remained high for many generations until late in the twentieth century when the part that Marshall had defined for it began to unravel under the pressures of increasing partisanship. By the beginning of the twenty-first century, Marshall's position that the Supreme Court had the last word on whether a law was allowed under the Constitution had been radically altered to the point where the court had usurped the authority of the legislature and began to pass laws of its own. The equilibrium that had lasted for almost two centuries had been ruptured and the trust

218

in the court that Marshall had worked so long and hard to establish was threatened with destruction.

Born at Germantown, Virginia, on September 24, 1755 Marshall was the first of 15 children born to Thomas and Mary Marshall, who later moved the family closer to the frontier in the Blue Ridge Mountains. Being a surveyor, the elder Marshall soon gained the respect of his neighbors and fell in with a young George Washington, a relationship that would later come in handy for his son who loved to read and had access to Washington's library. When he was twelve, Marshall had the opportunity to snatch a bit of formal education when a visiting pastor stayed with the family for a time. Later, some time was spent in a local school, but his father had ambitions for Marshall in the field of law and started his son off in that direction with the purchase of a copy of Blackstone's *Commentaries.* But the young Marshall's legal education was interrupted when the Revolutionary War broke out in 1775.

John Marshall

With his father already serving as a major in the county's militia company, Marshall was chosen as his lieutenant. Action soon followed when Governor John Dunsmore declared martial law and offered freedom to slaves who joined him against the colonists. Thus emboldened, on the morning of December 10, 1775 Dunmore ordered British troops to march against a band of militia gathering at Norfolk and met the Marshalls and other militiamen at Great Bridge where they were repulsed with heavy losses to themselves and none for the Americans. For the next few years, Marshall accompanied his father across a number of battlefields including Brandywine, Germantown, and Monmouth and shared with his fellow soldiers the deprivations of Valley Forge. Promoted to captain, Marshall last saw action in the north when he joined Col. Henry Lee in a daring assault behind enemy lines at Paulus Hook on the Hudson River across from New York City. Returning to Virginia in 1780, Marshall arrived just in time to join the fight against an incursion into the state by the traitorous Benedict Arnold at the head of a ravaging British Army.

It was while on a visit to his father's headquarters in Yorktown that Marshall met Mary Ambler whom he later married in 1783. Before that, however, he decided to leave the military and pursue the law, which he became quite good at. Success raised his profile such that he was elected to the Virginia House of Delegates where he served off and on from 1782 to 1796. During the years of debate surrounding the creation of a stronger national government, from the Annapolis Convention of 1786 to ratification of the Constitution in 1788, Marshall found himself leader of the nascent Federalist Party and during the ratifying debates at the Virginia Convention, argued against the sentiments of such men as Patrick Henry and Thomas Jefferson and in favor of a strong federal judiciary. The debates had given Marshall national standing among the leaders of the country's Federalist Party and he was subsequently made numerous offers of public office including being named as one of three commissioners sent to negotiate with France in 1797.

In company with Elbridge Gerry and Charles Cotesworth Pinckney, Marshall refused to have anything to do with an offer by French Foreign Minister Charles Maurice de Talleyrand to deal with the Americans only upon payment of a $250,000 bribe for himself and a $10 million loan for France. Upon the commission's return to the United States, a political firestorm erupted over the failure of the mission culminating in President John Adams' release of its report whose contents were promptly labeled the XYZ Affair. Popular with the people, Marshall refused an offer by Adams to become an associate justice of the Supreme Court and instead, ran for and won a seat in the House of Representatives. Adams nevertheless continued his efforts to find Marshall a place in his administration and finally succeeded in 1800 when the Virginian accepted the position of Secretary of State. The next year, having lost a bid for a second term of office to former friend and then arch-rival Thomas Jefferson, Adams made a number of last minute legal appointments, among them naming Marshall as Chief Justice to replace an ailing Oliver Ellsworth. As a result, Marshall had the unique experience, at least for two months until Adams' term ended, of holding two federal offices at the same time.

Unfortunately, the "midnight appointments" of the federal judges by Adams triggered a power struggle between Republicans and Federalists when Jefferson ordered his own Secretary of State, James Madison, not to allow seventeen of the appointees, including William Marbury, to take their seats. The result was a showdown between the two factions in the persons of Jefferson and Marshall as Marbury and some of his colleagues brought suit against the president to force him to honor their commissions. When the dust cleared, the case of Marbury v Madison would establish clear lines of responsibility among the three branches of the federal government and in particular, staking out for the Supreme Court its role as final arbiter on the constitutionality of actions taken by the legislative and executive branches. In his historic 1803 decision, Marshall established for the court, the right of judicial review that took defining the meaning of the Constitution out of the hands of elected legislators and into those of judges who were appointed for life. Instead of a literal interpretation of the Constitution, Marshall's decision made it possible for future justices to find "implied" powers in the document that its framers perhaps never intended. It was a situation that at first seemed to create a more stable balance of power among the three branches of government, one that held for almost 200 years, but it also created the opportunity for abuse of power by judges whose decisions could not be questioned or disobeyed except by the long and difficult process of constitutional amendment.

Marshall, jealous of the power of the Supreme Court and always interested in strengthening the federal government, continually found himself at odds with Jefferson (whom he once referred to as a political "terrorist") first in the president's 1805 attempt to impeach fellow Justice Samuel Chase and then in 1807 when former Vice-President Aaron Burr was arrested and charged with treason in a plot to raise a private army and invade Mexico. Because Burr had long since become a political enemy of Jefferson's, the president moved to suspend the right of a fair and open trial by having the legislature pass a law not requiring it in matters of treason. With the right of judicial review established by Marbury v Madison, the decision gave Marshall the opening he needed to pass judgment on the measure. The rest of the Supreme Court agreed with him, deemed the law unconstitutional, and a trial was held with the verdict in favor of Burr.

Over the years, Marshall continued to add to the court's authority and the power of the federal government in a series of important decisions beginning with Fletcher v Peck in 1803 that established the court's authority to review and if necessary, invalidate state laws that it thought conflicted with the Constitution. In 1819, in the case of McCullock v Maryland, Marshall defined the concept of implied powers, thus furthering the court's rationale for interpreting the Constitution and the intent of the Framers. In 1821, in the case of Cohens v Virginia, the Supreme Court established its right to review state supreme court decisions and finally, in the 1824 case of Gibbons v Ogden, Marshall expanded upon the Constitution's interstate commerce clause to include rights of navigation as well as commerce and opening the way for later decisions that would vastly increase the reach of the federal government.

After a long career spent strengthening the hand of the central government and redefining the meaning and intent of the Constitution for generations to come, Marshall, after 34 years of service, died on July 6, 1835 still acting as Chief Justice of the Supreme Court.

Lachlan McIntosh

Unlike his contemporary, Aaron Burr, involvement in a duel that resulted in the death of a signer of the Declaration of Independence did little to damage the subsequent career of Lachlan McIntosh. Retreating from Georgia to Pennsylvania to escape his political enemies, he suffered at Valley Forge and tamed the frontier before returning to his home state to contest British occupation of Savannah.

Born in Scotland on March 17, 1725 young McIntosh was only eight years old when his father led 100 members of the clan to Britain's new colony of Georgia in the Americas. There, the elder McIntosh established the town of Darien and over the following decade, took turns developing the land and fighting the neighboring Spanish in Florida on behalf of Britain. In 1740 McIntosh senior was captured by the enemy and taken prisoner to Spain. As a result, Lachlan was sent to a local orphanage until he was removed by James Oglethorpe, a friend of his father's, who sent him on to serve as a cadet in a local military regiment. It was Oglethorpe who encouraged McIntosh in his studies and helped him with the mathematics he needed to enter the surveying trade. When he came of age, McIntosh left his position with the regiment and moved to Charleston, South Carolina where he found employment with Henry Laurens, a wealthy merchant and prominent citizen of the city. It was Laurens who had the greatest influence on McIntosh as popular discontent with England grew in the thirteen colonies. Having proven a success in business, McIntosh was eager to strike out on his own and after marrying a local maid returned to Georgia, helped survey Darien, and bought land along the Altamaha River. Meanwhile, his sympathies for the patriotic movement continued to grow stronger so that by 1775, the year of Lexington and Concord, he was in a position to become involved in the preparation of delegates from Darien to the colony's Provincial Congress.

By dint of his past experience with the military, McIntosh's own revolutionary career turned in the direction of combat rather than politics as he was made a colonel of the Georgia Battalion. As such, he helped organize a defense against an attempt by the British Navy to sail up the Savannah River to seize provisions denied them by local patriots. In the battle of the Rice Boats fought on March 2 and 3 of 1776, store ships were set afire and allowed to drift downstream into the British fleet. In the course of the action, four enemy ships caught fire and the royal governor was forced to flee the colony. With that triumph, McIntosh was promoted to brigadier general in the Continental Army and began planning to defend Georgia from any incursions to the south. It was during this period of his career, when an expedition was being mounted for a preemptive strike into Florida that McIntosh angered Button Gwinnett, a powerful politician and a signer of the Declaration of Independence. Gwinnett had ambitions of his own to lead the expedition into Florida but when he failed to raise sufficient numbers of militia, he shifted the blame to McIntosh citing a lack of cooperation. But McIntosh, as an officer in the Continental Army, was

Lachlan McIntosh

not beholden to state officials and distrusting Gwinnett's lack of military experience, had refused to allow him command of his men.

The dispute only exacerbated a political split in the state with Gwinnett's country folk in opposition to the city party to which the McIntosh family was associated. In the end, Gwinnett challenged McIntosh to a duel and when the two met on May 16, 1777 in a field outside Charleston, both were wounded but only Gwinnett mortally. With Gwinnett's death, his political allies were out for blood and McIntosh was charged with murder. Although he was cleared of the charges in a subsequent trial, McIntosh was urged to leave the state for a time until tempers cooled. Thus, the winter of 1778 saw McIntosh off to Pennsylvania to join Gen. George Washington's army at Valley Forge.

By the time spring rolled around, McIntosh had earned the trust and respect of Washington who rewarded him with command of the country's western department. There, McIntosh was to proceed to western Pennsylvania and organize resistance to repeated incursions by the British and their savage Indian allies. Arriving at Fort Pitt with 500 men, McIntosh wasted no time and quickly established Fort Laurens at Sandusky and Fort McIntosh at Beaver Creek and garrisoned them with 150 men. With the frontier protected, McIntosh proposed a plan to attack Detroit, the enemy stronghold on the frontier from which supplies and money exchanged for scalps streamed to the Indians. Unfortunately, with most of its thin resources focused in the east and an invasion of the Carolinas imminent, Congress felt the plan too expensive and decided against it. McIntosh remained in the west a year before surrendering his command in the spring of 1779 in order to return to Georgia where the British had finally captured Savannah.

By the time McIntosh returned to his home state, political animosities had died down enough for him to take a vigorous part in retaking Savannah. Plans were laid for a combined force of Continentals and militia under the command of Gen. Benjamin Lincoln to lay siege to the city. In addition, Admiral Charles d'Estaing fresh from victory over the British in the West Indies, would reinforce the army with his fleet and 6,000 French troops. Surrounding the city, the allies gave the British one last chance to surrender. Instead, the enemy asked for a day's truce which was granted by the French against Lincoln's wishes. Those hours of inaction proved crucial as the British used them not only to improve their defenses, but to receive much needed reinforcements. When it was learned that as a result, it would take longer to force a surrender than originally anticipated, d'Estaing, fearful that a British fleet could arrive at any time, insisted on an all out attack on the city.

Still protesting but with no choice when faced with the threatened withdrawal of the French troops, Lincoln gave in and ordered the attack. Among those who assaulted the city was McIntosh commanding the 1st and 5th South Carolina regiments and in the fighting that followed, d'Estaing himself was killed leading his men. In the end however, the attack failed, the French sailed away, and Lincoln was obliged to call off the siege and retreat north to Charleston.

But the imagined safety of South Carolina proved only temporary as, after consolidating their hold on Georgia, the British shifted their attention north and moved on Charleston in force. A combined land and sea operation cut the city off from the mainland and this time it was the Americans who found themselves surrounded. However, unlike the British at Savannah, there was no hope of being reinforced. Compelled to give in, the city was surrendered on May 12, 1780 and among the prisoners taken was McIntosh.

Although other important prisoners were released after a relatively short captivity, McIntosh would be held for two years before being exchanged on February 9, 1782. By then, with the war's end in sight, his health had been permanently damaged and he returned to his estate, ravaged by war, to begin rebuilding the life he had before 1775. By 1783, he had been promoted to major general and in 1784 was elected to Congress. The next year, he was named a member of a special commission appointed to settle a boundary dispute between Georgia and South Carolina and later, worked to draw up a treaty between the government and the Indian tribes of western Georgia. McIntosh continued to serve Georgia until his death in Savannah on February 20, 1806.

Thomas McKean

A creature of the overlapping and intertwined political systems of Pennsylvania and Delaware, Thomas McKean held a dizzying array of offices over his long career that would have been more than enough for any three people. Serving as Pennsylvania's chief justice at the same time as he held a seat in the Delaware legislature, McKean still found the time to act as a delegate to the Continental Congress for Delaware, lead troops into battle in New Jersey, and father 11 children by two wives!

Born in New London, Pennsylvania on March 19, 1734 McKean received his early education from a tutor in Newcastle, Delaware before getting a job with the local government and reading law in his spare time. At the age of 21 he passed the bar and only a year later entered politics as deputy attorney general of Sussex County. He never looked back. In 1757 he served for two years as clerk of Delaware's legislature (at the time, Delaware was known as the three Lower Counties which were claimed by both Pennsylvania and Maryland). Quitting that job, he took time off to travel to England to broaden his legal studies and in 1762, returned home to join Caesar Rodney (with whom he later served in Congress) as a reviser of laws written before 1752. Later that same year he was elected to the Delaware general assembly or legislature where he served continuously for the next seventeen years.

McKean leaned radical in his politics and when residents began to protest passage by Parliament of new tax measures, his reputation was such that he was chosen to represent them at the Stamp Act Congress of 1765. There, McKean distinguished himself immediately by making sure that voting would be made by colony and not based on population or size thus assuring that smaller members such as Delaware had an equal voice at the conference with those of

Thomas McKean

the larger colonies. By then a staunch supporter of the rights of Americans, McKean had no trouble signing a memorial of rights and grievances issued by the congress to Parliament. It was more of the same over the next few years for the busy McKean as he added a commission as justice of the peace for Newcastle County, collector of the port of Newcastle, and notary of

the Lower Counties to his list of official positions. As judge of the orphans' court, McKean displayed his patriotic bona fides by ordering that all court business be recorded on unstamped paper. Thus, by 1774, it was almost a foregone conclusion that McKean would be on the short list of delegates to represent Delaware at the Continental Congress.

The only member of Congress to have served there till it was dissolved with the establishment of the United States Constitution in 1783, McKean found time to participate in a number of committees including those listing the rights of the American colonies, regulating the importation of munitions, and drafting the Articles of Confederation. And when it came to the most important accomplishment of the Congress, McKean expended whatever influence he had to get the Declaration of Independence signed and passed. When George Read, one of Delaware's three delegates, refused to vote for independence, McKean hurriedly sent word to Caesar Rodney to join him immediately in Philadelphia to vote in its favor. The two votes formed a majority of the colony's delegation and Delaware ended up in the pro-Declaration of Independence column. All of which proved to be ironic in that although McKean's name appears on the historic document, there is some controversy about just when he actually signed it. He was not present when the Congress as a whole signed the Declaration on August 2, 1776 because at the time he had been commissioned a colonel and had left town to lead militia units in the field around Perth Amboy, New Jersey where Gen. George Washington was harassing British outposts. In fact, it is entirely possible that McKean did not get around to signing the Declaration until January of 1777 the same year that he confused future biographers even more by accepting the position of chief justice of Pennsylvania…even as he continued to serve as Speaker in the Delaware legislature!

After McKean returned from New Jersey, he was asked to draft a constitution for Delaware as it prepared to become its own independent state. Soon after, during the summer of 1777, the state was invaded by the British and many elected officials were forced to flee including McKean who took his family west to hide in a log cabin on the frontier. Not all were lucky enough to evade capture and the state's governor, John McKinley was made a prisoner. With speaker of the legislative council George Read still on the run, McKean stepped in as acting governor for a month before returning to Congress in 1778. In 1781, his colleagues voted him as their president. Serving only briefly, McKean nevertheless was on hand to receive a dispatch from Washington notifying Congress of the surrender of British Gen. Charles Cornwallis at Yorktown.

McKean left Congress in 1782 but was back on the national scene as a delegate when Pennsylvania held its state convention for ratification of the Constitution. An advocate of a strong central government to replace the rickety Articles of Confederation, McKean fought for approval of the Constitution and had the satisfaction of seeing it ratified by the state in December of 1787. Following ratification, McKean continued to serve as chief justice of Pennsylvania until he was nominated by the Federalist Party for governor and won election to that office in 1799. Despite attempts by political enemies to have him impeached for reasons of nepotism, McKean kept winning elections and remained in office until 1808 until finally retiring in 1812. He turned down a request to run for vice president of the United States on the grounds that it would be undignified for a former president (of Congress) to seek an office he considered of lesser importance. Finally running out of steam, McKean died in Philadelphia on June 24, 1817.

Arthur Middleton

Daring to sign the Declaration of Independence, Arthur Middleton was captured by the British along with two other signers with the surrender of Charleston, South Carolina and, after being exchanged a year later, returned to find his home ransacked and all his possessions destroyed. It was the price he paid for being one of South Carolina's most ardent patriots.

Like many leaders of the Revolution, Middleton was a rich man, being a member of one of the wealthiest families in South Carolina, the owners of 50,000 acres and 800 slaves. He was born on June 26, 1742 in his father's mansion at Middleton Place along the banks of the Ashley River outside Charleston. Fabulously rich as one of the colony's legendary rice kings, the senior Middleton sent his son to England to acquire an education and to prepare him to take over the family estate. Graduating from Cambridge University in 1773, Middleton lingered in Europe for another two years, visiting around England before drifting to France and Italy where he indulged an interest in art, music, and sculpture. At last however, the time came for his return home where he was expected to begin his public career.

Arriving in South Carolina in 1763, he wasted little time in marrying Mary Izzard, the daughter of another wealthy family and entered politics as a member of the colony's legislature. Realizing that his anticipated responsibilities as the master of his family's estates would largely prevent travel in the future, Middleton decided in 1768 to embark with his wife on a second tour of Europe this time including Spain in his itinerary. Upon his return to South Carolina in 1773, Middleton began to oversee his family's vast estates but unrest among the people that had been growing over the years culminated in 1774 with the passage of a series of "intolerable acts" by Parliament, measures that protected royal officials from local justice, extended the southern borders of Canada to the Ohio River, and granted Roman Catholics in Canada freedom of conscience.

Despite having a personal interest in opposing the various tax

Arthur Middleton

measures that had also emerged from Parliament, Middleton, like his father, still found himself among the front ranks of patriots and over the following years, had ample opportunity to demonstrate his zeal. And so, as the Revolution approached, Middleton was drawn into the struggle until he was finally appointed to South Carolina's Committee of Safety which was charged to begin secret preparations for armed resistance to England should war break out. Middleton helped in appointing officers to the local militia and in one instance was involved in planning for a subsequent raid on stores of government munitions. At the same time, he was also part of a committee working on crafting a new constitution for the colony. Finally, in 1776, Middleton was elected to take his father's place in the Continental Congress and arrived in Philadelphia just in time to take part in the debates surrounding independence. Although he disliked committee work, Middleton had no problem with speaking his mind on the floor of Congress and when the time arrived to make a decision, he settled firmly on the side of separation from England and signed the Declaration of Independence.

Although he was reelected to Congress in 1777, Middleton ended up not going back. With South Carolina under growing threat of enemy invasion, he chose instead to stay home and joined the local militia. The presence of British armies in next door Georgia touched off a virtual civil war between the south's patriots and friends and neighbors still loyal to England. Although the struggle between fellow Americans would eventually devolve into bloody, small unit conflicts on back roads and lonely farmsteads, local patriots tried to prevent trouble before it started by suppressing the loyalists. Among the most zealous of these was Middleton who advocated such tactics as tarring and feathering and the seizure of property abandoned by loyalists who had fled the state. His firmness would come back to haunt him when the invading British would later ransack Middleton Place, destroy all of his own possessions, and trample an elaborate English garden built by Middleton's father that had been designed according to the principles of Andre Le Notre and built at great expense and the labor of 100 slaves over ten years. It was during this time too, that Middleton was offered a position as governor of South Carolina, a position he chose to decline due to disagreement with the shape of the state's newly adopted constitution.

In 1780, after an earlier repulse, the enemy returned to South Carolina in force and Charleston was invested. Soon, with the city surrounded, Middleton found himself trapped inside along with thousands of Continental troops and militia. Upon the city's surrender, he was captured as a combatant with fellow signers of the Declaration Edward Rutledge and Thomas Heyward and shuffled off to St. Augustine, Florida as a prisoner of war. After almost a year in captivity, Middleton was taken to Philadelphia and exchanged. While in Pennsylvania, he learned that South Carolina had once again appointed him to Congress but he remained barely long enough to contribute to the creation of one of the great iconic images of the new United States.

Before leaving for home later in 1782, Middleton served on a committee that eventually submitted to Congress a design for the Great Seal of the United States that included an eagle brandishing a clutch of arrows in one claw and an olive branch in the other. With the design approved in June of 1782, Middleton, anxious to return home and see his family, left Congress soon after. Back in South Carolina, Middleton learned of the damage to his home and was reunited with his wife who had fled before the advancing British lines with their children in tow. Preferring to concentrate on his family and restoring his estates, Middleton declined a request that he rejoin the Continental Congress. Instead, he became an intermittent legislator until January 1, 1787 when he died unexpectedly after being exposed to inclement weather.

Thomas Mifflin

Although he never wavered in his support for the Revolution, Thomas Mifflin did suffer a crisis of faith regarding George Washington as commander in chief of the Continental Army. As a result, despite his undisputed credentials as a Founding Father, Mifflin has also been associated with those who supported Gen. Horatio Gates as a replacement for Washington. The discontent however, never grew beyond some griping about Washington in private letters and a serious campaign to relieve the Virginian never coalesced into any real threat. His support for Gates and his earlier performance as the army's first quartermaster general presented rare failures in judgment for Mifflin whose career was otherwise a stellar one.

Born in Philadelphia, Pennsylvania on January 10, 1744, Mifflin was raised as a Quaker, the son of a wealthy merchant with political connections. After attending a local school, Mifflin was sent to the College of Philadelphia to complete his studies and graduated in 1760. Still a teenager, he began work in a local counting house before quitting and traveling to Europe. Returning to America, he married and partnering with his brother, went into business for himself as a trader. In 1765 he became a member of the American Philosophical Society and with the success of his business, found the time for some politicking. In 1773, he summered in Massachusetts where he met Samuel Adams and other patriots who reinforced his growing unease with British policies toward the colonies. First elected to the Pennsylvania legislature only the year before, Mifflin soon became one of the most ardent voices raised among local Sons of Liberty.

By 1774, Mifflin's reputation as a firebrand was such that he was chosen to serve in Pennsylvania's delegation to the First Continental Congress. Still popular with the people, he was reappointed to the Second Continental Congress but after war broke out in Massachusetts in the spring of 1775, his martial spirits prompted him to leave politics to help in the effort to recruit and train men for the Pennsylvania militia. Although his activities cost him membership in the Society of Friends, he was recognized by patriot leaders and appointed a major. Joining the new Continental Army, his first assignment was as an aide to Washington but only months later, in the summer of 1775, the general named him as the army's first quartermaster general. The job was an important one but largely thankless and loaded with pitfalls. Preferring action as a line officer rather than pushing papers, Mifflin tended to neglect his duties as quartermaster in favor of leading men in combat. That

Thomas Mifflin

autumn, for instance, he led a unit that surprised a group of enemy soldiers out looking for plunder at Lechmere's Point in Massachusetts. Pleading for an active command, he briefly left his position as quartermaster for the field and commanded American forces ordered to cover the retreat of the army from Long Island. Those deeds, as well as his successful effort to keep New England veterans from leaving the army at a critical point, resulted in his being promoted first to colonel, then to brigadier general.

In 1776, Mifflin was back in Philadelphia on a recruiting campaign when problems finding a replacement for him as quartermaster prompted a request both by Washington and Congress for him to return to his desk. But again, his duties as quartermaster did not prevent him from leading a brigade into the subsequent battles of Trenton, Princeton, and those around Philadelphia. Late in 1777, Mifflin was promoted to major general but after a congressional committee investigating complaints about the quartermaster department found it near collapse, he decided to quit the army.

Over the next two years, Mifflin served as a civilian member of the Congressional Board of War and, joining many others in his dissatisfaction with Washington's performance as commander in chief of the Continental Army, began to consider the possibility of replacing him. Mifflin may have been influenced in his estimation of Washington from his experience on Long Island when confusion in orders coming from the commander in chief almost resulted in disaster for the Americans. At the time, Mifflin had been ordered to cover the army's retreat from Long Island until he received orders from headquarters to abandon his prepared positions. His men were in the process of falling back when Washington himself approached and asked why they were retreating. "I did it by your order," replied a testy Mifflin whereupon Washington denied giving the order. It was only luck that allowed Mifflin's men to return to their former positions before the British could discover that they had been abandoned. So it was possibly no surprise that Mifflin could later consider Gen. Horatio Gates as a replacement for Washington. Gates at the time, seemed a good alternative having come fresh from a stunning victory in 1777 over British Gen. John Burgoyne at the battle of Saratoga. Also eating away at Mifflin was possible resentment of rival Gen. Nathanael Greene who had superceded him in Washington's councils. The effort however, never amounted to much more than talk and Washington remained in command.

Mifflin, angered at rumors that he had had a greater involvement in the attempt to remove Washington from command than he let on, resigned from the Board of War and attempted a return to the army. But his reappearance there was a disappointment both because he was prevented from fully participating by Washington who disdained him as a "sunshine patriot," and after his former role as quartermaster general came back to haunt him. Accused of mismanagement and embezzlement while quartermaster, Mifflin bristled. He had always been more interested in combat after all and never really paid much attention to the details of his quartermaster duties. Instead, he preferred to leave those to subordinates whom he blamed, along with an indifferent Congress, for any questionable dealings there may have been during his tenure. His protests however, did little good, but when Congress ordered Washington to investigate the charges with a formal inquiry, none was ever held. Perhaps the partisan origins of the accusations were proved when, even after he had resigned from the army for good on August 17, 1778, Congress continued to seek Mifflin's services for such duties as helping to reorganize the Army.

As a result, Mifflin was in Philadelphia during the summer of 1779 when supplies of all sorts were running low and public anger against speculators had reached the breaking point. Together with other officials suspected of profiteering, Mifflin was forced to take refuge in the home of attorney James Wilson and was only rescued by the local militia after some blood had been spilled. Returning to civilian life, Mifflin became trustee of the University of Pennsylvania and was again elected to the Pennsylvania legislature. In 1782, he was returned to Congress where he served as its president until mid-1784 and presided over ratification of the Treaty of Paris. Considering how he once contemplated removing Washington from the position of commander in chief of the Continental Army, it was ironic that as president, one of Mifflin's duties was to accept the general's official resignation upon the close of the war, something he did, by some accounts, with poor grace.

Following his stint in Congress, Mifflin returned to Philadelphia in 1787 as a member of the Constitutional Convention. With belief in a strong central government, he supported approval of the Constitution at Pennsylvania's ratification convention and succeeded Benjamin Franklin as president of the state's supreme executive council. Next, he chaired the convention charged with formulating a new state constitution under whose articles he was elected governor in 1790. Identifying himself with the Jeffersonian/Republicans, Mifflin became a supporter of the French Revolution and served as a strong executive for the next decade until returning as a member of the legislature in 1799. Active in politics until the end, Mifflin was still a legislator when he died in reduced circumstances at Lancaster, Pennsylvania on January 20, 1800.

Richard Montgomery

Right from the beginning of open hostilities between America and Britain on Lexington green blood was spilled. The next day a great deal more was shed as thousands of minutemen from all over Massachusetts congregated on the "battle road" leading from Concord back to

Boston. Over the following weeks leading up to the battle of Breed's Hill, which climaxed the opening chapter of the Revolutionary War, both sides were forced to acknowledge the harsh reality that winning the war would come at a high price in human life. And though all who fell in the name of the noble cause were heroes with most known and mourned and their exploits in the war celebrated only in their home towns or states, others became national heroes achieving their reputations by word of mouth or, more often, through literature and poetry. An example of the former might be the Massachusetts firebrand Joseph Warren who died atop Breed's Hill early in the war. Another who met his end early in the conflict but who has achieved a somewhat wider notoriety was Richard Montgomery.

Born to Irish gentry in Dublin on December 2, 1736, Montgomery followed one of the traditional career paths for a younger son and entered the military. Commissioned an officer at the age of twenty, he was already familiar with much of the social philosophies popular at the time and once a soldier, immersed himself in military history and culture. The resulting mix of influences heightened Montgomery's sense of honor and duty, personal attributes that would later influence his decision to make common cause with the Americans during the Revolution. More immediately, he found himself in combat at Louisbourg in 1758 and Quebec in 1759 during the French and Indian War and later in Havana, Cuba in 1762. Debilitated from life in the tropics, he was invalidated to New York to recuperate. There, he met his future wife Janet Livingston, who was related to future signer of the Declaration of Independence Philip Livingston and began to sympathize with the resentments Americans felt toward a British Parliament intent on finding some way to tax them without their consent. In fact, when ordered to enforce the Stamp Act, Montgomery

Richard Montgomery

resigned his commission. Returning to England, he became dissatisfied with his treatment there and decided to make his home in America.

Moving to New York, Montgomery purchased an estate along the Hudson River in Dutchess County, married Janet in 1773 and settled down to what he expected to be the life of a country gentlemen. Unfortunately, war interfered with his plans and his sense of duty to his adopted country prompted him to offer his services. He was appointed by Congress a brigadier general and reported for duty under Gen. Phillip Schuyler at Ticonderoga for the western portion of a two pronged attack on Canada which many hoped could be persuaded to join the American cause as a fourteenth colony.

Early on in the planning stages however, Schuyler, unenthusiastic as a military officer, became ill and retired from active duty. As a result, Montgomery, who was unimpressed with the quality of the troops that had been assembled, found himself in command of an army. Courageous, experienced, and bristling with energy, Montgomery threw himself into the task of preparing his 2,000 man force for its thrust up Lake Champlain to its first target: the town of St. Johns, a stepping stone to Montreal that had already been captured once by Gen. Benedict Arnold earlier in the war. After a frustrating delay at Ticonderoga, the army finally was underway and arrived in the vicinity of St. Johns in mid-September, 1775. After laying the fortress there under siege for nearly six weeks, its garrison of 700 soldiers finally surrendered. Montreal itself fell without a struggle on November 14 amid worsening weather as the year drew on toward winter.

Receiving word that a second column of 700 men under the command of Benedict Arnold had reached Quebec, the remnant of 1,100 that had originally started out from Massachusetts, Montgomery boarded a small fleet of boats seized at Montreal and traveled upriver with an additional 300 men. Arriving outside Quebec, he supplied Arnold's troops with much needed winter clothing and decided that the city could be easily taken. "Nothing shall be wanting on my part to reap the advantage of our good fortune," he reported optimistically in a letter to Schuyler. Meanwhile, behind Quebec's walls, Gen. Sir Guy Carleton had barricaded himself along with a mixed force of 1,700 men, ready to defend the city. This fact did not deter the two American generals who felt the city's defensive works too extensive for Carleton's army to defend, an army Montgomery characterized as "banditti," untried sailors and local residents without stomach to fight. Such was the New Yorker's confidence, even as he battled dissension among his own men some of whose enlistments were nearly up and others refusing to fight under Arnold, that he had even made plans for the occupation of a conquered Canada by 10,000 fresh troops!

And so, outside the city's walls, Montgomery sent a letter to Carleton demanding that he surrender immediately. It was refused and after resorting to bombardment, the Americans found the city impregnable to their fire. At last, in the early morning hours of December 31, under cover of a winter snowstorm, the Americans attacked. Arnold took his army north of the city to try and fight his way along the narrow streets while Montgomery led his fellow New Yorkers south along a trail that wound about the foot of a steep cliff beside the freezing waters of the St. Lawrence River. This route was thought to be the weaker of the two. At the head of his column of 200 soldiers, who were spread out almost single file back along the cliff side, Montgomery moved forward to clear the trail. At first, progress was good, but then the Americans came upon a fortified hut manned mostly by Canadian militia who had been warned by spies of the impending attack. As Montgomery led the way forward, there was a scatter of rifle fire and, just as the defenders decided to abandon their position, a lingering sailor touched off a primed cannon. There was a great roar and when the smoke cleared, Montgomery and a number of his officers lay dead or dying. With his last breath, Montgomery urged Captain Aaron Burr to continue the assault, but the young officer, unable to persuade the men to follow him, contented himself with a heroic effort to rescue Montgomery's body. But the robust general proving to be too heavy, Burr was forced to leave him behind and join the retreating New Yorkers. The failure of Montgomery's men to press the attack left Arnold's force to face an undivided enemy resistance. There too, luck was against the Americans as first Arnold was wounded and then co-commander Daniel Morgan captured. Leaderless, the American army gave up the fight for Quebec and began a retreat down the St. Lawrence back to Montreal where disease and desertions further reduced their number until, finally, the pitiful remnants of the army found themselves once more at Ticonderoga.

Could things have ended differently if Montgomery had not been killed before his troops made their way into the city? Could an enemy, divided between two attacking forces, been strong enough to withstand the American assault? It is hard to say, but more than once the tide of a battle has turned on the courage, leadership and force of personality of a single man and both Arnold and Montgomery certainly possessed those qualities. One thing is for sure however; although the Americans lost their first attempt to make Canada the fourteenth state, they gained their first hero of national standing. Montgomery's body was buried within the walls of Quebec where he had fallen and remained there for 42 years until 1818 when he was exhumed and returned to New York for burial with all the solemn panoply due a returning hero.

Daniel Morgan

Of all those who served in a military capacity during the Revolutionary War, no one seems to have participated in as many key battles and in as many different theaters as Daniel Morgan. From the snow bound Plains of Abraham in Canada, to the fortifications surrounding Boston, to the green fields of rural New York, to the sultry forests of the South, Morgan's towering, often buckskin clad figure became, to all who knew him, a symbol of American individualism and steely resolve. Never formally educated, the rugged frontiersman learned about fighting first hand against Indians and by observing how the British Army did it. More importantly, he learned from the mistakes of his enemies and more than once was able to turn the tables on the battlefield to spectacular effect.

Morgan was born in Hunterdon County, New Jersey in 1736 and judging by the evidence, was an undisciplined youngster who proved too much for his parents to handle. One day, after a particularly heated dispute with his father, he abruptly left home and ran away to Virginia. There, in the state's rough inland country, his unruly nature fit in perfectly with the gambling, drinking, and no holds barred style of fistfighting indulged in by the locals. Strong and unafraid of hard work, Morgan built his strength as a hired hand and later with a stint as foreman at a sawmill. Finally, he seemed to satisfy his wanderlust with a job driving goods over the mountains from the eastern part of the state to the frontier. It was while occupied as a wagoner that he had his first experience with military life transporting supplies for the British Army during the French and Indian War. An incident in which Morgan was sentenced to receive 500 lashes across the back for striking an officer probably went a long way in convincing him to take up arms against the British twenty years later when the Revolution broke out. However, the incident did not immediately drive him from the military. That came in 1757 after he had applied for and won a commission as an ensign and then found himself ambushed by Indians at Hanging Rock. In that action, two of

Morgan's companions were killed while he took a rifle ball through the back of the neck that exited from his mouth, taking many of his teeth with it. His mouth ruined and scarred for life, Morgan left the army. After the war, his wild streak was domesticated somewhat after he bought a house, found a wife, and fathered two children. But soon enough, his rougher qualities would once more be allowed full rein.

Almost as soon as word reached Virginia of the running battle between Massachusetts farmers and British soldiers at Lexington and Concord, Morgan determined to join the hundreds of volunteers from other colonies streaming north to join the army of minutemen surrounding Boston. By now well known and admired in his adopted community, he was named captain of a company of riflemen whose buckskinned dress and incredibly accurate Kentucky rifles caused quite a stir when they finally reached the new Continental Army outside Boston.

Quickly growing tired of camp life, Morgan and his men decided to volunteer for an ambitious operation that would see Canada invaded by a pair of American armies led by Generals Richard Montgomery and Benedict Arnold. The plan called for the two armies to invade Canada from two directions converging in time for a twin assault on Quebec. Joining Arnold's wing of the invasion, Morgan survived one of history's most grueling winter marches during which starvation and freezing to death were a constant threat. At last, after covering almost 600 miles in eight weeks, the depleted and exhausted army reached Quebec in December of 1775, united with a few hundred of Montgomery's men, and attacked the fortress city under the cover of a blinding blizzard. From that point on, everything went wrong. First Montgomery

Daniel Morgan

was killed, prompting his men to retreat in disorder, then Arnold was wounded and forced out of the battle. Suddenly, Morgan found himself the senior officer in command and, making the decision to continue the attack, he led the remainder of the men into the heart of the city. But that day, fate was against the Americans. Outnumbered and cornered amid the narrow, twisting streets of the city, they were forced to surrender and Morgan spent the next eight months as a prisoner of war.

Finally, after agreeing not to fight the British until a prisoner exchange could be arranged, Morgan and his men were paroled. A year later, recovered from his ordeal and newly promoted to Colonel, Morgan found himself in a different theater of the war and about to become a key player in one of the great battles of the Revolution. Dispatched to upstate New York by Washington in response to a request by Gen. Philip Schuyler for reinforcements, Morgan marched his company of 500 frontiersmen from New Jersey to the vicinity of Saratoga. There, a mixed force of almost 10,000 Continentals and local militia faced a British army of 5,000 men under the command of Gen. John Burgoyne that had come down from Canada by way of the Hudson River Valley. The British plan was to have Burgoyne link up with a second army that would move up from the south and cut off the hotbed of revolution in New England from the rest of the colonies. But a third army that had been turned back in the western part of New York by Benedict Arnold and the defeat of a strong detachment from Burgoyne's army near Bennington, Vermont threatened the plan with failure setting up a last, desperate attempt by the enemy to defeat the Americans in the field at Saratoga. Such was the situation upon Morgan's arrival when Gen. Horatio Gates, who had replaced Schuyler, ordered his detachment to support the American left. By coincidence, the order ended up having Morgan once again sharing the fight with Arnold, who was in command of the left wing.

Thus it was that early on the morning of September 19, as the British were observed preparing to advance up Bemis Heights towards Freeman's Farm, Arnold suggested that instead of placing his men behind prepared fortifications, Morgan position them amid the cover afforded by some nearby woods. From that position, the frontier sharpshooters would be able to lay down a harassing fire on the enemy as they came up the heights. What began as a skirmish quickly escalated to full scale battle as more and more American units were fed into the developing fight. When the long day finally ended, Burgoyne was left in possession of the field but at a cost of a third of his army. On October 7, after having expected his enemies to continue their attack, Burgoyne ventured out of his camp with 1,500 men to reconnoiter the American lines and discover what the situation was. Recognizing Burgoyne's vulnerability, Gates moved his units to the attack and once again ordered Morgan's men to open the battle from the cover of nearby woods. Morgan himself suggested having his men take a wide circuit to the left to hit the enemy on the flank, which was done. "The plan was the best which could be devised, and no doubt contributed essentially to the prompt and decisive victory we gained," wrote Col James Wilkinson later. As hostilities escalated, Arnold, confined to headquarters, could not hold his martial enthusiasm in check and rode toward the sound of the guns arriving in time to lead the climactic charge into an enemy redoubt. Just before he did so however, Arnold asked Morgan to have his sharpshooters target British Gen. Simon Fraser who was in immediate command of the enemy formations. The Virginian obliged and Fraser was killed at the head of his men. When the day was done, the Americans, who had outnumbered the British 6 to 1, held the field and Arnold was in hospital with a broken leg. The next day, Burgoyne abandoned his positions and took his main army north to Saratoga where he was eventually surrounded. There matters rested until, having run out of supplies and his pack animals dead of starvation, Burgoyne surrendered.

Perhaps due to Morgan's role in the important victory at Saratoga not being sufficiently recognized by the Continental Congress, he was later denied command of an elite military unit and passed over for promotion to the rank of general. Angered, Morgan left the army and returned to Virginia. Recognizing his value, however, Congress later offered him command of the war's southern theater but because the appointment came without a promotion, Morgan refused. Instead, the post was given to Gates, still basking in the glow of Saratoga, who soon disappointed his admirers by mishandling the very different conditions that characterized the war in the south. On August 16, 1780, Gates' forces met the enemy at Camden, South Carolina and were soundly and humiliatingly defeated.

With the south now completely open to the ravages of the enemy, Morgan felt compelled to emerge from retirement and reenter the fray. He was finally given a promotion to brigadier general and under the overall command of Gen. Nathaniel Green, who had succeeded Gates in the southern theater, Morgan climaxed his career with victory in one of the war's greatest set piece battles. It began late in the year of 1780 when British Gen. Lord Charles Cornwallis, eager to end the rebel threat in the Carolinas once and for all, fostered a plan to move his forces in two columns. The main force would move north of Winsboro, South Carolina while a second, lighter column under the command of the hated Col. Banastre Tarleton, would march along a more inland route. The hope was to catch Morgan's command between them and crush him before moving on to put the coup de grace to Green's main body. Things did not turn out that way however, because when Tarleton finally caught up to Morgan, the tables would be reversed. It happened at a place called Hannah's Cowpens on January 17 and despite a pessimism that had gripped him a few days earlier and deep misgivings about how local militia units would perform under fire, Morgan decided to challenge Tarleton head on.

The key to the resulting victory lay in Morgan's excellent judgment of the quality of his men. Knowing the unreliability of the untrained militia, he placed them in two lines at the center of his formation, below a gently rising hill. Behind them, he placed his regulars of the Continental Army and in reserve, out of sight behind the hill, Col. William Washington's cavalry. He had only one request of the militia: give him two fires and they could retire behind the safety of the regulars. Around 7 a.m., Tarelton's legion of American Tories and British regulars numbering about 1,200 men appeared at the southern end of the cowpens. Nervously, the militia watched as an attempt to sweep the skirmish line from the field failed and an impatient Tarleton ordered his infantry into ranks for an advance toward the American lines. As requested, most of the second line of militia delivered their two fires and withdrew in order to the American left. Those farthest to the right however, had time to fire only once before Tarleton's dragoons were among them; but just as they were, Col. Washington's cavalry swooped down from behind the hill and routed them. In the meantime, the British infantry had moved forward again, this time exchanging fire with the Continentals near the crest of the hill. Then, at the height of the exchange, part of the American line began to fall back, the result of an order being misinterpreted. Thinking their enemy breaking under the pressure, the British infantry charged the retreating men. "Face about boys!" cried Morgan, riding out in front of the regulars. "Give them one good fire and the victory is ours!" The men did as they were bid and when the smoke cleared, the field was littered with British dead and those left standing were chased down with the bayonet. Wheeling to the right, the Continentals then marched toward the enemy units still fighting among Washington's horsemen. In the meantime, the militia who had retreated after their first fire had circled the rear of the hill and emerged behind Washington to engage the enemy from that direction.

The remaining British on the field were caught between two advancing bodies of Americans and when Tarleton was unable to rally his remaining cavalry for a rescue, grounded their arms and surrendered. The battle had cost the Americans but 12 men killed while inflicting over 100 casualties on the enemy and wounding and capturing 800 more. The myth of Tarleton's invincibility was shattered.

By thinking outside the convention of accepted military tactics and adapting himself to the particular strengths and limitations of his fellow frontiersman, Morgan won as complete a triumph at Cowpens as any battle of the war. But despite further service in the south, Cowpens would prove to be the climax of the old wagoner's career. Ill even before the battle, Morgan now found it too much to continue and was granted a leave of absence. Returning to his home in Virginia, he would never again accept active service during the war. And although he briefly took to the saddle one more time to help suppress the Whiskey Rebellion of 1797, he moved on to the less active halls of Congress as a member of the House of Representatives where his sympathies were more for the Federalists rather than for fellow Virginian Thomas Jefferson's Republicans. Morgan left office in 1799 and died at his home in Winchester, Virginia on July 6, 1802. Of him, Nathaniel Green, his commanding officer during the southern campaign, said simply but truly, "Good generals are scarce…There are few Morgan's to be found."

Gouverneur Morris

One of the most intransigent problems afflicting those of the revolutionary generation was the struggle to overcome sectional loyalties and to cultivate a genuine sense of nationalism. As subjects of the king, Americans felt they owed their first loyalty to England and secondarily to their individual colonies. Once the king was removed from the equation, loyalty to colony, which many began to refer to as their "country," took center stage. Throughout the early resistance to the king's policies efforts were made by various patriots to make Americans in other colonies not suffering directly under the oppressive measures to feel kinship with those that were. It was an uphill battle until such larger colonies as

New York and Virginia joined Massachusetts as targets of British ire. It was only once they shared the common cause of oppression that Committees of Correspondence gained popularity and patriots from different colonies began to see the wisdom of joining together to form a common front against the mother country. Even then, however, sectional interests and jealousies often superceded those of the confederation: New York and New Hampshire sparred over the Hampshire Grants, the rural South suspected the mercantile North, the frontier resented the attention given to the seaboard in men and supplies. Thus, in the early days of the revolution, it was the rare man who could rise above such provincialism and see that the geography of America compelled a close relationship among the colonies for reasons including economy, communication, and security. One of those men was Gouverneur Morris.

Morris was born on January 31, 1752 at Morrisania, his family's estate in Westchester County, New York. The only son of a second marriage, Morris knew early on that if he were to continue to live the lifestyle he enjoyed as a member of one the colony's wealthiest families, he would have to earn the money to do it by himself. It was fortunate then, that he possessed an intelligence that was first displayed in his early education and that continued when he moved on to King's College at the age of twelve. Graduating in 1768, he went on to study the law and upon passing the bar in 1771, found easy entry into the colony's leadership circles.

Gouverneur Morris

Along the way, Morris was instilled with a strong sense of individual freedom and love of liberty that was only strengthened after he began to associate himself with similarly minded would-be revolutionaries.

Morris' involvement with the resistance movement kicked into high gear in 1775 when he was elected as a member of New York's Provincial Congress which supplanted the colony's legislative assembly by default after royal Governor William Tryon retreated to the safety of a British warship. As he was drawn deeper into the revolutionary movement and talk of independence from England grew, Morris faced a difficult decision, one made all the harder due to the fact that many in his family would choose to remain loyal to England during the coming conflict. In 1776, Morris chose to remain faithful to his belief in the principals of liberty and joined the local militia as a lieutenant colonel knowing full well that in the wake of Lexington and Concord and the siege of Boston, he was taking an action considered treasonous. There was no turning back and after the Declaration of Independence had been signed by members of the Continental Congress in Philadelphia (of which his half brother Lewis, was a member), Morris made sure of it by working with the Provincial Congress to fashion a new government for the state of New York. Joining close friends John Jay and Robert Livingston, he helped to draft the state's constitution, the last to be adopted by the thirteen states.

Quitting the militia after it refused to be absorbed into the Continental Army, Morris involved himself ever deeper in the workings of New York's new state government, slowly emerging as its expert on fiscal affairs as chairman of the Ways and Means Committee. His energy and willingness to work hard and long at the dull but crucial job of crunching numbers to balance the books while finding the money to cover the state's wartime responsibilities brought him increasingly to the attention of his peers who quickly appointed him to the state's Committee of Safety where he acted as liaison to the state's militia and kept track of residents opposed to the revolution. His duties with the militia naturally placed him in contact with George Washington, commander in chief of the Continental Army, who guessed correctly that New York would be the enemy's next target after the British evacuated Boston in 1776. Despite suggestions that the city of New York be burned to the ground to deny it to the enemy, Congress judged that such a desperate move would be a crushing blow to patriot morale. Instead, Washington was ordered to defend the state from invasion. Over the ensuing weeks, Morris worked with Washington and his staff to prepare for the defense of the city as well as the rest of Manhattan and Long Island. In anticipation of the battle to come, he even rejoined the state's militia and may have seen some action. Unfortunately, all of it came to nothing as the invading British took advantage of its naval power to outflank the defenders chasing them first from Long Island and then from Manhattan. The disappointment of the campaign was made all the keener for Morris whose family estate in Westchester was overrun and his home opened up by his loyalist mother for use by the enemy.

Cut off from New York and his family, Morris turned down a seat in the state's legislature but in 1778 accepted an appointment as a member of New York's delegation to the Continental Congress where he signed the Articles of Confederation. As a result of his experience in New York working with and making sure the militia was supplied, Morris was made a member of a committee sent to inspect the Continental Army and conditions at Valley Forge. The sight that met his eyes at the winter camp shocked and moved him to fight every chance he could for the welfare of the common soldier. His experience in the Congress and its failure to address even such basic needs as supplying the army, convinced Morris that the new government, based on the Articles of Confederation, was too weak to properly address the problems of the nation, a nationalist point of view that his constituents had yet to embrace. Thus, his outspoken attitude toward such matters went unappreciated by his constituents who decided to replace him in Congress.

Estranged from the people in his own state, Morris took up permanent residence in Pennsylvania, entered private law practice and in 1779 wrote *Observations on the American Revolution*. Somewhat of a bon vivant, his enjoyment of the good things in life was hardly slowed even after a carriage accident in 1780 left him with the loss of a leg and its replacement with a wooden substitute. In the meantime, he embarked on a series of articles for local newspapers writing on financial issues. The letters brought him to the attention of Robert Morris (no relation), perhaps the wealthiest man in the country at the time and when Robert was appointed by Congress in 1781 as its Superintendent of Finance with virtually limitless power over the nation's fiscal policies, he asked Morris to join him as his assistant. In that capacity, Morris developed the country's current system of decimal coinage and in 1787, his superior pulled strings to have him appointed as a member of the state's delegation to the Constitutional Convention.

His appointment to such an important post seemed to justify his nationalist position and the convention's debates, which were closed to the public, made it easier for him to give voice to his beliefs. Those beliefs however, were not always shared by his fellow delegates who for the most part, as in the lengthy discussions involving the admission of new states, were still concerned about the rights of their individual states. "It is at all times difficult," wrote Morris, "to draw with precision the line between those rights which must be surrendered, and those which may be reserved; and on the present occasion this difficulty was increased by a difference among the several states as to their situation, extent, habits, and particular interests." Rising to speak a record 173 times, Morris worked hard both to explain his nationalist position and to keep his often impolitic outbursts in check and in the process, aware as many others were, that what emerged from the convention would likely set an example for the rest of the world, stood firm against slavery, defended such basic tenets as freedom of speech and religion, property rights and the rule of law and consent of the governed. Morris, however, was sanguine about democracy itself versus republicanism, fearful as many learned men were at the time of direct rule by the common people. Morris was also wary of the backwoods settlers on the frontier who he believed would sooner or later drag the country into a war with Spain over control of the Mississippi River. Perhaps in appreciation for his leading role in the debates, Morris was chosen along with Alexander Hamilton, James Madison, William Samuel Johnson, and Rufus King as a member of its Committee of Style and Arrangement to draft the constitutional instrument. In the end, although not completely happy with the result, Morris supported the Constitution and was responsible for much of its written text including its historic preamble: "We the People of the United States, in order to form a more perfect Union..."

Following the convention, Morris turned down an invitation by Alexander Hamilton to participate in writing the Federalist Papers and moved back to New York. After mending bridges with the rest of his family, he set off for Europe in 1789 on business. He would remain there for almost ten years, witnessing the first repercussions of the American Revolution as France, the country's wartime ally, underwent the early upheavals of its own revolution, one that would soon devolve into an orgy of violence. In 1790, Washington, as the new President of the United States, asked Morris to travel to London in a diplomatic capacity to see what he could do to settle outstanding issues involved with the treaty that had ended the Revolution. In 1792, Morris replaced Thomas Jefferson as ambassador to France, but because of the constant unrest in the country over the next two years and his own hostility to the revolution, he was unable to accomplish much beyond keeping to his post during the infamous Reign of Terror that subsequently gripped Paris. Eventually, the French revolutionary authorities demanded he be recalled in retaliation for a similar request by the United States concerning its own ambassador, Edmund Genet. Genet had made himself *persona non grata* in America by interfering with domestic matters just as Morris had done in France when he involved himself in a plot to free the imprisoned royal family.

Returning to the United States in 1798, Morris bought the family home in Westchester from his brother and with his beliefs in a strong central government still strong but wary of the rising power of the Republicans, found himself drawn to the Federalist Party headed by his friend and New York political kingmaker Alexander Hamilton. As a result, in 1800, he was appointed to fill the unexpired term of Congressman James Watson in the United States Senate but after almost three years in office, was unable to hold on to his seat and lost it in 1803. The next year, he had the sad privilege of eulogizing Hamilton following his old friend's death in a duel with political enemy Aaron Burr. His sense of nationalism undimmed by political rejection, Morris was still eager to see the strengthening of the country's economy through investment in public works projects that would expand regional trade and help bind different parts of the country together. Although it was a positive vision for the future that moved him to accept a position as chairman of the Erie Canal Commission in 1810, Morris grew more pessimistic about the union he helped forge with the outbreak of the War of 1812 and the domestic rancor that accompanied it, prompting him even to suggest its dissolution.

Morris' participation in the Erie Canal project however, would remain unfulfilled as he left the commission in 1813, well ahead of the project's official completion in 1825. But if anyone thought that the senior revolutionary had any idea of slowing down in his old age, they were mistaken. Even as he worried about the future of the United States, he climaxed a life of public service and the quest for pleasure with his marriage in 1812 to Anne Cary, a woman half his age. The fact that she was surrounded by a scandal involving possible incest and murder was of little concern to him. Finally, on November 6, 1816, Morris died at Morrisania, the same place where he was born.

Lewis Morris

An old revolutionary of the generation of James Otis, Lewis Morris would have been content to live out his life as a gentleman farmer on his New York estate but for what he saw as the growing oppression of the British government. Joining early with the patriot cause, he earned the resentment of his wealthy neighbors and after signing the Declaration of the Independence, suffered the loss of his fortune and the destruction of his beloved Morrisania.

Born at Morrisania on April 8, 1726, Lewis Morris was the eldest son of a wealthy and influential clan that included step brother Gouverneur Morris. His education began at the hands of private tutors and was continued when he left home to attend Yale College where he graduated in 1746. However, being the eldest of the family carried with it certain obligations and upon leaving school, he returned to Morrisania to help his father run the estate, a fate he enjoyed. Although he would have preferred to remain in the country tending to the farm, as an educated man and a member of the wealthy class, he was called by the colonial government to serve on New York's admiralty court where he remained until rising disagreement over British policies in the Americas forced him to resign in 1774. Meanwhile, Morris chose to run for office in his own right and was elected to the colonial legislature in 1769. His position in the legislature however, placed him in close proximity to royal authority from where he could judge first hand the oppressive nature of unpopular rulings emanating from Parliament and their effects upon local business and ordinary citizens. Soon, he became an outspoken opponent of the various measures and a strong supporter of the growing patriot cause. Although not chosen as a member of the Stamp Act Congress that met in New York during 1774, Morris was surely a supporter of it because the next year he was instrumental in organizing a provincial convention at White Plains that was to select a delegation for representation at a new Continental Congress to be held in Philadelphia in 1775. His efforts

Lewis Morris

with the convention were rewarded when he found himself appointed as a member of New York's delegation.

A valued member of the Congress, Morris was immediately assigned to the Secret Committee charged with acquiring weapons and munitions for the new Continental Army and later, was appointed to a special commission sent to make peace with the Indians and ensure their non-participation if the hostilities that had broken out in Massachusetts between colonists and Britain expanded into a general conflict. Absent from Philadelphia for several months as a result of his duties, he returned to Congress in time to make the most momentous decision of his life. Although firmly in favor of independence, Morris had to wait until his fellow citizens in New York could overcome their hopes for an eventual reconciliation with Britain before joining him in his zeal for liberty. Eventually they did and Morris became free to sign the Declaration of Independence, an action that left him open for reprisal by the enemy, which in time happened.

After the British occupied New York and invaded New Jersey, Morris' property at Morrisania was targeted for spoliation and during the course of the war, he would experience the loss of the great part of his fortune as well as the destruction of the land he loved. It was perhaps with even greater pain that Morris heard from Lewis Morris, Jr., one of three sons serving in the Continental Army, of how their home was plundered first, not by the British, but by fellow patriots seeking desperately needed supplies for the army. "I assure you, sir, your affairs at Morrisania, however secure you may think they may be, are in a very critical situation..." wrote the younger Morris, describing how the American army had occupied the property, turned his home into a barracks, and confiscated livestock and auctioned off furniture.

Undaunted, Morris continued with his duties in Congress while often taking time out to serve as a brigadier general in the New York militia. Later, he became a deputy with the state's provincial convention and then a member of the provincial congress in 1776. In 1777, he gave up his seat in Congress to his brother Gouverneur and was appointed a county judge back in New York. Elected as a senator in the state's new legislature, he served there, except for a brief hiatus, from 1777 to 1788. He was appointed a regent of the University of New York and as a delegate to the state's constitutional ratifying convention in 1788, voted in favor of the new federal Constitution. Ten years later, after spending much of his retirement working to restore his estate, he met his death back on the grounds of his beloved Morrisania on January 22, 1798.

Robert Morris

Perhaps none of the Founding Fathers epitomizes the pledge to give up their lives, their fortunes and their sacred honor more than Robert Morris who went from being one of the richest, most successful businessmen in the thirteen colonies and ended as an inmate of a debtors' prison. Although the reasons for his incarceration were not directly related to his efforts in the service of his country, Morris nevertheless did sacrifice much of his time and wealth for the cause of American freedom. Many were the times that the purchase of extra barrels of flour or quantities of lead made on Morris' own credit when that of the United States government was almost worthless, made the difference between victory and defeat for Washington's hard pressed army.

Robert Morris

Born in Lancashire, England in 1734, Robert Morris was the son of a tobacco exporter who had moved to Oxford, Maryland for commercial reasons. When his son reached the age of 13, the elder Morris summoned him to America with the intention of including him in his business. Part of the younger Morris' preparation included his first formal schooling in Philadelphia, but before he had a chance to get too far, his father died. Leaving school, Morris obtained work with a local shipping-banking firm owned by Charles Willing. There, he proved his worth, learning the ins and outs of the trade until he was made a full partner in 1754 and later, formed his own company with Charles' son, Thomas. As the years passed, Morris paid little attention to the increasing friction between the colonies and the land of his birth, only rousing himself when measures such as the Stamp Act of 1765 threatened the smooth operation of his business which by that time included a fleet of trading vessels that plied the seas between Europe, Africa, and the Caribbean and diversified investments in real estate, manufacturing, and mining. But a nascent hostility to royal authority was slowly growing in him and when fighting broke out at Lexington, Massachusetts in 1775, the event galvanized his patriotic feelings as well as his business instincts. Soon after, his company had been charged with the lucrative trade in arms and other supplies for the Continental Congress and in that same year of 1775, Morris was named to Pennsylvania's Committee of Safety. Membership in the colony's Committee of Correspondence and provincial assembly soon followed culminating in his appointment to the Continental Congress. It was while serving there that Morris' still lukewarm feelings toward the Revolution made themselves apparent when he voted against independence on July 1, 1776. Not wishing to stand in the way of an obviously advancing tide however, he recused himself on the next vote, thus allowing the Pennsylvania delegation to vote for independence. Once the historic vote was taken however, he rejoined his fellow delegates and on July 4 signed the Declaration of Independence.

Once the die was cast, Morris had no reservations about the course chosen by his peers in the Congress and worked diligently as a member of numerous committees involved with overseeing the importation of supplies for the war effort and the arming of naval vessels; not an easy task for a young nation that was cash poor and whose income was earned primarily through agriculture. But Morris, who would become known as the financier of the Revolution, was equal to the task, using his long experience as a successful merchant to deal with suppliers, distribute goods and later, arrange credit by establishing the first federal Bank of North America of which he was among the first depositors. Not as sensitive to conflict of interest issues as later generations, many public figures, Morris included, saw nothing wrong with taking advantage of their positions in government to make a personal profit. The general public however, saw things a little differently. As the war went on and the rising price of food became unbearable, many in cities like Philadelphia took their anger out on those whom they suspected of profiteering, including Morris. In October of 1779, an angry mob briefly besieged he and others in the home of James Wilson until they were rescued by the city's military commander, Benedict Arnold.

Ironically however, it was the confluence of his public and private activities that was perhaps crucial to Morris' ability to succeed in his duties for Congress, enabling him to acquire much needed credit from other businessmen on the basis of his personal reputation. It was just such an understanding that may have saved the Continental Army late in 1776 when Washington desperately needed a victory to hold it together. In a letter written to Congress, Washington explained his plan to strike back against the British who had driven him from New York but in order for it to succeed, a sum of $10,000 was needed in order to buy intelligence of the enemy's movements. Unfortunately, the letter arrived in Philadelphia just after Congress had fled the city against it being seized by the British. Left behind with a handful of his fellow committee members, Morris was helpless to raise the funds without congressional authorization. Instead, he personally guaranteed a private loan from a fellow businessman for the money. The result was that Washington was able to cross the Delaware River and strike at the British at Trenton, reinvigorating the army, lifting the spirits of the public, and ensuring that resistance against the enemy would continue through the long winter. Confidence in Morris' word and personal credit came in handy again later in the war when the army was in desperate need of lead for its guns. When one of his own privateering vessels arrived in port bearing ninety tons of lead, Morris gave half the cargo to the army. Although the remaining half had already been sold to buyers, it was bought back by another businessman with the same intention. That purchase, however, had to be personally guaranteed by Morris. In another instance, Morris spent his own money to buy over 5,000 barrels of flour to provision a starving Continental Army that had been on the verge of mutiny. The move also forestalled a draconian measure by Congress that would have allowed the army to confiscate whatever provisions it needed from private citizens within a twenty mile radius of their campsite.

In 1778, Morris had given up his seat in Congress for a stint in Pennsylvania's legislature and after emerging in 1781 from an investigation into accusations of profiteering while serving in Congress, he was immediately appointed by that same body as its Superintendent of Finance. A condition of his appointment was that he would have sweeping powers to place the new nation's economic house in order and that he would be permitted to continue to conduct his own business concerns. His conditions met, Morris immediately proceeded to cut spending (which included soldiers' wages), track all of the government's revenues and expenditures, negotiate with the states over their individual apportionments, disperse private as well as European loans and saw that money was spent as intended by Congress and that the government was not cheated. Morris was also responsible for seeing that the army and navy were properly supplied, that the agencies of government were duly funded, that payments on outstanding loans were covered, and to keep track of the nation's financial interests at home and abroad. Although Morris had been granted vast powers over the country's financial system, he needed them in order to deal with a ruined economy that threatened American credit in Europe and an inflationary spiral at home that placed the cost of the simplest consumer goods out of reach of ordinary citizens. Even government employees were threatened with debtors' prison due to their not having been paid in months. Out of this shambles, Morris, through hard work, a native intelligence, and the strength of his own reputation, was not only able to provide the funds necessary to bring Washington's army from New York to Yorktown for the climactic battle of the war, but brought order to the nation's finances and placed them on a sound footing that would position the country to take advantage of the freedoms so dearly gained on the battlefield.

After the war, Morris returned to the Pennsylvania legislature for the term beginning in 1785 but clearly was more interested in immersing himself in his own business affairs. Although he clearly preferred the world of private finance to that of public service, he could not escape the fame of his fiscal wizardry and was chosen as a delegate first to the Annapolis Convention and then to the Constitutional Convention where his participation was minimal. Not a political animal, he remained on the sidelines during the growing struggle between Federalists and Republicans turning down an offer by President Washington to serve as his Secretary of the Treasury (suggesting instead the young Alexander Hamilton whom he characterized as "damned sharp") while at the same time taking a seat in the new United States Senate in 1789.

It was in the following years of his term in the Senate that Morris' financial judgment began to wane. He invested in real estate around the site of the future city of Washington D.C. and began to build a grand mansion in Philadelphia. Heavily leveraged, and caught in the general slump of the post-war economy, Morris found himself hounded by creditors who finally had him arrested and condemned to the ignominy of debtors' prison where he remained for three years until 1801. By the time he was released, the man who had given so much to ensure that his country might be free, in time, experience, and personal fortune, had grown feeble, old before his time, and penniless. Almost forgotten by his peers of the Revolutionary era, Morris, who had been respected but never liked, survived on a small pension acquired by the wife of a friend until he died in 1806.

John Morton

Not all of those who signed the Declaration of Independence were well known even in their own times let alone earning fame as one of the Founding Fathers. Take John Morton for instance, who had the misfortune of being the first of the signers to pass away, dying less than a year after passage of the Declaration, a death that cut short any chance he might have had of making a mark on the new country that he helped to create.

Born on a farm in Ridley Township, Pennsylvania in 1724, young Morton suffered the loss of his father early on but in John Sketchley, gained a stepfather who recognized his inborn talent for learning and personally supervised his education. After a few months in a local school, Morton was removed and taught the surveying trade by Sketchley himself and, after mastering the subject, went to work on his own. Morton was past thirty years old before he entered politics as a member of Pennsylvania's legislature in 1756 where he remained sometimes serving as speaker with only a single absence until 1775. In 1757, Morton became a justice of the peace and while on hiatus from the legislature between 1766 and 1769, was appointed as high sheriff of Chester County.

John Morton

In the last days of his first stint in the legislature, Morton became involved in rising protests against policies emanating from Britain aimed at taxing the American colonists. As a result, he was chosen to represent Pennsylvania at the Stamp Act Congress in 1765. Concerned over Britain's intentions and fearful that growing discontent in the colonies could lead to a civil conflict that would set "parents against children, and children against parents," Morton's cautious approach to further protest won him a position as a member of Pennsylvania's delegation to the First Continental Congress in 1774. At first aligning himself with those who wished to take a cautious approach to independence, preferring to give the king every chance at reconciliation, Morton's attitudes slowly evolved until, on that fateful day in July when a decision needed to be made on whether the thirteen colonies should declare independence, he voted in its favor, later becoming a signer of the Declaration of Independence. Morton's decision to vote in favor of independence was a crucial one, being the swing vote within the Pennsylvania delegation, one that earned him a number of political enemies among those who opposed the drastic step.

After independence, Morton was assigned to and became chairman, of a committee charged with drafting a frame of government under which the new United States would operate. Unfortunately, he never lived to see the Articles of Confederation approved by Congress, dying of fever at Ridley Township on April 1, 1777. Aware of the criticism he yet suffered from those who disagreed with his historic vote for independence, Morton's last utterance was one of prophecy: "Tell them they will live to see the hour when they shall acknowledge my signing of the Declaration of Independence to have been the most glorious service that I ever rendered my country."

William Moultrie

Not all who were called decided to serve. Such was the case with William Moultrie who twice was chosen by the residents of South Carolina to serve in the Continental Congress and both times ended up not going. The first time he was appointed, the war itself interfered and, as an officer in the army with the threat of enemy invasion imminent, Moultrie chose to remain at home and help prepare his state's defenses.

The second time he was asked to serve in Congress, he simply turned down the offer, choosing instead to help stiffen the spines of local politicians who had lost their nerve. With a British army outside Charleston, Moultrie was asked by the state's suddenly fearful grandees if South Carolina should consider surrender. Instead, he replied in one of the most ringing declarations of the Revolution: "We will fight it out!" Those who heard the words breathed a sigh of relief. "Thank God!"

William Moultrie

gasped a wounded John Laurens upon hearing of Moultrie's reply. It was the kind of attitude sorely needed in a theater of the war where the patriot cause, threatened by the enemy and divided from within, found itself on the ropes more often than not.

The son of a physician, William Moultrie was born in Charleston, South Carolina on November 23, 1730. Although he managed an early and advantageous marriage in 1749, it did not prevent him from accepting a captaincy in a local militia unit and marching off in 1761 to fight the Cherokees in an expedition under British Lt. Col. James Grant.

Distinguishing himself on the frontier, Moultrie returned home an experienced soldier but like most American officers, probably came away from his association with British officers with a bad taste in his mouth. More a moderate than a radical, the patriot cause nevertheless earned his sympathies as rising tensions between England and its American colonies neared the boiling point. When that time came, Moultrie had sufficiently earned the respect of local patriots to be appointed by them as a delegate to the First Continental Congress in 1774; but before he had a chance to attend, hostilities broke out in Massachusetts and he chose to serve with his fellow militiamen rather than enter politics. Commissioned as a colonel in the 2nd South Carolina Regiment, Moultrie was immediately charged with the defense of Charleston and the construction of Fort Sullivan guarding the approaches to its harbor. Moultrie however, was never able to complete work on the fort and a lack of building materials, including stone, forced him to improvise in its construction. Building a double wall of soft palmetto logs and filling the space between with sand, it turned out to be the very thing to withstand cannon fire when British warships eventually appeared offshore. It was an unlikely defense and one which Gen. Charles Lee, commander of the southern theater, considered a "slaughter pen" that should be abandoned. That suggestion was turned down by South Carolina Governor John Rutledge while Moultrie himself expressed confidence that the fort would hold against an attack. That assertion was put to the test early in June of 1776 when the British under Maj. Gen. Henry Clinton, landed an invasion force on nearby Long Island with the aim of crossing a narrow spit of water and assaulting Fort Lincoln from its undefended rear. Intending his men to wade across the divide on foot, Clinton soon discovered that not only was the militia on the opposite shore prepared for him, but that the water was too deep for his plan to succeed in any case. Frustrated and finding his men stranded on the island, Clinton sent word to Commodore Sir Peter Parker for the navy to take over. As a result, at mid-morning of June 28, 1776, a number of British warships with a total of almost 250 guns appeared offshore. "The sight of these vessels alarmed us very much," stated Moultrie in his memoirs. The ships soon began a heavy bombardment of the fort but with little effect as the cannonballs were simply absorbed by or bounced off of the soft wood and sand of its walls. In the meantime, three of the attacking ships tried to enter the harbor proper and strike the fort from behind but ran aground on a hidden sand bar leaving them sitting ducks for the Americans on shore. Gesturing with a pipe he had been smoking, Moultrie calmly directed that the fort's guns be turned on the helpless ships. Blasting away, the enemy vessels were struck with deadly accuracy, laying waste their rigging and washing the decks in blood; even the *Bristol*, Parker's flagship, did not escape the devastation with its captain losing an arm in the battle and the commodore his pants. When the action ended later that night, the Americans had suffered only a single gun knocked out while the British fleet was forced to retreat and enemy plans for the capture of Charleston delayed until 1780.

Following the action at Fort Sullivan, Moultrie became a national hero and his dramatic defeat of the enemy helped raise the morale of patriots everywhere. The fort was renamed in his honor and in 1777,

Moultrie himself was promoted to Brigadier General in the Continental Army. The next year, the British returned to the South, but this time to Georgia, seizing Savannah on December 29, 1778. Quickly, efforts began to prepare for an invasion of South Carolina and Moultrie found himself with the army of Gen. Benjamin Lincoln as it moved south to oppose the British. Detaching himself from the main army, Moultrie led a force of militiamen to Beaufort, South Carolina where on February 3, 1779 he defeated British Col. Augustine Prevost in a battle where the Americans fought from the open and the British from the cover of brush and swamp. But Moultrie's victory stopped Prevost only temporarily. When Lincoln drew his army further away, Prevost took advantage of Moultrie's sudden loss of support to once more move on Charleston. The suddenness of the British appearance outside the city prompted Gov. Rutledge to order Moultrie, who was in command of the city's defenses and outnumbered four to one, to negotiate with Prevost, offering him the state's neutrality in return for its safety. Prevost, however, decided that it was not in his power to negotiate and demanded the city simply surrender. Fearful and faced with the possibility of becoming prisoners of war, Rutledge and his supporters again turned to Moultrie, who had never wanted to surrender in the first place, and asked for his advice. "We will fight it out!" declared the general in no uncertain terms. Fortunately, the return of Lincoln's army prompted Prevost to retreat to Stono Ferry where an attack by Moultrie was thwarted due to a lack of manpower. Thereafter, Prevost was able to fall back along the coast back to Georgia. Later, a counterattack by a combined Franco-American force to recapture Savannah failed and the army was forced to retreat back into South Carolina.

By early 1780, the British noose again began to tighten around Charleston and Moultrie, who was second in command of the city, was once again appointed to serve in the Continental Congress. He turned down the offer but accepting the appointment might have spared him grief when, after the city fell to the enemy in May, Moultrie was captured and spent the next two years as a prisoner of war. Resisting attempts to get him to betray his country, he was eventually exchanged in 1782 for Maj. Gen. John Burgoyne, who had been defeated and captured at Saratoga in 1777. Upon his release, Moultrie was promoted to major general but with Cornwallis' defeat at Yorktown in October of 1781, never saw action again.

His reputation undimmed during the time he spent as a captive, Moultrie was elected to the South Carolina House of Representatives in 1783 and became lieutenant governor the next year. In 1785, he was elected governor and presided over the move of the state capitol from Charleston to Columbia, his success marred when his brother John, who had remained loyal to the king during the war and even served as governor of East Florida, decided to move to England. Moultrie returned to the legislature in 1787 but was re-elected governor in 1792. Retiring in 1794, he managed to complete his *Memoirs of the American Revolution so far as it Related to the States of North and South Carolina and Georgia* before his death on September 27, 1805.

Thomas Nelson, Jr.

The eldest son of one of the wealthiest landowners in Virginia, Thomas Nelson, Jr. was born on his father's estate in Yorktown on December 26, 1738. As the scion of one of the colony's most illustrious families, it was a foregone conclusion that following a period of personal tutoring, the junior Nelson would be shipped off to England to complete his education. Graduating from the university of Cambridge in 1761, Nelson returned to Virginia where he slipped easily into a life of the landed gentleman: helping to conduct his father's affairs and eventually entering upon a good marriage. Although having been elected to the colony's legislature by 1774, it has never been clear exactly when or how Nelson became politically active, let

Thomas Nelson, Jr.

alone siding with local patriots in the growing revolutionary struggle. Later, Nelson would not only boast of being the only person among those that had been at school with him in England who later joined the American side of the Revolution, but nearly impoverished himself in helping to subsidize Virginia's military preparedness.

Perhaps it was the new taxes imposed by Parliament on the American colonies that first excited Nelson's patriotic sentiments. As a large landholder that depended heavily on the sale of agricultural products overseas, the Stamp Act passed by Parliament would have impacted the Nelsons' bottom line. In any case, the junior Nelson soon became known for his opposition to royal authority which led to his participation in Virginia's provincial convention. There, in 1775, as colonists in Massachusetts fired for the first time on British troops, he proposed that the colony organize an independent militia force. Despite how threatening such a move would appear on the opposite side of the Atlantic, the suggestion was adopted and Nelson himself appointed as the militia's first commander. But Nelson had little time to attend his military duties as he was obliged to travel to Philadelphia as a member of Virginia's delegation to the Continental Congress. There, Nelson was an advocate for separation from England and became a signer of the Declaration of Independence. He continued to serve in Congress for another two years before illness forced him to resign in 1777. With symptoms resembling those of a stroke, Nelson retired to his Yorktown estate where he made a gradual recovery. No sooner was he back on his feet however, than he was called once more to public service, this time to again take up his duties as commander of Virginia's state militia. Ranked as a brigadier general, Nelson used a great portion of his wealth to outfit his soldiers and guarantee loans from other wealthy landowners.

Nelson's command of the militia came at a time of crisis for Virginia as the focus of British military strategy shifted from the north to the south. Even as the enemy invaded Georgia and South Carolina and moved inland to threaten North Carolina, a raiding army under the command of the traitor Benedict Arnold landed at Hampton Roads late in 1780 and began burning and looting virtually without opposition. Early in the new year, advance elements reached as far as Richmond where legislators were forced to flee at a moment's notice and Governor Thomas Jefferson nearly captured at Monticello. Soon after, Jefferson chose not to stand for reelection and partially on the strength of his successful command of the militia, Nelson was chosen to take his place. With the state still under siege and threatened by an army commanded by British Gen. Charles Cornwallis advancing from the south, Nelson used the authority of his office to raise troops and requisition supplies in anticipation of opposing the enemy. When Gen. George

Washington arrived in Virginia at the head of the Continental Army, Nelson joined him as commander of the state's militia and together with an accompanying French army, surrounded Cornwallis at Yorktown. During the siege that followed, after learning that the British general had set up headquarters in his own home, Nelson insisted it be targeted and shelled by allied artillery.

The victory at Yorktown proved to be the climax of Nelson's public career as, soon after, he had a recurrence of the illness that had forced him from Congress and he retired permanently to property he owned in Hanover County. There, he spent his final years restoring his estate and rebuilding his shrunken fortune until his death on January 4, 1789.

James Otis

All revolutions have to begin somewhere and although the American Revolution can be said to have had its roots in the religious, political, and social upheavals of earlier popular movements from the Renaissance to the Protestant Reformation, in terms of a rising political consciousness and sophistication, it really began in the years between the French and Indian War that began in 1754 and the beginning of hostilities at Lexington and Concord in 1775. It was in those years that the generation immediately preceding that of the better known Founding Fathers first grappled with a mounting oppression from Britain and an increased realization that Englishmen in America were not quite the equal of those in the mother country. Deprived of representation in the British Parliament, under the direct rule of royally appointed governors and with little voice in their own affairs, some Americans began to question the status quo and even to challenge it. One of those proto-revolutionaries was James Otis, attorney, sometime royal official, and mentor to Samuel Adams, perhaps the greatest firebrand, rabble-rouser, and politically savvy leaders of the Revolution.

Born in Barnstable, Massachusetts in 1725, Otis was well ahead of the curve of revolution by the time he was appointed to the Committee of Correspondence in 1764. Educated at Harvard, he began his career as an attorney in Boston before being appointed the colony's advocate general of the vice admiralty court. It was while serving the court that he first publicly opposed official policy by speaking out against the arbitrariness of writs of assistance which, intended to combat smuggling, could actually be used as general search warrants. Refusing to have anything to do with the writs, Otis resigned his position and then argued before the colony's Superior Court against the policy on the grounds that the writs violated the natural rights of Englishmen. Extending the logic of his argument, Otis even claimed that any measure passed by Parliament that was in violation of those rights, was void. He hardly realized it

James Otis

at the time, but Otis had run into the understanding in Britain that for all intents and purposes, American colonists were not the equal of Englishmen living in the mother country and thus, did not share in "the natural rights of Englishmen."

As the true situation became more apparent, opposition by a growing number of colonists to any moves made by King and Parliament increased and as time passed, Otis was joined by other like minded patriots who began to organize. In 1761, his supporters managed to elect Otis to the colonial assembly and in 1764 were prepared to make him its speaker when his appointment was struck down by royal governor Francis Bernard.

As the colony's royal governor, Bernard's concerns about Otis were well placed as by 1764, the would-be speaker had become a leader of a rising group of patriots unified in their opposition to what they saw as the arbitrary application of power by a distant sovereign and parliament. The Stamp and Townshend Acts were two early attempts by London to coerce its American colonists into paying what it saw as the costs of securing the continent against the French in the recent war and then in policing the frontier against the threat of an Indian population aroused at violations of their land by white settlers. But the colonists did not see it that way; to them, passage of the measures had been unfair and designed to restrain their rights. In response to the Sugar Act, the first of the taxation measures, Otis crystallized the colonists' argument in a 1764 pamphlet entitled *The Rights of the Colonies Asserted and Proved* in which he argued again that since the colonies were not represented in Parliament, that body had no right to tax them. After the repeal of the Sugar Act, Parliament passed the Stamp Act and as they did for the Sugar Act, Massachusetts called for a Stamp Act Congress to be attended by representatives of all the colonies. Otis with Samuel Adams wrote the letter of invitation. But by the time the congress met in 1765, Otis had begun to show signs of the mental instability that would eventually lead to his decline as a leader in the revolutionary movement. Otis reached the zenith of his influence soon after 1767, the year Parliament passed the Townshend Acts that imposed duties on such commodities as paint, lead, paper, and tea. As tensions between patriots and loyalists continued to mount, Otis became more outspoken and was accused of treason by the colony's customs commission. Retaliating in print, Otis threatened commissioner John Robinson and when the two finally met, a fight ensued in which Otis received a serious wound to the head. He was never the same after that. The injury exacerbated a personality that had grown increasingly erratic over the years and forced Otis to give up his leadership role to other, younger men. After sitting out the active years of the revolution, the old patriot reemerged only briefly after independence to meet Massachusetts governor John Hancock. In 1783, Otis was killed by a freak bolt of lightning.

William Paca

William Paca was born on October 31, 1740 on his father's estate of Wye Hall in Harford County, Maryland. After receiving an early education at home, he entered the College of Philadelphia and graduated in 1759. From there, he followed the usual path taken by the sons of wealthy families and began studying the law in Annapolis before completing his education at the Middle Temple in England. Upon returning to Annapolis, he passed the bar in 1764 and went into practice for himself; the same year Parliament passed a number of unpopular tax raising measures and Boston retaliated by calling for a boycott of English goods. For the next several years, Paca concentrated on his legal work until elected to Maryland's legislature as a member of the House of Burgesses. There, having been elected directly by the people, he often found himself at odds with the Upper House whose members were appointed by the colony's proprietor and royal governor. As the decade wore on, this dichotomy of interest between himself and the upper house widened and Paca often found himself allied with Samuel Chase and on the side of patriots who opposed tax gathering measures not only passed by the English Parliament, but also such local measures as a mandatory poll tax made in support of local Anglican clergy.

Notwithstanding his struggles with the Upper House and the governor and his patriot sympathies, Paca's radicalism at this time did not extend so far as to agitate for separation from Britain. It did, however, demand that what he saw as injustices emanating from the mother country be confronted. In 1773 he became a member of the colony's Committee of Correspondence and defended resisters of the poll tax. By that time, his position on the issues being well known among local patriots, he was chosen in 1774 to be a member of Maryland's delegation to the First Continental Congress. There, Paca and his fellow delegates were constrained by their instructions from openly supporting any effort to declare independence from England even going so far as to support an olive branch petition begging the king to reconsider his position on issues that had angered the colonists. But with the failure of the petition, a motion was made in Congress in favor of independence, putting Paca and his fellow delegates on the spot. Seeing no other choice, Paca joined fellow delegate Chase and his friend Charles Carroll in an effort to change Marylanders' minds on the subject and at a hastily arranged provincial convention, they succeeded, and the colony's delegates were given liberty to vote as they chose on independence. Consequently, Paca was freed to vote in favor of the motion and ended up in August of 1776, joining Chase and Carroll as a signer of the Declaration of Independence. Following independence, the three friends would join together again, this time to help draft a new state constitution for Maryland.

Paca next served briefly with the Maryland militia and donated funds to the war effort. Remaining in Congress until 1779, Paca only left when he was appointed chief justice of Maryland's supreme court and left that job in 1780 after accepting a position from Congress as chief justice of Maryland's admiralty court of appeals. He had only served on the admiralty court another two years when he was elected governor of the new state of Maryland in 1782 serving until 1785. After leaving office, he helped found Washington College in Chestertown, Maryland and in 1786 reentered public life to serve as a delegate at the state convention held to deliberate ratification of the United States Constitution. There, concerned that the Constitution lacked a bill of rights, he sided with the anti-federalists proposing a list of 22 amendments to the document. Later, despite the fact that all of his amendments were eventually turned down, he had the satisfaction of seeing motions similar to his approved in other states. He nevertheless chose to support ratification and, in 1789, with the establishment of the new government of the United States, was asked by President George Washington to serve as a judge on the federal court for Maryland. Paca accepted and served until his death at Wye Hall on October 23, 1799.

William Paca

Robert Treat Paine

Although history recalls bold patriots such as Patrick Henry or John Adams who spoke out unflinchingly against the abuses of royal authority and later called for flat out independence from Britain, little is ever said of those like Robert Treat Paine, who took a more cautious approach to the Revolution.

Robert Treat Paine, not to be confused with Thomas Paine, the author of *Common Sense*, was born in Boston, Massachusetts on March 11, 1731 to a family with historic connections to the religious life. Expected to become a member of the clergy, he attended Boston's Latin School before entering Harvard. Graduating in 1749, he became a teacher for a time before taking up theology. Still expecting to become a minister, Paine acted as a chaplain during the French and Indian War serving in the frontier campaigns to the north and west. But suffering from a weak composition as well as a loss of interest in the ministry, he left the army and his vocation and went to sea in the merchant marine with an idea that the hard work and sea air would improve his health. It was while overseas that he had the opportunity to visit other countries including Spain and England. When he returned home, he decided to study law and in 1757 passed the bar. Moving to Portland in what is today the state of Maine but at the time was still part of Massachusetts, Paine set up his own practice but soon relocated to Taunton where he reacquainted himself with Harvard classmate John Adams and joined him in working to rouse support against the Stamp Act. His law practice grew successful and in 1770 he was prevailed upon by local patriots to join the team of prosecutors charged with bringing to trial British soldiers accused of murder in the infamous "Boston Massacre" that occurred on March 5 of that year. Although fellow attorney John Adams, who had taken up the challenge of defending the soldiers, succeeded in having them acquitted of the charge of murder, Paine's performance at the closely followed trial brought him much public attention and resulted in his election to the colonial legislature later that same year.

Robert Treat Paine

As a politician in Massachusetts, Paine could not avoid being at the center of patriot agitation and defiance of royal authority in those increasingly passionate times. Having the public trust, he was chosen in 1774 as one of the colony's representatives to the First Continental Congress to be held in Philadelphia. Although serving on a number of committees and voting to appoint George Washington as commander of a new Continental Army, Paine's performance during the various deliberations on the floor of Congress was less than stellar. Known as the "objection maker," Paine seems to have spent all of his time objecting to the proposals of others while offering none of his own. In truth, like others in Congress, Paine became reluctant to accept what even such fellow Massachusetts delegates as John and Samuel Adams had been advocating, the radical step of declaring independence from Britain. Instead, Paine, who had become increasingly isolated from the Adamses due to a combination of family concerns and personal criticism from other patriots, sided with Pennsylvania representative John Dickinson who argued at length against separation and giving the crown one last chance to make peace with the colonies. Impatient with the accommodationists, but feeling that the time was not yet right for declaring independence, hardliners such as the Adamses and their Virginian allies, decided not to raise any objections to the so-called "olive branch petition" firm in their belief that the king would never accept it. Paine's position on the issue apparently did him little harm among his constituents who promptly reelected him to Congress in 1776. But by then, events had proven the hardliners right. When the olive branch petition was refused by the king, they pushed for independence and on July 4, 1776, the resolution was passed by Congress and Paine became one the signers of the historic document.

Returning to Massachusetts, Paine's popularity among the people continued as he was elected once again to Congress. This time however, he preferred to remain in Massachusetts to serve in the new state's legislature. In 1777, he participated in the convention that drafted the state's constitution. That same year, he was also elected attorney general, an office he held until 1790. In 1779 and 1780, he served on the governor's council, moved back to Boston, and found the time to help establish the American Academy of Arts and Sciences. In 1783, Governor John Hancock wanted to appoint him to the state's Supreme Court. Although he refused the offer that first time, Paine decided to accept it when the position was offered again in 1790. He served on the bench for the next fourteen years until his retirement and died on May 11, 1814.

John Penn

In the deep south of the Carolinas where the Revolutionary War against British rule more often appeared to be a civil war between patriots and loyalists with all of the divisiveness, waste, and often savage brutality, that went along with it, John Penn's service to his adopted state was perhaps more crucial at home than in the halls of Congress.

Although he signed the Declaration of Independence on behalf of North Carolina, Penn had not been born there. Originally, he had been a native of Virginia, a member of a well to do but not grandiosely wealthy planter family related to the influential Pendleton clan. An only child, Penn was born in Caroline County, Virginia on May 17, 1741 and while his father was alive, received only a basic education in a local country school. What more there was to learn, the young Penn discovered it on his own as he browsed through the substantial private library of his Pendleton relatives. When he was 18 however, Penn's father died and an opportunity to widen his education finally opened up. Encouraged by his uncle and mentor Edmund Pendleton, Penn began to apply himself to the study of law using his uncle's legal library as his classroom. Eventually, he felt himself prepared to face the bar and was admitted in 1762. In Virginia however, Penn found himself only one among scores of other attorneys and although successful, he still found competition for clients stiff. As a result, he decided to remove himself and his family to Granville County, North Carolina in 1774. It proved to be a wise move as his legal skill and personal qualities allowed him to build not only a successful practice, but earned him a reputation in his new community that catapulted him to the forefront of its politics.

In 1775, Penn found himself elected to North Carolina's provincial legislature then meeting in Hillsboro and with his well known opposition to Parliament's attempts to tax the American colonies, he was soon after appointed as a member of the colony's delegation to the Continental Congress. Although never known as a public debater, Penn found his niche in committee work making his support for separation from Britain well known; and when the time arrived to replace words with action, he joined his fellow congressmen in signing the Declaration of Independence. By 1777, Penn had become the leader of North Carolina's congressional delegation and added his signature to the Articles of Confederation as well. The only dark cloud that ever appeared over Penn's career in Congress came about when he was drawn into a duel with South Carolina's Henry Laurens, then president of Congress. Luckily however, Penn's friendly ways managed to avoid a potentially deadly encounter when at the very last minute, he convinced Laurens that a duel was unnecessary.

After serving in Congress for almost five years, Penn returned to North Carolina in 1780 where he was immediately appointed to the new state's Board of War. The position was an extremely important one as by that time, the British had brought the war from the

John Penn

northern states to the southern. Encouraged by reports that support for the crown was strong in the south, the enemy seized the city of Savannah, Georgia in 1778 and Charleston, South Carolina in 1780. From there, the British immediately moved west and north in a campaign that rapidly descended into one of unheard of savagery and desperation as patriots and loyalists, often brothers and cousins and long time neighbors, confronted each other in the region's swamps, narrow unpaved roads, and dense forests that made sudden raids and ambush the order of the day. With the attention of Congress and the Continental Army still concentrated around the mid-Atlantic states and after the capture of Gen. Benjamin Lincoln together with his entire army of 5,000 men at the fall of Charleston, South Carolina and the defeat of Gen. Horatio Gates at Camden, the southern states were mostly left to fend for themselves as the war in the Carolinas devolved for the most part into small unit, mostly hit and run, actions. It was amid this generally dismal situation that Penn, as a member of the Board of War, was called upon to find the resources from a weary, demoralized public in order to continue resistance and keep the revolutionary cause alive in

North Carolina. In the end, he succeeded, as the British suffered major losses at Cowpens and King's Mountain and was checked by Gen. Nathanael Greene in a campaign designed to delay and weaken the invaders. Eventually, American tactics forced British Gen. Charles Cornwallis to detach his army from its southern moorings and march it into Virginia where it was eventually trapped at Yorktown. Initially established only to help the governor in the conduct of war related matters, the Board of War with Penn as chief among its three members, soon began to exert its influence over all things military in the state, a development that drew increasing concern among state officials. Wary about losing control over the conduct of the war in North Carolina, Governor Abner Nash decided to abolish the board early in 1781.

After his experience with the Board of War, Penn declined a position on the governor's council and instead returned to his legal practice. He emerged from his private affairs briefly in 1784 when he accepted an appointment as North Carolina's receiver of taxes under the Articles of Confederation but resigned soon afterward citing too much resistance from the public. After quitting as receiver of taxes, Penn returned to his legal practice but mounting ill health forced him to retire and he died at his home near Stovall on September 14, 1788.

Timothy Pickering

In the Revolutionary War era when many found the opportunity to rise to national distinction, others, seemingly on the same track, fell short of that pinnacle and so failed to be singled out by later historians. Such men as Timothy Pickering, who served in the military and held numerous local, state, and federal positions before and after the war, seemed on the surface to have had the kind of career suitable for remembrance as one of the better known Founding Fathers. Instead, he was unable to meet that standard. Although such men as Thomas Jefferson and Alexander Hamilton may have had their faults, Pickering never made his mark as a great thinker, fighting officer, or architect of political systems; rather, his outspokenness, strongly held positions, and especially his tendency to carry loyalty to a man or a cause to the point of being subversive, made him less than an attractive historical personality.

The son of a well to do family, Pickering was born on July 17, 1745 in the seafaring town of Salem, Massachusetts. Sent to Harvard for his education, he graduated in 1763 and took a job as a clerk in Salem's registry of deeds, the first of a string of local civil and political positions he would hold leading up to the Revolution. Taking up the study of the law, he passed the bar in 1768 but never really practiced.

Instead, he continued to hold a number of public offices including town clerk, assessor, and selectman and in 1766, after studying military history and working unsuccessfully to convince local officials to take the state's defense seriously, he was made a lieutenant in the Essex County militia. In 1775, his readings and subsequent experience with the militia led him to write *An Easy Plan of Discipline for a Militia* which was used by the Continental Army in the early years of the war.

But military matters were not the only thing on Pickering's mind during the 1770s; his anxiety for making sure the

Timothy Pickering

militia was prepared for war grew out of his increasing hostility to Britain as Parliament continued to force its will on the American colonies. As a result, Pickering began to express himself in pamphlet form and his increasing name recognition won him a place on the Committee on the Rights of Colonists and Committees of Correspondence and Safety.

Pickering's first confrontation with the enemy came in February of 1775, only a few months before hostilities opened in earnest at Lexington and Concord when his militia unit confronted a British Col. Leslie across the North Bridge in Salem. Leslie had been ordered to Salem in search of military stores but when he arrived at the bridge, he was confronted by the militia and local residents who refused to lower the draw and let him pass. The situation was defused without violence when Pickering and others agreed to allow Leslie to save face by crossing the bridge and immediately turning around. When actual war finally broke out, a reluctance by Pickering to lead his men from Salem to attack the British as they retreated from Lexington and Concord back to Charlestown damaged his reputation. His decision later to take his unit back to Salem instead of staying on to surround the British in Boston did not help either. Nevertheless, he was promoted to colonel and eventually saw action in New York, New Jersey, and Pennsylvania. In 1777, he was promoted again, this time to adjutant general and later in the year, was appointed to the Board of War by the Continental Congress.

In 1780, Pickering was released of his duties as adjutant general and became quartermaster general for the Continental Army, a position he served faithfully, but as time went on, with increasing frustration. With little help available from a cash poor Congress, Pickering did what he could, including using his own money, to keep supplies flowing to the army. Finally, with sources of supply drying up, Pickering convinced Congress to allow him to issue what he called "specie certificates" which acted as promissary notes from the government to merchants in exchange for products. The notes promised repayment for supplies in silver or gold by a certain date and if payment was not forthcoming, interest on the note would build by 6 percent annually until the government made good. Despite continued shortages and a constant lack of funding, Pickering remained quartermaster general until the end of the war, spending the last years following Washington's victory at Yorktown trying to balance the books and pay off debts, including his own.

When the war ended, Pickering decided to take advantage of his experience and contacts made when he was quartermaster and went into business for himself as a merchant in Philadelphia. Later, he moved to western Pennsylvania where his reputation was such that he was elected to serve as his county's representative at the convention held to ratify the United States Constitution. Remembered by the nation's first president, George Washington appointed Pickering postmaster general in 1791 and in 1795, he took over from Henry Knox as Secretary of War. Later the same year, after playing a key role in securing embarrassing letters that hinted Edmund Randolph was in the pay of the French, Pickering took over as Secretary of State after Randolph was forced to resign. Pickering stayed on as Secretary of State, along with the rest of Washington's cabinet, after John Adams was elected president in 1796.

A supporter of a strong central government who was wary of the duplicity of a newly radicalized France, Pickering became a close ally of Alexander Hamilton who, even though he no longer held a position as Secretary of the Treasury in the president's cabinet, still remained a power broker and leader of those opposed to Thomas Jefferson who preferred a weak federal government and sympathy for France. The opposing views soon polarized the country and two political parties emerged: the Federalists led by Hamilton and the Jeffersonian Republicans. Sympathetic to the Federalists, but still independent of either party, President Adams tried to steer a common sense course between the two using as his guide what he judged as best for the country. His efforts, however, were met with scorn by the Republicans and disdain by the Federalists including Pickering who, along with the rest of the president's cabinet, gave his first loyalty to Hamilton as the former Secretary continued to dictate policy behind the scenes. Infuriated by Pickering's refusal to support him in his attempts to defuse rising tensions between France and the United States, Adams finally caught on and after a heated confrontation, fired Secretary of War James McHenry and then, after he refused to resign, Pickering.

Unrepentant, Pickering decided to leave Pennsylvania and return to Massachusetts where, after the resignation of Dwight Foster, his Federalist credentials were enough to get him appointed to the United States Senate in 1803. He resigned his seat in 1811 however after being censured for breach of confidence when he made public secret documents sent by the president to Congress. Pickering opposed the policies of President Jefferson as well as those of his Republican successors, James Madison and James Monroe. In particular, Pickering was strongly opposed to war with Britain and even advocated the secession of New York and the New England states from the rest of the union conspiring with the likes of Vice-President Aaron Burr and even British emissary to the United States, George Henry Rose, to make it happen. But despite being sent back to Congress for one more term in 1813, Pickering's support for secession proved unpopular as a rising tide of Republican feeling swept the nation and Federalists lost their influence. Deciding against running for another term and retiring to his farm in Wenham, Pickering still refused to remain quiet, dashing off in 1824 a scathing critique of John Adams. His voice was only stilled upon his death in Salem on January 29, 1829.

Enoch Poor

Enoch Poor was born in Andover, Massachusetts on June 21, 1736 and, perhaps after hearing tales from his father's days soldiering against the French a decade earlier, joined the local militia as a private during the French and Indian War of the 1750s. After being involved with the removal of the French residents of Nova Scotia, Poor returned to Massachusetts and promptly eloped with Martha Osgood. Retreating to Exeter, New Hampshire, Poor entered the shipbuilding trade and became a moderate success. But as the British Parliament began to impose various tax measures, the seafaring community felt their effects immediately and tensions rose.

As a veteran, Poor was called upon by local officials to help in keeping the peace and later to enforce a prohibition set by the Continental Congress on buying imported tea. He was a member of the New Hampshire Provincial Congress when he was appointed as a colonel, along with John Stark and James Reed, in command of one of the colony's three regiments of militia. Detailed to Boston early in 1775 when that city was surrounded following the battles of Lexington and Concord, Poor's regiment was eventually redeployed to Portsmouth, New Hampshire to guard against an attack by sea. That posting proved only temporary and, after it became clear that the British intended to concentrate their forces in Boston, Poor's regiment returned there to take up positions in the siege lines that ringed the city.

In March of 1776, the British evacuated Boston and for some time, it was a mystery where they would strike next. The suspicion however, was that the target would be New York, a suspicion that proved correct. But before the enemy arrived, a bold plan to launch a surprise invasion of Canada was hatched and Poor's regiment was reassigned from the vicinity of New York to the army of Gen. Philip Schuyler as it marched north through the lakes country to Montreal. Schuyler, however, was forced to drop out due to illness and his place in the field was taken over by Gen. Richard Montgomery who completed the mission by leading the army into Canada and capturing Montreal. But exhaustion, disease, and lack of supplies prevented many of Montgomery's men from continuing on to Quebec and so it was a greatly reduced force that finally joined up with a second American army under Gen. Benedict Arnold that had come from the opposite direction through Maine. But Arnold's army too had been weakened and sharply reduced in numbers after a terrible winter march through the wilderness so that even combined, the two armies lacked the strength to conquer Quebec. Instead, on December 31, 1776 Montgomery was killed in the assault, Arnold wounded, and the army forced to retreat back to Montreal and then all the way back into New York and Fort Ticonderoga.

Back with Washington, Poor was promoted to brigadier general and given command of a brigade that not only included his own New Hampshire regiment, but those from Connecticut and New York as well. He had not been in command long when his brigade was ordered back north to Fort Ticonderoga. There, Poor once again found himself in the thick of the action when an invading army under the command of British Gen. John Burgoyne descended from Canada with the object of cutting off the northern states from the rest of the country by effecting a juncture at Albany with two other armies, one coming up the

Enoch Poor

Hudson River from New York and another mixed force of British and Indians under the command of Col. Barry St. Leger coming in from the west. But even as the plan unfolded, it began to fall apart as the western army was later routed by Arnold and the army from New York never materialized. Left alone, Burgoyne managed to force the evacuation of Fort Ticonderoga and chase its defenders into Vermont. The public, shocked at the turn of events, forced Schuyler from command and his replacement, Gen. Horatio Gates, became the beneficiary of the subsequent defeat of British forces by local militia at the battle of Bennington on August 16, 1777 and Arnold's victory against St. Leger a few days later on August 22. Suddenly, with thousands of militiamen from

New England and New York concentrating around Albany, Burgoyne found himself surrounded and cut off from help at a place called Freeman's Farm. From there, on October 7, 1777, Burgoyne sent out a reconnaissance in force from his position atop Bemis Heights. Gates responded by dispatching Poor with five regiments to the British left and Daniel Morgan's riflemen to the right. As Morgan's men poured a lethal fire on the enemy's flank, Poor's men stood toe to toe with them on the left, loosing close up volleys of rifle fire until suddenly, his men rushed the enemy line and overwhelmed it sending the British flying back to a prepared redoubt where Burgoyne had his headquarters. It was then, as the Americans pressed the advantage, that Arnold rode onto the field and personally led a pair of attacks on the redoubts that persuaded Burgoyne to pull back his entire force to positions at Saratoga where surrender of the shattered enemy forces was received on October 17.

With Burgoyne's defeat, Poor's brigade was ordered south where it helped to oppose a relief force sent up the Hudson River by British Gen. William Howe which eventually gave up the effort and returned south. Poor then rejoined the main army under Washington and spent the winter of 1778 at Valley Forge. The following spring, in order to demonstrate to the British, who spent their own winter in the comfort of Philadelphia, that the Continental Army was still a force to be reckoned with, Poor accompanied Gen. Lafayette to Barren Hill, a position within in sight of the city. Not wishing to have the enemy occupy a position so close to their own lines, the enemy marched 5,000 men out of the city to sweep the Americans from the hill. They succeeded, but thanks to a rear guard action by Poor, there were few casualties as a result. The next year, Poor accompanied an expedition under the command of Gen. John Sullivan into the western wilderness to punish the Indians of the Six Nations for their continued raids on local settlers. Sullivan's 4,000 man army was but one of three separate columns comprising the operation but it was the one that ended up inflicting the most harm on the Iroquois whom they met on August 26, outside New Town. Moving on the left of the American line, Poor's brigade encountered a steep hill which it climbed hoping to catch the enemy in the flank. Half way up the men began taking fire from Indians and their Tory allies hiding behind prepared works at the top. Moving from tree to tree, the Americans forced the enemy from their positions and watched as they "fled with the utmost precipitation." With the Indians routed, the army set about burning villages and destroying crops ensuring that the Indians would have too much to do simply surviving the next winter to think about going on the warpath anytime soon.

For his part, Poor spent the following spring training an elite force of light infantry that would have seen service with Lafayette but over the summer, he fell ill and died suddenly of "putrid fever" while encamped at Paramus, New Jersey, on September 8, 1780. Buried at Hackensack, his funeral procession was well attended by numerous officers and soldiers including Washington himself who characterized Poor as "an officer of distinguished merit, one who as a citizen and soldier had every claim to the esteem and regard of his country."

William Prescott

Although many in Europe were surprised when it was learned that Washington, the most famous and admired man in America following the Revolutionary War, intended to simply retire to his home at Mount Vernon and resume the bucolic duties of a "farmer" rather than take advantage of his position to make himself the ruler of the new United States, he was not the first military man to turn his back on power. In fact, seeing action in combat and returning to the plow when the need for military service had ended had become a tradition in the former colonies. Possessing frontiers threatened by wild Indians and French and Spanish imperialism necessitated the formation of irregular militia units made up of citizen-soldiers who could be raised at need and then sent home when the emergency faded. Thus, there were many former "colonels" and "majors" scattered in small towns all over the colonies who had fought the French and Indians on various occasions and, their services no longer required, simply retreated to their homes and farms to pick up their lives where they had left off. One such man was William Prescott, a veteran of the French and Indian War who, after twenty years of "retirement," took up arms again to oppose the British in the Revolutionary War.

Although born in Groton, Massachusetts on February 20, 1726 Prescott later inherited a large estate in neighboring Pepperell and moved there when he was twenty years old. He spent the next few years working his property until 1755 when he joined the local militia and saw action during the siege of the French fortress of Beausejour in

Nova Scotia during the French and Indian War. Promoted from lieutenant to captain, Prescott came to the attention of General John Winslow, commander of the expedition, who offered him a commission in the British Army. Prescott, however, wanted nothing to do with it and returned to his farm after the war. There he remained in relative obscurity, his war record known only to a few local residents until the tumultuous events of the 1770s thrust him into the forefront of a new nation's pantheon of heroes.

William Prescott at Burgoyne's surrender after Saratoga

(Prescott is the first to Gates' left standing behind Daniel Morgan in white)

With the quartering of troops in Boston and continued efforts by Parliament to raise taxes in the colonies, tensions in New England mounted and local leaders began to take prudent measures in anticipation of possible hostilities. In Massachusetts, minuteman companies were formed and those men with military experience were called upon to act as officers. Thus, in 1775, Prescott found himself appointed to lead the Pepperell militia and when the British finally left the safety of Boston for the countryside surrounding Lexington and Concord, he led his men into battle. Unfortunately, by the time the Pepperell militia arrived in the vicinity of Concord, the enemy had already begun their retreat. Retiring back to Boston faster than minute companies from outlying towns could keep up with, the harried British forces finally regained Boston just as Prescott's unit arrived in nearby Cambridge.

With hostilities having begun and gone so well for the Americans, neither Prescott nor his men were in any hurry to return to the prosaic surroundings of Pepperell. Instead, Prescott wasted no time in signing up for the Massachusetts Provincial Army with many of his men following suit. In the meantime, word from intelligence sources in Boston indicated that the British planned to seize some hills along Charlestown Neck in order to deprive them to Americans who had begun to encircle their positions. In response, General Artemas Ward ordered Prescott to take a thousand men onto the Neck and dig in atop Bunker Hill. Arriving on the scene however, Prescott decided that a better location would be nearby Breed's Hill that overlooked Boston across a narrow gap of water formed by the Charles River. Working through the night of June 16, the men presented the British the next morning with a complete set of fortifications including redoubt and breastworks.

Alarmed that the high ground occupied by the Americans atop the hill placed his own men in jeopardy, British General Thomas Gage ordered warships stationed off shore to bombard the patriot lines. Unable to acquire the proper elevations, the resulting cannonade had little effect on the minutemen, but managed to burn Charlestown to the ground. Frustrated and unwilling to leave the enemy in occupation of the hill, Gage decided to assault the position and drive the patriot rabble from the crest. Thus, on the morning of June 17, 1775, elements of the British Army crossed the Neck and landed at the base of Breed's Hill. At first, an attempt was made to flank the hill by the shoreline to the north, but a spirited resistance led by New Hampshire's John Stark threw back the British with heavy losses. Now, forced to turn his attention to the center of the American line at the top of Breed's Hill, General William Howe, in immediate command of the British assault, ordered his regiments to attack. As the Americans watched the enemy organize themselves into line of battle, they were cautioned by Prescott "not to fire until you see the whites of their eyes." Although other officers atop the hill were more senior, by virtue of his experience and force of personality, Prescott had assumed actual command of the American defense. Up the hill, in the hot summer sunshine marched the soldiers in their bright red uniforms only to be unmercifully mowed down by massed musket fire. Again, the advance was sounded and again the soldiers went down by rows. A third time they came, and now, with powder and shot running low, the farmers at the top of the hill decided that the time had come for the better part of valor and as the enemy approached, one by one the Americans melted away. Prescott himself remained until the last minute, his coat spattered in the blood and brains of fellow patriots killed in the preceding action. Immediately, his 6' 2" frame became a target for enemy bayonets which sought to run him through. More than once his life was saved by quick use of his own sword to parry the savage thrusts. After his performance atop Breed's Hill, Prescott had earned the respect of the professional soldiers he'd opposed, fulfilling a prediction made to Howe that he would "fight as long as a drop of blood remains in his veins."

Indeed, no sooner had the British seized the American positions than Prescott asked that he be allowed to counter-attack and retake them with the larger part of the army which had not participated in the battle. Ward, however, turned down the request. In the meantime, Howe quickly claimed victory, but everyone knew that Britain could never sustain such "victories" for long. "The loss we have sustained is greater than we can bear," wrote Gage of the loss of half his army of 2,500 men to that of 400 by the Americans. "...you cannot succeed in this mad and wicked attempt to conquer," read a letter from a supporter of the Patriot cause to acquaintances in England. "Every hill will be disputed with you, and every inch of ground. Two more such actions (as the battle of Breed's Hill) will destroy your army..."

In the wake of the battle of Bunker Hill (as it has ever since been mistakenly labeled), Prescott continued to serve in the Continental Army seeing action in the New York campaigns of 1776. Later, he resigned from the army but no sooner had he returned home than he volunteered to join the local militia to meet the British in upstate New York and ended up participating in the battle of Saratoga. At home again, he was once more called to serve in a number of public offices including the Massachusetts legislature. Prescott died in 1795 at the age of 69.

Israel Putnam

Of all the former veterans of the French and Indian War who later served on the American side in the Revolution, the career of "Old Put" in that previous war was perhaps the longest and most illustrious.

Israel Putnam, the tenth of eleven children born to a prominent Salem, Massachusetts family, was born on January 7, 1718 and proved growing up to have an abundance of energy and a daring that extended into his own business dealings. In 1739, when he was twenty years old, he entered into partnership with his brother-in-law in the purchase of a 514 acre tract of land located in Windham County, Connecticut. Only a few years later, after buying out his partner, he found himself sole owner of Mortlake Manor that he worked hard to improve including hunting down and killing one of the last remaining wolves in that part of the country. However, large as his holdings were, they were not enough to take up all of Putnam's restless energy. Thus, in 1755, when the French and Indian War broke out, he finally found an outlet equal to his ambitions. Already a well known local leader, he was appointed captain of a company of Connecticut militia and marched

Israel Putnam

off to what would become a ten year military career. Following his participation in the battle of Lake George, Putnam joined Robert Rogers' famous Ranger company and honed his wilderness fighting skills. Eventually promoted to the rank of major, Putnam became involved in much of the action in the northwest until his luck almost ran out when he was captured by the Indians, tortured, tied to a stake, and prepared for immolation. It looked grim for the young fighting man until luck, in the form of a French officer, intervened and he was rescued. Taken to Montreal, he was eventually exchanged and in 1759 was promoted again and placed in charge of a full regiment. The next year, he traveled with the army to Canada and returning by way of the St. Lawrence River, led a small raiding party that succeeded in grounding an enemy schooner protecting Fort Oswego. That action allowed the British to capture the vulnerable fort. Next, Putnam traveled to the West Indies where he became one of a handful of survivors shipwrecked off Cuba when the English fleet was lost at sea. Back in

America again, he joined Col. John Bradstreet in an expedition to relieve Fort Detroit from siege by the Indian chieftain Pontiac before returning finally to Connecticut in 1764. His return home was a bittersweet one however as he arrived just in time to attend his ailing wife, who died the next year. Over the next ten years, Putnam remarried and concentrated on raising his ten children, improving his neglected farm and running an inn. But as the memories of the French and Indian War faded, the public's resentment toward England began to grow and although Putnam became involved in the Revolutionary movement and even joined the local Sons of Liberty, neither prevented him from accompanying one of his former commanders on a trip to the Gulf of Mexico and the Mississippi delta.

When the electrifying news of Lexington and Concord reached him on his farm in the spring of 1775, Putnam left the plow he had been working and immediately rode to Massachusetts where, seeing that men were needed to help keep the British penned within Boston, sent word back to Connecticut to raise the militia and bring them north. Rushing to Hartford, he explained the situation to the colonial legislature and was appointed brigadier general in command of all the Connecticut militia. Returning to Massachusetts, his position placed him in the top ranks of the military forces gathered around Boston. Realizing the importance of holding the hills overlooking the Charles River, Putnam ordered his Connecticut militia to occupy both Breed's Hill and Bunker Hill but was subsequently ordered to remove his men by Gen. Artemas Ward who thought the Americans unprepared to meet the enemy if the British chose to challenge them. Later, there would be disagreement between Putnam and Col. William Prescott as to which hill was which but when the dust cleared and both hills were finally occupied, it was Prescott and Gen. John Stark who ended up in command atop Breeds Hill when the fighting started. Putnam meanwhile, busied himself in occupying a second position at nearby Bunker Hill while at the same time trying (and failing) to move reinforcements up to Breed's Hill. Later, after the Americans had been forced from Breed's Hill and the militia became the nucleus of the new Continental Army under the command of Gen. George Washington, Putnam, who may have been wounded during the battle, was named one of four major-generals and assigned responsibility for the center of the line encircling Boston. With the British withdrawal from the city, Putnam was first placed in charge of the American occupation and then traveled to New York to take command of the American line at Brooklyn Heights when Gen. Nathanael Greene took ill. But Old Put's luck it seemed, had finally run out.

No sooner had the old soldier assumed command at Brooklyn Heights than the British, who had concentrated a vast armada in the area of New York, landed on Long Island and outflanked his position by use of the Jamaica Road, which had been left inexplicably undefended. Frightened by the sudden appearance of the enemy in their rear, the inexperienced Americans panicked and broke. Washington himself, when he appeared on the scene, joined Putnam in trying to force the men to turn and fight but their efforts were to no avail. Faced with a disadvantage in numbers of as many as 4 to 1, there was little anyone could do to save the situation. Abandoning Long Island for Manhattan, Washington took up new positions north of New York City while placing Putnam in command of the force occupying the town. But like Brooklyn Heights, the Americans were once again outflanked when the British landed in their rear at Kip's Bay and threatened to cut off the southern end of the island. The move came as no surprise to Putnam who had foreseen the move and advised Washington to give up New York to the enemy and concentrate on fortifying the upper reaches of the island instead. Later, after covering the retreat back to the American positions at Harlem Heights, Putnam participated in the series of battles that eventually saw the Continental Army forced completely off Manhattan. Fearing that Philadelphia would be the enemy's next target, Washington made Putnam military commandant of the city only to order him back to cross the Delaware River with him as part of a plan to strike the Hessian garrison at Trenton, New Jersey. Although a small portion of his force made it across, increasingly dangerous weather conditions prevented the main body of Putnam's army from making the crossing near Cooper's Ferry about 30 miles south from where Washington went across at McConkey's Ferry. In 1777, when Washington recrossed the Delaware, Putnam found himself recalled and placed in command of the army's right wing at the battle of Princeton. Later that spring, he was ordered to the New York Highlands to help prepare defenses against any enemy incursion up the Hudson River. That threat became real after British Gen. John Burgoyne led an army southward from Canada with the intention of hooking up with a second force moving north from the direction of New York City. That plan was foiled when a lack of enthusiasm for the scheme prevented fellow Gen. William Howe from sending sufficient forces to make the plan workable. As a result, although Howe captured Forts Montgomery and Clinton on the lower Hudson, they did nothing to prevent Burgoyne's defeat at

Saratoga in the autumn of 1777. Once that happened, Putnam launched a campaign to recapture the two forts and succeeded when Howe's men were unable to mount more than a half hearted defense.

Following Burgoyne's defeat, Putnam spent the balance of his military career headquartered in western Connecticut concentrating on recruiting and managing the defense of that part of the country. In 1779, Old Put suffered a stroke and was forced to retire from the army. Returning to his home in Pomfret, he died on May 19, 1790.

Rufus Putnam

Some heroes of the Revolution, for reasons of temperament, interest, or ego, managed to lead erratic but uneventful careers in the years between the French and Indian War when they were young men and the American war of independence when they were middle aged and presumably wiser. One such person was former millwright, surveyor, politician, soldier, entrepreneur, and pioneer Rufus Putnam who became a key figure in helping to open up the west and making possible the nation's unprecedented expansion following the war.

Putnam, a cousin of fellow French and Indian War veteran and Revolutionary War general Israel Putnam, was born on April 9, 1738 in Sutton, Massachusetts. His father having died while he was still young, Putnam was apprenticed out to learn the milling trade but as a young man, dreams of glory in faraway lands dominated his thoughts and when the French and Indian War broke out in 1757, he immediately signed on as a member of the local militia. After serving in four campaigns and the Fort Ticonderoga sawmill, Putnam returned from the war in 1760 and used the wages he had saved to buy a farm and take up the milling trade. But after seeing the wider world, he found that he was unsatisfied with the quiet life and determined to improve himself by studying mathematics and becoming a surveyor. At the same time, he took up the cause of his fellow veterans, pleading to the king that they be compensated in land for their military services. But the only open land available was in Indian country and the crown feared with justification, that any settlement there would only arouse the savages to violence. In response, England refused the request and established the Proclamation Line which forbade any settlement west of the Appalachians. Frustrated, Putnam later accompanied his cousin Israel and other military officers to West Florida to investigate the possibility of land being available there for veterans. But that venture too, fell through. The two instances however, left Putnam with an interest in land speculation that would remain with him the rest of his life and lead to his greatest claim to fame. But first, there was the intervention of the Revolutionary War.

No doubt, Putnam's frustration with the royal government in his search for land formed part of the reason for his taking up the cause of liberty and after the minutemen had driven the British army from Lex-ington and Concord and surrounded it in Boston, Putnam used his knowledge of surveying to supervise the construction of the defenses around the city. So impressed was Gen. George Washington with the results, that he recommended Putnam to Congress for appointment as the Continental Army's chief engineer. Named a lieutenant colonel in the army, Putnam became responsible for constructing all of the American defenses in New York but a promising beginning was abruptly ended when a difference of opinion

Rufus Putnam

arose between himself and Congress over the creation of a separate corps of army engineers.

Leaving engineering behind, Putnam took command of the 5th Massachusetts regiment and joined Gen. Horatio Gates' command at Stillwater before moving with the army north to upstate New York and participating in the battle of Saratoga. Later, he was attached to the command of his cousin Israel in the New York Highlands and once more employed his engineering skills to help fortify West Point. He then served with Gen. Anthony Wayne, scouting out the defenses of Stony Point before its successful assault by Wayne's men, but saw little more action for the remainder of the war. In 1783, Putnam's interest in land resurfaced when he helped to write the infamous Newburgh Petition in which officers in the army, disgruntled at not being paid by Congress, demanded compensation in land and threatened action if satisfaction were not forthcoming. Washington, in a famous speech, defused the potentially dangerous situation but the desire for western land would remain with Putnam.

After the war, Putnam left the army with the rank of brigadier general and was hired by the federal government as a surveyor. Taking advantage of the information he learned while on the job, Putnam was finally able to indulge his interest in land speculation and began to invest. In 1786, he joined others in founding the Ohio Company of Associates which was bent on large scale investment in the Ohio territory that had come under American control following the war. In 1787, after concluding negotiations with the government under the authority of the Northwest Ordinance, the company succeeded in winning a grant of 1,500,000 acres of land at a cost of little more than 8 cents an acre. Named superintendent by the company, it was Putnam who led the first group of war veterans down the Ohio River by flatboat to the present site of Marietta at the mouth of the Muskingam River. Putnam soon became a major player in the ongoing development of the region and was appointed as a judge to the territory's federal bench. When Indians massacred a nearby settlement at Big Bottom in 1791, Putnam petitioned the government for help and Gen. Arthur St. Clair was ordered to raise an army to chastise the Indians responsible. St. Clair's efforts ended in failure and defeat and when Gen. Anthony Wayne was charged to succeed where his fellow officer had failed, Putnam reassumed his rank as brigadier general. After Wayne defeated the Indians at the battle of Fallen Timbers, Putnam served as a peace commissioner and in 1796, was appointed Surveyor General of the United States.

By 1803, Ohio had become sufficiently populated to qualify for statehood and after holding a constitutional convention, at which Putnam participated, the former territory was declared the 17th state. A supporter of the Federalist Party, Putnam lost his surveyor's job in 1808 when President Thomas Jefferson, removed him over charges of incompetence. Although his interest in western land may have begun for self-serving purposes, it finished by opening up the Old Northwest for settlement and paved the way for the country's historic leap westward over the great plains to the coast of California. The courage to lead pioneers down a waterway vulnerable to Indian attack to settle upon ground still dark and bloody from a thousand unspeakable acts,

the faith that prompted him to establish the first religious schools and
Bible societies in the western lands, and the confidence he felt in the
new nation's future were the essential elements that brought a people
united and free through the rigors of Revolutionary War and would see
them in the next hundred years, carry those virtues across a continent.
Putnam, "the Father of Ohio" and the last surviving American general
of the Revolution, died in Marietta on May 1, 1824.

Edmund Randolph

Edmund Randolph was typical of many patriots who supported
unstintingly independence from Britain while also believing in the necessity of a strong central government for the new nation that would
arise as a result of that separation. But, also like many of his fellow
patriots, Randolph feared a federal government that would be too
strong. Jealous of the liberties that had been won in the wake of the
Revolution and unhappy with the compromises and some of the inno-
vations included in the proposed Constitution, Randolph initially held
the instrument at arm's length even after having served at the Convention that had created it. But when push came to shove, or when rejection of the Constitution would mean a dissolution of the union between
the thirteen states, Randolph was realistic enough to see that there was
no better alternative and worked hard to have Virginia ratify it.

Randolph was born in Williamsburg, Virginia on August 10,
1753 to John Randolph, a King's Attorney whose loyalty to the crown
during the Revolution prevented him from condoning his son's patriotic sympathies and compelled him to move to England rather than
remain in the new United States. It was to his father that Randolph
owed his legal education after he graduated from the college of William
and Mary but a sensitivity to his rights as an Englishman, rights that he
felt strongly were being trampled by Parliament, drove a wedge between father and son and when news of the outbreak of war came from
Massachusetts, there was a sundering of their relationship.

After his father had left the colonies to return to England, Randolph moved in with his uncle, Peyton Randolph, himself a patriot who
was active in local politics. Perhaps it was through his influence that
the younger Randolph was able to secure a position as aide de camp at

the headquarters of Gen. George Washington. The year 1776 was a busy one for Randolph who not only managed to get married, but also took part in the convention that adopted Virginia's constitution. Leaving the army, Randolph was elected mayor of Williamsburg and then became Virginia's attorney general, all before he was 26 years old. In 1779, he was chosen as a delegate to the Continental Congress and in 1786, following in the footsteps of Patrick Henry and Thomas Jefferson, he became governor of Virginia. But all of his accomplishments were but prelude to his most enduring legacy.

It was while serving as governor of Virginia that Randolph became directly involved in the process that would eventually end in the adoption of the United States Constitution. In 1786, he attended the Annapolis Convention, called by Alexander Hamilton to consider changes in the Articles of Confederation which many, including Virginia's James Madison, thought inadequate for conducting the affairs of the thirteen states. Convinced that Madison and Hamilton were right, Randolph supported making a change, and when a Constitutional Convention was called in Philadelphia the next year, he attended as a delegate and opened the proceedings by presenting what has become known as the "Virginia Plan" or Resolves, a fifteen point proposal for a new federal government that was probably drafted by the members of Virginia's own delegation. In large measure, the plan Randolph presented to his fellow delegates that day, became the basis of the Constitution that was accepted by the states in 1788. In it, Randolph proposed a government composed of executive, legislative, and judicial branches. The legislative branch would be made up of two sections, a House of Representatives and a Senate with members of the House being elected directly by the people and the members of the Senate chosen by the House. In addition, the executive would be made

Edmund Randolph

up of more than a single person and the federal government would have the right to use force on any state to enforce its rulings.

Entering the convention an advocate for a strong federal government, Randolph's position on the issue evolved as he began to worry that the proposed Constitution did not include enough safeguards for the protection of such individual liberties as religion. He was also wary of a single person executive, fearful that such power, concentrated in one man, could be used to create a monarchy. By the time the final draft emerged from the Committee of Detail, of which he was a member, Randolph had determined not to put his name to the document even though he still believed that the country needed something more than the Articles of Confederation. In the subsequent struggle over ratification, Randolph championed an amendment process that would provide a way for the states to modify the Constitution when circumstances demanded. It was through the amendment process that a Bill of Rights was eventually appended to the document the first of which included the freedom of worship that was sponsored by Randolph himself. Although lukewarm about the Constitution through most of the ratification process, Randolph's support grew such that in the end, after it had already been officially enacted by a majority of the states, he put the full force of his reputation behind its acceptance. At that point, he concluded that rejection of the document by Virginia, one of the country's four most populous states, would mean no second chance to form a central government and eventual dissolution of the union. And so, on June 25, 1788 after weeks of debate that included legendary orations by himself and James Madison in the defense and Patrick Henry in opposition, Randolph had the pleasure of seeing Virginia become the ninth state to ratify the Constitution.

Once the Constitution was ratified, Randolph put his money where his mouth was and accepted the position of Attorney General in Washington's first cabinet and later, became Secretary of State from 1794-1795 after he agreed to fill out the remaining months of Thomas Jefferson's term. Jefferson had chosen to resign the office when his political disagreements with Hamilton and Washington became intolerable. Although Randolph had always tried to maintain a neutral course between the Republican and Federalist factions, he fell victim to their struggle for dominance when political enemies played on Washington's suspicions to get rid of him. In a meeting with the president, Randolph was confronted with letters written by Joseph Fauchet, French minister to the United States, that implied in vague language that the Secretary of State was peddling information for money. The wording of the letter was such that any interpretation could be placed on them. In addition, it seemed that Fauchet was not above exaggerating what influence he had with American officials in order to impress his superiors. Already suspicious of Randolph due to their disagreement on the suppression of the Whiskey Rebellion of 1794, Washington was prepared to believe the worst. Seeing the impossibility of continuing to work with a superior who considered him an enemy and Federalist colleagues who had engineered the situation to force him out of office, Randolph resigned.

Returning home, he resumed the practice of law and filled his leisure time by writing a history of Virginia. In 1807, he joined a team of the most prominent attorneys in Virginia to defend Aaron Burr, who had become notorious for killing Alexander Hamilton in a duel, breaking his word to Thomas Jefferson and almost stealing the election of 1800, and being accused of treason. In his arguments before Chief Justice of the Supreme Court John Marshall, Randolph insisted that Burr could not be accused of treason due to the fact that he had not been present when other arrests in the case were made and that testimony regarding his involvement in the plot amounted to hearsay. Burr was acquitted and Randolph once again retreated from public view, this time permanently and after a struggle with recurring paralysis, died in 1813.

Peyton Randolph

A revolutionary consciousness came slowly to Virginia's Peyton Randolph who, as a member of one of the colony's most important families, was educated in England and graduated from Oxford's inner Temple with honors in the study of law.

Born in 1721, Randolph pursued a not unexpected career path that began with his return to the colonies and an appointment as both a crown attorney and election in 1748 to the Virginia House of Burgesses. It was while serving in the legislature that he had his first brush with unyielding royal authority when he opposed what he considered an unjust tax on local landowners imposed by the colony's Governor Robert Dinwiddie. Up until the issue of the pistole fee, Randolph and the governor had been on somewhat friendly terms, but when their difference of opinion over the new tax became obvious, Randolph had an early taste of the arbitrary power of royally appointed officials. Chosen by his fellow burgesses in 1754 to travel to England to make a personal appeal to the government, Randolph succeeded in killing the land tax but making an enemy out of Dinwiddie who, in the meantime, had suspended him from his seat in the Burgesses.

Reinstalled in the legislature after an admission to the governor that his trip to England had been made without Dinwiddie's permission, Randolph had retaken his seat just as news of Major General Edward Braddock's defeat at Fort Duquesne reached Williamsburg in 1755. Randolph was chosen to lead a company of fellow lawyers who promptly marched off to the frontier and took part in halting the advance of the victorious French and Indians.

Peyton Randolph

Although he had chaffed under the sometimes arrogant attitude of royal authority, by 1766, Randolph had yet to become as radicalized as other colonists in their growing opposition to British rule. More in tune with such moderates as Pennsylvania's John Dickinson, who were reluctant to take hasty steps that the colonies might come to regret, Randolph was one of those in the House of Burgesses who had voted against anti-British resolves sponsored during the Stamp Act crisis by local firebrand Patrick Henry. "If this be treason, make the most of it!" cried Henry in an impassioned speech that frightened some of his fellow burgesses, including Randolph who joined nineteen of his peers in voting against what became known as the Virginia Resolves that declared Parliament did not have the right to tax colonists who had no representation in its deliberations. The resolves however, were passed by a bare majority of twenty after which a young Thomas Jefferson, who was in sympathy with Henry, said he heard Randolph remark "My God, I would have given 100 guineas for a single vote!"

Dunmore retaliated against the vote by declaring the legislature dissolved on May 26, 1774. Led by Randolph, the Burgesses then met unofficially at Williamsburg's Raleigh Tavern and voted its support for a congress of all the thirteen colonies. Randolph left the Burgesses soon after the momentous decision, but because of his continuing suspicion of the crown's arbitrary use of power as well as his undoubted legal expertise, was soon called upon by local patriots to head various revolutionary committees including the Virginia Convention that, later in 1774, named him as a delegate to the First Continental Congress. There, impressed by his demeanor and reputation, members from the thirteen colonies unanimously elected him as their president.

The next year, after guiding the congress through its first meeting and managing to avoid the inflammatory issue of independence, Randolph returned to Virginia and was immediately plunged into a confrontation between John Murray, Lord Dunmore, and local patriots aroused over the new governor's unannounced seizure of gunpowder stored at a Williamsburg armory. In the wake of recent news about the fighting at Lexington and Concord, the seizure and transfer of the gunpowder to a British schooner waiting out on the James River struck residents as a particularly ominous move. Randolph had to use all of his persuasive powers to convince an angry mob not to assault the governor's home and later, assured hundreds of armed men led by Patrick Henry that their services would not be required as he believed that the mere threat of violence would persuade the governor to relent and return the gunpowder. Randolph's confidence proved well placed after negotiations with Dunmore resulted in payment for the missing gunpowder. Although open revolt against royal authority in Virginia was delayed, a frightened Dunmore later fortified his home and took the precaution of moving his family offshore.

Unfortunately, in the wake of his successful negotiations with Dunmore, Randolph's services to the emerging nation that would become the United States would be cut short before Congress took the momentous step of declaring independence from the mother country. In 1775, Randolph was chosen to serve with the Second Continental Congress and although he arrived in time to be elected its president for a second term, he was forced to resign only 14 days later due to failing health. In the meantime, John Hancock was chosen to serve in his place under the assumption that the Bostonian would relinquish the office upon Randolph's return. But showing no sign that he intended to relinquish the post, which was considered a breach of good faith by John Adams among others, Hancock threatened to cause an unpleasant scene if he were forced to give it up. A showdown over the issue was only avoided when Randolph died suddenly of a stroke on October 22.

Such was the regard for Randolph that Congress immediately arranged for a grand funeral that was, according to the observations of New Hampshire congressman Josiah Bartlett, attended by 12-15,000 residents and 2,000 soldiers. Cousin to Thomas Jefferson, a patron of Patrick Henry, and close friend of George Washington, although Peyton Randolph could never be counted at the forefront of the more colorful and well known heroes of the American Revolution, his steadiness, honesty, knowledge of the law, and calm determination in the face of crisis made him as indispensable a brick in the edifice of the new nation as any of his peers.

George Read

It is a fact that not all Americans supported the Revolution and that even among those who did, there were degrees of radicalism that included at one end those who urged a complete break with all ties with the mother country and those at the other who counseled caution, advising that every attempt should be made to reconcile the two sides. Among the latter was George Read who, unconvinced that the time was right for severing ties with England, was the sole member of the Continental Congress to vote against independence on that historic day in 1776.

Although Read spent his entire career in Delaware, he was actually born in next door Maryland on September 18, 1733. Read was still a youngster when his father, a prosperous landowner, moved the family to Newcastle, Delaware (before it had become completely independent of claims by Pennsylvania and Maryland) and became a gentleman farmer. From there, Read was soon dispatched to a private school in Chester, Pennsylvania and then to Philadelphia Academy in New London from which he graduated in 1752. The next year, he passed the bar and moved back to Newcastle to begin his own practice and where he later built Stonum, which at the time became one of the most impressive homes in Delaware. His reputation as a lawyer quickly spread and in 1763 he was appointed attorney general for the three lower counties that would some day become the state of Delaware. Doing so, he replaced his father-in-law John Ross who would later join him in signing the Declaration of Independence. But his dealings as a local attorney and as attorney general combined to heighten his awareness of the injustice of such laws as the Stamp Act passed by a distant Parliament. Feeling that having no voice in their passage made the colonists no better than slaves, Read began to speak out on the issue and became associated with the patriot movement. Meanwhile, his political career continued to move forward as he joined Delaware's provincial legislature in 1765. Although continuing to hold his seat in the legislature, Read was compelled in 1774 to give up his position as attorney general to join instead Delaware's Committee of Correspondence and then its delegation to the Continental Congress meeting in Philadelphia.

The delegation however, was in a delicate situation in that Delaware at the time Read was sent to Congress was not a completely independent colony. Far from being the neatly settled thirteen political entities that later signed the Declaration of Independence and fought the Revolution, England's colonies in America had over the years bickered with each other over jurisdiction and boundaries. Delaware, like New Hampshire, was one of those that found itself caught in a tug of war of competing claims. In the case of Delaware, those claims were between Pennsylvania and Maryland whose original proprietors, William Penn and Lord Baltimore, each believed that as part of their original grants, what they called the three lower counties of Delaware rightfully belonged to them. The issue was only settled in 1776 when, in addition to declaring for national independence, the three counties also declared themselves free of any claims by their two neighbors and after acknowledging

George Read

boundaries that had been surveyed in 1763-68, set up their own state government.

It was under such circumstances that Delaware's delegation arrived in Congress and although his attendance there was intermittent in the three years that he was a member, Read's position on the prevailing issues was clear, especially that dealing with independence. Often allying himself with his friend and Pennsylvania delegate John Dickinson, Read made it known that he thought any talk of independence was still premature and preferred continued efforts at reconciliation with Britain. But after the king's rejection of Dickinson's "olive branch" petition, the momentum for independence became too strong to resist and those congressmen who had opposed it found themselves outnumbered, and some even replaced with new delegates by constituents impatient of any further hesitation. Nevertheless, when the time came for the historic vote on independence, Read held out as the only member of Congress to decide against it. However, no less patriotic than his colleagues, and gracious in defeat, Read bowed to the will of the majority and on August 2, 1776 placed his name with the others on the Declaration of Independence.

Soon after the signing, Read left Philadelphia to return to Delaware to preside as president over the new state's constitutional convention. Later, he acted as chairman of the sub-committee which drafted the constitution that was eventually approved. In the summer of 1777, with Gen. George Washington headquartered in Wilmington, an army of 15,000 British soldiers under Gen. William Howe entered Chesapeake Bay and invaded Delaware. Turned aside on September 3 by the Continental Army at the battle of Cooch's Bridge, the British passed north into Pennsylvania where they defeated the Americans at Chad's Ford on the Brandywine River that eventually led to the capture of Philadelphia. With the setback of Chad's Ford however, Delaware was left vulnerable and when the enemy returned, they entered the capital at Wilmington and captured Governor John McKinley. Nearly caught himself, Read managed to elude the dragnet and remained at large. Eventually, as speaker of the state's legislative council and de facto lieutenant governor, he took over the state's government in McKinley's absence. By 1778 he was back in the legislature and writing directions to Delaware's representatives in Congress to give their support to the Articles of Confederation.

The incessant traveling from Philadelphia to Wilmington, the pressures of the various offices he held, and the threat of capture, all combined to take a toll on Read's health compelling him into a short retirement in 1779. Over the next few years however, he slowly re-emerged into public view first by returning to the legislature and then with the acceptance of a judgeship on the United States admiralty court. In 1786, Read traveled to Virginia to attend the Annapolis Convention to discuss the need for reforming the Articles of Confederation. Read's public career climaxed in 1787 when he was chosen to represent Delaware at the Constitutional Convention held in Philadelphia. There, he was among the first to argue for a completely new form of federal government to take the place of the Articles of Confederation which he considered inadequate. In fact, during arguments involving representation in Congress by small versus large states, he went so far as to predict that no matter what form of federal government was chosen, it would eventually swallow up all local government, reducing the states to the role of simply electing members of Congress. "If we do not establish a good government on new principals, we must either go to ruin or have the work to do over again," he warned on the floor of the convention. Later, he would go so far as to suggest the elimination of state boundaries as they existed and redistricting the United States, a position that was also held by Hamilton who expounded upon it as part of a day-long speech before the Convention. When he found that no one was interested in his radical proposal, Read fell back on protecting the rights of the smaller states and once threatened to lead a walk-out of the convention if a means were not adopted to insure them. At the same time, he also found himself agreeing with Hamilton on the need for a strong central government as the only solution to the problems created by the looser Articles of Confederation and was little disturbed, as many others were, by the New Yorker's too favorable opinion of British forms of government including his suggestion of a chief executive appointed for life.

Taking the issue back to Delaware, Read reiterated his arguments for a strong federal government and led the fight for state ratification of the new Constitution. In the end, on December 6, 1787, Delaware became the first state to vote for its acceptance. In 1789, Read was rewarded for his unflagging efforts by being elected as Delaware's first representative in the Senate where he proved himself a staunch Federalist supporting Hamilton's positions on federal assumption of the states' wartime debts and the creation of a national bank. Having served in the Senate until 1793, Read resigned to become chief justice of Delaware's supreme court where he remained until his death in Newcastle on September 21, 1798.

Joseph Reed

A native of New Jersey, Joseph Reed managed to navigate the tricky waters of Pennsylvania politics which frequently involved the struggle between radicals and conservatives to attain the highest office in the state.

Born in Trenton, New Jersey on August 27, 1741 to a merchant of modest means, Reed's education began in Philadelphia, where the family had moved for a brief time and continued at Princeton University after it had returned to New Jersey. Graduating from college in 1757, Reed turned to the law and was admitted to the bar in 1763 before topping off his legal education with another two years studying in England. When he returned to America in 1765 he began his own legal practice. Later, he entered public service with positions in the colonial government that gave him the ear of royal authorities. At the same time, he acted as assistant to Dennys De Berdt who had acted as his father's agent in London and in 1770 traveled again to England to marry De Berdt's daughter, Esther. When the couple returned to America, Reed decided to take up residence in Philadelphia and by the time of the Revolution, had established himself as an important figure in Pennsylvania politics.

As friction between the colonies and Britain in-

Joseph Reed

creased, Reed drifted from a conciliatory attitude toward the British to one of outright opposition so that by 1774 he was a member of Pennsylvania's Committee of Correspondence, president of the colony's Provincial Congress, and served in the legislature. In 1775, following the events at Lexington and Concord in Massachusetts, he cemented his patriotic credentials when he became a lieutenant colonel in the Pennsylvania militia and later transferred to the new Continental Army as military secretary to Gen. George Washington. In that position, his legal training and organizational mindset proved ideal in establishing an office routine, including preparing state papers, writing official letters, and setting headquarters protocol. Promoted to colonel, he was with the army when chosen in the summer of 1776, along with fellow officers Henry Knox and Samuel Webb, to receive a message under a flag of truce from British Admiral Richard Howe. But when Howe's note failed to recognize Washington's rank as general, Reed refused to accept it. In the subsequent battle for New York, Reed saw heavy action leading frontline troops at Harlem Heights and then accompanied the army as it fought at Trenton and Princeton in New Jersey, and met the enemy in his adopted home of Pennsylvania. It was Reed's contacts in his native state that prompted him to suggest to Washington the surprise attack on the enemy at Trenton. In New Jersey with the army, Reed also led raids to capture prisoners and scouted the approaches to Princeton. He only left the army in 1777 after he was chosen as a member of Pennsylvania's delegation to Congress. There, he became its president and was present to add his signature to the Articles of Confederation.

Managing to stay in the treacherous middle ground of the volatile Pennsylvania political scene, Reed emerged as a compromise candidate for the position of president of the Supreme Executive Council, in effect, the state's governor. Inclined to treat loyalists severely, Reed became increasingly disenchanted with Philadelphia's military commandant, Benedict Arnold who had taken over when British occupiers left the city. When the general, who cavorted openly with Tories, was court martialed over accusations of profiteering, he accused Reed of maligning his reputation, a charge that had some validity as it was known that Reed had been briefly involved with intrigue when he criticized Washington's judgment in letters to Gen. Charles Lee. As a result, Arnold was merely reprimanded and found guilty only of minor charges. The governor was also on hand to lead the militia personally in relief of "Fort Wilson" where a group of politicians and businessmen accused of profiteering were holed up and surrounded by an angry mob. After helping to defuse a crisis among mutinous soldiers of the Pennsylvania Line, Reed left office in 1781 and busied himself with legal work highlighted by a case in which he himself was a defendant replying to charges by political enemy John Cadwalader that he had once considered betraying the Revolution. It was true that at one time, an attempt had been made by the British to bribe him with an offer of 10,000 pounds in cash and any position he cared to hold within the empire, but Reed turned it down saying that he was "not worth purchasing, but such as I was, the king of Great Britain is not rich enough to do it." Overcoming those charges, confidence in him by the people was expressed when they elected him once more to Congress in 1784. Unfortunately, ill health prevented him from accepting the position and after a brief trip to England, he returned to Philadelphia and died on March 5, 1785.

Paul Revere

Paul Revere's brush with Revolutionary heroism was brief but memorable, made the more so by Henry Wadsworth Longfellow's famous poem about his midnight ride. If it weren't for the celebrity given Revere by that poem, the Boston silversmith would have probably remained a footnote in American history, known primarily as one of many local Patriots active in the Boston area. As it is, however, Revere's fame serves to illustrate the parts played by thousands of ordinary Americans, some active Patriots, some merely sympathizers, whose stories are rarely if ever told or only known by those living in the small towns of rural Massachusetts or New Jersey or North Carolina that were their homes. But taken together, these Patriots and lovers of freedom form a mosaic whose big picture comprises the vast tapestry of the American Revolution itself.

Born in Boston near the end of December, 1734, Revere was the eldest son of Apollos Rivoire, an immigrant from France who had settled in Massachusetts to escape religious persecution. Upon arrival in the New World, Rivoire had anglicized his name to Revere and set himself up in the silversmith trade, a line of work his son Paul soon entered. The younger Revere was nineteen and nearly finished his apprenticeship when his father died, leaving him the family business. In 1756, like many other young men thirsting for adventure, Revere had his first taste of military life when he served in the local militia as a lieutenant of artillery during the French and Indian War. Returning from the war, he married and proceeded to have the first of sixteen children by two wives and bore down to make his silversmithing business one of the most successful, personally producing items of such exquisite craft that over 200 years later, they are still highly regarded by collectors and connoisseurs of eighteenth century workmanship. A successful businessman, Revere was naturally involved with a number of business associations including the local Masonic Lodge where he came into contact with the nascent resistance movement and local Patriots such as James Otis and James Warren. As a businessman, he was already sensitive to the effects many of the British Parliament's proposed tax measures would have on his livelihood and it probably did not take much convincing for him to become an active member of the growing resistance movement.

Not active in politics and not necessarily disposed to expressing himself pseudonymously in print as others did, he became first a spy, keeping Patriot leaders informed of British activities around Boston, then a dispatch rider, delivering letters among local Committees of Correspondence and Safety and the Continental Congress. In between, he acted as one of the "Indians" during the Boston Tea Party and used his engraving talents to produce propaganda for the cause with his most successful, and notorious, effort being an engraving of the "Boston Massacre," copies of which were distributed far and wide inspiring popular outrage against the British.

It was in his capacity as a spy that Revere had arranged a signal system from the steeple of Christ Church to give advance warning of British troop movements from Boston to the mainland. On the night of April 18, 1775 just such movements were observed and the signal given to local Patriots out in Charlestown. Revere and another rider named William Dawes were

Paul Revere

warned by Warren of the activity in the British camp and instructed to ride to Lexington by separate routes to warn Samuel Adams and John Hancock, the presumed targets of the enemy movement, to flee the area. Before he left, Revere went to Christ Church to make sure the pre-arranged signal was given (in this case, two lanterns, indicating that the British would be moving by sea). With two companions and oars muffled using strips from the undergarments of one of the men's sweetheart, Revere was rowed across the Charles River to Charlestown where he verified that the signal from Christ Church had been received by local Sons of Liberty. From there, he left at top speed for Lexington on a borrowed horse, avoiding British patrols and arousing minuteman companies and Patriot sympathizers along the way. Arriving in Lexington around midnight, he found Adams and Hancock and warned them in time to escape (Hancock wanted to stay and face the British, but was talked out of it by Adams). Shortly after, Revere was joined by Dawes who had been ordered by Warren to follow the land passage to Lexington. Knowing of a hidden supply of gunpowder and other military stores in the next town, the two men decided to go on to Concord and warn the minutemen companies there to beware a possible attempt by the British to seize the supplies. On the way, they met Samuel Prescott, a resident of Concord who volunteered to join them, but before the little group could reach their destination, they were intercepted by a British patrol and held under suspicion of being spies for the Sons of Liberty. But their captors were soon distracted and Dawes and Prescott took the opportunity to escape (Dawes, however, was thrown from his horse and never reached Concord; Prescott succeeded in staying in the saddle as his horse leapt a stone wall and eventually reached Concord to raise the alarm). A frustrated Revere continued to be held along with a few other men who had been stopped by the patrol until the sound of distant shots prompted the soldiers to loose their prisoners in order to ride to the sound of the guns. After forcing him to switch horses with one of their own, the soldiers released Revere and left him. His primary mission accomplished, Revere turned around and headed back to Lexington where he arrived in time to help Hancock and Adams finish packing up their things. On the nearby green, the town's minutemen had assembled and were receiving orders from their commander. Meanwhile, with church bells pealing and the alarm sounding in every town, the British officer in charge of the first companies to enter Lexington was made more nervous when Revere's former captors reported that hundreds of local militia had been called out in response to the British incursion. As he rode away to catch up with the departing Hancock and Adams, Revere heard the first shots fired in the Revolution come from the green as a great cloud of gun smoke rose over the village.

Following the excitement of that historic "midnight ride," Revere resumed his old wartime position as an officer of artillery and was posted with the rank of colonel at Castle Island out in Boston harbor where he saw no action. After accompanying his regiment on an abortive attempt to invest Newport, Rhode Island in 1779, he commanded troops at Penobscot, Massachusetts where British ships had been sighted offshore. When the commander of American naval vessels refused to engage the enemy, Revere marched his men back to Boston where he was accused of cowardice and disobeying orders. It took a half dozen applications before he received a court martial and eventual exoneration. Out of the military again, Revere continued his efforts on behalf of the Revolution by establishing a sorely needed mill for the manufacture of gunpowder and later a foundry for the production of cannon.

After the war, Revere continued to prosper, establishing a copper rolling mill by which he manufactured brass fittings and copper plate for the USS Constitution, copper sheets for the dome of the state capital in Massachusetts, and fashioned parts for Robert Fulton's steam driven ferry boats. He also switched from making cannon at his foundry to casting church bells. Prosperous and well regarded in his community as a loyal Son of Liberty, Revere retired in 1811 and died of old age on May 10, 1818.

David Rittenhouse

Astronomer, engineer, surveyor, inventor, David Rittenhouse might be considered an American "renaissance man" of the type whose creative energies would be released in the blossoming of freedom following the Revolutionary War and that would in turn, help build the most powerful national economy in history.

Born on April 8, 1732 near Germantown, Pennsylvania, Rittenhouse was the son of a local manufacturer who had built the first paper mill in the British colonies. Perhaps inspired by the machinery involved with his father's mill, Rittenhouse, at an early age, began to construct mechanical models including a water mill when he was only eight years old. As he grew older, he discovered books and became an avid reader, teaching himself the basics of many subjects including mathematics for which he seemed to have a natural affinity. Over the years, the young Rittenhouse managed to get his hands on more advanced literary works such as Isaac Newton's *Principia* and grew in his knowledge of mathematics, geometry, and astronomy. At the same time, he retained his interest in machinery and with a set of tools given to him by an uncle, began to build clocks first in wood, then in brass. Working from his parents' home, he opened a shop and sold mechanical instruments of his own manufacture including clocks and devices called orreries that simulated the motions of the solar system. In 1767, after his work came to the attention of the local intelligentsia, he was given an honorary masters degree from the College of Pennsylvania and in 1768 joined the American

David Rittenhouse

Philosophical Society. It was to be the beginning of a long association with the group during which Rittenhouse would serve as librarian, secretary, vice-president, and finally president. With the Society's support, Rittenhouse embarked on a project that would take advantage of the expected transit of Venus in 1769 which included the building of special measuring instruments, the establishment of a number of observation platforms (one of which would later be used to proclaim the signing of a new Declaration of Independence), and possibly the design and construction of the first telescope made in America. During the course of his observations, Rittenhouse confirmed an earlier surmise that Venus had an atmosphere. In 1770, after suffering the loss of his wife in childbirth, the budding scientist left his home in Germantown and took residence in Philadelphia.

Although to this point, Rittenhouse had earned a local reputation for his native genius, political events would soon thrust him onto the national stage as disagreement between Britain and the thirteen American colonies reached the flash point in Massachusetts. In 1774, the year Parliament passed the "Coercive Acts" and the First Continental Congress met in Philadelphia, Rittenhouse was made city surveyor. By the time minutemen had fired on British troops at Lexington and Concord, he had entered politics as a member of the Pennsylvania legislature. Finally, as the year 1776 began, the Second Continental Congress decided that events had gone too far for a reconciliation with Britain and signed a Declaration of Independence. Open war suddenly made the scientific talents of men such as Rittenhouse a valuable national commodity and he was importuned by fellow patriots to help. As a result, Rittenhouse became deeply involved in organizing the development of the new nation's military supply system from the design and casting of cannon and huge harbor chains to the manufacture and storage of gunpowder. His involvement with military supply led to his being made a member of the Board of War and in 1779 his mastery of mathematics made him a natural choice for Pennsylvania's state treasurer. At the same time, Rittenhouse continued as a leading member of the state's academic community, serving on the board of trustees for the University of Pennsylvania and in 1780, teaching astronomy at the school.

With the end of the war in 1783, Rittenhouse was able to return to purely academic pursuits, delving ever more deeply into the world of mathematics and eventually publishing a number of works on the subject that proved the earliest ever written in the United States. Having surveyed many of the state's boundaries, Rittenhouse worked with James Madison in 1784 to locate the Mason-Dixon line running between Pennsylvania and Virginia and extending it west into the Ohio country. In 1790, following the death of Benjamin Franklin, Rittenhouse, became second president of the American Philosophical Society, a position he would hold until his own death six years later. In 1792, he was called by President George Washington to serve his country one last time as the first director of the United States Mint.

Established by Congress under the Coinage Act as part of a plan submitted by Secretary of the Treasury Alexander Hamilton, the Mint enjoyed offices located in the first building to be constructed by the federal government and by the end of 1793, Rittenhouse had overseen the issuance of the first copper, gold, and silver coins that finally gave the country a uniform currency and the basis for a sound economy. But it was not until 1795 that Rittenhouse capped his professional career when he was elected as a fellow of the Royal Society of London, the premier scientific organization of the time. The recognition, however, came just as ill health forced Rittenhouse into retirement. Not long after, he died at his home in Philadelphia on June 26, 1796.

Caesar Rodney

John Adams once described Caeser Rodney as "the oddest looking man in the world" an appearance that would not be improved by the development later of a cancerous sore on his face. But despite appearances, Rodney was one of America's most ardent patriots and a man who was convinced early on of the need for the thirteen colonies to declare their independence. A quality also noted by the observant New Englander when he went on to note that Rodney possessed a "sense of fire, spirit, wit, and humor in his countenance."

Born on his father's farm near Dover, Delaware on October 7, 1728 Rodney received no formal education when he was young. Instead, such training had to wait until his father's death when Rodney was placed under the guardianship of Nicholas Ridgely, a clerk of the peace for Kent County. Rodney's subsequent education, and no doubt his nascent political connections, yielded him the first of a long list of public offices when he was appointed Kent County's high sheriff in 1755. Registrar of wills, clerk of the orphan's court, recorder

Caesar Rodney

of deeds, and justice of the peace soon followed, his prestige in the community rising with each new responsibility. The succession of offices was crowned in 1758 when Rodney was first elected as a representative in Delaware's legislature. With a single year's exception, there he remained, through succeeding elections until 1776, witness to his colony's growing struggle with royal authority as Parliament and the king sought to impose a series of increasingly unpopular tax raising measures.

Rodney's attitude toward arbitrary authority was perhaps first inspired by Delaware's position in relation to neighboring Pennsylvania. Having exchanged hands earlier in its history between the Dutch and the Swedes, when Delaware was finally secured by England it was placed under the stewardship of the Penn family, royal proprietors of Pennsylvania. That situation created tension between the proprietors and leaders in Delaware that came to a head in 1776 when the colony's legislature dissolved and was reconvened in a new state convention which Rodney, as Speaker of the Assembly, took the lead in sponsoring. But by that time, the change seemed less radical than it would have earlier in Rodney's career when he first became involved in revolutionary activity. The defining moment for Rodney's radicalization seemed to come when he was chosen as a delegate to the Stamp Act Congress of 1765, significant as the first gathering of representatives from most of the thirteen colonies in a common purpose. Spur for calling the congress came from a wave of violence that began in Massachusetts in protest of the new Stamp Tax imposed by Parliament. Mobs roamed the streets of Boston, burning officials in effigy, intimidating stamp tax collectors, and even forcing Lt. Governor Thomas Hutchinson out of the city when they attacked and destroyed his home. Soon, a loose society of protestors began to form calling themselves Sons of Liberty and Committees of Correspondence sprang up among the colonies to keep each other abreast of the struggle against the imposition of the hated tax measures. Rodney, already recognized as one of Delaware's most outspoken leaders, was made a member of the colony's own Committee of Correspondence and later, was chosen as a delegate to the Stamp Congress to be held in New York. The historic meeting, which would serve as the model for the later Continental Congress, was attended by nine of the thirteen colonies and lasted about three weeks. At the end of that time, the delegates had produced a document, the *Declaration of the Rights and Grievances of the Colonies*, that listed the colonists' complaints and determined that they could not be taxed without representation in England's Parliament. Following that line of reasoning, the *Declaration* concluded that due to the distances involved between the colonies and the mother country, representation of the colonists was vested in their individual legislatures. The demand dashed the hopes of liberals in Parliament for a compromise on the issue of representation and forced some older revolutionaries to abandon similar ideas.

Thus matters stood until 1774 when, finding the crown's position toward the colonies unchanged, a Continental Congress was called to meet in Philadelphia. Rodney, who, in addition to his duties in the legislature, had also become an officer in Delaware's militia, was chosen as a member of the colony's delegation. That first session of the Congress, which was also attended by such ardent nationalists as John and Samuel Adams from Massachusetts and Richard Henry Lee and Patrick Henry from Virginia, was dominated by pleas from moderates to give England every chance to seal the widening breach between itself and its colonies. When a second Congress was called to meet in 1776, the attitude toward independence had shifted considerably in the wake of fighting around Boston and the mother country's refusal to consider any offer of reconciliation. Convinced of the uselessness of continued negotiation, Rodney became well known as a staunch supporter of a Declaration of Independence.

The issue came to a head late in June of 1776 when the Congress entertained a resolution for independence. A crucial factor to any decision on the issue was a voting rule limiting each colony's delegation to a single vote representing the entire group. Thus a unanimous vote by the entire Congress would amount to thirteen. The problem with the rule was the possibility of having a tie vote within the membership of a single delegation should a member abstain or be absent. If that happened, the delegation's vote on the issue at hand would be canceled out. Thus, a decision by Rodney to return to Dover to tend to his ailing wife set the stage for a tie vote on the independence issue between the two remaining members in Delaware's delegation. Although member Thomas McKean, like Rodney, supported independence, the third member of the delegation, George Read, did not. If the possibility of a unanimous decision for independence by the thirteen colonies were to be preserved, it was crucial that Rodney return immediately to Philadelphia in order to preserve Delaware's vote on the issue. Knowing the importance of the vote, McKean sent a note to Rodney urging him to return to Philadelphia as fast as he could. Upon receiving the message, Rodney took to horse almost immediately and began the 80 mile ride from Dover to Philadelphia through the night of July 1-2. Around noon the next day, after having ridden the whole way in a thunder storm, Rodney made his dramatic appearance in the Congress booted and spurred, a scarf wrapped around his head to hide the increasing deformity of his cancer and still soaked from the steady rain. Because of his action, Rodney's presence allowed the Delaware delegation to break its deadlock and make the vote for independence a unanimous one among the thirteen colonies.

In 1777, Rodney was appointed major general in Delaware's militia and the next year was elected as the new state's governor. Rodney's continued zeal for American liberty carried over to the performance of his public duties which included making sure the state met and often exceeded its quota for soldiers serving in the Continental Army. Although Rodney left the office of governor in 1781, he remained in politics as speaker of the Upper House in Delaware's legislature. Unfortunately, his role in the legislature would be cut short by the disease that had plagued him for years. Despite a risky operation to remove the cancerous sore on his face by a prominent Philadelphia surgeon, Rodney at last succumbed to the illness and died on June 29, 1784.

George Ross

George Ross was born on May 10, 1730 in New Castle, Delaware, the son of a clergyman with a large family. After receiving a solid grounding in the classics at home, he was shipped off to the offices of an older brother in Philadelphia where he was taught the law. Passing the bar in 1750, he decided to move further west to Lancaster where presumably, competition for legal business would not be as stiff as it was in Philadelphia. There, Ross was quick to establish a reputation for himself as well as a marriage to a young lady who had been one of the first to seek out his services as a lawyer. Ross spent the next eighteen years building up his practice, serving as a crown prosecutor, and becoming a well respected citizen of the county before finally being elected to the colonial legislature in 1768. He served there for the next eight years as tensions grew between the American colonies and Britain over attempts by Parliament to impose unwanted tax collecting measures on the people. Although his sympathies were initially for the mother country, Ross slowly changed his attitude to the point where he served as a member of Lancaster's Committee of Safety and was appointed an officer in the army. In 1774, his growing patriotism was recognized when he was asked by Pennsylvania's provincial assembly to draft the instructions by which the colony's representatives to the

Continental Congress would conduct themselves. When the instructions were approved by the assembly, Ross was then chosen by the same body as a member of Pennsylvania's delegation.

As the first Continental Congress opened, Ross followed the instructions given to his delegation to avoid support for any move to declare independence from Britain; but by 1775, with the news from Massachusetts of Concord and Lexington and Breed's Hill, his attitude changed and he became a supporter of independence. His new stance was not received well and he was removed from Pennsylvania's delegation. But by that time, events were moving rapidly and following a groundswell of popular opinion in favor of independence, Pennsylvania modified its instructions to its delegates in Congress

George Ross

and Ross found himself reappointed. He returned to Congress too late to vote for independence, but was present to add his name to the Declaration.

Although Ross was forced to resign from Congress in 1777 for reasons of health, that did not prevent him from participating in Pennsylvania's constitutional convention which was charged with forming a new government following independence. Representing Lancaster County, Ross was assigned to draw a set of rules under which the convention would operate, prepare a declaration of rights, and drafting a definition of treason. In 1779, after helping to organize the state's defense against invasion, Ross was made a judge of Pennsylvania's admiralty court. Unfortunately, he was able to serve for only a few months before an attack of gout killed him on July 14, 1779.

Benjamin Rush

Many Patriots, although united in their fervor to conduct the war and see the thirteen colonies independent, nevertheless, often did not see eye to eye whether in their politics or their professional lives. In the case of Benjamin Rush, that kind of contradiction was especially obvious in his relations with George Washington and the Congress as surgeon general to the Continental Army and later, his difference of opinion with fellow physicians on the practice of medicine. Despite his progressive attitude toward the democratization of health care and his belief that following the Revolution, people would have to adjust their attitudes to a new political reality, the continued use by Rush of the practice of bleeding for the treatment of illness, a technique that had begun to receive widespread condemnation, was perhaps symbolic of the divide between the colonial era and the new age that began following the Revolution. Rush, like many of his contemporaries, had become pessimistic about the new order they had helped to bring about and feared for the future of the infant United States. Even though many like Rush had been staunch supporters of both independence and the federal Constitution, wariness of foreign alliances, party politics, democratic tendencies, or a voracious central government still gnawed at people's minds and sometimes prevented them from fully accepting the new conditions under which they found themselves living.

Rush was born on December 24, 1745 just outside of Philadelphia, in Byberry, Pennsylvania and was only six years old when his father died. At loose ends, his mother decided to have her son educated at an academy in Nottingham, Maryland headmastered by her brother. There, Rush earned his early education and was steeped in the classics of Greek and Latin before moving on to Princeton College where he graduated in 1760. Only fifteen years old at the time, Rush decided to study medicine and returned to Philadelphia to apprentice under the eye of an established physician while at the same time attending lectures given by Dr. William Shippen who was noted at the time for his progressive treatment of mental illness and for founding the country's first public hospital. In 1766, Rush left Pennsylvania for Europe and by 1768, had earned a degree in medicine from Edinburgh University.

After a brief tour of the continent, he returned to Pennsylvania and began his own medical practice. In no time, his reputation was such that in 1769 he was offered the chair in chemistry at the College of Philadelphia where he joined Shippen on the faculty of America's first medical school. Later, after the college had become a full university, Rush was made a full professor of medical and clinical practices.

Although his European education, the success of his educational career, and his work among the poor were factors in the favorable impression he was making among Philadelphians, Rush was also earning himself a name among local Patriots. Having set pen to paper to write a textbook on chemistry, Rush soon broadened the subject of his writings to include politics and his work began to appear in local newspapers. He started joining things, first the American Philosophical Society and then the local Sons of Liberty. From there, his fellow patriots chose him to represent them at the colony's provincial congress and again as a member of Pennsylvania's delegation to the Continental Congress in 1776 where he became a signer of the Declaration of Independence. One of the

Benjamin Rush

few members of Congress who kept extensive records of the activities of that body, Rush also wrote descriptions of many of its members including John Adams ("a most sensible and forcible speaker"), Samuel Adams ("a republican in principle and manners") and Thomas Jefferson ("he possessed a genius of the first order").

In 1776, Rush met Thomas Paine and, impressed with a tract the Englishman had written against slavery, encouraged him to write something just as forceful in support of independence. What resulted was a booklet Rush entitled *Common Sense* which went on to become one of the most widely read documents of the Revolutionary era and often cited as instrumental in reviving the new nation's morale in the darkest days of the war.

Recognizing his medical credentials, Rush was appointed by Congress as surgeon general for the middle department of the Continental Army. That position placed him under Shippen, his old teacher and professional colleague who had been named in charge of the Army's medical service. After producing a new manual on preserving the health of soldiers by emphasizing cleanliness, Rush began to criticize Shippen for the deplorable conditions he found in military hospitals, conditions Shippen himself had inherited from his predecessors. But the younger Rush refused to consider Shippen's position and complained to Gen. George Washington, commander in chief of the Continental Army, about "our hospitals crowded with 6,000 sick but half provided with necessaries or accommodations, and more dying in them in one month than perished in the field." His concerns were bumped up to Congress which ended the affair by siding with Shippen. Disappointed and harboring resentments against those who failed to support him, Rush chose to resign his office but remained in contact with many influential politicians whose acquaintance he made while serving in Congress. In the dark days of the New York campaign and Valley Forge when Washington's fortunes and personal reputation were at their lowest, Rush wrote letters to such men as Patrick Henry urging them to reconsider Washington's position as commander in chief. "A dreary wilderness is still before us, and unless a Moses or a Joshua are raised up in our behalf, we must perish before we reach the promised land," wrote Rush in an unsigned letter to Henry. Henry, however, was not interested and forwarded the letter to Washington who recognized the handwriting and confronted Rush with the evidence. Caught in his backstairs lobbying, Rush decided to give up his efforts and return to medicine, leaving politics and the war behind.

Reentering politics after his writings appeared in local newspapers in defense of the proposed United States Constitution, Rush was chosen as a representative to Pennsylvania's state ratifying convention. Admitting the need for a strong federal government, Rush believed that fighting the Revolutionary War was the easy part while forging a new conception of government the more difficult with citizens needing to change the way they thought about what such an entity was supposed to do in order for it to work.

In the following years, Rush continued to teach and practice medicine. As a member of the American Philosophical Society, he spoke in favor of emphasizing science in popular education, advocated health care for the poor, and stood against the institution of slavery. These positions however, were not enough for Rush to escape the harsh criticism that followed his treatment of patients during a yellow fever epidemic that gripped Philadelphia in 1793. Called into question was his steadfast belief in the benefits of bleeding, which had been considered for centuries as a practical method of treating the symptoms of almost any kind of sickness and one Rush used on Washington himself in 1799 when the president was on his deathbed. The practice, by a physician who had been known for most of his professional life as progressive, was unfortunate in an age where medicine, like science in general, was on the verge of being transformed. As a result, his reputation suffered a blow from which it never fully recovered as newspapers labeled him a murderer and he was even threatened with legal action. His practice fell off sharply until, nearly destitute, he was saved from complete ruin when President John Adams took pity and appointed him treasurer of the United States Mint in 1797, a position he held for the next sixteen years.

In the meantime, Rush helped found the Pennsylvania Bible Society and was honored by various European governments for his medical achievements, supported popular medicine while continuing to emphasize cleanliness in the avoidance of sickness and found the time to write such popular tracts as an *Inquiry into the effects of ardent spirits upon the human body and mind* and *Observations upon the influence of the habitual use of tobacco upon health, morals, and property*. Rush was also an advocate for public education and when a proposal to found a public school system in Pennsylvania failed, he organized a group aimed at educating homeless boys. But perhaps of even greater service than his philanthropic endeavors was the role Rush played in reconciling the breach that had grown between John Adams and Thomas Jefferson since the rancorous days when each had occupied the White House. Acting as intermediary, Rush put the two giants of the Revolution in touch with each other again and the result was one of the most exhaustive and enlightening series of correspondence in American history as the two men reviewed a lifetime of world shaking events and their estimation of the results. Near the end of his life, Rush seemed to have second thoughts about his role in the Revolution, remarking in correspondence with John Adams that he often looked "back upon the hours I spent serving my country...with deep regret." Rush died of typhus on April 19, 1813, his career as physician, teacher, writer, and politician remembered by the mourners who crowded his home upon news of his demise.

Edward Rutledge

The youngest of the signers of the Declaration of the Independence, Edward Rutledge was considered nothing but a callow youth by fellow congressman John Adams but in time proved otherwise as he rose from successful attorney, revolutionary soldier, politician, and eventually governor of his state.

Rutledge was born on November 23, 1749 in Charleston, South Carolina, a city that would loom large over the course of his subsequent career. The youngest of seven children and a member of one of the colony's wealthiest and most influential families, Rutledge received a good education that began at the hands of a tutor and then continued in the law offices of older brother John. When it was decided that he was ready, the younger Rutledge was sent off to England to complete his legal education at the Inner Temple where a good deal of his time was spent in the halls of Parliament observing the creation of law first hand. At last, his education complete, he became a member of the English bar and returned home in 1773 where he began his own legal practice. As a member of the colony's upper classes, Rutledge naturally hobnobbed with his peers and from among them, married Henrietta Middleton, the daughter of Henry Middleton with

Edward Rutledge

whom he would later travel to Philadelphia as a member of the colony's congressional delegation. After winning the admiration of local patriots by securing the release from prison of a local newspaperman who had published articles critical of royal authority, Rutledge won a seat in the South Carolina legislature and soon after, with the influence of his brother John and father-in-law, was allowed to join them as a delegate to the Continental Congress.

Although fellow congressman John Adams held a dim view of the younger Rutledge, his opinion may have been prejudiced by the South Carolinian's position on independence from England which leaned on the side of caution and which even led him to support the Galloway Plan of Union which was described as a "British American legislature," independent but still under the authority of the crown. As debate on the issue progressed, Rutledge made motion after motion to delay a final decision and when the time came at last, kept the South Carolina delegation from casting its vote in favor of independence. It was only after a first ballot indicated that the measure would pass that Rutledge asked for a second vote on the issue and after advising his delegation that passage was inevitable, led its members in making the final decision a unanimous one. When it was time to sign the actual Declaration of Independence, at age 27, Rutledge became the youngest of that elite group of signatories.

After the signing, Rutledge accompanied John Adams and Benjamin Franklin for peace talks with British Admiral Richard Howe who hoped for a last minute settlement of the issues dividing Britain and its former colonies. But with formal independence declared, it was too little too late and nothing was resolved. After that, Rutledge left Congress and returned to South Carolina where he continued his law practice until rejoining the state legislature in 1778. The next year, he was once again chosen to represent the state in Congress, but his duties as an officer in the state's militia prevented him from attending. With the enemy showing a rising interest in the south and the seizure of Savannah, Georgia in December of 1778, North Carolina belatedly began to prepare for war. It was almost a year later when the enemy began to advance north and among their movements was a raid on Port Royal Island. There, on February 3, 1779, about 200 British soldiers were met by 300 militiamen under the command of Col. William Moultrie, the hero of Sullivan's Island. Among the defenders was Rutledge and his artillery battery which was placed in the center of the American line. As it turned out, Port Royal was a victory for the militia and was distinguished by a role reversal in which the British fought from cover while the Americans attacked in the open. In May of 1780, the British returned in force and this time managed to cut off Charleston from the mainland trapping over 5,000 militia and Continentals inside the city. Among the captives taken were American commander Gen. Benjamin Lincoln and artillerist Lt. Col. Edward Rutledge. Sent to St. Augustine, Florida for confinement, Rutledge remained a prisoner for the better part of a year until the summer of 1781 when he was taken to Philadelphia and exchanged.

After the war, Rutledge served in South Carolina's legislature until 1798 when he was elected governor. Like many of the Founding Fathers, Rutledge remained wary of pure democracy and as such, supported ratification of the Constitution and gravitated to the Federalist party in national politics. That, however, was not held against him when he became governor and later, he supported the leader of the Republican Party Thomas Jefferson in his bid for the presidency. Rutledge was at the zenith of his career when his health began to fail him and after suffering from exposure on the way back to Charleston from Columbia, he died on January 23, 1800.

John Rutledge

The older brother of Edward Rutledge, signer of the Declaration of Independence, John Rutledge rose to distinction in the revolutionary movement to become governor of South Carolina.

The exact date of his birth unknown, Rutledge was born to a successful physician near Charleston, South Carolina sometime in September of 1739. Educated at first by his father then by tutors, young Rutledge was sent off to England to study law and admitted to the bar in 1760. Returning home, he started his own legal practice and was successful enough that in a few years he was able to begin making business investments that would eventually make him a rich man. In 1761, he entered politics as a member of South Carolina's legislature and two years after that, married. By 1765, Rutledge had begun to think seriously of the relationship between Britain and its thirteen American colonies and when talk of a pending Stamp Tax arose, he was chosen to be a part of South Carolina's delegation to a Stamp Act Congress that met in New York that year. Although Rutledge became increasingly radicalized as the years passed, he began his revolutionary career as a moderate, a position he occupied when he joined the First Continental Congress in 1774 as a member of South Carolina's delegation. Satisfied with his cautious approach to relations with Britain, residents of his colony reappointed Rutledge to the Second Continental Congress in 1775. Later, when he chose to leave Congress, he was replaced by his younger brother Edward.

By the time Edward had joined the rest of Congress in signing a Declaration of Independence, John had mourned the break with England but accepted the decision. He joined the South Carolina Committee of Safety and later shared in the creation of the new state's constitution, one that many understood to be only a temporary device pending an eventual settlement of differences between the colonies and Britain. Under the new constitution, Rutledge found himself elected president in 1776 but resigned in protest two years later when wording was changed to bring South Carolina into conformance with the Declaration of Independence. In 1779, his protests notwithstanding, Rutledge was again chosen to lead South Carolina this time as its governor and was in office when the state's seaport city of Charleston was invested by the enemy.

When the British had attacked the city three years before, Rutledge had stood steadfast in support of Col. William Moultrie who succeeded in frustrating the British attempt to conquer the city, but this time, facing what he thought was a superior enemy force, things were different. Given almost dictatorial powers to defend the city, Rutledge enraged many patriots when he offered the state's neutrality for the rest of the war should Charleston be spared. Luckily, the deal never had to be made after an army under Gen. Benjamin Lincoln

John Rutledge

appeared on the scene and the enemy was forced to retreat. But the governor's luck ran out the next year when, despite a successful recruiting campaign in the countryside, he failed to get much help from the city's residents and Charleston fell to the British on May 12, 1780. With the British in control of the countryside surrounding the city, Rutledge lost his property and was forced to flee to North Carolina. There, he tried to rally elements of the South Carolina militia to strike back, but was stymied when the British inflicted yet another humiliating defeat on revolutionary forces when they shattered an invading army under Gen. Horatio Gates at the battle of Camden and sent the general flying almost 200 miles ahead of his troops. Undeterred, Rutledge resumed his efforts to raise men and supplies and by the time a new commander was named to take charge of the southern theater, there was an infrastructure in place to receive him. In a slow, but deliberate campaign, Gen. Nathanael Greene led his small army back into the Carolinas and by 1781, after a series of victories and harassment of enemy outposts, scouting parties, and supply lines, was able to regain control over most of the state.

With the defeat of Gen. Charles Cornwallis at Yorktown on October 19 and victory in the war in sight, Rutledge stepped down as war governor and became a legislator again. Except for a year long return to the Continental Congress in 1782, he remained in the legislature until 1790. In between, Rutledge was once again sent to Philadelphia, this time as a delegate to the Constitutional Convention held in 1787. There, he supported efforts not simply to revise the Articles of Confederation, but to replace them entirely with a new Constitution that would strengthen the federal government. It was Rutledge who moved that the affairs of the Convention be held behind closed doors and then worked in committee to set its agenda. He supported the assumption of state debts that had been incurred during the war, popular election of federal legislators, and continuance of the slave trade. Following the Convention, Rutledge returned to South Carolina to take up the fight again during the state's own ratification convention. After the Constitution had been ratified by the states and a new president and Congress elected, Rutledge served for a year on the United States Supreme Court before becoming chief justice of the South Carolina Supreme Court in 1791.

Four years later, he became the object of controversy when he was appointed by President George Washington to replace retiring chief justice John Jay on the United States Supreme Court. The appointment was made while Congress had been in recess, but by the time it was in session again, Rutledge had ruined his chances for confirmation by making an intemperate speech denouncing a new treaty between Britain and the United States brokered by John Jay that reestablished commercial ties and required the British to abandon forts in the

Northwest Territories. Since the treaty already had the support of Washington and the Senate, some called his mental capacities into question and when the votes were counted, his nomination was rejected making Rutledge the first nominee to the Supreme Court to be turned down by Congress. Returning to South Carolina, Rutledge died there on June18, 1800.

Philip Schuyler

In the end, Philip Schuyler's wealth and position as one of New York's most prominent citizens was not enough to overcome the sectional prejudices that ran like fault lines beneath the surface of the political landscape that would one day become the United States. A New Yorker as well as a friend and confidant of George Washington, his loyalties placed him in a position counter to those forces, mainly from New England, who were suspicious of the Empire State in general and disappointed with the military performance of the commander in chief in particular. The result of this toxic mix was that Schuyler became an early casualty of the political infighting in Congress that would harden after the war into a contest between Federalists in favor of a strong central government led by mercantile interests and free citizen farmers in the North and Republicans concentrated in the southern and western states who commanded the support of slave holding aristocrats, small landowners, and backwoods pioneers suspicious of officialdom and the moneyed classes. The revolutionary strug-

Philip Schuyler

gle from the very beginning had never been a monolithic movement: different people, factions, and colonies all had varying motivations for supporting rebellion, all of which could be served under the call for freedom from oppressive royal authority. But those conflicting interests were never far from the surface, emerging in the debates surrounding such early documents as the Declaration of Independence, the Articles of Confederation, the Treaty of Paris, and later, the Constitution itself. It was only unfortunate that Schuyler's fate as a military officer found itself caught between a sampling of those competing interests.

Born on November 20, 1733, Philip Schuyler was the offspring of an old Dutch family that had come to New York when it had still been known as New Amsterdam. At the time, the Schuyler family was already the most prominent in the upper Hudson Valley area and possessed of large land holdings and a lucrative trade with the local Indian tribes who were firm allies of the British against the expansionist French in Canada. With the successive deaths of his father and other, more senior, family members when he was still young, it grew increasingly obvious that Schuyler would some day be the one to assume leadership of his clan. As a result, he was taught by a series of tutors until, turning 18, his education was completed with his first trip into the deep forest for a taste of the family's Indian trade. It was around that time also, that he made the acquaintance of John Bradstreet, a British supply officer stationed in Albany who would prove to be one of the great influences in his career. But Schuyler's life took a drastic turn in 1755 when he married Catherine Van Rensselaer (with whom he sired 15 children) and was commissioned captain in the local militia with instructions to help prepare defenses around Albany in expectation of hostilities by the French and their own Indian allies. When the French and Indian War did break out, he accompanied Bradstreet to Oswego where he learned firsthand both how to raise and manage supplies for an army and weather the disappointment of defeat as the British suffered early setbacks in the war. Returning to Albany the next year, he was chosen for a number of minor civil positions before going off again with the army for the war's final, and more successful chapter. Victory, however, did not come without cost. He was with the army on its approach to Fort Ticonderoga (known by its French defenders as Fort Carillon), when it was taken by surprise by a French patrol and its commander Lord George Howe, killed. Accompanying the body back to Albany, Schuyler remained there for the balance of the war serving in the quartermaster department.

Following the war, Schuyler concentrated on building up his family business and in 1768 was elected to New York's General Assembly. During these years, he grew increasingly annoyed with the constant stream of laws and taxation measures emanating from London that he not only found oppressing to his constituents, but that prevented the expansion of his own business interests. He spoke out forcefully against what was called the "intolerable acts," the closing of the Boston port and the imposition of admiralty courts which severely restricted colonial trade. Finally, in 1775, he followed his fellow legislators into the Provincial Congress which replaced the General Assembly when that body was dissolved by New York Governor William Tryon. By that time, Schuyler had acquired a reputation as a leader in the opposition movement and had been appointed as a member of New York's delegation to the second Continental Congress where he first made the acquaintance of George Washington, working with him in a committee charged with laying the groundwork for the creation of a Continental Army. That experience, his service in the French and Indian War, and sectional politics, all were factors in his fellow congressmen appointing him as one of the first four major generals to head up the new army. Taking advantage of his position and his familiarity with northern New York, Congress placed Schuyler in charge of that department with orders to defend the region against possible Indian attack and to prepare for an American invasion of Canada. In this capacity, Schuyler was in his element, having experience not only in the organization of his business affairs, but in the quartermastering he had learned during the French and Indian War. Unfortunately, a long battle with gout and lung disease which he had been waging since he was a young man, finally caught up to him and prevented his accompanying the army into Canada. That duty fell to his young second in command, Gen. Richard Montgomery, who succeeded despite fearful odds in taking the fight to the very gates of Quebec before being forced to retreat in the face of disease, cold, and lack of supplies.

Just prior to the start of the failed Canada expedition, Schuyler was instructed by Congress to pacify the state's Tryon County area which, being the seat of British Indian agent Guy Johnson and his Indian ally Joseph Brant, still had strong loyalist tendencies. With his knowledge of local Indians, Schuyler met with representatives of the Six Nations and other tribes and managed to arrange a temporary truce and rebuild Fort Stanwix as a strongpoint in the area. Left behind in charge of the Mohawk Valley was Johnson's son, John, who was regarded by local patriots as a Tory sympathizer. Arriving at Johnson

Hall with a force of militia, Schuyler read him the riot act and ordered his arrest.

Unfortunately, the energy he displayed in suppressing a possible Indian uprising fell short in the matter of Fort Ticonderoga when, due to a chronic shortage of men and supplies, he failed to secure the heights overlooking the fortress after it was captured in 1775. A general belief that the heights were impossible to scale with cannon played into the hands of former British General Horatio Gates who had been scheming for months to wrest control of the northern department away from Schuyler. Failure to secure the heights cost the Americans possession of Ticonderoga when elements of an invading British army descending from Canada under Lt. Gen. John Burgoyne managed to haul guns to the top of nearby Mount Defiance and force the evacuation of the fort. When the news reached Congress, there was an outcry against Schuyler, especially among New England delegates who disliked the New Yorker for his indecisive and aristocratic manner and his state's continued claims to the Hampshire Grants. They preferred Gates instead. "...my crime consists in not being a New England man in principle, and unless they alter theirs I hope I never shall be," wrote Schuyler in a letter. "Gen. Gates is their idol because he is at their direction."

In the wake of his failure, Schuyler's defenders were unable to protect him and in August of 1777 he was replaced by Gates who went on to one of the greatest victories of the war at Saratoga due in no small measure to Schuyler's delaying actions to slow down the enemy advance, his organization of men and supplies, and his vigorous recruitment efforts. No longer in command of the northern department, Schuyler nevertheless continued to serve his country especially in regards to the continuing threat of Indian attack in the west and at Burgoyne's surrender, even opened his Albany home to the general and his officers who afterward, expressed regret at destroying much of their host's property during their advance.

A subsequent investigation of Schuyler's actions surrounding the fall of Fort Ticonderoga cleared him of the accusations that had led to his being replaced as commander of the northern department, but in 1779, he resigned his commission and returned to Congress. There, he once again became involved in military matters, conferring with Washington on the new alliance with the French and later, all unknowing of his treasonous intentions, suggested Benedict Arnold be given command at West Point. It was Schuyler who had dispatched Arnold to the relief of Fort Stanwix in 1777 and the two became close friends when the former was a congressman in Philadelphia and the latter was the city's military commander.

After the ratification of the Constitution, of which Schuyler was an early supporter, he was elected in 1788 as one of New York's first two senators to the new United States Congress but was subsequently defeated in 1791 by Aaron Burr, a political foe of his son-in-law Alexander Hamilton. Hamilton had come to Schuyler's attention through a prior acquaintance with fellow New Yorkers Gouverneur Morris and Robert Livingston as well as an earlier contact in 1779 when the young man had written to Schuyler about the creation of a national bank and to comment on a pamphlet the businessman had prepared entitled *Causes of Depreciation of the Continental Currency*. The young man's obvious knowledge of financial matters impressed Schuyler and the result was that Hamilton cemented his entrée into an influential circle of Empire State politicians who in turn introduced him to Pennsylvania's William Morris, possibly the wealthiest man in the country and as Superintendent of Finance, the most powerful figure involved with the country's monetary affairs. With those connections, and his marriage to Schuyler's daughter Elizabeth in 1780, Hamilton sealed a political alliance with Schuyler that yielded him a place among the state's delegation to the Constitutional Convention of 1787 where he was able to present a draft plan for a new federal government prepared by himself and his father-in-law. Returning to Congress again in 1796, Schuyler was eventually forced to retire due to an increasing illness that would dog him until his death on November 18, 1804, only a year following the devastating loss of his wife, Katherine.

John Sevier

One of the most popular and respected men on the frontier, John Sevier engaged in dozens of wilderness battles against Indians and at least once directly against the British during the years of the Revolution, never losing a battle. Such was his reputation as a leader and fighter, that when he gave the word, hundreds of his fellow frontiersmen would immediately look to their rifles and follow him anywhere he led. And where he led was often controversial at one time flirting with the

Spanish for control over what would later become the state of Tennessee.

Sevier was born near Harrisonburg, in Rockingham County, Virginia on September 23, 1745, the descendent of French immigrants to England who later found their way to the American colonies. From Maryland, the family moved to Virginia's Shenandoah Valley where Sevier, one of several siblings, went to school. In the area of Fredericksburg, Sevier followed the usual pattern of backcountry folk, doing a little farming, a little merchandising, and a good deal of hunting. By the time he was sixteen, Sevier had not only married, but his woodcraft and skill in the use of a gun earned him a position as an officer in the local militia. However, as with so many men in the settlements, Sevier was lured to the frontier by the promise of land for anyone bold enough to take it. And so, by 1773, he and his brothers made their way to the area of the Holston River in what would later become the state of Tennessee but at the time was technically unclaimed and belonged by treaty to the Indians. There, Sevier concentrated on staking a claim and establishing a homestead all the while participating in the defense of the tiny community as a member of the militia. By 1774, he had risen to the rank of captain and left home to serve under George Washington in Virginia Governor Lord Dunmore's war against the Shawnee in the Ohio country.

John Sevier

Back home in 1776, Sevier supported a petition to the North Carolina legislature signed by settlers in Holston as well as nearby Watauga, to bring the area under the jurisdiction of the new state. The petition was approved and Sevier not only attended the state's Provincial Congress, but was promoted to lieutenant colonel in the North Carolina militia. The appointment came just in time as Indians in the region, angered over violation of the treaty, went on the warpath and Sevier was among many caught in Fort Watauga when it was placed under siege. When the tide of battle had receded somewhat, Sevier was promoted to full colonel and later suffered the death of his first wife.

As the Revolution raged in the east, Sevier spent the next few years in a new marriage, developing the Holston settlements, and earning a reputation for fearlessness fighting the Cherokee in an ongoing wilderness war that had set the whole frontier ablaze. Although Indian warfare kept him busy as an officer in the militia, Sevier had had little opportunity to face the main enemy of the Revolution face to face. That situation changed dramatically in 1780 when Col. Isaac Shelby put out the word that he needed men to oppose a large body of British and Tories that was beating the brush in the South Carolina back country. Adding to the threat was word that British Major Patrick Ferguson, in command of the enemy force, had boasted that Shelby dared not challenge him in open combat and that if he did, his men would whip him soundly. Angered by the taunts, when Ferguson finally entered the neighborhood, Shelby met Sevier at a local horse race and the two agreed to attack the British together. Accompanied by their respective followers, the two men met again at Sycamore Shoals on September 25, 1780 and, joined by Col. William Campbell, they set off for an immediate campaign against Ferguson with a combined force of 1,000 men.

As the little army crossed the mountains east, more men joined it swelling its ranks to 1,400. Wasting little time, the Americans caught up to Ferguson at King's Mountain, South Carolina on October 7. There, they split into four columns and extended themselves around the base of the mountain. Commanding the right flank, Sevier met the left as his men rounded the mountain and began advancing up the slope. In the meantime, the British had retreated to the top of King's Mountain where they thought the high ground would give them the advantage. Instead, it proved just the opposite as the over mountain men moved up the slopes, dodging from tree to tree for cover and picking off the enemy one by one. At last, nearing the crest, Shelby ordered a charge. There, he was joined by Sevier and their combined commands soon overwhelmed the defenders.

Following King's Mountain, Sevier returned home and again campaigned against remnants of the Cherokee tribes who had since allied themselves with the British. In 1781, he may have marched east to join Gen. Nathanael Greene who was placed in charge of the southern theater and was in the process of gathering a force strong enough to oppose a British army under Gen. Charles Cornwallis moving up from South Carolina. After the war, Sevier once again returned to Holston where the streak of independence that had moved local settlers to petition North Carolina to take the region under its jurisdiction now prompted them to form a separate state. In June of 1784, North Carolina had ceded claims to its western lands to the United States government. But the move frightened residents of the area who, concerned that they would be cut off from the benefits of organized government, gathered in Jonesborough to fashion one of their own. Thus was born the "lost" state of Franklin with Sevier elected its first governor. But plans for the new state proved premature and the scheme fell through in 1789 when North Carolina voted to reabsorb the area. As a result, Sevier was labeled an outlaw and his reputation in the east cast under a shadow. But in 1788, the intrepid frontiersman emerged from the affair as a strong supporter of the country's new Constitution and was elected to the North Carolina legislature. Soon pardoned for the Franklin mess, Sevier next found himself in Congress and associated with the emerging Federalist party. Serving until 1791, he left Congress to take up the post of brigadier general of militia for the Southwest Territory. The appointment placed him in a position to be chosen in 1796 as the first governor of the new state of Tennessee which included the area once declared as the state of Franklin. He occupied the office until 1801 and again from 1803 to 1809 after which he was returned to Congress until 1811. In 1815, by reason of his long experience with Indians, he was appointed a member of a commission charged with settling the boundary between Georgia and Creek land in Alabama. It was while staying at Fort Decatur in Alabama that he died on September 24, 1815 the day after his seventieth birthday.

Isaac Shelby

The frontier facet of the Revolutionary War was one that was even more ill financed than the main theater of combat along the eastern seaboard of the thirteen colonies. Chronically short of money and supplies, which came primarily from cash strapped state governments rather than the more distant national Congress, the forward lines on the frontier were ill defined at best and non-existent at worst. It was a war where every man, woman and child could be a target of the enemy, both red and white, and a man often survived with reliance on his own wits as much as the support of distant governments across the mountains. Fortunately for the United States however, life on the frontier had a habit of raising men both courageous and self reliant, many of whom could be counted on to coalesce into fighting bands whenever the need arose and to disintegrate just as quickly. Among the men comprising these often rag tag forces were a few natural leaders around whom the rest would rally; frontiersmen knowledgeable of the Indians and familiar with their ways, experienced in woodcraft and possessing a good working knowledge of what later generations would call psychology. Just the qualities possessed by Isaac Shelby who, by the time of the Revolution, had no trouble finding men willing to follow where he led.

Shelby was born on a farmstead in rural Maryland on December 11, 1750. His early life was spent working the family farm where he learned all the skills expected of a boy in those days: hunting, shooting, and riding. His real education however, came from his father who not only had a reputation as a formidable woodsman, but also practiced surveying and often participated in the public life of his community, an example his son followed when he served the area as

Isaac Shelby

deputy sheriff. Shelby's life changed radically in 1773 after his father moved the family to the raw frontier of western Virginia in what is today, the state of Tennessee. The next year, Shelby had his baptism of fire when he took part in Lord Dunmore's War as an officer in the Fincastle County militia commanded by his father. It was while serving with the militia that Shelby participated in the battle of Point Pleasant which took place at the mouth of the Great Kanahwa River and that involved close, and often desperate fighting with the Shawnees led by their great chief Cornstalk. In recognition of his performance in combat, Shelby was named to the command staff of Fort Blair, which was built on the site of the Point Pleasant battle. He remained at the fort until 1775 when the lure of Kentucky proved too great and he left his command to survey land for himself and the government in the forbidden Indian hunting grounds.

When the Revolution began, Shelby, like most people on the frontier, had no trouble choosing sides and was immediately made captain of a local minuteman company by the Virginia Committee of Safety. In 1777, the state named him commissary of supplies for frontier defense in which capacity Shelby supported numerous military campaigns against the British Army and its Indian allies as well as finding the boats needed by George Rogers Clark for his historic conquest of the Illinois country. In 1799, Shelby was chosen by fellow residents to represent them in the Virginia legislature and the next year, after the settlement of a boundary dispute between Virginia and North Carolina, was commissioned a colonel with the North Carolina militia. By that time, the war in the north had settled to one of wary watching and waiting as active combat moved to the southern states where the British had seized Charlotte, North Carolina. Aided by great numbers of loyalists and a British cavalry commander named Banastre Tarleton who terrorized the countryside, the enemy had handed the United States a series of defeats that left a great portion of the southern states under its control. That however, did not slow down Shelby who had a most active year in 1780 as he and his "over mountain men" began by reducing loyalist positions at the Pacelot River on July 30 and pursued British forces under Major Patrick Ferguson who commanded a large group of American loyalists. On August 18, Shelby met and ambushed part of Ferguson's mostly Tory force at Musgrove's Mill, North Carolina where he served it a body blow resulting in over 200 enemy killed, wounded, or captured to only 4 of his own men killed. Shelby met Ferguson's men again at Cedar Springs and completed the year by arranging for a final showdown with the arrogant major at King's Mountain, North Carolina.

Riled by a challenge from Ferguson to either surrender or face death, Shelby met with Col. John Sevier who agreed to join him in a final effort to destroy Ferguson's army. To that end, the two men set off in pursuit of the British force and by the time they caught up to it, their army had swelled to over 1,000 men. Driven by Shelby, the force of rugged mountaineers pursued Ferguson's army of 1,125 men through a driving rainstorm until they caught up to it atop King's Mountain. With the rain stopped, the Americans moved up the slopes of the mountain from different directions with Shelby attacking the British left center. Near the summit, after suffering a bayonet charge and engaging in hand to hand combat with the enemy, Shelby's men joined those of Sevier and pressed the action home. In the end, Ferguson was killed and the remnant of his force captured. "The slaughter of the enemy was great, and it was evident that further resistance would be unavailing," stated Shelby in a report of the battle. "A more total defeat was not practicable." The next year, Shelby refused to slow down, joining the command of Francis Marion, "the Swamp Fox," he served as a partisan leader till the end of the war.

After the Revolution, Shelby returned to Kentucky and married. He participated in negotiations that resulted first in the separation of Kentucky from Virginia, in the convention that framed its constitution, and then in making it the new nation's fifteenth state. At that point, residents honored Shelby in 1792 by making him Kentucky's first governor. In 1813, after being elected governor a second time, Shelby once more led men into combat, commanding a force of 3,000 Kentucky volunteers at the battle of the Thames, located on Canada's Ontario Peninsula. There, his men participated in the attack that killed famed Indian warrior Tecumseh. In 1826, he was asked by President James Monroe to serve as his Secretary of War, but the aging patriot was forced to turn down the offer. Finally, revered as a hero of the Revolution and one of the buckskinned leaders in Kentucky's charge to statehood, the famed stamina of the old frontiersman at last faltered and after suffering a stroke, he died on July 18, 1826.

Roger Sherman

In the shadows of Thomas Jefferson, John Adams, and Benjamin Franklin, Roger Sherman is often overlooked as a fellow member of the committee assigned by Congress to draft the Declaration of Independence. A member of Congress before, during, and after the Revolutionary War, and an architect of some of the key provisions of the federal government that came into being with the United States Constitution, Sherman was the only Founding Father to have signed all the major documents of the era including the Declaration, the Articles of Confederation, and the Constitution. A key figure in the early years of the Republic, Sherman became a staunch federalist and a champion for smaller states such as Connecticut for whose rights he worked indefatigably to protect.

Sherman was born on April 19, 1721 in Newton, Massachusetts, near Boston, before being taken by his parents to Stoughton, a much more rustic community. There, he divided his time growing up between working the family farm and learning the cobbler's trade from his father. But early on, the young Sherman displayed a strong interest in learning, reading through his father's limited library with a voracious zeal. Later, he spent some time in the local school after one was finally established, but he owed most of his learning to the local minister who helped him with mathematics, philosophy, and other subjects. Then in 1743, following the death of his father, Sherman's life changed forever when he went to join an older brother in New Milford,

Roger Sherman

Connecticut. There, he continued the cobbler's trade until, earning enough to go into business for himself, he opened a store. In addition, using the mathematical skills taught him by the minister back in Massachusetts, he managed to be named county surveyor which gave him the money as well as the contacts and inside information to invest in land making him one of the area's most prominent businessmen. From there, he launched himself into public service, holding down a number of positions including town clerk and School Committee member. A brush with a local attorney encouraged him to look into the law as a career and after teaching himself what he needed to know, passed the bar in 1754. The very next year, he was elected to the colonial legislature where he served until 1761 while at the same time publishing a popular annual almanac, being named a county judge, and acting as military supply officer for Connecticut during the French and Indian War. In 1761, he gave up the almanac as well as the practice of law and his seat in the legislature and moved to New Haven where he opened a chain of two stores, one catering to the needs of students attending nearby Yale University. So profitable did his new venture become that he was able to retire and concentrate on public service once more, going back to the legislature where he remained until 1785. During that time, he was able to observe firsthand the struggle between local government and attempts by the British Parliament to enforce its will on the colonies and although wary of violence, Sherman became strongly opposed to royal authority and was recognized early as an outspoken patriot. A member of Connecticut's committee of correspondence, it was a short step from there to Congress when Sherman was chosen in 1774 as a member of Connecticut's delegation.

Active in Congress through 1784, Sherman became involved in many important committees and was not shy about expressing his opinion in debate. Recounting once a story about Sherman's zeal for liberty, fellow patriot Benjamin Rush called him "a republican machine." From the beginning, he let it be known that he thought Parliament did not have the right to impose its will on the colonies and perhaps because of his position on the issue, was chosen as a member of the committee charged with drafting a declaration of independence. Later, he was active in the formation of the Articles of Confederation even though many of his ideas for union were ultimately turned down. Shuttling back and forth from Philadelphia to Connecticut, Sherman wore himself out contributing to Congress in such capacities as being a member of the War Office as well as tending to the work needed to transition Connecticut from a dependent colony to an independent state.

But despite the toll his activities had taken on his health, Sherman returned to Philadelphia in 1787 as a delegate to the Constitutional Convention where in 138 speeches he expounded on some of the same ideas he had once proposed for the Articles of Confederation, including taxation and the creation of a supreme court. Of particular importance, he may have played an important part in crafting the New Jersey Plan which paved the way for the Connecticut Plan or Great Compromise that protected the rights of smaller states by dividing the legislative branch of the proposed federal government between a House of Representatives the election of whose members was to be based on population and a Senate, whose members were to be apportioned equally among the several states. It was not a new idea for Sherman who first suggested it in the debates surrounding the formation of the Articles of Confederation. Later, despite a basic distrust of the people whom he felt were constantly "liable to be misled," reservations on aspects of the Constitution such as direct election of congressmen that he felt were too democratic, and a conviction that provisions in the Articles of Confederation precluded the need for popular approval, Sherman fought hard for ratification of the Constitution back home in Connecticut.

In 1784 Sherman became the mayor of New Haven and in 1789, was rewarded for his efforts during the ratification process by being elected the state's first representative in Congress. Later, in 1791, he moved from the House to the Senate. In Congress, Sherman became a staunch Federalist, the party of Secretary of the Treasury Alexander Hamilton who favored a strong central government. Although Sherman supported Hamilton's plan for the federal government to take over the responsibility of paying off the remainder of the states' wartime debts, he opposed a compromise with the southern states to locate the future federal capital on the Potomac River in exchange for passage of the assumption bill. Sherman remained a member of the Senate until failing health and typhoid finally caught up to him. He died in New Haven on July 23, 1793.

James Smith

The victim of a capricious fate which destroyed all of his personal papers in an untimely fire, little is known about the interior life of James Smith but what can be discerned from the public record is a career that began unassumingly in the backwoods of Pennsylvania and ended in the halls of Congress and his signature on one of the most important documents ever written.

Although in his lifetime, Smith refused to reveal the exact date of his birth in northern Ireland, it is believed to have taken place between 1713 and 1715. About a decade later, his father removed the family to America and settled in Pennsylvania near Philadelphia. There, the elder Smith wasted no time in providing an education for his second son, sending him to nearby Philadelphia Academy where he studied the classics of Greece and Rome and mathematics useful in the surveying trade. In addition, Smith also prepared for a career in the law and after leaving the school, apprenticed in a Lancaster law office run by his brother. Passing the bar in 1745, Smith moved west to Shippensburg in Cumberland County where a young man had a chance of establishing himself without fear of having to worry about more established competition. He was not there long however, before he moved again, this time to York, a fast growing town that would one day serve as a temporary home for the Continental Congress. There, with little call for his legal services, he mostly practiced the surveying trade with iron mongering on the side, until, with increased friction between Britain and its American colonies, he found himself drawn into the patriotic camp and was chosen in 1774 as a delegate to a provincial assembly representing York County. There, he made his sentiments known in no uncertain terms with a paper entitled *Essay on the Constitutional Power of Great Britain over the Colonies in America* in which he called for a total boycott of British imports and the convening of a general Congress of all the colonies to further con-

James Smith

solidate efforts at resisting what he considered unjust laws emanating from Parliament. Putting action to his words, Smith next organized Pennsylvania's first volunteer militia company for the purpose of defending the colony's rights by force of arms if necessary.

In the meantime, at a provincial convention held in 1775, Smith joined in a resolution calling for resistance against any attempt to strip Americans of their rights as Englishmen. Soon afterward, the colony's general assembly met and, alarmed by talk of independence coming from the convention and the new Continental Congress meeting in Philadelphia, issued instructions to the colony's delegates to resist any call for permanent separation from Britain. Angered by those orders, a crowd met in the city and after voicing its support for independence, voted for the creation of a provincial convention in which Smith participated and supported a resolution in favor of independence. By 1776, Smith had been chosen as a member of Pennsylvania's delegation to the Continental Congress and reaffirmed his position on separation from Britain by signing the Declaration of Independence.

Smith remained in Congress until 1778 when he retired to serve a single term in Pennsylvania's new state legislature and later a few months on the bench of the court of appeals. Reelected to Congress in 1785, he refused to serve on account of his age but continued to practice law in York until about 1800. He was still there six years later when he died on July 11, 1806.

John Stark

Rarely has a hero matched the qualities enshrined in Daniel Chester French's famous sculpture of the Concord minuteman, but New Hampshire's General John Stark is one of them. A true son of liberty, a citizen-soldier whose admonition "Live free or die, death is not the worst of evils" became the motto of his native state, Stark, like the minuteman statue, was equally comfortable behind a plow or the length of a rifle barrel.

Born in Londonderry, New Hampshire in 1728, Stark was toughened by working his father's farm after the family moved to present day Manchester, hunting and trapping the nearby forests and even familiarizing himself with the ways of local Indians. When the French and Indian War broke out in 1754, Stark's position in his community was such that it was only natural that he be commissioned a lieutenant in Rogers Rangers, the famed guerilla force raised and trained by William Rogers to fight the enemy in the style of their Amerindian foes.

Although Stark distinguished himself among the hardened members of the rangers, friction between the colonials who made up the bulk of the force and British regulars presaged resentments that would only grow over the following twenty years as Britain sought to impose measures on its colonies that residents found increasingly onerous. Stark carried these nascent resentments back with him when he returned home from war in 1758 and remembered them in 1775 when he, along with thousands of other residents of Massachusetts and New Hampshire responded to the echoes of Paul Revere's cry that "The British are coming!" and joined the fight building along the route of British retreat leading from Concord Bridge back to Boston. Now a general, Stark played a key role in the battle of Breed's Hill on Charlestown Neck when he recognized a weakness in the patriot lines where they descended to the shore of the Mystic River. Quickly ordering that a fence running down from Breed's Hill to a strand by the river be draped in concealing grass, Stark had his men drag stones forward to continue the line of the fence right up to the edge of the water. It was fast thinking and a prescient move for hardly had the work been completed than the British attempted to storm the position and flank the patriot lines. But when the redcoats reached a point where the Americans could "see the whites of their eyes," they were met by a hail of lead that left nearly 100 dead on the beach. Two more attacks followed, each bloodily repulsed before the enemy gave up the attempt. Stark's victory on the beach forced the British commanding general William Howe to concentrate his attack on the center of the patriot lines atop Breed's Hill where they eventually won the day but at a heavy cost.

John Stark

As an officer in the newly created Continental Army, Stark participated in the New Jersey campaign of 1777 commanding the army's crucial right wing during the attack on Trenton and was a member of the board of inquiry that tried and executed the infamous British spy Major John Andre after he was captured in the possession of secret correspondence proving the guilt of the traitorous Benedict Arnold. Stark's skill and resourcefulness were recognized by Gen. George Washington who later chose to send him back to New Hampshire to drum up recruits for the army. But Stark did not achieve what he did by having a bashful nature, his was a forceful personality with no small ego and when he learned that he had been passed over for promotion for someone he considered a lesser man, he resigned his commission and retired to his farm. Appalled, members of the New Hampshire legislature offered him instead the rank of brigadier general in the state militia which, to their relief, Stark accepted on condition that he answer only to them.

His independent command proved fortuitous when New England militias were ordered in 1777 to report to General Schuyler in New York to help repulse an incursion by British General John Burgoyne who was descending from Canada with 5,600 men and threatening to divide the thirteen colonies in half. Hearing that almost 1,000 men had been detached from Burgoyne's army to forage in southern Vermont, Stark took it upon himself to organize an attack on Lt. Colonel Frederick Baum's mixed force of German Hessians, loyalists, French Canadians, and Indians. His own force having swelled to more than 2,000 local militia, Stark chose a risky plan that involved surrounding the enemy by dividing his own force into four sections. The plan worked, and after two hours of heavy fighting, Baum was defeated at a place called Bennington. The battle was "the hottest I ever saw in my life," remarked Stark in his after-action report. Thus, with his victory in Vermont coupled with Benedict Arnold's earlier rout of Lt. Col. Barry St. Leger at Fort Stanwix and Gen. William Howe's failure to move reinforcements up the Hudson River from New York City, Stark had contributed to a severely weakened and isolated Burgoyne who was finally driven to ground at Saratoga.

Having made his own decision to attack Baum instead of joining the main body of the American army gathering in New York, Stark again displayed his independence when he acceded to the wishes of his men to stick to the letter of their enlistment and return to their homes when they felt their duty done. Thus, Stark did not participate in the great battle of Saratoga and returned instead to New Hampshire. Although he participated briefly in other wartime incidents, from that moment on, he mostly retired from active duty and in 1783, at the close of the war, Washington awarded him the rank of major general.

Stark died in 1822 at the age of 94 and was understood not only to have been the last surviving general of the Revolution, but one who could have been better remembered as one of its greatest if not for the fierce sense of independence that removed him from the historical spotlight. A toast he offered in writing to a reunion of the veterans of the battle of Bennington 32 years after that great victory became famous and was adopted in 1945 as New Hampshire's state motto. "Live free or die; death is not the worst of evils," summed up not only the strong feelings of the old soldier, but of all his fellow patriots of that Revolutionary generation.

Arthur St. Clair

Arthur St. Clair was a problematic figure in the history of the Revolution having begun his career in America as a hero of the French and Indian War and ended it under a cloud with his evacuation of Fort Ticonderoga and later defeat at the hands of Indians when an army under his command was ambushed and decimated by a numerically inferior foe.

St. Clair was born on March 23, 1736 in Caithness County, Scotland becoming the heir to some wealth. As a young man, he studied medicine at the University of Edinburgh but found that the academic life did not satisfy his craving for adventure. In 1757, he left his studies and bought himself a place in the British Army as an ensign in the 60th Regiment of Foot. With the French and Indian War raging in America, he soon found himself on the frontier serving with Gen. Jeffrey Amherst. It was while with Amherst that St. Clair participated in the assault and capture of the great French fort of Louisbourg in 1758. The next year, he climaxed his experience with the British military on the Plains of Abraham where he distinguished himself by taking up the flag from a fallen comrade and holding on to it for the remainder of the battle. With the fall of Quebec and the defeat of New France, St. Clair ended up assigned to Boston where he met and married Phoebe Bayard in 1760. Two years later, he resigned his commission in the army and relocated to Bedford, Pennsylvania where he had landed a job as a surveyor for the Penn family. Falling in love with the country, he and his wife decided to make Pennsylvania their permanent home and bought land in the Ligonier Valley. There, St. Clair developed his property, operated mills, and expanded his real estate holdings. As a prominent resident in his neighborhood, he soon became involved in public life as a justice of the peace, a clerk of the orphans' court, and official surveyor. But the military life was never far from his thoughts and when the Revolutionary War broke out, St. Clair had no reservations about joining the local militia and marching against the army he had formerly served.

Commissioned a colonel in the Pennsylvania militia, his first assignment in 1775 was with the American army then in full retreat from its abortive invasion of Canada. He must have performed his duties well as the next year, he

Arthur St. Clair

found himself with the Continental Army serving as a brigadier general under Gen. George Washington. In 1776, the year that gave birth to the United States, St. Clair crossed the Delaware River into New Jersey with the rest of the army and participated in the battles of Trenton and Princeton. At Trenton, he demanded and received the surrender of the last Hessian regiment that had been trapped by the victorious Americans and later, at an officers' meeting with Washington, urged an attack on Princeton. St. Clair suggested that if the Americans could seize a little known crossing at Quaker Bridge, they could steal a march on the unsuspecting British and take Princeton by surprise. With the success at Princeton, St. Clair earned the trust of his superiors and was rewarded with promotion to major general and his own command at Fort Ticonderoga which, in one of the earliest actions of the war, had been captured by the Americans without firing a shot. It was ironic then, that St. Clair would end up surrendering the fort in almost the same fashion himself. "If the enemy intend to attack us...we are very ill-prepared to receive them," he wrote to Gen. Philip Schuyler, his immediate superior. "The whole amount of Continental troops, fit for duty is one thousand, five hundred and seventy-six..." Thus, when the country was invaded by British Gen. John Burgoyne's army moving south from Canada down the Hudson River Valley and cannon dragged to the top of Mt. Defiance, which overlooked the fort, the fate of the American garrison was sealed. Undermanned, ill supplied, and with no way to return fire, St. Clair realized that his position inside the fort was hopeless and gave the order to abandon it. Retreating to the eastward, elements of St. Clair's army under Colonels Ebenezer Francis, Seth Warner, and Nathan Hale fought a desperate rearguard action against an enemy who constantly pressed the attack. Then, at Hubbardton, Vermont, on July 7, 1777, the two sides clashed in a pitched battle that threw the pursuers off the scent. In giving up Ticonderoga, perhaps St. Clair recalled what had happened to Gen. Nathanael Greene just the year before. Confident that he could hold Fort Washington located on the banks of the Hudson River in New York, Greene had waited until too late to abandon it in the face of superior enemy forces and ended up losing the fort along with 2,900 of its defenders. In any case, St. Clair would later explain that at the time, he thought it preferable to save his army rather than lose it in a hopeless defense of Ticonderoga. Whatever the reason for the fort's evacuation, the news still came as a shock to the rest of the country and St. Clair was court martialed as a result. Cleared of fault, St. Clair found himself back in action and was on hand with Washington when British Gen. Charles Cornwallis surrendered at Yorktown in 1781.

Following the war, St. Clair served two years as a delegate for Pennsylvania in the Continental Congress becoming its president in 1787. Two years later, after the nation had ratified the Constitution, which he had opposed, St. Clair was appointed governor of the vast Northwest Territory, an area that would eventually include the states of Ohio, Indiana, Illinois, Wisconsin, Michigan, and Minnesota. As governor, his most pressing concern was to ease friction between the Indians and the thousands of settlers who began to pour into the region after the war. The treaty of Fort Harmar, signed on January 9, 1789, that was supposed to have opened most of Ohio to settlement, did little to solve the problem and in 1791, in response to continuing depredations by the Indians, St. Clair was forced to mount an expedition against them. That effort ended in embarrassing failure on November 4 when the army, reduced to about 1,500 men, was ambushed by a smaller force of Miami Indians under the leadership of Little Turtle and defeated on the banks of the Great Miami River. The defeat did not result in St. Clair's removal from the governor's chair; that event had to wait until 1802 when his vocal opposition to Ohio statehood prompted President Thomas Jefferson to have him fired. Although Jefferson was prepared to wait until St. Clair's term of office expired to remove him, the governor's declaration that the enabling act passed by Congress that would pave the way to Ohio statehood had no force in law proved to be the last straw. Having lost most of the wealth he had earned before the Revolution, St. Clair retired in reduced circumstances to the Hermitage, his home in the Ligonier Valley. He died fourteen years later, on August 31, 1818.

Richard Stockton

One of the saddest stories involving the Founders was that of Richard Stockton who was born to wealth and influence, became one of the colonies' most successful attorneys and only reluctantly came to embrace revolution. When the time came, however, he signed the Declaration of Independence and thereby sealed his fate by falling into the hands of the enemy losing his home, his fortune, and finally, his reputation.

Stockton was born on October 1, 1730 on the grounds of his ancestral home in Somerset County, New Jersey. Later named "Morven" by his poetess wife, the 6,400 acre estate, which had originally been given to Stockton's Quaker grandfather by William Penn, encompassed part of what is now Princeton, New Jersey. While still a youngster, Stockton left Morven to receive an early education at the Nottingham Academy in Maryland before moving on to the College of New Jersey where he became the sole member of his class to take up a career other than the ministry. Choosing the law, he graduated in 1748 and completed his studies under a prominent local attorney before passing the bar in 1754. Setting up his own office in Princeton, Stockton eventually became one of the most successful attorneys in America before tiring of the game in 1766 and deciding instead to embark on an extended tour of Europe. In the meantime, never having completely cut his ties with his alma mater, he had become a trustee of the college after it had moved to Princeton and been renamed Princeton University. When it was learned that he would be going to Europe, Stockton was asked by fellow board members to seek out the Rev. John Witherspoon in Scotland and offer him the post of president of the college. Doing so, he found the reverend receptive to the idea but his wife remained adamantly opposed. Enlisting the aid of a young medical student named Benjamin Rush, Stockton was finally able to convince the lady to set aside her objections and accept the move.

Returning to New Jersey in 1768, Stockton began a more public career when he became a member of the colony's executive council and later a judge on the state's supreme court where he served until chosen as a delegate to the Continental Congress in 1776. Before that time, as tensions rose between the colonies and Britain, Stockton had leaned toward reconciliation

Richard Stockton

with the crown, even suggesting to the royal authority a compromise involving colonial home rule. Disillusioned by the lack of response, Stockton at last began to take a more radical position and when the citizens of New Jersey became dissatisfied with the moderate position taken by its delegates to the Continental Congress, it voted to recall two of them and chose Stockton as one of the replacements. Stockton arrived in Congress in mid-session, just as John Adams was winding up a lengthy summary of the arguments in favor of independence. Prevailing upon the Massachusetts delegate to repeat his speech, Stockton declared Adams the "Atlas of American independence" and followed up with a few words of his own before joining the other delegates in signing the Declaration of Independence. Interestingly, two of Stockton's fellow signers included the very same John Witherspoon whom he had recruited from Scotland for the presidency of Princeton College ten years before and Benjamin Rush, the medical student who had helped him in that effort and who had since become his son-in-law.

Not long after the signing of the Declaration, Stockton was nominated as a candidate for governor of New Jersey, but losing the race in a run-off, he found himself instead heading north in September of 1776 as a member of a congressional committee sent on an inspection tour of the military. It was while he was away that the British invaded New York and moved into New Jersey after the retreating Continental Army. Returning home in the nick of time, Stockton bustled his family from Princeton to Monmouth County and Federal Hall, the home of his friend John Covenhoven. Unfortunately, Federal Hall lay in an area of the country with strong loyalist sympathies and late in November, Stockton was taken by surprise when in the middle of the night, a party of loyalists burst into his friend's home, seized him, and handed him over to the British. Having been informed that their prisoner was a signer of the Declaration of Independence, the British considered Stockton a traitor and treated him accordingly. Although 46 is not old, neither is it a young age, and held for months first in freezing weather at Perth Amboy where he was nearly starved and then in shackles in New York City under the worst of conditions, Stockton, under duress and frightened for his life, agreed to sign a document swearing loyalty to the king before his release was finally arranged by Congress via George Washington in January of 1777.

But freedom came too late for Stockton. The damage to his reputation was already done and he became infamous as the only signer of the Declaration to renege on his oath to sacrifice his life, his fortune, and his sacred honor in the fight for American freedom. Thus, Stockton's release from captivity only signaled the beginning of his problems. As a result of his repudiation of the American cause, he was forced by local patriots to undergo a humiliating process of repatriation conducted by the New Jersey legislature in order to restore his good standing. In the meantime, he returned to what was left of Morven which over the years served as the headquarters of Gen. Charles Cornwallis and later was ransacked by British soldiers who, using it for a barracks and stable, destroyed its paintings and furnishings and burned the books in its library to feed their cooking fires. In addition, heavy investment in depreciated Continental currency had depleted his considerable fortune. And so, living amid the ruins of his once proud estate and in health that left him a broken man, Stockton tried to revive his legal career. But time was against him and, dying of cancer on February 28, 1781, he would not live to see the American victory in a revolution he had helped to ignite but whose fruits he would fail to enjoy.

Thomas Stone

Yet another Founding Father who was an attorney before fate cast him as a signer of the Declaration of Independence, Thomas Stone was born to wealthy parents on the family's Poynton Manor estate in Charles County, Maryland some time in 1743. The uncertainty about the date of his birth is not coincidental as very little is known about the man in general and what is known seems to indicate a relative disinterest in the political storm that raged before the Revolution and the historic events following independence.

A love of learning dominated Stone's teenage years as he rode ten miles to and from a local parish school each day until he left for Annapolis to read law with one of the city's attorneys. In 1764, he passed the bar and opened his own office in Fredericktown. Not much is known of Stone's life before he was suddenly chosen as a member of Maryland's delegation to the Continental Congress in 1774. By accounts, his practice did well if not spectacularly, he married a local belle named Margaret Brown, produced three children, bought land near Port Tobacco, Maryland, and proceeded to build a home and grow crops.

When he was appointed as a delegate to Congress, he arrived in the spring of 1775, just as events moved into high gear with fighting breaking out in Massachusetts and talk of independence from Britain on every-

Thomas Stone

one's lips. The Maryland delegation however, were under strict orders from the colony to do nothing to promote separation from Britain so it was not until late in the game that sentiments changed and Stone and his fellow delegates were given liberty to vote as they chose on the subject. When the time came, Stone voted for independence and became a signer of the Declaration. Immediately afterward, he was assigned to the committee charged with drawing up the Articles of Confederation, the framework under which the United States would operate during the years of the war and immediately afterward. Stone remained with the Congress until the Articles were completed and approved upon which he returned to Maryland in 1779 and found himself elected to the new state's legislature. There, he worked to assuage local fears about the Articles of Confederation until seeing them finally approved. In 1783 he left the legislature to serve in the new Congress but in the next year, resigned in order to concentrate his energies on his legal practice.

Declining to act as a representative to the state's ratification convention called in 1785 to consider a proposed United States Constitution, Stone chose to remain in private life. That life however, was rudely disrupted when his wife failed to recover from the effects of a small pox inoculation and died in 1787. Heartbroken and himself physically weakened from the ordeal, Stone was advised by his doctors to embark on a sea voyage but after traveling to Alexandria, Virginia and preparing to take ship for England, he suddenly died there on October 5, 1787.

John Sullivan

Although one of Washington's most competent officers, a degree of impetuousness and bad luck often combined to make John Sullivan's career seem less stellar than those of his fellow generals. Possessed of a spirit of independence, greed, and a "tincture of vanity," qualities that in fellow officer Benedict Arnold would lead to treason, Sullivan avoided the abyss of betrayal and ignominy by virtue of also being possessed by a deep and genuine love of liberty and personal patriotism. It was his misfortune that a cold blooded outlook on business affairs early in his career resulted in his being disliked by neighbors (an attitude that returned in retirement after he had been extolled as a hero of the Revolution) and cast a shadow over his reputation that has persisted ever since.

Sullivan's problems started early, almost as soon as he began to practice law as a young man. Born in Somersworth, New Hampshire on February 17, 1740 Sullivan developed a streak of avariciousness early and upon buying a homestead in Durham, New Hampshire in 1764, immediately began suing his neighbors for outstanding loans. His reasons were simple: he wanted to get rich quick and the fastest way to do that was to take advantage of the law. Only two years after moving to Durham, his neighbors filed a petition with the local court for relief but Sullivan survived the challenge. In any case, as he became more successful, Sullivan eased off on his litigious nature until, fences mended between himself and his neighbors, he was appointed a major in the Durham militia by the colony's royal governor John Wentworth. But as relations between the colonies and royal authority disintegrated in the early 1770s, Sullivan became increasingly radicalized. In 1774, his neighbors in Durham chose him to represent them at the colony's Provincial Congress and later appointed him as a delegate to the First Continental Congress. Rubbing shoulders with such firebrands as John and Samuel Adams and Patrick Henry radicalized Sullivan such that upon returning to New Hampshire, he took it upon himself to lead a raid on Fort William and Mary in Portsmouth harbor. There, he seized the fort's store of arms and ammunition for use by the local militia, an action that came well in advance of a similar, and much popularized attack on Fort Ticonderoga by Ethan Allen and Benedict Arnold made six months later. Early in 1775, perhaps in recognition of his daring action, Sullivan was appointed a brigadier general in the new Continental Army by his fellow delegates attending the Second Continental Congress.

John Sullivan

His vanity at last satisfied, Sullivan began his military career in earnest when he reported to Washington during the siege of Boston. Soon, however, he was ordered to embark on an important mission to Canada where he was to help take charge over an American army reeling after its failure to capture the city of Quebec. When he caught up with it however, he discovered that its commander, Gen. John Thomas, had died of smallpox. Suddenly, as senior officer on the scene, he found himself in command of the army. Wasting little time, Sullivan promised Washington that he would do all he could to continue with the invasion of Canada. His optimism, however, was premature. Crippled with disease and suffering from lack of food and other basic supplies as well as being demoralized after the death of its charismatic general Richard Montgomery, his army was in no condition to fight. After a failed attack on Trois Rivieres, the army was forced to retreat back to the United States. Left open to criticism by some in Congress, Sullivan was nevertheless promoted to major general while his northern command was handed over to Gen. Horatio Gates.

In 1776, Sullivan was returned to Washington's command in time for the battle of Long Island where an ill trained American army that was still learning the ropes of eighteenth century warfare, was routed by the more professional British. Not helping matters was Sullivan, who was accused by some of neglecting warnings that his position on the left of the American lines could be outflanked by the enemy. When it happened, the army had to fall back in full retreat. To his credit, Sullivan remained behind to help hold back the advancing enemy but was captured in a wheat field by a handful of Hessian soldiers. In captivity, Sullivan unwisely agreed to carry offers of surrender to Congress from British admiral Lord Richard Howe; the offers failed, but their delivery once again left Sullivan open to criticism.

In an exchange of prisoners, Sullivan was released from captivity late in 1776 just in time to join Washington as he crossed the Delaware to hit the enemy at Trenton, New Jersey. Once more facing the German mercenaries who had captured him on Long Island, Sullivan led his men in a key part of the attack plan, capturing a bridge across the Assunpink Creek that sealed the enemy's fate. Early the next year, he performed similar services at Princeton but his performance on the battlefield was overshadowed by earlier controversies as he was passed over for promotion. Sullivan's ill luck continued when he was investigated for moving against the enemy on Staten Island without orders and later, was judged responsible by North Carolina Congressman Thomas Burke for the army's disastrous defeat at Brandywine. In a stinging rebuke, Burke charged Sullivan with a failure to properly scout for the presence of the enemy and an inadequate disposition of his men to defend against a flanking attack very similar to the one inflicted upon him on Long Island. Germantown followed, and then in 1778, he was chosen to lead the first large scale military operation with the country's new French allies against Newport, Rhode Island. The Americans' high hopes for that campaign came to nothing however when arrival of militia units from Massachusetts was delayed and a decision was made by French Admiral Count D'Estaing to reembark his troops in expectation of sea battle. When a storm ended plans for both battle at sea and relanding the French troops, the British in Newport took advantage of the situation and attacked. Left alone to fend off the enemy counterattack, the Americans succeeded but losses on both sides were about equal and when word was received that the British were being reinforced, Sullivan ordered a retreat. Frustrated, Sullivan was then assigned a second independent command, this time to lead a force on a punitive expedition deep into western New York and Pennsylvania to end the power of the Iroquois to wage war on the frontier where recent massacres at Wyoming and Cherry Valley prompted Congress to take action.

Part of a three pronged plan to reduce the Six Nations of the Iroquois and retain control of the frontier for the United States, Sullivan led an army of 4,000 men into the wilderness and at Newtown, defeated a mixed force of Indians and loyalists under the leadership of Joseph Brant on August 29, 1779. Following the battle, he met little opposition and successfully completed his mission after building a fort at Tioga, razing as many as forty villages and destroying enough crops to keep the Indians too busy just staying alive in the wilderness to cause any immediate trouble. It was a remarkable feat in that most expeditions of the kind were usually ill planned and often ended in disaster, but Sullivan's is noted for its efficiency as he penetrated up to 90 miles into a trackless wilderness to put an end to the Indian threat. But his string of disappointing military campaigns, fights with Congress, and finally the rigors of frontier warfare seemed to quench Sullivan's desire for glory on the battlefield. And so, after his mission to New York, he offered to quit the army and somewhat to his surprise, Congress agreed.

Ironically, however, after being hailed as a local hero upon his return to New Hampshire, Sullivan was promptly elected to serve in the same Congress that had given him such a hard time in the past. But old animosities and suspicions died hard and when it was discovered that he had accepted a loan from the French ambassador, Sullivan was forced to leave Congress in 1781. The experience did nothing to lessen his patriotic zeal however as, upon returning to Durham, he fought hard for New Hampshire's ratification of the Constitution. He served as the state's attorney general for four years and as governor for three terms before President Washington named him a federal judge in 1789. Unfortunately, in his later years, Sullivan seemed to have lapsed into those habits that had earned him the animosity of his neighbors early in his career and after a series of legal disputes coupled with a drinking problem that contributed to a decline in his health, he died estranged from his family on January 23, 1795.

Benjamin Tallmadge

One of the least known or understood aspects of the Revolution was that of intelligence gathering, or spying. Against the cynical European powers with their long established secret services and espionage experience, the Americans were relative babes in the woods but babes who could and did learn quickly. So much so that by the end of the war, a British intelligence official could say that it was the quality of American intelligence that was the true measure of their victory in the Revolution and not superior battle strategy.

In charge of the United States infant intelligence network was a little known school teacher from Wethersfield, Connecticut. Born on February 25, 1754 Benjamin Tallmadge grew up in Brookhaven, New York and attended college at Yale University. Graduating in 1773, he took a job as headmaster of a high school in Wethersfield where he remained until 1776. In the previous year, excited at the news of hostilities breaking out at Lexington and Concord in Massachusetts, Tallmadge left home and traveled to Bos-

Benjamin Tallmadge

ton to confer with a friend in the militia. Expressing interest in serving himself, when Connecticut raised troops for service with the Continental Army the next year, Tallmadge was asked to join a regiment of the Connecticut Brigade as a lieutenant. As a resident of New York, he was familiar with the Long Island countryside that would soon become a battleground between the invading British and American patriots turned soldiers. Tallmadge saw plenty of action during these campaigns including White Plains where he fell into the Bronx River and was almost captured by the enemy. Later, he was promoted to captain in the 2nd Continental Light Dragoon Regiment, an elite, well appointed light cavalry unit, and participated in battles at Brandywine, Germantown, and Monmouth until he was promoted again this time to major in 1777 and then to colonel in 1779.

It was while with the dragoons that Tallmadge began his career in espionage under Gen. George Washington's then chief of spies Brig. Gen. Charles Scott. But in 1778, when Scott was forced to give up his duties, Tallmadge was appointed to take his place. Impressed with his detailed reports and knowledge of the New York area, Washington gave Tallmadge a mandate not only to gather intelligence on the British army but to report his findings directly to him. Motivated by the death of a brother while in British captivity and a father who was forced to flee his home, Tallmadge entered on the task with gusto disguising his identity first under the pseudonym of John Bolton and then with the simple code number of 721. Using his connections and knowledge of the New York area, Tallmadge built up a number of spy rings in the New York area that were kept compartmentalized for added security and communicated in secret code written in a special kind of invisible ink devised by James Jay, brother of future Supreme Court justice John Jay.

One of the first and most important spies recruited by Tallmadge was Abraham Woodhull who, stationed at a boardinghouse in New York, became one of Washington's most valuable sources of information. Codenamed, "Samuel Culper," the Culper ring that formed around him proved one of the most valuable of the war providing important information on British naval activity, troop strength, and fortifications. With tools and methods in place, Tallmadge was in business and began to track enemy movements across the New York/Philadelphia axis. Although there were many successes, there were failures too including that of Nathan Hale, a friend of Tallmadge's, who was captured by the British as a spy and hung. But such setbacks did not keep Tallmadge's other spies from keeping Washington well informed about British troop movements in New York and New Jersey, the defenses around Trenton, and an attempt by the British to surprise him while in winter quarters at Valley Forge.

In addition to human agents, Tallmadge also intercepted mail, spread disinformation, and had code breakers reading British military dispatches. And when he was not going through the enemy's mailbag, he was in the field leading troops on raids he often planned and executed himself. In September of 1779 for instance, Tallmadge led his dragoons across Long Island sound to Lloyd's Neck, Rhode Island and captured 500 Tory raiders; and the next year, after crossing to the island of Oyster Bay, Long Island, attacked and captured Fort St. George.

One of the most famous cases of espionage during the Revolution was that of the betrayal of Gen. Benedict Arnold. Returning to a military post below West Point in September of 1780, Tallmadge ran into Lt. Col. John Jameson who had just released a man he knew only as "John Anderson" back to Arnold at West Point. This, despite the fact that the men who had brought him in found incriminating documents on his person. Tallmadge, already acquainted with the twilight world of espionage, was immediately suspicious and advised Jameson to bring Anderson back. After a reply was received from Washington about what to do with the prisoner, Tallmadge along with 100 dragoons was placed in charge and ordered to escort Anderson, now revealed as British Major John Andre, to safer quarters. When Andre was eventually convicted as a spy and sentenced to hang, Tallmadge was there with him until the end, moved, despite the similar fate of his friend Hale, to regret that the handsome Englishman had to die. Tallmadge was to hear from Arnold one more time before the end of the war after he received a letter from the traitor encouraging him to switch sides and to take "as many men as you can bring over with you." Needless to say, the entreaty failed in its purpose. Later, Tallmadge also became the target of Silas Deane, former American diplomat to France who had become disenchanted with the Revolution and wrote a number of letters to prominent patriots urging them to reconcile with the mother country.

As the war wound down, Tallmadge returned to New York only briefly to make sure American spies who had been posing as Tories were kept safe after the British pulled out; after that, he married and settled in Litchfield, Connecticut. There, he entered business and became president of the Phoenix Branch Bank. After ratification of the United States Constitution, he was elected to Congress as a Federalist and remained there until 1817 when he refused to stand for reelection.

Returning to his business interests, Tallmadge died in Litchfield on March 7, 1835.

George Taylor

An early example of the dizzying heights to which a newcomer to the shores of the American colonies could rise, the story of George Taylor (whose career admittedly, was helped by a strategic marriage to his employer's widow), was one that would become more typical in the nineteenth century, when a prevailing belief among a growing immigrant population that anything was possible in the United States evolved into national dogma.

His origins in Ireland clouded in uncertainty, Taylor is believed to have been born around 1716 and given a solid early education before entering medical school. However, it seemed that medicine had not been to the liking of the young Taylor who suddenly absconded to the American colonies at the age of twenty. Having made arrangements to indenture himself to cover the cost of his passage, Taylor began work for Samuel Savage at the ironworks in Warwick, Pennsylvania and then at the Coventry Forge. Taylor began by stoking coal into furnaces but his slight figure proving unequal to the heavy labor involved, Savage moved him indoors as a clerk. There, Taylor's early education served him well and as he began to rise in the company, first as bookkeeper, then manager, he gained more of the trust and esteem of his employer as well as his employer's wife. In 1742, after Savage died, Taylor married his widow and became the owner of the forge. Now in charge, he worked to make the company more profitable and later entered a partnership that enabled him to lease an ironworks in Durham. He lived in nearby Easton, Northampton County until the death of his wife in 1768 when he bought a 331 acre estate a few miles outside town and proceeded to sire a brood of illegitimate children by his housekeeper. Meanwhile, his expanded ironworks succeeded so well, that he was able to retire from active business.

As a wealthy member of the area's upper class, Taylor was naturally looked to by his neighbors for civic leadership and after serving intermittently as a justice of the peace, he was elected to the colony's legislature in 1764 where he remained for the next five tumultuous years; years in which the British Parliament attempted to enact a Stamp Tax and other fund raising measures in the face of growing popular resentment. Taylor, up to that point a moderate, became increasingly radicalized as the tax measures and subsequent boycotts took a bite out of his faltering iron working company. When he was voted out of the legislature in 1770, Taylor concentrated on business while also serving in the local militia. Summoned back to the legislature in 1775, he served on Northampton County's Committees of Correspondence and Safety and helped to frame Pennsylvania's instructions to its delegates to the Continental Congress. It was an indication of the colony's wariness of the patriotic fervor that had gripped some of the other colonies that the instructions included firm language ordering delegates to resist any talk of independence. But the quick pace of events soon outstripped that attitude and only the next year, residents began to press for independence and the original instructions were changed to reflect that desire. However, a number of the colony's delegation still refused to support a formal separation from England forcing their recall and others named in their place among them George Taylor. The new delegates arrived in Congress too late to take part in voting for independence, but on August 2, 1776, joined their fellow congressmen in signing the Declaration of Independence. Following that historic event, Taylor's career in Congress was brief with his only notable contribution being the completion of treaty negotiations with the Iroquois which ended up not being ratified by Congress.

George Taylor

Taylor remained in Congress only a short time, leaving in early 1777 after being elected to the Supreme Executive Council of the new state of Pennsylvania. He was on the job for only a few weeks before pleading ill health and concentrated instead on rebuilding his iron working business which he had lost when the new federal government had failed to pay him adequately for the manufacture of war materiel such as shot, shell, and cannon. Leasing another forge in New Jersey, Taylor was trying to make a go of it when he died at his home in Easton on February 3, 1781.

Matthew Thornton

Matthew Thornton, noted physician and landowner from New Hampshire, was one of a handful of congressmen who missed out on the deliberations and subsequent drafting of the Declaration of Independence but whose names nevertheless appeared boldly on the final document, no less firm supporters of that great resolution as those who had actually hammered it out.

Born in Ireland sometime in 1714, Thornton came to America with his family in 1717 and settled at first in Wiscasset, Maine. Soon however, his parents uprooted again and moved to Worcester, Massachusetts where many fellow Scotch-Irish immigrants had gone to live. Displaying some aptitude for learning, Thornton attended local schools before being sent to the Worcester Academy to learn medicine. By 1740 he had graduated and relocated to sleepy Londonderry, New Hampshire where his medical skills served him well and he was able to invest his earnings in real estate. In 1745 he was appointed medical officer in a 500 man New Hampshire militia regiment and accompanied it to Louisbourg, the formidable French fortress off Cape Breton, Nova Scotia. Thornton was so skillful in his responsibilities, that by the time the campaign was over and the fort captured, only a handful of the men had died while under his charge. Returning to Londonderry, he soon entered local politics becoming a selectman and then in 1758 was elected to represent the town in the colony's Provincial Assembly.

As relations between the colonies and England deteriorated during the 1770s, Thornton's sympathies increasingly drifted to the patriot side and in 1775 he was chosen as a member of the state's local Committee of Safety. It was while serving on the committee and as president of the assembly that he drafted a plan of government by which the affairs of New Hampshire would be conducted after the legislature officially cut its ties to royal authority. Approved, the plan later became the basis for the constitution of the new state of New Hampshire. By 1776, Thornton's stature within the state had risen such that he became its unacknowledged leader and was chosen to represent New Hampshire in the Continental Congress.

Contrary to popular belief, not all those who signed the Declaration of Independence did so immediately upon its acceptance by Congress on July 4, 1776. On July 5, only President of Congress John Hancock signed the document with a more general signing occurring almost a month later on August 2. But even then, many signatories were still absent and signed individually later on. Among them was Thornton who only arrived in Philadelphia to begin his term of office late in the year and affixed his name to the Declaration on November 4, 1776. Having been a longtime advocate of separation from England, for Thornton, signing the Declaration was an act that required little soul searching.

Matthew Thornton

As was the way with men of social prominence in those days, Thornton was appointed to the New Hampshire Superior Court around the same time that he was serving in Congress. After leaving Congress in 1777, he returned to his native state and picked up where he had left off in both the legislature and the Committee of Safety. Busying himself in the writing of political essays and tracts, Thornton finally retired in 1782 when he declined to continue as a member of the Superior Court.

By 1780, Thornton could be counted as one of the state's great landowners and added to his wealth upon the purchase of a Merrimack estate that had been owned by a local Tory. When the war ended, he moved to Merrimack, New Hampshire and once again entered politics by representing his new community in the state legislature. At the same time, he did time on the governor's council and continued to practice some medicine on the side. Finally, however, he decided to retire from public life to concentrate on developing his estate and running a ferry operation along the Merrimack River. By 1786, Thornton had outlived his wife and son and while on a visit to see his daughter in Newbury-port, Massachusetts, died on June 24, 1803.

Tench Tilghman

It is said that one third of the population of the thirteen colonies at the time of the Revolution were patriot sympathizers, one third were loyalists, and one third just wanted to be left alone. Such a statistic may or may not have been accurate, but it would help explain the very real existence of deep divisions on the politics of the war not only among the general population, but among families as well. Take the Tilghman family of Pennsylvania for instance, in which three of six brothers supported America's war with England and the others, headed by the family patriarch, stood against it. It was a situation not uncommon and although in many instances, the difference of opinion would prove too wide a breach for some families to seal, resulting in a permanent sundering of relations, in the case of the Tilghmans great effort was made by the siblings on the side of the patriots, especially the eldest, Tench, to maintain close relations with their father. In letter after letter, before the opening of hostilities in Massachusetts and throughout the war, Tilghman would try to persuade his father to see his side of the argument but to no avail. James Tilghman would not budge, an obstinacy respected by his son even if he did not agree with the reasons for it.

Tench Tilghman was born on December 25, 1744 on the family plantation in Talbot County, Maryland. The eldest of twelve children, Tilghman was the scion of one of the most prominent families in the colony. A successful attorney, his father resettled in Philadelphia, Pennsylvania where he eventually assumed many important positions relating to the affairs of the colony's proprietors including the Pennsylvania Proprietary Land Office. It was his loyalty to the proprietors, and the British government that had granted them sovereignty over Pennsylvania, that perhaps fostered in the elder Tilghman his unshakeable support of the crown that would later come between he and his sons. The younger Tilghman, meanwhile, having grown up amid the political struggle between the proprietors and the Assembly Party of Benjamin Franklin and Joseph Galloway, which in some ways resembled the larger struggle the thirteen colonies would later have with England, found his sympathies moving in the opposite direction of his father's. As a result, when tensions between England and its colonies began to mount, Tilghman joined a local Philadelphia based militia unit that loyalists derided as the "Silk Stockings," so called because of its members having been recruited from the city's most prominent families. But before Tilghman had a chance to enter active duty, he was named as secretary and treasurer to a commission charged with seeking the neutrality of the Indian tribes in any conflict between the colonies and England. Succeeding in arranging a treaty with the Indians, the commission returned in September of 1775 and Tilghman formally entered the Silk Stockings and was promoted to lieutenant. By the time the unit joined the Continental Army under George Washington, Tilghman had been promoted again, this time to captain.

Tilghman's dedication and energy brought him to the attention of his superior officers and through influential connections came to the notice of the commander in chief himself. Impressed with his reputation, as well as his education and social standing, Washington allowed the young man to join his "family," the close knit group of aids-de-camp and other officers that made up his personal staff. As a member of Washington's family, Tilghman would enjoy a close relationship with the commander in chief that later he would have to share with Alexander Hamilton and the Marquis de Lafayette. Although the position usually came with a promotion, because of the cumbersome system used by Congress, Tilghman had to wait almost four years to be promoted to Lieutenant Colonel. Only the ongoing efforts of Washington pleading his case finally moved Congress to make the promotion official, making it retroactive to April 1, 1777. In the meantime, Tilghman had continued to serve with his new, unofficial rank without pay, serving "in every action in which the main army was concerned" according to a letter written by Washington.

Over the years, Tilghman became extremely close to Washington, serving as his personal assistant as well as confidential secretary, accompanying him everywhere, including the battlefield. Tilghman was with Washington on October 19, 1781 when British General Lord Cornwallis surrendered at Yorktown, Virginia and was privileged to carry the great news to Congress. Although news of the victory reached Philadelphia ahead of him, a Congress already used to rumors and false hopes had refrained from completely accepting it until it arrived through more reliable channels. Thus, when Tilghman finally arrived in the city with his news, the resulting celebrations were complete and heartfelt. Impressed with the young man's poise during questioning about the battle and surrender, an overjoyed Congress presented him with a horse and new sword. That same night, an official celebration was held both in honor of the great victory and for Tilghman, who had been the bearer of such glad tidings as well as one of Philadelphia's native sons.

Tench Tighlman

After the war, Tilghman continued to add to his family's luster by forming Tench Tilghman & Company, joining in partnership with Robert Morris, one of the wealthiest men in America who had played a key role in arranging the finances of Congress and the army. Based out of Baltimore, Maryland, where the Tilghman family had had its origins, the company proved successful in the mercantile trade and prospered until Tilghman's early death, brought on by exposure suffered during his military career. His passing on April 18, 1786, greatly affected his wartime colleagues including his commander in chief who had grown close to all of the young men who had served in his "family."

In a letter to Tilghman's father, who had retired to an estate in Maryland, Washington assured the old loyalist that: "Of all the numerous acquaintances of your lately deceased son, and amidst all the sorrowings that are mingled on that melancholy occasion, I may venture to assert (that excepting those of his nearest relatives) none could have felt his death with more regret than I did, because no one entertained a higher opinion of his worth or had imbibed sentiments of greater friendship for him than I had done. That you, sir, should have felt the keenest anguish for this loss, I can readily conceive; the ties of parental affection, united with those of friendship, could not fail to have produced this effect. It is however, a dispensation, the wisdom of which is inscrutable; and amidst all your grief, there is this consolation to be drawn, that while living, no man could be more esteemed, and since dead, none more lamented than Colonel Tilghman."

John Trumbull

As a young man, John Trumbull's experience as a soldier in the Continental Army influenced his work as one of America's most distinguished artists. Over a long career, Trumbull created a great number of monumental paintings depicting important scenes of the American Revolution and many portraits of its key participants whom he had known personally. "The greatest motive I had or have for engaging in or for continuing my pursuit of painting has been the wish of commemorating the great events of our country's revolution," Trumbull once said, a lofty goal to which he dedicated his life.

John Trumbull

Born the youngest of three brothers on June 6, 1756 in Lebanon, Connecticut, Trumbull was the son of Jonathan Trumbull, the colony's patriot sympathizing governor. Although he attended Harvard College and graduated in 1773, it was a visit to the studio of John Singleton Copley while on his way to Cambridge before entering college that had the greatest influence on his career. "...his paintings, the first I had ever seen deserving the name, riveted, absorbed my attention, and renewed all my desire to enter upon such a pursuit," recalled Trumbull of his first meeting with the artist. But even as the young Trumbull completed his studies and took a job teaching, resistance to British attempts to force different taxation measures on the thirteen American colonies began to enter the public consciousness and nowhere were revolutionary sentiments as strong as they were in Massachusetts. As local militia units began to drill with more earnestness, actual hostilities finally broke out at Lexington and Concord prompting neighboring colonies to send contingents to Massachusetts in support of their fellow countrymen. Like many other young men, Trumbull found the call to arms irresistible and, joining the 1st Regiment of the Connecticut militia as an adjutant, he was soon promoted to major and arrived in the vicinity of Boston in time to witness the battle for Breeds' Hill.

It was while in Massachusetts that Trumbull's artistic talents first came to the notice of his superiors including Gen. George Washington who, impressed with his detailed sketches of British defenses and emplacements, recruited him as one of his aides-de-camp. Trumbull stayed with Washington through June of 1776 when he was promoted to colonel and transferred from Pennsylvania to the command of Gen. Philip Schuyler then in charge of the army's northern department. Assigned first to Crown Point and then to Fort Ticonderoga, Trumbull helped in preparing defenses and rebuilding military forces shattered in the wake of the failed Canadian campaign. Later, when Schuyler was replaced by Gen. Horatio Gates, Trumbull became a member of the general's staff. But by 1777, embroiled in a disagreement over the date of his commission, Trumbull's earlier enthusiasm for the military life had begun to cool and he became impatient to leave in order to pursue his study of art. Resigning from the army that year, he left to take up painting. Back in Connecticut, however, he could not ignore a plan to oust the British from next door Rhode Island and joined Gen. John Sullivan as a volunteer aide in 1778. Following the failure of the Rhode Island campaign, Trumbull returned home but his experiences over the next few years proved disappointing and in order to seek a more vital atmosphere for his studies, he decided to leave the United States for Europe.

Trumbull reached England by way of Paris in 1780 with the object of studying under the American painter Benjamin West. In London, he had hardly settled in when ill judged comments in support of the ongoing Revolution caused him to be arrested for treason and placed in jail for seven months. When he was finally released, he was deported back to the United States where he joined his brother in a venture to supply provisions to the Continental Army. But the war had no sooner ended in 1783 than he once again found himself in England and in West's studio to pick up where he had left off. There, after meeting John Adams who was serving as ambassador to Great Britain, Trumbull's interest in documenting the great events and figures of the American Revolution first manifested itself with such paintings as *The Death of General Warren at Bunker's Hill* and *The Death of General Montgomery in the Attack on Quebec.*

In 1785, Trumbull left England for France where he began assembling sketches of French officers in preparation for his execution of *The Surrender of Cornwallis.* While in France, he also studied the work of artists Jacques-Louis David and Jean-Antoine Houdon and visited museums in Germany and the Netherlands. In Paris, he made the acquaintance of Thomas Jefferson who was then serving as United States ambassador and with his encouragement, later painted *The Signing of the Declaration of Independence.* That work was followed by *The Surrender of Burgoyne* and *The Resignation of Washington* which, along with *Signing*, were later re-executed at gigantic twelve by eighteen foot sizes for display in the country's new Capital building in Washington, D.C. Meanwhile, back in England, Trumbull completed *Signing* and the *Surrender of Cornwallis.* After a second visit to France during the early years of that country's own revolution, he returned to the United States determined, as he wrote to Jefferson, "to commemorat(e) the great events of our country's revolution." In following years, Trumbull would do just that, supplementing his historical scenes with monumental portraiture that included full length executions of George Washington (whom he would eventually paint over a dozen times), John Adams, Alexander Hamilton, John Jay, and Rufus King.

In 1794, Trumbull took a brief hiatus from his work to join Jay as secretary on a diplomatic mission to England to negotiate a treaty which among other things, was intended to end the impressment of American seamen. Although the issue of impressments was never settled, other outstanding matters were including compensation of war debts by Americans to British citizens, the removal of British troops from the northwest territory, and the granting to the United States of most favored nation trading status. When Jay returned to the United

States, Trumbull was promoted and remained in England to oversee administration of the accords.

Taking advantage of his extended stay in Europe, Trumbull took the opportunity to make another visit to France before returning to the United States where, in 1804, he set up a studio in New York concentrating on portraiture. The next year he was named president of the New York Academy of Fine Arts and in 1808 became vice president of the American Academy of Fine Arts. Failing eyesight prompted him to spend the next six years, from 1809 to 1815, in London seeking treatment while broadening his artistic subjects into the area of religion and other historical periods. When he returned to the United States, he brought a number of these new paintings with him for exhibition. In 1816, he was named president of the American Academy of Fine Arts, a position he would hold for the next twenty years. In the meantime, he met with President James Madison and suggested that the rotunda of the federal Capital building be decorated with a series of monumental paintings depicting key events in the Revolution. The suggestion was approved and Trumbull was commissioned by the federal government to recreate some of his most famous paintings in heroic twelve by eighteen foot dimensions. When completed over the course of the next two decades, they would cement his reputation as the chief pictorialist of the American Revolution.

Trumbull ended his long career by selling his personal collection of art to Yale University, designing the Trumbull Gallery where they would be displayed, and writing an autobiography. Finally retiring, he died at his home in New York on November, 10, 1843.

George Walton

Although many of the Founding Fathers had other interests in seeing America throw off the rule of England other than purely patriotic ones, including real estate speculation on the frontier, few ever allowed themselves to take advantage of the Revolution for personal aggrandizement. Unfortunately, one of those whose reputation became tarnished in such a way was George Walton.

Not much is known about Walton's early life other than that he was born about 1749 in Farmville, Virginia and that he was orphaned soon after. Taken under the wing of an uncle, he was apprenticed to a carpenter, but somewhere along the way, he must have become dissatisfied and determined to improve himself. Somehow, he was educated, and in 1769 showed up in Savannah, Georgia where he acquired legal training and admitted to the bar in 1774, a momentous year for America. At the time, Georgia, the last of the thirteen colonies to be established in 1732, was still a wide open place and so, attractive to young men with ambitions. Walton was no different; as soon as he could, he opened a law office in Savannah and then, as popular resentment of Britain began to grow, became involved in local politics. He joined what was known as the "city party," those Georgian patriots allied with the McIntosh clan and other conservative leaning mercantilist elements who soon became involved in a bitter running fight with more radical patriots made up of the colony's planter class and country folk represented chiefly by Button Gwinnett and Lyman Hall.

By 1775, the year active fighting in the Revolution broke out in Massachusetts, Walton was secretary of Georgia's Provincial Congress and president of its Council of Safety, later he also joined the colony's Committee of Intelligence. Despite the existence of these revolutionary organizations however, Georgia was slow to throw its full support behind the effort to resist British oppression and even as the more radical elements in the state voted to send Lyman Hall to the Continental Congress as a non-voting member, the city party held back. That changed in 1776 when the decision was finally made to join the other colonies in resistance and an official delegation was appointed to represent Georgia in Congress. Among those chosen for the group was Walton who arrived in Philadelphia in June and had only occupied his seat in Congress for a single day

George Walton

before he was called upon to sign the Declaration of Independence.

With the Declaration of Independence, the new United States could expect even more determined efforts by Britain to retain its American colonies and amid heightened fears that the enemy could strike anywhere, some members of Congress decided to return to their respective states to help in the defense of their homes. Among those who did was Walton. He returned to Georgia in 1777 and joined the 1st Regiment of the Georgia Militia as a colonel. In the battle for Savannah, Walton commanded about 100 men on the American right flank and was taken by surprise after the British discovered a little known trail that led into his rear. Wounded in action before Savannah, he was taken prisoner while the enemy seized the city.

In 1779, Walton was released in a prisoner exchange and promptly elected governor of Georgia. His term of office proved one of the shortest on record however when he was removed under a cloud of political infighting. His questionable dealings as governor notwithstanding, Walton was returned to Congress and when his term ended, found himself once again in trouble for his participation in a duel that ended in Gwinnett's death at the hands of Lachlan McIntosh in 1777. Still in Philadelphia, he was chosen to help negotiate a treaty with the Cherokee Indians in Tennessee. In 1783, he was appointed as Georgia's chief justice, an office he held until 1789 when he was once again made governor. That stint also ended quickly when the state's constitution was rewritten and Walton was forced to leave office. From there, he was again named as judge, this time to the state's superior court, a position he held until 1798. In between, he was named as the state's senator in Congress filling out the unexpired term of James Jackson in 1795.

Ironically, Jackson had left office to return to Georgia to head up a reform movement investigating what has become known as the Yazoo Land Act fraud. The scandal, which Walton had become involved with when he was governor in 1789, included the sale over the legal limit of 40 million acres of state owned land to fellow politicians and a number of large land investment firms for only one and half cents an acre. The deal sparked outrage and dismay throughout the country and growing popular resentment among Georgia residents prompted the return of Jackson from Congress and the convening of a reform legislature. When it was over, all records dealing with the land fraud were burned on the steps of the state capital and the political careers of many of Georgia's most prominent politicians were ended. It was a political fight Walton was doomed to lose and after completing Jackson's term in Congress, he lost reelection and retired from public life. Walton died at College Hill, his home outside Augusta, on February 2, 1804.

Artemas Ward

It would probably come as a surprise to most that George Washington was not the first commander in chief of the armies of what would eventually become the United States. Artemas Ward, who shone oh so briefly in the national spotlight before coming under the massive shadow of the planter from Virginia, commanded all that there was of a "national army" prior to June of 1775. Overweight and past his physical prime, Ward was yet an experienced soldier and ardent patriot and when he found himself the senior officer among the minuteman forces converging on Boston, he took a chaotic situation and the most unpromising material for a future army and turned them both to America's advantage. When Washington finally arrived in the vicinity of Boston to take command of the new Continental Army, he found that the raw recruits and volunteers of Lexington and Concord, Menotomy, and Breed's Hill, had been set on a firm foundation from which he could immediately begin to fashion a professional army.

Artemas Ward

Born in Shrewsbury, Massachusetts on November 26, 1727, Ward spent little time pursuing private business upon graduating from Harvard in 1748 being chosen almost immediately as his home town's representative in the colonial legislature. With the coming of the French and Indian War, he was commissioned a major in the provincial militia and served under Col. Abraham William during the ill fated Ticonderoga campaign of 1758. Sharing the frustration of his fellow soldiers in British General James Abercrombie's inexplicable retreat from New York, Ward nevertheless found himself promoted to lieutenant-colonel by the time the war ended. Back in Massachusetts, he resumed his political career but as the years passed, found himself increasingly at odds with the British authorities and Parliament's attempts to tax the colony for its share in the expenses of conducting the late war. His efforts in defiance of the Stamp Act in 1765 resulted in his being stripped of his rank as colonel in the militia, a circumstance, Ward told Governor Francis Bernard, that he considered more of an honor than having been commissioned in the first place "Since the motive that dictated it is evidence that I am...a friend of my country." But his decommissioning was only the first of many attempts by the colonial authorities to silence the Shrewsbury native, denying him a seat in the legislature until Bernard's successor, Thomas Hutchinson, gave up and finally allowed him to sit in 1770.

Unrepentant, Ward continued to be involved in Patriot activities taking part in the conventions of 1774 that concluded Massachusetts owed no allegiance to Parliament and took steps to wrest control of the colony from the royal governor including preparing for its defense against invasion by British troops. Later, Ward was named a delegate to the provincial congress that took over from the general court when that body was suspended by British General Thomas Gage. On October 27, 1774 the Provincial Congress, recognizing Ward's military experience and patriotic zeal, made him a brigadier-general in the colony's militia under Jedediah Preble.

Ward did not have long to wait before he and the militia were called out by the Committee of Safety later in the spring of 1775. That June, the British army had emerged from Boston on an extended raid deep into the countryside around Lexington and Concord. They were met and stopped at Concord Bridge after local minutemen fired upon them and ignited a protracted, running battle that dogged the British as they retreated back the way they had come. Perhaps little realized at the time, but it was the opening battle of the Revolutionary War and Ward suddenly found himself at the center of the maelstrom. With Preble's failure to assume the duties he had been nominated for, responsibility for the army that had coalesced on the outskirts of Boston fell to Ward and as its commander in chief, he found himself dealing with the most basic elements involved in fielding an army including the power to recruit.

Without the ability to sign up new recruits or reenlist men, Ward could not plan on having a certain number of men to call upon for service when they were needed. In addition, with the stark choice of deciding whether they were for the Patriot cause or still loyal to England, many of Ward's roughly 10,000 men could not even be counted upon for their complete support; in fact there was a good chance that some would turn out to be informers. Adding to Ward's concerns was that the ad hoc army had arrived in the Boston area with only the clothes and equipment on their backs; all the food, clothing, bedding, and ammunition needed to keep them in place were lacking and had to be found, transported and distributed. And while he was keeping track of all that, Ward still had a war to fight with elements of the most powerful military machine of the day positioned only a few miles away. Finally, taking the position of commander in chief of the rebel army was not one to be assumed lightly: for sure, if he was ever captured by the British, it would be the hangman's noose for Ward.

Meanwhile, colonial forces under Ward had been in position outside Boston for some weeks when word was received by the Committee of Safety that the British intended to strengthen their position by crossing the Charles River and seizing some hills on Charlestown Neck. To deprive the enemy of such strategic ground, the committee instructed Ward to take it first as well as other positions on Dorchester Heights to the south of the city. Ward called in one of his most experienced officers and ordered Col. William Prescott to take a thousand men and occupy Bunker Hill out on the Neck. But by remaining behind at his headquarters and allowing Prescott to become the ranking officer on the scene, Ward forfeited immediate control of the direction subsequent events would follow. Thus, it was the experienced Prescott who decided on his own authority to fortify not Bunker Hill but nearby Breed's Hill instead which, being closer to Boston, he considered more strategic. And so it was that the stage was set for the so-called historic battle of Bunker Hill in which an inexperienced militia held off the cream of the British Army in three costly assaults before the enemy finally could claim possession of the high ground.

Unfortunately, the battle of Bunker Hill did not end with active fighting between Americans and British, but continued in another form as recriminations for the loss of the battle were bandied about by various American commanders. In the end, Ward's popularity with his men suffered and when it came time for the Continental Congress to officially appoint a commander in chief, conditions were such that it was made much easier for George Washington to take over when he arrived in Massachusetts on July 2, 1775. And although Ward stayed on as second in command after the British evacuated Boston and Washington took the army south, ill health forced him to resign his commission.

Ward spent the remainder of his life serving in a number of public offices including a judge and a long standing member of the Massachusetts state legislature. He was chosen as a delegate to the Continental Congress in 1779 but never took his seat due to bad health. Later, after the Constitution was ratified, he went to Congress as a Federalist and served there from 1791 to 1795. Ward did have one more brush with heroism however, when on September 5, 1786 he courageously defied a group of armed men in front of his own courthouse.

The years immediately following the military phase of the Revolution were difficult for small landowners as the new nation struggled with a lagging economy. As a result, many former veterans of the war were faced with land foreclosures and, frustrated with their powerlessness, rose up in what has since been called Shay's Rebellion after one of its leaders, Capt. Daniel Shays, a veteran of Bunker Hill. Worcester County, Massachusetts was at the epicenter of the troubles and the armed men who had kept Ward from entering his courthouse were attempting to keep any rulings ordering the seizure of local farms from taking place. Ward, daring the men to run him through with their bayonets, turned and addressed an angry crowd that had gathered before the courthouse and pleaded with them for nearly two hours to abandon their illegal course. Failing, he retreated to a nearby tavern and held court from there. Finally, recognizing the inevitable approach of old age, Ward retired from public life in 1797 and died on October 28, 1800.

Seth Warner

Although growing friction between Britain and its American colonies dominated the attention of residents living along the larger seacoast towns and cities and to a lesser extent, homesteaders and land speculators impatient with restrictions placed on westward expansion by royal authority, there were other, regional concerns, unrelated to the looming national struggle that would soon explode into open revolution. Concerns such as the disconnect between people living in the backwoods areas of the southern colonies and the tidewater plantation

John Stark directs pursuit of the enemy at the battle of Bennington

owners who governed them, the struggle by residents of Pennsylvania to free themselves from the rule of the proprietary Penn family, the repression of Catholics by the Protestant dominated government of Maryland, and the ongoing threat of Indian warfare all along the frontier. But one area of contention common to most of the thirteen colonies arose from a continuing uncertainty regarding their exact boundaries. Over the years, disagreement about just where the boundaries between various colonies lay became the source of much debate with many not being definitively settled until after the Revolution. Arising out of those disagreements, was New York's claim on what was known at the time as the "Hampshire Grants," an area west of New Hampshire and north of Massachusetts that would eventually become the state of Vermont. At the time however, the region was occupied by a breed of stubborn frontiersmen and yeoman farmers possessing a strong streak of independence and who were intensely resentful of authority. And so when New York insisted on governing the region as if it were its own, there was a strong response from residents which took the form of armed resistance. Organized by frontier giant Ethan Allen (who had land interests in the Grants), a loose band of volunteer militia calling themselves the Green Mountain Boys took it upon themselves to offer armed resistance against any attempt by New York to force its will on them. The group, like Daniel Morgan's Virginia riflemen, established for itself an elite reputation that was due in no small part to a number of experienced frontier fighters such as sometime botanist Seth Warner.

Far from the wilds of Vermont, Seth Warner was born in Roxbury, Connecticut on May 17, 1743 and early on learned to enjoy the outdoors while developing an interest in nature beyond simple hunting and fishing. When he was twenty years old, he moved with his father from Connecticut to the Hampshire Grants and the area around Bennington. There, Warner grew attached to the surrounding hills and farmland and developed a resentment against New York officials who entered the region in an attempt to force residents to abide by the colony's laws. Angered by New York's heavy handed insistence that the Grants belonged to it, Warner joined a group of resistance fighters called the Green Mountain Boys which had been organized by fellow Vermonter Ethan Allen. With his farm located barely a mile from the New York border, his intimate knowledge of the surrounding geography, and his skill as a woodsman, there was little argument among his neighbors when Warner was named captain of his local company of Green Mountain Boys. Specializing in harassing New Yorkers who came to the Grants, chasing them out and sometimes doing violence to them, it was not long before Warner and Allen each were wanted outlaws with prices on their heads. Thus, when hostilities finally broke out between America and Britain in 1775, Vermonters were primed to join the fight against a royal authority that had sponsored New York's claims against the Grants.

Armed with an order from the Continental Congress, Allen and Warner led the Green Mountain Boys on an assault of Fort Ticonderoga. On the way, they were joined by Benedict Arnold who had similar papers from the Massachusetts Committee of Safety and together they proceeded to take the fort from its unsuspecting defenders. After the surrender of Ticonderoga, Warner led his men north to the fort at Crown Point and succeeded in capturing that post as well. Promoted to Colonel as a result of that action, Allen and Warner next joined Gen. Richard Montgomery's army on its ill fated invasion of Canada in 1776. It was while moving north toward Quebec that Allen was captured leaving Warner in command of the 300 Vermonters who were instrumental in turning back an 800 man relief force under British Gen. Guy Carleton during the siege of St. John's. Following that fight, Warner and his men were allowed to return home and so were not on hand when Montgomery was killed during the failed assault on Montreal and the American retreat from Canada.

The American failure to capture and hold Canada strengthened the enemy's position there and provided the springboard for a British invasion of the northern states. Led by Gen. John Burgoyne, the plan called for the capture of Ticonderoga and an eventual link up with a second army moving up the Hudson River valley from New York City. Accordingly, Burgoyne entered New York with an army of 10,000 men and by placing his artillery on high ground overlooking the fort, forced the Americans to abandon Ticonderoga on July 5, 1777. With British Gen. Simon Fraser in pursuit, Warner's men fought a successful rear guard action that allowed the main body of about 4,000 Americans to withdraw toward the town of Hubbardton. There, Fraser managed to surprise a group of local militia but was in turn caught in an unexpected movement by Warner's Green Mountain Boys as they struck the enemy's center. The action quickly escalated to an all out battle with Warner's men, now reinforced by another 1,000 militia, going almost hand to hand with the enemy. In danger of being surrounded, the Americans pulled back only to counterattack again and were on the point of carrying the day when Fraser was rescued by the sudden appearance of a squad of German mercenaries under Baron Von Riedesel.

After the mauling given the British at Hubbardton, which cost the enemy about half their force of 850 men in casualties and captured, the Americans retreated to nearby Manchester, Vermont. From there, most decided to join the gathering forces around Albany, New York but Warner chose to remain in Vermont, fearful that the British would try to invade the area again and threaten its citizens. Warner's caution was justified as a few weeks later, Burgoyne ordered a second force of 800 regulars, Indians, and loyalists into New England to forage for supplies. By then, however, Warner's small army of Vermonters had grown to 500 and had been joined by 1,500 militia from New Hampshire under the independent command of Gen. John Stark, a veteran of Breed's Hill and the Continental Army. Bowing to Stark's seniority, Warner placed himself under his command but retained a strong leadership role by virtue of being intimately familiar with the area around Bennington where the enemy was headed. In fact, after hearing of the enemy's approach, the Americans made camp atop a hill not a mile from Warner's farm. When the British force came within sight, Hessian Gen. Baum ordered his men to fortify a nearby hill overlooking the American position. Meanwhile, Stark and Warner met in Bennington to plan their strategy, a three pronged pincer movement designed to surround the British while pinning them down in the center.

The plan worked to perfection and on the morning of August 16, 1777, after some initial hard fighting between rebels and loyalists at the base of the hill, the Americans crossed the Walloomsac River and overran the enemy, mortally wounding its commanders. With the remnants of the British army scattering in all directions, the Americans began to celebrate and failed to notice the approach of a British relief column under Col. Heinrich Von Breymann. In minutes, the rebels were in danger of being swept from the field and would have been if not for Warner's timely arrival with reinforcements he had gathered from Manchester while the first part of the battle had been in progress. Marching his men onto the field in perfect order, Warner ordered them to fire with devastating effect. While the British force was kept at bay by Warner's men, Stark was able to reorganize his units and have them rejoin the battle one by one. Soon, Breyman found himself outnumbered and was forced to abandon the field. The resulting chase went on for ten miles and with only 40 American casualties to nearly 900 British killed or captured there was no doubt who had won the battle of Bennington. News of the great victory spread all over New England and with morale soaring, thousands of volunteers began to stream toward New York for the expected showdown with Burgoyne's main army. By the time of the second battle of Saratoga in October, American forces would have swelled to more than 20,000 men.

After Bennington, Warner led his men to Stillwater where he joined the main American army that had been gathering at Gen. Schuyler's call and later led an operation at Lake George Landing that captured a small fleet of boats that Burgoyne had intended for use in making his escape from Saratoga. In the battles that followed, Warner's command consisted of over 1,800 men.

Remaining with the Continental Army until 1782, the six foot tall Warner, who had always boasted robust health, fell ill and returned to his farm. After years of fighting with the Green Mountain Boys and neglecting his personal affairs, Warner found himself near destitute and even a grant of land awarded him by a grateful Vermont, was sold off to pay his taxes. With his health getting worse, he moved back to Roxbury where he continued to suffer malarial hallucinations and died on December 26, 1784. Warner died before he had a chance to see Vermont become the first new state to be added to the original thirteen. His resistance efforts with the Green Mountain Boys allowed the Grants to establish its own government in 1777 and declare itself an independent republic after the war thus paving the way for statehood in 1791.

Joseph Warren

Of all the Founding Fathers, it seems that few, if any, have actually had to live up to that oath in the Declaration offering their lives to the cause of American independence. Of course, those who survived the war would have had the opportunity to build reputations filled with military glory and political achievement that would come to the notice of subsequent generations and so be recognized as a Founder, but how many others would have qualified for that honor if not for promising careers cut short as a result of the Revolutionary War? How many of those who died, had they lived, would be counted today among such heroes and survivors of the war as George Washington, Thomas Jefferson, John Adams, or Daniel Morgan each of whom, some more often than others, came close to making the ultimate sacrifice? It's impossible to say. Examples however, might have included Virginia's John Laurens, New York's Richard Montgo-mery, or Massachusetts' fiery Joseph Warren, described by one British officer as "the great-est incendiary in all America."

Joseph Warren

Warren was born to a well to do farming family in Roxbury, Massachusetts on May 11, 1741. After attending Harvard College, he graduated in 1759 and while continuing his studies in the field of medicine, took a job in charge of a local grammar school. By 1764, he was established in his own medical practice with a growing reputation of selflessness and great skill and had married Elizabeth Hooten who brought to their union a substantial inheritance. Meanwhile, in common with fellow residents, Warren had begun to cultivate a resentment toward the English Parliament over its attempts to tax the colonies without their approval. Joining the growing debate, he railed against the newly passed Stamp Act in a series of letters published in the *Boston Gazette* newspaper which brought him to the notice of Samuel Adams. Thus, a close partnership began in which the two men would become key players in the nascent Revolutionary movement.

In 1767, following passage by Parliament of the Townshend Acts, Warren, writing anonymously in the *Gazette* as "a True Patriot," once again took up the pen and so angered royal administrators that Governor Francis Bernard asked the local legislature to have the paper's publishers arrested for libel. The effort failed and over the next few years, often making speeches at public events described by one British officer as "seditious" and "inflammatory," Warren would become ever more deeply involved in the resistance movement, rising to leadership positions alongside Samuel Adams and James Otis. A pivotal year for Warren was 1774 when, upon Samuel Adams' appointment as a delegate to the first Continental Congress, he became chief of the resistance effort in Boston and thus de facto patriot leader for all of Massachusetts. Also that year, at a Suffolk County convention held on September 9, Warren presented a paper he had written, later known as the "Suffolk Resolves," that placed Massachusetts in open rebellion against the crown. Asserting that the king had violated the rights of the colonists as free Englishmen in his acquiescence of the various tax raising measures and quartering acts, Warren charged that Britain could no longer claim their allegiance. With those bonds cut, the Resolves ordered all public officials to seize cooperation with the royal administration and even threatened seizure of hostages should any colonist be arrested for political reasons. Warren's hand was strengthened and his position vindicated after a copy of the Resolves was delivered by Paul Revere to the Congress in Philadelphia which voted to endorse the document on September 18.

Following the Suffolk convention, Warren was named chairman of the powerful Committee of Safety which was in charge of organizing local militia units for resistance against the British and for rounding up military supplies. It was news in April 1775, of a British plan to seize just such supplies hidden in Concord that prompted Warren to order William Dawes and Revere to ride westward to alert the countryside and warn patriot leaders John Hancock and Samuel Adams in Lexington that they could be possible targets as well. With the element of surprise lost and finding itself under a constant fire by thousands of local militia, the British incursion was turned back and Warren, hearing of the running battle between minutemen and soldiers retreating back to Boston, rushed to Menotomy to confer with commander of militia General William Heath. Some of the heaviest fighting of the day took place at Menotomy with Warren in the thick of it treating the wounded, at one point having a hairpin shot from his head. With the British once more ensconced in Boston, Warren circulated an urgent message to surrounding communities to send every fighting man they could to the capital and then spent the next few weeks helping to organize into an army the 20,000 men that had answered his summons. At the same time, Warren was also involved in the decision that sent Benedict Arnold west to seize Fort Ticonderoga and dispatched messages to Congress pushing for recognition of Massachusetts' new independent government and for it to take charge of the army. At the end of May, he was made president of the colony's Provincial Congress, the provisional government of Massachusetts that had arisen in the wake of the Suffolk Resolves, and the following month, he was named a major general of militia. It was while serving in that capacity that he found himself atop Breed's Hill on the afternoon of June 17. While meeting with the army's new commander, General Artemas Ward, at his headquarters, Warren learned that the British had begun to cross the Charles River to Charlestown with the intention of denying the Americans the high ground on Breed's Hill. Not one to stand by while others did the fighting, Warren rushed to the scene of impending battle, perhaps with the lines of a poem he'd written running through his mind:

> Lift up your hands ye heroes,
> And swear with proud disdain,
> The wretch that would ensnare you
> Shall lay his snares in vain:
> Should Europe empty all her force,
> We'll meet her in array,
> And fight and shout, and shout and fight
> For North America.

Refusing to interfere with Col. William Prescott's command of the troops atop the hill, Warren instead stood with the men within their improvised earthworks and helped repel the enemy's first two attempts to storm the American lines. In the meantime, to the rear, his brother John, also a physician, treated the wounded. It was on the third assault of the hill, with ammunition running out on the American side, that the 34 year old Warren was struck in the head by an enemy ball and instantly killed, the first high ranking patriot to die in the birth pangs of the new United States and a man greatly loved by all who knew him.

George Washington

Labeled the "indispensable man" by some scholars, George Washington alone of the founding generation was able to command the confidence of a majority of his fellow citizens both north and south, and in small states as well as large. His participation first in a weak confederacy of former colonies and then as a leader of thirteen united states divided by regional differences, was a key factor in the eventual success of the American experiment in popular republicanism. Described by fellow Virginian and Revolutionary War veteran Henry Lee as being "first in war, first in peace, and first in the hearts of his countrymen," Washington's career spanned the entire revolutionary era, touching on every aspect of the struggle except perhaps, direct diplomacy, which he guided from afar during his two terms as president of the United States. But despite the central position Washington has since achieved in the American consciousness and pantheon of national heroes, he was a man before he became an icon and, as with all mortals, he began life as a callow youth.

He was born at Wakefield Farm, Virginia, in 1732 and

George Washington

grew up in the shadow of his adored elder brother Lawrence who inherited the family estate at Mount Vernon. As a younger son, Washington found himself at a social disadvantage in aristocratic Virginia and, wishing to be included in the sophisticated circles in which his brother moved, studied closely books on proper etiquette for upwardly mobile social climbers. Eager for adventure and the local prestige automatically inferred onto those in uniform, Washington also decided to enter the local militia. However, with little formal schooling under his belt and without an estate of his own, Washington had to earn a living and so learned the surveying trade under Lord Thomas Fairfax, a wealthy landowner whose example inspired the younger man to pursue his own investments in real estate.

Washington's fortunes changed radically in 1752 when he became the master of Mount Vernon upon the death of his older brother and one of four majors in the Virginia militia. Two years later, promoted to a lieutenant colonel and experienced in outdoor life, he led a force into the Ohio country to establish a British presence there but instead, ended up starting a war when he rashly attacked a French diplomatic mission. The French and Indian War, although ending some years later with British victory and dominion over Canada and all of the eastern seaboard of North America to the Mississippi River, began badly with Washington's defeat at the hands of the French at Green Meadows. Following his involvement in a second defeat of British forces under Major General Edward Braddock in 1755, the personal courage displayed by the twenty-three year old Virginian won him command of all the colony's militia. By the end of the war, the young Washington had learned that there was a good deal more to fighting than boyhood dreams of adventure and glory; a lesson that would stand him in good stead when he took the field again for an entirely different cause ten years later.

Over the next decade, Washington spent most of his time managing his estates, speculating in land in the unsettled west, and positioning his farms and workshops so that they would continue to prosper against the vicissitudes of market forces. In the meantime, he took a seat in the colony's legislature and became concerned as Britain began to issue measures designed to raise money from its recalcitrant colonies in America. In addition to resenting taxes imposed on Virginia by a Parliament in which it had no representation, Washington also grew increasingly resentful of restrictions placed on settlement west of the Proclamation Line that ran along the Appalachian Mountains preventing him from profiting from his land holdings there. As opposition to Britain grew, Washington aligned himself with political radicals that called for resistance against the mother country and in 1774 was eventually chosen to represent Virginia at the Continental Congress called to decide how the thirteen colonies should react to the British measures. But events soon outpaced politics when the first shots of the American Revolution were fired in Massachusetts and a British army was surrounded by local militiamen in Boston. Because he was viewed as America's most prominent and experienced military officer and a figure that could help unify the northern and southern colonies, Washington was chosen by the Continental Congress in 1775 as the first commander in chief of the newly created Continental Army. Pleased with his appointment, Washington was nonetheless appalled by the lack of military discipline he encountered in Boston and as cannon from Fort Ticonderoga were hauled across the colony from New York for a final showdown with the British, he began to whip his soldiers into a respectable military force.

The arrival of the big guns on Dorchester Heights overlooking Boston placed the British in an untenable situation, forcing them to abandon the city for Canada. Anticipating the enemy's next move, Washington moved his army south to New York and began to prepare a network of defenses on both Long Island and Manhattan. But, perhaps still encumbered with the same reckless self-confidence he displayed at the start of the French and Indian War, Washington counted too much on the staying power of his army of militia and newly recruited Continental soldiers. As a result, the Americans suffered a series of disastrous defeats at the hands of the British that ended up sweeping them clear out of New York and into Pennsylvania. With his confidence shaken and Congress in doubt over his abilities, Washington struck back with an unexpected foray across the Hudson River in the winter of 1776-1777, successfully attacking enemy positions in New Jersey at Trenton and Princeton. Later, the army's reputation was again tarnished when British forces effortlessly occupied Philadelphia in the autumn of 1777 but somewhat restored the following year at the battle of Monmouth.

By then however, most of the action in the war had shifted to other theaters where the United States won victories in the west and at Saratoga, New York. Disappointments were also to be had in the deep south as British forces seized Charleston, South Carolina and raided Virginia fostering a vicious civil war there between patriots and loyalists. Gradually, however, Continental forces reestablished control over the south and forced British General Lord Charles Cornwallis into a corner at Yorktown, Virginia. Leaving some of his men behind to convince General Henry Clinton in New York that the Continentals remained in place, Washington led the better part of his army south to Virginia and, joined by French soldiers on land and with a French victory at sea, forced Cornwallis' surrender and effectively ended the active phase of the war.

Washington remained with his troops until the Treaty of Paris was signed with Britain in 1783 and in a parting service to the new nation, quelled a simmering uprising by army officers disenchanted with their treatment at the hands of Congress. After that, the general stunned the world by returning to his home instead of taking advantage of his position and seizing power for himself.

After the war, Washington had every intention of retiring from public life but in 1787, when proponents of a stronger union among the states managed to convene a Constitutional Convention in Philadelphia, he was once again called upon to serve. Chosen as the Convention's chairman, Washington then presided over the creation of the United States Constitution, one of the most important documents ever written, and in 1789, under its provisions, was elected as the country's first president.

Serving two consecutive terms of office, Washington became president with near universal approval among his fellow citizens and was conscious that every move he made would set precedents for his successors. Unfortunately, as his first term ended and his second progressed, the seeds of discord planted when he chose Thomas Jefferson and Alexander Hamilton as his Secretaries of State and Treasury respectively bore bitter fruit. In the final months of his presidency, after Washington sided with Hamilton and the rising Federalist Party on issues involving relations with a revolutionary France, finance, and the assumption by the federal government of state debts left over from the war, Jefferson resigned his office and became a leader of the opposition. Thus, by the time Washington left the presidency in 1797, even he was not above being pilloried in an increasingly partisan press.

Nevertheless, despite his wish to spend his remaining days at Mount Vernon, Washington was called upon to serve his nation one more time in 1798 when he was named commander in chief of a new Provisional Army created by Congress in response to fears of being caught between a militant France and the British army that continued to occupy American land in the Ohio country. The ex-president, however, never took the field and after a brief illness, died at Mount Vernon on December 14, 1799.

In an era populated by giants, Washington, as he did in real life, towered over his peers not simply because of a career that spanned and influenced nearly every aspect of the American Revolution, but because of his universally recognized human qualities: his fellow soldiers admired his courage and coolness under fire, his fellow congressmen and members of the Constitutional Convention trusted him to be fair and deliberate, his fellow citizens were impressed with his dedication, polite bearing, and personal dignity. Everywhere he went, he inspired loyalty and affection, an affection that would increase down the years since his death and more than earn him the deserved appellation "Father of his country."

William Washington

There was not much in the early life of William Washington, a second cousin of George Washington who was twenty years his senior, to indicate that he would become one of the most active, and successful officers in the fledgling Continental Army. Educated but unambitious, a man of action who was to be wounded numerous times but described as "corpulent" by fellow cavalry officer "Lighthorse Harry" Lee, Washington at first glance did not seem like promising material for martial greatness. Nevertheless, like his more famous cousin, he had inherited a large build, a likeable manner, and a talent with horses that, coupled with a keen intelligence and fearless demeanor, enabled him to lead men through a dozen chancy engagements in the most demanding theater of the Revolutionary War while, more often than not, emerging triumphant. Washington was born on February 28, 1752 on his family's 1,200 acre plantation in Stafford County, Virginia. One of several children, including three brothers, Washington early on displayed an interest for outdoor activities including fishing, hunting, and riding. At a loss for a profession to follow, Washington seems to have fallen back on that old standby, the ministry, and although he worked at it long enough to acquire a proficiency in Latin and Greek, the Revolution interrupted and he wasted no time in abandoning his books for the saddle.

William Washington

After the first shots in the war were fired at Lexington and Concord in Massachusetts, Washington joined the 3rd Virginia Regiment that was formed later in the summer of 1775. His big size, good cheer, and known skill on horseback helped in his being chosen as captain of one of the unit's companies. The next year, the regiment moved out to New York where Washington's cousin had assumed command of the Continental Army and was busily arranging for the defense of Long Island. After sharing in the action and disappointments of New York, including receiving his first wound, Washington joined the rest of the army as it retreated into New Jersey. At the nadir of the country's fortunes, he took part in the battle of Trenton where he was once again wounded but played a pivotal role in capturing a battery of enemy artillery. His courage and resourcefulness in that action as well as the growing respect he had from his officers and men, resulted in a promotion to major in 1777 and he was placed in command of the 4th Continental Light Dragoons. Washington took part in many of the major battles that took place between New York and Philadelphia including Brandywine and Germantown before receiving his next promotion to lieutenant colonel and command of the 3rd Dragoons. In 1779, he received his most fateful orders and was transferred with his cavalry to South Carolina where the British had invaded hoping to find strong support among the south's loyalists. There, out from under the shadow of his older cousin, Washington would come into his own.

In South Carolina, Washington soon found himself stationed outside Charleston which was placed under siege early in 1780 and fell to the enemy on May 12. Nearby, was Sandy Hill, the plantation of Charles Elliott, one of the wealthiest men in the state. During one of the many opportunities Continental officers had to meet the local gentry, Washington made the acquaintance of Elliott's daughter, Jane Riley Elliott, who lamented the fact that Washington's regiment did not sport its own flag. To remedy the situation, Jane fashioned one from a piece of drapery and an impressed Washington slipped it onto a hickory pole and carried it in battle for the remainder of the war. But after the fall of Charleston and the capture of Gen. Benjamin Lincoln's Continental Army of almost 5,000 men, the war in the south went from bad to worse as the British emerged from the city and prepared to move inland.

With major Continental units smashed or captured, the war became one conducted mostly by partisan bands commanded by such men as Francis Marion on a hit and run basis. At first, Washington's regiment concerned itself mostly in defensive operations around Charleston but as the situation deteriorated, he finally met the enemy's most resourceful cavalry leader at Rantowle's Bridge not far from Sandy Hill. There, on March 27, 1780 Washington routed a unit of North Carolina royalists and when Lt. Col. Banastre Tarleton and his dreaded British Legion appeared, charged them as well, forcing them back in disarray but failing to capture them for lack of infantry support. The two men were to meet again, but with less fortunate results for Washington as his regiment, along with the rest of the American army to which it was attached, was caught by surprise in a number of skirmishes with the Virginian barely making his escape from a pursuing Tarleton.

With the fall of Charleston in May and later, the rout of a new Continental Army under Gen. Horatio Gates at Camden, Gen. Nathanael Green was placed in charge of the southern theater and one of the first things he did was to persuade Gen. Daniel Morgan out of retirement and give him an independent command in support of the main army. Attached to Morgan's unit, Washington's regiment operated on Greene's western flank and took part in many small, but successful operations including his defeat and capture of nearly 200 loyalists near Camden, South Carolina after deceiving them into thinking he was armed with artillery, and his decimation of a second loyalist force of 250 men at Hammond Stores where a cavalry charge supported by infantry ended in a lopsided victory with 50 enemy captured and 150 killed, many only after the battle had ended.. In that action, Washington's units did not lose a single man.

It was at the battle of Cowpens on January 17, 1781 that Jane Elliott's flag earned the name of "Tarleton's Terror" when Washington's cavalry, ordered by Morgan to remain hidden behind a hill, emerged at a crucial point in the battle and struck the enemy formations on the American left sweeping aside the 17th Light Dragoons and, turning about, doing the same to a second British formation on the right. Washington's men then pursued the fleeing enemy into nearby woodland where they were met by Tarleton's Legion which had been held in reserve. Far ahead of his men, Washington was the first to engage the enemy, splintering his sabre in the first rush and having his life saved when his men shot an enemy horseman who was about to bury a sword in his head. Then, suddenly clear, Washington found himself face to face with Tarleton himself and managed to parry a sword thrust with the hilt of his broken sabre. Frustrated, Tarleton drew his pistol and shot but missed Washington, hitting his horse instead. After that, the rest of the Americans were all around and the encounter ended with Tarleton fleeing for his life.

As Greene's strategy for his campaign in the south unfolded, he sought to draw the enemy farther and farther inland, extending their lines of supply to the breaking point. Along the way, there were many skirmishes and a number of battles including Guilford Courthouse on March 15, 1781 where Washington's regiment drove the enemy before him, capturing valuable artillery pieces and at Hobkirk's Hill on April 25, 1781, when a timely charge not only recovered captured American field pieces, but helped to save the army from falling apart. But Washington's luck ran out at Eutaw Springs where, on September 8, 1781, he was wounded for the third time and captured after leading his regiment in a disastrous and bloody charge against strong enemy positions.

It would be the last action Washington saw in the war. Held prisoner in Charleston, he again met Jane Elliott, whose father had since died, and married her on April 21, 1782. After British Gen. Charles Cornwallis was defeated at Yorktown and the war wound down to its finish, the couple moved to Sandy Hill and Washington, after fathering two children, settled into a decades long pursuit of agriculture and administering the estate's 12,000 acres. Washington's popularity in his adopted state was such that he was eventually compelled to serve in the South Carolina legislature for 17 years, but refused any higher office. In 1791, his famous cousin, the elder Washington, visited South Carolina and spent a few days with William and Jane from which a long exchange of letters resulted concentrating on agriculture, a subject that greatly interested both men. The cousins once more joined together as warriors in 1798 when, with rising tensions between France and England with the United States caught in the middle, President John Adams asked George Washington to once again serve as commander in chief of the nation's armies and appointed William a brigadier. The two saw no action however, and after returning to his peaceful pursuits, the younger Washington died on March 6, 1810.

Anthony Wayne

Rash, impetuous, bold, were all words that have been used to describe "Mad" Anthony Wayne, but as one of Washington's most able and trustworthy officers, he could also be careful, deliberate, and open to the advice of subordinates, all qualities he learned while seeing action in every theater of combat both during the Revolution and after when he was called back to duty in order to put down once and for all the Indian menace that had bedeviled the Old Northwest for years. His subsequent triumph at Fallen Timers and its denouement at Greenville only solidified his reputation as one of the country's top fighting men.

Named after his grandfather, Anthony Wayne was born on January 1, 1745 at the family home of Waynesborough, in Chester County, Pennsylvania, only a few miles from Valley Forge. Wayne received his early education at a school run by an uncle and later, was sent to Philadelphia where a talent for numbers allowed him to practice as a professional surveyor, a job that in those years often required spending days and even months in the outdoors. By the time he was 20 years old, Wayne had already acquired a sufficient reputation to be hired by a consortium of businessmen including Benjamin Franklin for a job that took him to Nova Scotia for over a year. Returning to Waynesborough, he continued to survey while improving the farm and starting up a tannery. His

Anthony Wayne

local prominence and patriotic sympathies earned him a place on the local Committee of Safety and later, he became a natural choice for the state legislature in which he served for a year or so. That service came to an end in 1775 when hostilities broke out at Lexington and Concord and Wayne, always interested in military matters, promptly helped raise a regiment of local militia.

Chosen as colonel, Wayne was with his men when they joined the command of Gen. Richard Montgomery for the ill fated invasion of Canada. Charged with the capture of Montreal and an eventual link up with a second army led by Gen. Benedict Arnold for the seizure of Quebec, Montgomery lost his life in a failed assault on the city. Wayne and his men arrived in time to help stave off enemy counter attacks during the long retreat from Canada and at Trois Rivieres, located on the St. Lawrence River between Quebec and Montreal, the Pennsylvanian took part in a joint operation that scattered his men and forced them to make their escape into a vast, mosquito infested swamp. When the debacle was over, Wayne emerged slightly wounded in the leg and, his actions having come to the attention of his superiors, found himself promoted to brigadier general early in 1777.

Reassigned to Washington's command around New Jersey, Wayne moved with the army southward to Pennsylvania in a plan that was intended to protect Philadelphia from being taken by the British. On the east bank of the Brandywine, Wayne's division was charged with the defense of Chad's Ford, a key crossing along the river. In the action that followed, his men fought for hours to hold back a tide of the enemy's German mercenaries, action which proved to be merely a diversion from the real attack farther upriver on the American right. There, due to confused information regarding enemy movements, the line collapsed forcing the army to fall back. The retreat however, was an orderly one and after holding the enemy advance in check, Washington decided that the best his outnumbered army could do was to fight guerrilla fashion. Ordering Wayne to take 1,500 men, Washington instructed him to conduct raids on the enemy rear. On the night of September 20, 1777 Wayne was camped near Paoli, Pennsylvania, only a few miles from the enemy when deserters informed the British of his whereabouts. Despite being warned, the Americans were taken completely by surprise when the enemy struck. Ordered not to use their guns but the bayonet instead, the British overwhelmed Wayne's men and when it was over, the Americans had taken almost 150 casualties, many suffered after the battle had ended.

A subsequent court martial cleared Wayne of any responsibility for what became known as the Paoli Massacre and after the near victory of Germantown in October, the army found itself encamped at Valley Forge while the British settled down in Philadelphia. Perhaps due to his familiarity with the area (his home was close enough to visit every night), Wayne was assigned by Washington early in 1778 to search the countryside for provisions to supply his starving and freezing army. It was perhaps due to the unusual vigor with which Wayne followed his orders that his men began to call him "mad."

Later that spring, when the British emerged from Philadelphia on a march to Sandy Hook from where they could take ship to New York, Wayne was alone in insisting that the army take advantage of the long line of march to attack the enemy. Washington approved, despite strong protest from Gen. Charles Lee who was assigned a key role in the coming battle of Monmouth. But when the day of battle arrived on June 24, 1778, Lee failed to press the attack, even ordering a retreat that stranded Wayne's unit on the field. When Washington finally rode up, he was enraged at Lee's failure to perform his part of the plan and, rallying the retreating troops himself, ordered them in support of Wayne who had positioned his men in an orchard. Thus reinforced, Wayne was able to repulse a number of enemy assaults with massed musket fire until, finally outnumbered, he was able to retreat in good order.

After following the British back into New Jersey and New York the two sides once again settled down to a watching and waiting game as small units continued to spar in limited actions. One such action occurred on July 15, 1779 after Wayne convinced Washington that with his new command of an elite corps of light infantry, he could capture a British fort along the Hudson River at King's Ferry known as Stony Point. Well defended by 500 men and protected by reinforced outposts and surrounded on three sides by water and on a fourth by a swamp, Stony Point presented a formidable challenge for Wayne's men. With absolute silence and tight security a vital part of the scheme, two American columns managed to maneuver through the dark to meet as planned beneath the brow of the fort's walls. There, they were at last discovered and, in the face of a heavy barrage of rifle and cannon fire, made the final assault. Suffering an ugly wound to his head, Wayne led his men into the fort and captured the enemy flag. At a cost of 15 lives, the Americans made prisoner up to 543 of the enemy and killed 63. The battle was a brilliant victory and the most thorough for Wayne until his successful campaign against the Indians conducted many years later.

In 1780, it was Wayne's unit that rushed to West Point to secure the post against Benedict Arnold's treachery and in 1781, after contending with mutiny and discontent among the soldiery, he was ordered to the troubled southern theater of the war where the British, with strong support from local Tories, were long able to move at will and control much of the countryside. Wayne arrived in Virginia just in time to meet an army under the command of Gen. Charles Cornwallis coming up from the Carolinas. In an action more bold than well judged, Wayne, attacked the British army as it crossed the James River at Green Spring Farm and although his men performed well, they were outnumbered 6 to 1 and eventually ordered to retreat. Wayne's attack had a benefit however: it gave Cornwallis doubt and caused him to halt his advance. When he began to move again, the British general determined to encamp at Yorktown where he could be resupplied or evacuated by sea as the fortunes of war dictated. Unfortunately for Cornwallis, his defensive position became a trap after the arrival of a French fleet under the command of Admiral de Grass. After disembarking an army to join that of Washington around Yorktown, the French fleet then won a battle at sea against the British Navy, thus sealing Cornwallis' fate.

With Cornwallis' surrender on October 19, 1781, Wayne proceeded to the relief of South Carolina to help drive out the remaining British occupiers. When that was done, he took his army to Georgia and began a series of battles designed to draw the noose around enemy occupied Savannah. After a series of skirmishes that involved an encounter with local Indians and a last, desperate sortie by the British, a final siege of the city was avoided when the enemy chose to abandon it on July 11, 1782.

Wayne retired from the army as a major-general and returned to Waynesborough to pick up where he left off eight years before. More respected than ever, he served in the Pennsylvania legislature and participated in the state's constitutional ratifying convention. Later, he traveled back to Georgia to oversee the plantation with which he was rewarded by that state and while there, ended up being elected as the state's delegate to the House of Representatives. That election however, was soon voided after allegations of fraud. Deciding not to run again, Wayne was soon recalled to military duty by Washington, who had since become the new nation's first president under the Constitution. Made commander in chief of the army, Wayne was asked to lead an expedition to the Northwest against a league of Indians involving the

Shawnee, Potawatomi, Delaware, and Miami tribes which had been terrorizing settlers for years.

Wayne, with all the experience garnered after years of warfare, took his time in making his preparations, setting up a chain of forts including Fort Washington located on the future site of Cincinnati, Ohio; Fort Greene, named after his wartime friend and commanding officer; and Fort Recovery at the site of the disastrous defeat suffered by his immediate predecessor Gen. Arthur St. Clair at the hands of the Indians in 1781. Leaving little to chance and so avoiding St. Clair's mistakes, Wayne led a well trained army of 3,000 men into Indian territory, building more forts and driving the enemy all the way to the Maumee River where the British occupied Fort Miami, located on the future site of Toledo, Ohio. There, on August 10, 1794, caught between the advancing Americans and their supposed British allies who, in the end, refused to help them, the Indians were defeated in a final clash at Fallen Timbers, so named from a vast tangle of fallen trees downed during some past storm. When the battle was over, the power of the Indians had been broken and at a peace conference held the next year at Fort Greenville, a treaty was signed that allowed for the final settlement of the Old Northwest. Also that year, with the ratification by Congress of a treaty arranged with England by John Jay, the British were at last compelled to abandon the string of forts that they had continued to occupy in defiance of the Treaty of Paris, the instrument that ended the Revolution over ten years before. Their presence in the northwest had been a major source of trouble for the United States as they had been major abettors of Indian warfare in the region ever since the end of the Revolution. Now, with the victory at Fallen Timbers and his subsequent return in 1796 to take over the forts from the departing British, Wayne had removed the two prime sources of trouble on the frontier, paving the way for a wave of settlement that would prove one of the most rapid and remarkable in history. Only fifty years later, the states of Ohio, Michigan, Wisconsin, Minnesota, Iowa, Indiana and Illinois would prove to be a major source of manpower for the Union army and contribute greatly to the North's victory in the Civil War.

Following his successful campaign, Wayne returned to the nation's capital in Philadelphia and home to Chester County to receive a hero's welcome but his stay was destined to be brief when he was called west again. He died unexpectedly of "a severe fit of gout" at Fort Presque Isle on December 15, 1796.

William Whipple

Jack of all trades, William Whipple did it all: sailor, merchant, soldier, politician, judge…signer of the Declaration of Independence, and all with what amounted to no more than a grade school education. But Whipple's overriding passion was the welfare of his country which rapidly became the United States after what he, in common with many of his peers, regarded as a betrayal of the public trust by the royal authority in England.

William Whipple was born on January 14, 1730 in the small New Hampshire town of Kittery that later would become part of the state of Maine. As a young boy, he was educated in the local public school before a streak of independence prompted him to sign up with a local merchantman and go to sea. By the time he was 21, he was rated as a ship's master or captain and sailed the difficult triangle trade that involved trading New England wood for British rum and then trading the rum in west Africa for slaves who were then transported to the West Indies or back to Portsmouth, New Hampshire. When he was 30 years old, Whipple decided to abandon the sea and invest his savings in a shore based mercantile venture with his brother, Joseph. Soon however, the troubles with England began as the mother country attempted to impose on the American colonies various tax raising measures including those on stamps and tea, fiscal measures that had a direct impact on Whipple's business. Incensed, Whipple became a strong supporter of the patriot cause and as a successful merchant and prominent member of the community, he was persuaded in 1775 to join the provincial congress. He hardly had time to settle in however, when New Hampshire severed its relationship to royal authority and set up its own independent legislature. When the dust settled, Whipple found himself not only a member of the new government's executive council, but a member of the powerful Committee of Safety that was involved, among other things, in military planning. In 1776, after hostilities had broken out between the colonies and Britain, Whipple was chosen as one of New Hampshire's delegates to the Continental Congress.

Whipple's service in Congress however, was spotty at best. In Philadelphia to participate in the debates over independence, he voted in its favor and signed the Declaration of Independence before returning home in time to help repel a British invasion down New York's Hudson River valley by Gen. John Burgoyne. Appointed a brigadier general, Whipple led the New Hampshire militia west and joined fellow General John Stark in repelling enemy columns at Bennington. Unlike Stark however, Whipple continued on to join the American forces gathering under Gen.

William Whipple

Horatio Gates for the climactic victory at Saratoga, New York on October 17, 1777. In recognition of his battlefield performance, Whipple was chosen as one of the members of the team assigned to negotiate terms with the defeated Burgoyne and later, for escort duty taking prisoners back east.

Back in Congress the next year, Whipple the ex-seaman, pressed the Marine Committee to abandon plans for the construction of large warships in favor of smaller, faster frigates. Whipple also warned of the ill effects of privateering on the people calling it "no kind of business (that) can so effectually introduce luxury, extravagance, and every kind of dissipation that tend to the distraction of the morals of the people. Those engaged in it soon lose every idea of right and wrong and, for want of an opportunity of gratifying their insatiable avarice with the property of the enemies of their country, will, without the least compunction, seize that of her friends."

Taking up his duties as leader of the New Hampshire militia once again, Whipple joined American Gen. John Sullivan for a planned assault on Newport, Rhode Island. The attack was planned to include support from the French Navy which had been ordered to the aid of the United States following the convincing victory at Saratoga. But after a storm blew in scattering both the French and English fleets, French Admiral Count D'Estaing decided his storm damaged vessels were too vulnerable to remain in the area and abandoned the attack for safe harbor in Boston. Despite the insistence by officers such as Whipple to press the attack even without French aid, the American force was considered inadequate to seize Newport and a counterattack by the British occupiers only hastened the decision to give up on the operation.

In 1780, his neighbors sent Whipple back to the state legislature and two years later, he reluctantly consented to act as federal financial agent or tax collector for New Hampshire. Naturally, such a position was an unpopular one and Whipple had to expend much of the goodwill he had built over the years to persuade the state's residents to live up to their obligations to the union. So difficult and onerous did his duties become, that in 1783, Whipple tried to resign but his boss, Robert Morris, superintendent of finance under the Articles of Confederation, refused to go along with him. Finally, in 1784, Whipple managed to deliver the state's first payments and used failing health and the end of the war as an excuse to quit the tax collector position.

Concurrently with his responsibilities to the legislature and the federal government, Whipple was named a commissioner to help settle a dispute between Pennsylvania and Connecticut over possession of the Wyoming Valley one of several boundary questions among the states left unsettled before the war. That experience, in addition to his service as a legislator and congressman, qualified him for a position as an associate judge on the New Hampshire Superior Court. As judge, he was required to spend much of his time riding circuit from town to town but the increasing pressures related to his various duties finally caught up to him and fainting spells that sometimes ended with him tumbling from his horse forced him into retirement. As it turned out, his physical problems were due to a bad heart to which Whipple at last succumbed while home in Portsmouth on November 28, 1785.

Marinus Willett

One of the most uncertain areas on the Revolutionary War battlefield was the United States' long and largely unmarked frontier west of the Appalachian Mountains that stretched from New York in the north to Georgia in the south. But in all that wild country perhaps the most volatile was located in western New York and Pennsylvania. There, various Indian tribes predominated by the Iroquois and Mohawk, already in a constant state of agitation due to the incessant encroachment of white settlers on their land, were disposed to ally themselves with the British as the lesser of two evils. But the Indians made for unpredictable allies at best and became uncontrollable once the hatchet had struck the war post; raiding and killing without regard to age or sex. More disturbing to many who lived on the frontier were those times when fellow white men, Tories, loyalists or simple renegades, joined or even led the Indians on their raids. In those cases, the names of such figures as Simon Girty and Walter Butler became synonymous with the worst kind of betrayal and whose names have remained in the American vocabulary of villainy for two hundred years. In contrast, citizens of the early republic admired as heroes those among themselves who rose in opposition to the turncoats and, having mastered the bloody art of frontier warfare, were able to strike back at the enemy in equal measure.

One such man was Marinus Willet who was born in Jamaica, Long Island, in New York on July 31, 1730. Long since left behind as the frontier moved west, Jamaica was a sleepy corner of British America and as one of thirteen siblings, the young Willet probably found few opportunities there save a life of work on his father's farm. Instead, he chose to seek his fortune in the city and after moving to New York, became a merchant and otherwise made his name known about town. When the French and Indian War broke out in 1758, a restless Willett returned home to Jamaica to recruit family and friends as militiamen and as reward, was named a lieutenant in one of three companies attached to British Lt. Col. Richard Abercrombie. Willett saw action and gained his first experience of wilderness warfare in western New York when he took part in assaults on Forts Ticonderoga and Frontenac. Eventually incapacitated due to illness, Willett was invalided to Fort Stanwix which at the time was in the process of being constructed. After the war, he returned to New York.

With the experience of serving with the haughty British officer class still fresh in his mind, Willett found it easy to fall in with the growing patriot movement and became a member of the local Sons of Liberty. Specializing in street politics that frequently involved mob action, Willett at one point led a group of patriot sympathizers against an attempt to remove military supplies from New York for use by British soldiers trapped in Boston. Intercepting the transfer, the weapons and powder found their way into the hands of local militia instead. Soon after, Willett was commissioned as a captain in a regiment commanded by Alexander McDougall and took part in the ill fated invasion of Canada. Made the commanding officer of the fort at St. John's after Montgomery continued north to Montreal, he was eventually promoted to lieutenant colonel and attached to American forces charged with the defense of upstate New York. Key to protecting the western frontier was a line of outposts including Fort Stanwix, renamed Fort Schuyler by the Americans, which had fallen into disrepair since Willett had spent time there during the French and Indian War. Ordered by Gen. George Washington to be repaired and garrisoned, Willett, in command of the 3rd New York Regiment and his immediate superior Col. Peter Gansvoort, arrived at the site in the summer of 1777 with 750 men and began to rebuild the fort. The work was completed just in time to welcome an army of 1,200 Indians, loyalists, and British soldiers under the command of Col. Barry St. Leger who promptly placed it under siege.

Marinus Willett

Leger's force, having come east from Fort Oswego located on Lake Ontario, was one part of a three pronged strategy intended to cut the thirteen states in half. After reducing Fort Schuyler, the British officer was to march his men eastward to link up with another army led by Gen. John Burgoyne then descending from Canada down the Hudson River Valley to Albany. The two forces would then be joined by a third, that of Gen. William Howe moving north from New York City. Thus, with the reduction of Fort Schuyler vital if the plan were to succeed, Leger could not leave an American force in his rear to threaten his flanks. After Gansvoort refused to surrender the fort, a formal siege was laid on August 3, 1777.

Two days later the defenders were relieved to learn that 800 militiamen under the command of Gen. Nicholas Herkimer were not far off. To help them on their approach, a plan was made to have the defenders ride out to meet the relief column but after Willett and his men reached the British camp, they found it deserted. Although the Americans took advantage of the situation to loot the enemy encampment, it did little to offset the defeat suffered by Herkimer when his army was ambushed at Oriskany on August 6 by Indian leader Joseph Brant. With the siege renewed, the defenders again refused to surrender. Later, under cover of darkness, Willett and Maj. Levi Stockwell left the fort, passed through enemy lines, and headed to Fort Dayton, 50 miles away, where they learned that Gen. Benedict Arnold would soon arrive with a second relief force consisting of 1,000 men. Because he and Stockwell had been ordered back to Albany to raise more men, Willett was not on hand when Arnold sent a local resident known to the Indians ahead of the army to spread stories that the approaching Americans were "more numerous than the leaves on the trees." Frightened, already satisfied with their victory at Oriskany, and impatient with the siege, the Indians abandoned their British allies. Without his native auxiliaries, Leger knew his force was not strong enough to face both Arnold's approaching column and the men inside the fort. Impelled to retreat, his absence in the Hudson Valley campaign would prove disastrous for the British.

Throughout the siege of Fort Schuyler, Willett's nemesis seemed to be Walter Butler, who became infamous as a loyalist leader of Indian raids across the frontier including the notorious Cherry Valley massacre. For a brief time immediately following the relief of the fort, it seemed that perhaps Butler would be placed permanently out of action after he was captured while recruiting men for his raiding parties. Ironically, Willett, who had been present when Butler demanded the surrender of Fort Schuyler, sat in judgment of the captive finding him guilty of espionage and condemning him to death. Unfortunately for the people of the frontier however, Butler later escaped captivity and resumed his bloody career.

Meanwhile, Willett briefly rejoined the Continental Army in the east. After taking part in the battle of Monmouth, he returned to the frontier where he joined an expedition against local Indian tribes. One of the targets of the campaign included the neutral Onondagas, a tribe who lived near present day Syracuse, a circumstance not uncommon on the frontier where settlers often refused to differentiate between friendly and hostile natives. In 1779, Willett was attached to still another campaign, that of Gen. John Sullivan who was ordered by Washington to punish the Indians of the northwest for their continuing raids on the settlements. Villages were destroyed and crops burned and a battle fought at Newtown.

In 1780, New York Governor George Clinton, recognizing his long experience in Indian warfare, placed Willett in command of the state's western frontier. He would have his hands full. Angered by the recent destruction of their villages, Mohawk and Iroquois braves were on the warpath and joined loyalist bands in bloody raids all across the Mohawk Valley. With the American military presence in the area drained by the ongoing war, Willett had inherited a weakened defensive position but quickly rose to the challenge. Hardly ever sleeping in the same place twice, he kept himself and his men constantly on the move, a mobility that matched that of the enemy who slipped through the murky forests like ghosts. His efforts paid off when his army of 400 defeated a mixed force of 800 British and Indians at Johnstown and pursued the remnants into the wilderness where "we left them in a fair way of receiving a punishment better suited to their merit than a musket ball, a tomahawk or captivity..." It was in a skirmish at Canada Creek that Willett finally caught up to his old enemy, Walter Butler, who was killed there on October 30, 1781. Willett remained on duty over a much quieter frontier until 1783.

After the war, George Washington, president of the new United States, respecting Willett's long years of experience dealing with Indians, asked him to negotiate a treaty with Georgia's Creek nation. In 1792, Willett was offered the rank of brigadier general for yet another expedition against the Indian tribes of the northwest, but for reasons of conscience, he declined the appointment which went to Anthony Wayne instead. Eventually, Willett returned to civilian life but after the war, he was no longer the unknown quantity he had been before the Revolution. Gravitating to politics, he attached himself to the "old incumbent" George Clinton, whom he had known while on campaign with Sullivan and was a supporter of local politician Aaron Burr in the struggle between Thomas Jefferson's Republicans and Alexander Hamilton's Federalists. His Republican sympathies came in handy after Jefferson was swept into office as president on a wave of anti-Federalist feeling in 1800. With Jefferson's reelection in 1804, Willett himself was elected in 1807 as Mayor of New York City. Over 90 years old, Willett died at Cedar Grove, his home in the city, on August 23, 1830.

William Williams

William Williams, the man with the redundant name, seemed to be the exception in a family of otherwise Biblically named kin which included such Old Testament standbys as a brother called Eliphalet, a cousin named Ephraim and a father known as Solomon. But despite the nondescript nature of his name, it would be Williams, although trained for the ministry and a dabbler in retailing, who would find immortality in the nation's panoply of revolutionary heroes when he briefly left a lifetime spent in local politics for a few years in Philadelphia where he arrived in time to become a signer of the Declaration of Independence.

Born in Lebanon, Connecticut on April 8, 1731, Williams received his early education in public school until entering Harvard at the age of sixteen. Graduating in 1751, he returned home to continue his studies under his father's tutelage with the intention of entering the ministry but a few years later war intervened and the young Williams joined a company of volunteers under the command of his cousin Col. Ephraim Williams as a surgeon. Marching off to the western wilderness, the army was ambushed by the French and Indians a few miles from Lake George in New York at a place called Rocky Brook where Ephraim was killed leading a counter charge. The survivors of the battle, which became known as "the Bloody Morning Scout," managed to fall back to the main body under Sir William Johnson and there turned back the enemy at the Battle of Lake George. Now a veteran, Williams returned to Connecticut in 1756 and decided that the ministry was not for him. He became a merchant and in due course, took his first political position as town clerk of Lebanon, a job he would hold through the ups and downs of revolution for the next 45 years. That small taste of politics must have been like a tonic for Williams because in a short time he had also become the town's treasurer, member of the Board of Selectmen, justice of the peace and finally a colonial legislator. Williams entered the Connecticut legislature at a difficult time for the colony when Americans were faced with increasing demands placed upon them by a Parliament eager to recoup the cost of its recent war with France. By then, Williams had begun filling in as speaker of the House and working with Governor Jonathan Trumbull, Sr. on such sensitive issues as reports to the King on the effects of the Stamp Act. But just because he worked closely with the colony's royal authority (and was

William Williams

married to Trumbull's daughter) did not mean that he was sympathetic to England's point of view.

Williams, like many other veterans, had experienced his first extensive contact with the British Army and its officer corps during the French and Indian War and learned first hand of the contempt in which they held Americans. Their insulting, haughty attitude made a bad impression on American volunteers, one they would never forget and predispose them to patriotic arguments against royal authority. Williams was no different, and as feelings rose against the British, he came into his own with essays and fiery public speeches denouncing what he believed were unjust edicts emanating from England. But Williams' energies weren't confined to words, in 1775, he joined members of the Committee of Safety in signing promissory notes to the colonial treasury in exchange for the withdrawal of funds that were then used to finance the seizure of Fort Ticonderoga by Ethan Allen.

Thus, when hostilities between America and Britain broke into open warfare, Williams used his position as selectman to mobilize efforts in his local community to raise money and supplies for the men who were volunteering in droves for the army that began to coalesce around Boston. Later in the war, when the currency issued by Congress was hardly worth the paper it was printed on, Williams would buy it up at his own expense, nearly bankrupting himself in the process. So strong was his patriotic zeal that it was almost a forgone conclusion that he would eventually be chosen as one of the colony's delegates to the Continental Congress and in 1776 it would not take much convincing for him to place his name on the Declaration of Independence. Named to the committee charged with drawing up a government for the newly independent thirteen states, Williams had a hand in crafting the Articles of

Confederation and later served on the Board of War before returning to local politics in Connecticut. There, his support for the war had not abated as his fellow politicians soon discovered.

At a meeting of the Committee of Safety held in Lebanon, it was remarked that if the war should be lost, Williams' life, as a signer of the Declaration of Independence, would be forfeit. One member of the committee noted that since he had not signed any incriminating documents nor was his name ever associated in print with any criticism of the King, he was safe from hanging. To which an incensed Williams declared, "Then, sir, you deserve to be hanged, for not having done your duty." But happily, America won the war and throughout, Williams continued to support efforts at raising funds and supplies while continuing to serve in a number of official capacities including county judge, judge of probate, and after 1780 on the Governor's Council. In 1782 he served as representative to the state's ratification convention in support of the United States Constitution and in 1783 was again chosen to represent Connecticut in Congress. Back home a year later, Williams later retired but after the death of his eldest son, suffered declining health until meeting his own demise while in his hometown of Lebanon on August 2, 1811.

James Wilson

One of the many founding fathers who were not born in the thirteen colonies, James Wilson arrived in America with a few letters of introduction and worked his way to the top, both politically and socially...only to end up in debtors prison near the end of his life.

Wilson was born on September 14, 1742 in Carskerdo, Scotland to a well to do farmer. Living near Glasgow, he ended up attending a number of local colleges including St. Andrews University, Glasgow University, and Edinburgh University from none of which he ever received a degree. Instead, he collected letters of introduction and took ship for America in 1766. Arriving in Philadelphia, he quickly found employment at the College of Philadelphia as a teacher of Greek and Roman history and such subjects as rhetoric and logic which he excelled at. The latter subjects served him well when, after only a few months, he left the college to pursue a legal career. (But not before prevailing on the school's administration to grant him an honorary Masters of Arts degree). He read law in the offices of John Dickinson, an early patriot who would later champion reconciliation with Britain when many others were clamoring for independence. Wilson was admitted to the bar in 1767 and began his own practice first in Reading then in Scots-Irish dominated Carlisle. In a very short time, his skill had earned him enough money to buy a modest farm and to begin speculating in land development, a weakness that would be his downfall decades later. It was about this time, around 1774 that Wilson became involved in revolutionary politics. Perhaps influenced by Dickinson, who had written the influential *Letters from a Farmer in Pennsylvania*, Wilson put his own ideas into words with the publication of *Considerations on the Nature and Extent of the Legislative Authority of the British Parliament* in which he took the position that Parliament had no right whatsoever to pass laws in the name of its colonies and that each colony was completely independent of Britain save in their loyalty to the crown. His bold declaration caught the notice of patriots everywhere, and earned him seats on the Carlisle Committees of Correspondence and Safety, a commission as colonel in the Pennsylvania militia, and a brief stay in the Pennsylvania legislature. Wilson's high profile eventually won him a place among the colony's delegation to the Continental Congress which Wilson joined in 1775.

James Wilson

In Congress, Wilson's oratorical skills and training in logic came in handy as he advocated forcefully for independence from Britain. "...his eloquence was of the most commanding kind," was how fellow congressman Benjamin Rush described his oratorical skills. So strong was his position, that fellow members in favor of separation felt betrayed when he sided with those in the Pennsylvania delegation urging a go slow attitude toward independence. Samuel Adams even referred these more cautious individuals as "servile and degenerate." Wilson himself was conflicted on the issue, feeling strongly that separation was the only answer while also thinking that his constituents, who were more cautious than he was, had a claim on his loyalty. "We are servants of the people," he explained, "sent here to act under a delegated authority." But the personal impasse was soon corrected when the citizens of Pennsylvania met and demanded that the colony's position against independence be reversed. His conscience thus freed, Wilson joined a majority of his fellow delegates in voting for, and later in signing, the Declaration of Independence.

With the passage of the Declaration, each of the former colonies began to fashion new forms of government for themselves and in criticizing Pennsylvania's proposed constitution on the basis that its unicameral legislature and lack of checks and balances could be an invitation to mob rule, Wilson found himself not only voted out of Congress, but chased from the state. In 1778 he moved back to Philadelphia from Annapolis, Maryland and resumed his legal practice taking on business clients and even defending Tories. It was perhaps among those associations that his zeal for investment veered from land speculation to that of profiteering. The next year, when the city was hit by severe food shortages, he and others were suspected of hoarding food for the purpose of making a profit (while his opposition to price controls added fuel to the fire). He was threatened with arrest more than once and the threat to his life became so dire, that he was forced to barricade himself in his home with friends (most of whom also happened to be businessmen and critics of the state constitution) after an angry mob surrounded the building. Relief in the form of local soldiery arrived only after blood had been spilled and his home broken into. Following the siege of "Fort Wilson," official duties were hard to come by and Wilson accepted an appointment from France to serve as its United States advocate general for maritime and commercial enterprises. Although Wilson quit the job soon after over a salary dispute, he continued to advise the French in its dealings with the new nation. By 1781, political tempers in Pennsylvania had moderated enough to allow Wilson to be named as a director of the Bank of North America and in 1782 to be reelected to Congress where he worked with Revolutionary financier Robert Morris (who had shared dangers with him in the siege of Fort Wilson). Finally, in 1787, he was chosen as a member of Pennsylvania's delegation to the Constitutional Convention where he advocated a number of radical positions including the cession of western lands to the federal government, increased powers of federal taxation, and the popular election of the president and congress calling the latter a "cornerstone" of democracy. In a long series of speeches (more than 140!), he advocated for a strong central government, and was not averse to compromise when needed even calling it "indispensable." Chosen as a member of the committee assigned with writing a draft of the Constitution, he chose to support the resulting document and argued for its acceptance at Pennsylvania's ratification convention claiming that it would set an example for "temples of liberty in every part of the earth." For his trouble, he was burned in effigy and later nearly beaten to death by a gang of "anti-federalists" at a bonfire in Carlisle held to celebrate the state's ratification. Recovering, he returned to the College of Philadelphia as a law teacher and, ironically, worked on the state's constitution to have it conform with the federal instrument; the same constitution which he had earlier criticized and that became the cause of his political ostracism and beating at the bonfire. In 1789, after appealing to President George Washington, he was appointed as an associate justice of the Supreme Court under John Jay but unable to resist dabbling in still more land speculation, he lost whatever fortune he had, spent some time in debtors' prison, and moved to New Jersey to avoid further arrest. By 1798, at the relatively young age of 56, Wilson was a broken and dispirited man and died on August 21 while riding circuit in Edenton, North Carolina.

Oliver Wolcott

Rare among those who served in Congress and no doubt the envy of some of them, Oliver Wolcott managed to divide his time during the Revolution between legislative affairs and the battlefield. And despite spending his entire career in politics, when he was not leading men in combat, Wolcott did manage to make time during 1776 to sign the Declaration of Independence thus joining an elite circle of Founding Fathers.

Born the youngest of fourteen children in Windsor, Connecticut on November 26, 1726, Wolcott began life as the son of a future royal governor of the colony before entering Yale where by all accounts, he became an excellent student. But before he graduated in 1747, King George's War intervened and he was commissioned a captain of militia. Wasting little time, he recruited a few hundred volunteers and marched with them to the frontier. Although that phase of the war proved unsuccessful for the British, Wolcott returned home with a reputation as a veteran and began to study for a medical career before changing his mind and pursuing the law instead.

Moving to Litchfield, he not only became the county's sheriff in 1751 (a position he would hold for the next twenty years) but his experience in the law also led to appointments as judge in both the court of common pleas and probate and in 1764, a long career as a member of the colonial and later state legislature. In the meantime, his military career continued to keep pace with his civilian career as he was promoted in 1771 first to major in the colony's militia then to colonel. But as tensions rose between the thirteen American colonies and England, a streak of rebelliousness in his family's blood as well as memories of his treatment at the hands of British officers during the war prompted Wolcott to side with the patriots and early on advocate for independence. In 1774 he was named as a member of a peace delegation to negotiate (unsuccessfully as it turned out) with the Iroquois to

Oliver Wolcott

remain neutral in any war between the American colonies and the British. Later, he was appointed by Congress to help settle a boundary dispute between Pennsylvania and Connecticut and New York and Vermont. It was perhaps those experiences as well as his military and political background that led his supporters to appoint him as one of the colony's delegates to the Second Continental Congress in 1775. Although he did not take an active role in public debate and missed the initial vote for independence, his support for the issue was clear. Later, leading Connecticut militia during the battle for Long Island, he missed the formal signing of the Declaration of Independence in August of 1776 but finally added his signature the following October. In the meantime, upon hearing of independence from Britain, the people of New York, unable to contain their enthusiasm, pulled down a famous equestrian statue of King George III and took it to Wolcott's home in Litchfield where it was melted down into thousands of lead bullets for use by the army.

However, despite the people's joy, the military situation had deteriorated further since the battle of Long Island as the British assault on Manhattan and later, its advance upon Philadelphia proceeded. Escaping the city, Wolcott accompanied the Congress to Baltimore, Maryland before leaving again in 1777 to raise troops for the continued defense of New York. Now promoted to brigadier general in the Connecticut militia, Wolcott led his troops north and joined an army gathering under Gen. Horatio Gates to oppose advancing British armies coming down the Hudson River to Albany. At Saratoga, Wolcott participated in the second battle of Freeman's Farm and was on hand for the final surrender of British Gen. John Burgoyne.

Wolcott returned to Congress in 1778 and except for a final absence the next year to help defend the Connecticut coast from enemy raids, he served there until 1784 when he was named a commissioner of Indian Affairs and participated in negotiations with the Iroquois and Wyandottes tribes for the cession of western lands and to bring a temporary peace to the frontier. Widely read and keenly interested in the sciences, Wolcott was chosen president of the Connecticut Society of Arts and Sciences and although he took some convincing, eventually supported ratification of the United States Constitution. "It is generally agreed that the present Confederation is inadequate to the exigencies of our national affairs," said Wolcott in a speech favoring ratification. "We must therefore adopt this plan of government, or some other, or risk the consequences of disunion." While a commissioner, he continued to serve in the Connecticut legislature and in 1787 was elected lieutenant governor, a post he held for ten years before succeeding fellow signer of the Declaration of Independence Samuel Huntington as governor in 1796. He held that office until his death on December 1, 1797.

George Wythe

Though George Wythe achieved immortality when he signed the Declaration of Independence, it was in the less colorful role of teacher and mentor to many of the younger generation of Founding Fathers including Thomas Jefferson and James Madison that his contribution to American republicanism will be most remembered.

Wythe was born on his parents' estate in Elizabeth County, Virginia sometime in 1726. Losing his father at a young age, his early education was provided at home by his mother who was unusually well taught for a woman of that era. Although his mother managed to give him a grounding in the classics, her death when Wythe was only a teenager interrupted his education and redirected him onto a path of licentiousness that delayed his personal development. Cut off from most of the family's wealth by an older brother who had inherited everything, Wythe spent the next few years blowing what money he had received and enduring a brief first marriage. Finally, short of funds, he was forced to return to school where he attended the College of William and Mary but never graduated. Instead, he left school to read law with a local attorney and by 1746 had passed the bar. He never looked back. The very next year, he was appointed as clerk to the legislature's Committee on Privileges and Elections and by 1753 had become attorney general for Virginia.

The year 1755 was a watershed in Wythe's life as he married for the second time; inherited his family's estate on the death of his brother; and was elected to the House of Burgesses, Virginia's legislature, representing Williamsburg. On the professional front, his law practice continued to flourish as he in turn began to accept students among whom the most famous would be a young Thomas Jefferson. Perhaps the most personally satisfying event in this period was his election to the College of William and Mary's Board of Visitors in 1761 and his being named later a full professor of law. For twenty years, his greatest pleasure would be teaching and

George Wythe

among his many prestigious students could be counted James Monroe, John Marshall, and Henry Clay. But as the political storm that would lead to revolution grew in the thirteen American colonies, Wythe found his attention increasingly drawn away from the halls of learning and focusing more on Virginia's response to the crisis. Angered at plans by the British Parliament to enact measures intended to raise taxes among the American colonies without their consent, Wythe was the likely author of a petition to the king called *Resolutions of Remonstrance* which detailed the Virginia legislature's opposition to the measures. The effort however, came to nothing as the Stamp Act was passed the following year in 1765. But by then, the legislature had acquired a fiery new member in the young Patrick Henry (whom Wythe had turned down following his bar examination) who called for a series of new resolutions condemning the British tax measures as unlawful. Although Wythe was among those who opposed the resolves due to their uncompromising language, they were approved nonetheless, by a single vote. The next day however, after Henry had left town, the legislature reconvened and voted to remove one of the more incendiary of the five resolves whose language claimed that Parliament had no right whatsoever to impose taxes on the American colonies. (All five resolves however, would appear together when they were printed for public consumption cementing Henry's reputation as a popular hero).

In 1775, his patriotic credentials in order, Wythe was named as a member of Virginia's delegation to the Continental Congress. There, he met John Adams and after listening to his arguments in debate, urged him to commit them to paper and Adams' influential *Thoughts on Government* was born. In 1776, Wythe joined his fellow delegates in signing the Declaration of Independence and over the course of the ensuing war, ended up losing much of his property including the unlawful release of his slaves to the British by an untrustworthy employee. Later, his home, being located in the vicinity of Yorktown, was made the headquarters of Gen. George Washington when the Continental Army lay siege to that city. It would take years to rebuild his estate and pay off his debts but in time, Wythe succeeded.

Meanwhile, he and former student Thomas Jefferson among others, left Congress to help reform the laws of the new state of Virginia. Together with Edward Pendleton, the two took three years to fashion a document that included the abolition of the ancient privilege of primogeniture (something with which Wythe had personal experience) and enshrined freedom of worship among the rights and liberties of residents. Six years after they completed their work, the legislature finally finished voting on their recommendations. Rejected, was a radical plan of public education and changes in criminal sentencing that were eventually stricken from the plan. In 1777, Wythe was elected speaker of the state's house of delegates while also serving as a judge on Virginia's high court. In 1787, he was chosen as a delegate to the Constitutional Convention and, believing that there was a need for some plan of national government that would be more binding than the Articles of Confederation, sided with federalists such as James Madison for the creation of a strong central government.

Forced to leave the convention before its conclusion to tend his ailing wife, Wythe's participation in public life following Virginia's ratification of the Constitution diminished slowly thereafter until he died on June 8, 1806 of apparent arsenic poisoning. In a scandalous court battle after his death, a nephew was tried for his murder but later acquitted. Speculation had it that the nephew, angered by conditions in Wythe's will that would have set his slaves free with enough monetary compensation to help them transition to a life of freedom (a separate condition bequeathed his library to Thomas Jefferson), decided to enlarge his share of the estate by murdering the slaves. Unfortunately, in the process, he also ended up killing his uncle.

www.ingramcontent.com/pod-product-compliance
Lightning Source LLC
Chambersburg PA
CBHW020520100426

42813CB00030B/3304/J